Rival Capitalists

A volume in the series

Cornell Studies in Political Economy

EDITED BY PETER J. KATZENSTEIN

A full list of titles in the series appears at the end of the book.

Rival Capitalists

INTERNATIONAL COMPETITIVENESS IN THE
UNITED STATES, JAPAN, AND WESTERN EUROPE

JEFFREY A. HART

CORNELL UNIVERSITY PRESS

Ithaca and London

First published 1992 by Cornell University Press.

International Standard Book Number 0-8014-2649-9 (cloth)
International Standard Book Number 0-8014-9949-6 (paper)
Library of Congress Catalog Card Number 92-52757

Printed in the United States of America

Librarians: Library of Congress cataloging information appears on the last page of the book.

⊗ The paper in this book meets the minimum requirements of the American National Standard for Information Sciences—Permanence of Paper for Printed Library Materials, ANSI Z39.48-1984.

Contents

Figures and Tables

TABLES

Preface

This book examines the five largest capitalist, industrial countries (the United States, Japan, France, Germany, and the United Kingdom) and their strategies for dealing with change in the national and international markets for steel, automobiles, and semiconductors. I selected steel, automobiles, and semiconductors because they represent three distinct historical periods of industrial change. The earliest of the three to emerge was the steel industry; the most recent was the semiconductor industry.

Many books on industrial policy deal with the effect of government policy on aggregate economic performance. They frequently argue that a centralized and explicit form of industrial policy, usually associated with Japan, is best suited to fostering overall competitiveness in international trade and therefore accounts for the higher rate of economic growth in these countries. That argument is firmly refuted in this book.

Instead, I argue that an exclusive focus on government policies to explain changes in international competitiveness is misleading. Government policies obviously affect international competitiveness. They cannot explain, however, why Japanese firms do so well in areas lacking administrative guidance or why German firms do so well inasmuch as Germany has nothing vaguely resembling administrative guidance. To build a credible explanation of changes in competitiveness, it is necessary nonetheless to know how government, business, and labor are organized in each country.

One of the core arguments of this book is that changes in international competitiveness must be observed at the level of individual industries but that they can be explained only at the level of the national system. Changes in international competitiveness tend to be similar across the three industries studied here for all five countries. The countries that have experienced declining competitiveness in all three industries—the United States and Britain—have had problems creating or diffusing new technologies in those industries. The countries that have experienced increasing competitiveness—Japan and Germany—have developed a variety of institutional mechanisms (not just governmental) to create and diffuse new technologies.

The book is divided into seven chapters. The first chapter lays out theoretical arguments to be pursued in the rest of the book and summarizes changes in national competitiveness in the three industries since World War II. Chapters 2–6 give detailed comparisons of national policies toward the three industries. These chapters include an introduction to the organization of government, business, and labor in each of the five countries. Chapter 7 summarizes the findings of the country chapters and shows how they provide evidence for the theory proposed in Chapter 1.

I received support and encouragement from many sources. Institutional support at Indiana University was provided by the Department of Political Science and the Center for West European Studies. Major financial support for my research came from the Boas Foundation and the Office of Technology Assessment of the United States Congress. Smaller grants came from the German Marshall Fund, the Friedrich Ebert Foundation, and the American Enterprise Institute. Substantial institutional and intellectual support was provided by the Berkeley Roundtable on the International Economy and its principals: Michael Borrus, Stephen Cohen, Laura Tyson, and John Zysman.

The following individuals commented on early versions of the manuscript: John Alic, Claude Barfield, Alfred Diamant, Glenn Fong, Ernst B. Haas, Stephan Haggard, John Ikenberry, Gerd Junne, Peter Katzenstein, Robert Keohane, Todd Laporte, Charles Lipson, Robert Putnam, Duncan Snidal, Jay Stowsky, Susan Strange, Hans Van der Ven, Stephen Woolcock, David Yoffie, and John Zysman.

Excellent editorial assistance was provided by Paul Weisser and Trudie Calvert.

Finally, I could not have completed this work without the help and encouragement of my family, especially my wife, Joan, and my son, Zachary.

JEFFREY A. HART

Bloomington, Indiana

Rival Capitalists

ONE

State-Societal Arrangements and International Competitiveness

The main argument of this book is that variations in state-societal arrangements best explain changes in international competitiveness since World War II among five major industrial countries—the United States, Japan, Germany, France, and Britain. I focus on three important industries: steel, automobiles, and semiconductors. The creation and diffusion of new technologies is the most significant intervening variable between state-societal arrangements and international competitiveness (see Figure 1). This chapter elaborates that argument and discusses its relation to alternative explanations for changes in competitiveness.

After defining the explanatory and dependent variables and giving some background on their theoretical and conceptual roots, I provide quantitative evidence for economy-wide and industry-specific changes in national competitiveness. The consistency of these data requires explanation at the level of national systems because, even though internationalization of markets exposes all countries to a global, industry-specific logic, national logic prevails across industries within each country.

The connection between the creation and diffusion of new technologies and changes in competitiveness must be made at the level of specific industries because technologies vary considerably from industry to industry. Chapters 2 to 6 describe and summarize overall and industry-specific state-societal arrangements. The demonstration of the linkages between these arrangements and the creation and diffusion of technologies is left to the final chapter.

Figure 1. The impact of state-societal arrangements on international competitiveness.

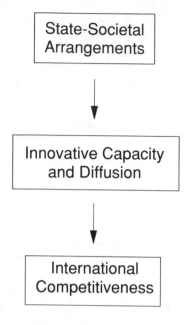

STATE-SOCIETAL ARRANGEMENTS

State-societal arrangements are defined as the manner in which state and civil societies are organized and institutionally linked. The state consists of a set of institutions mostly associated with the government but also including tripartite (government-business-labor) boards and commissions, state-owned business enterprises, and other parastatal organizations. Civil society is the domestic social environment in which the state operates. In contemporary advanced industrial countries, two groups in civil society, business and organized labor, are of primary importance, especially when considering competitiveness in manufacturing industries.[1]

The state-societal dichotomy is rooted in liberal political philosophy and premised on the notion that the power of the state should be and will be limited to prevent undue interference in the actions of individuals and selected collectivities.[2] In an ideal free enterprise economy, all

1. For a convincing argument that agricultural groups need to be included in descriptions of social dynamics in earlier historical periods, see Ronald Rogowski, *Commerce and Coalitions: How Trade Affects Domestic Political Alignments* (Princeton, N.J.: Princeton University Press, 1989).

2. For lengthier discussions of the concepts of state and civil society see Bertrand Badie and Pierre Birnbaum, *Sociologie de l'état* (Paris: Bernard Grasset, 1979); Martin

business corporations would be private and relatively independent of state agencies and thus part of civil society. All private individuals would also be members of civil society, unless they hold state offices. No capitalist country meets this liberal ideal; all use state-owned enterprises to perform certain functions of government and limit the autonomy of private firms through regulations.

The communist ideal for state-society relations subordinates the state to the interests of one class, the proletariat, in the expectation that the state eventually will wither away and a classless society be reached. The social democratic ideal gives the state sufficient power to reduce the inequities between classes that capitalism creates over time but tries to keep it accountable by maintaining a representative form of government.[3] The fascist ideal gives the head of state extraordinary powers, organizes societal interests from above, and prohibits the formation of autonomous groupings that might resist state leadership.[4] In the neocorporatist ideal the state and privileged groups—especially business and labor—work together to determine national policies.[5]

None of these ideals has ever been fully realized. Yet they have had a major influence on national and international politics in the twentieth century. National debates over state-societal relations tend to be defined in terms of these ideals. Not only do such debates become an important element of partisan politics; they become highly salient during and after major international wars, domestic social conflicts, and deep economic crises. At key moments in a nation's history, changes in state-societal arrangements may be embodied in new political, social,

---

Carnoy, *The State and Political Theory* (Princeton, N.J.: Princeton University Press, 1984); Eric A. Nordlinger, *On the Autonomy of the Democratic State* (Cambridge, Mass.: Harvard University Press, 1981); Reinhard Bendix, ed., *State and Society* (Boston: Little, Brown, 1968); Charles Tilly, ed., *The Formation of National States in Western Europe* (Princeton, N.J.: Princeton University Press, 1975); John A. Hall and G. John Ikenberry, *The State* (Minneapolis: University of Minnesota Press, 1989); and Alfred C. Stepan, *The State and Society: Peru in Comparative Perspective* (Princeton, N.J.: Princeton University Press, 1978).

3. See David Held and Joel Krieger, "Theories of the State: Some Competing Claims," in Stephen Bornstein, David Held, and Joel Krieger, eds., *The State in Capitalist Europe: A Casebook* (Winchester, Mass.: Allen and Unwin, 1984).

4. I owe this formulation of the fascist ideal to Gregory Kasza, *Administered Mass Organizations* (forthcoming).

5. A very clear statement of this ideal is in Wolfgang Streeck and Philippe C. Schmitter, "Community, Market, State—and Associations? The Prospective Contribution of Interest Governance to Social Order," in Wolfgang Streeck and Philippe C. Schmitter, eds., *Private Interest Government: Beyond Market and State* (Beverly Hills, Calif.: Sage, 1985), p. 10. See also Gerhard Lehmbruch, "Introduction: Neocorporatism in Comparative Perspective," in Gerhard Lehmbruch and Philippe C. Schmitter, eds., *Patterns in Corporatist Policy Making* (Beverly Hills, Calif.: Sage, 1982).

and economic institutions designed to settle the domestic debates, at least for a time.[6]

The ways state and society are organized and linked vary significantly from country to country as a result of historical and contextual factors. Different institutions are inherited from the past. Some states have more centralized bureaucratic systems than others, often recruiting from elite colleges and universities. Some states are more inclined than others to structure civil society through the exercise of state authority and, at times, direct intervention in the economy.[7]

SYSTEMATIC OBSERVATION OF STATE-SOCIETAL ARRANGEMENTS

State-societal arrangements vary across countries and across time. They may even vary across specific industries, although the empirical cases presented here suggest that this type of variation is not very important. To approach the observation of state-societal arrangements in the area of industrial competitiveness, I asked the following questions for each country examined in Chapters 2–6:

1. How is the government organized? Specifically, how centralized and influential are the bureaucracies that set industry-specific policies? What instruments are available to the government for making industrial policies? How inclined is the government to use these instruments? How successful is the government in getting its way with business or labor in conflicts over industrial policies?

2. How is the business sector organized? How powerful are business peak associations?[8] Do individual firms or subgroups have other channels for lobbying outside of business associations? Is there a system of "industrial families" (loose horizontal groupings) in the business sector? What is the role of the financial sector in underpinning these ar-

6. On this subject, see G. John Ikenberry, "Conclusion: An Institutional Approach to American Foreign Economic Policy," in G. John Ikenberry, David A. Lake, and Michael Mastanduno, eds., *The State and American Foreign Economic Policy* (Ithaca, N.Y.: Cornell University Press, 1988), pp. 223–25; and Stephen Krasner, "Approaches to the State: Alternative Conceptions and Historical Dynamics," *Comparative Politics* 16 (January 1984): 234.

7. The works that inspired this formulation are Andrew Shonfield, *Modern Capitalism* (London: Oxford University Press, 1965); Peter Katzenstein, ed., *Between Power and Plenty* (Madison: University of Wisconsin Press, 1978); John Zysman, *Governments, Markets, and Growth: Financial Systems and the Politics of Industrial Change* (Ithaca, N.Y.: Cornell University Press, 1983); and Peter Hall, *Governing the Economy: The Politics of State Intervention in Britain and France* (New York: Oxford University Press, 1986).

8. A peak association is an association that aspires to represent all organizations of a certain type (e.g., businesses or labor unions) in a given society. Examples of business peak associations are the U.S. Chamber of Commerce, the Japanese Keidanren, and the German Bundesverband der Deutschen Industrie. Examples of labor peak associations are the U.S. AFL-CIO and the German Deutsche Gewerkschaftsbund.

rangements? Are the articulated interests of business in the country so diverse that there is insufficient unity to influence government policies or legal regimes that affect business-labor relations?

3. How is labor organized? How powerful are labor peak associations? What percentage of the work force is unionized? Are unions organized on an enterprise or industrial basis? Can unions successfully block undesired government policies or managerial decisions?

4. What institutions link state and society? In particular, are individuals recruited for top positions in the government bureaucracy from elite colleges and universities? What role does the state play in financing those institutions? Does the government own major business enterprises or does it closely supervise the operations of "private" firms? Does the government help organize and fund consortia of businesses for the purpose of advancing industrial technology? Are there special institutions for transmitting abstract knowledge from universities to the business sector? What role do the state and business sectors play in providing training for workers? What parastatal institutions exist—especially those involving neocorporatist concertative mechanisms—and how important are they in specific policy realms?

In the final chapter of this book I argue that some state-societal arrangements are conducive to the creation and diffusion of new technologies and others are not. Differences in the state-societal arrangements among the five major industrial countries examined here emerge when one studies the distribution of power among government, business, and labor. I argue that the distribution of power among those three social actors is the basic underpinning of state-societal arrangements.

DEFINING INTERNATIONAL COMPETITIVENESS

Definitions of international competitiveness are controversial, but one proposed by the President's Commission on Industrial Competitiveness seems to satisfy many experts: "the degree to which a nation can, under free and fair market conditions, produce goods and services that meet the test of international markets while simultaneously maintaining or expanding the real income of its citizens."[9] This definition has three main elements that deserve elaboration.

9. *Global Competition: The New Reality,* Report of the President's Commission on Industrial Competitiveness, Vol. 2 (Washington, D.C.: U.S. Government Printing Office, 1985), p. 6; see also *The Cuomo Commission Report: A New American Formula for a Strong Economy* (New York: Simon and Schuster, 1988), p. 19; and Stephen S. Cohen and John Zysman, *Manufacturing Matters: The Myth of the Post-Industrial Economy* (New York: Basic Books, 1987), p. 60.

First, meeting the test of international markets means the ability to design, produce, and distribute goods and services at costs that are globally competitive. Factor costs and the application of the latest technologies are central here. If factor costs are high or rising, application of technologies that increase the productivity of factors will be crucial for maintaining or increasing competitiveness. If a country's factor costs are low, the application of productivity-enhancing technologies can improve its competitiveness.[10]

Second, there is the question of whether market conditions are free or fair. If they are not, then some countries will appear to be internationally competitive when they are not because their domestic markets are sheltered or their firms are receiving large subsidies. Any country can present a simulacrum of competitiveness by adopting illiberal policies. Similarly, truly competitive countries will appear not to be competitive because their unsubsidized and unprotected industries are forced to compete with subsidized or sheltered firms from other nations.

Third, there is the question of real incomes. If a country is experiencing a large increase in exports but real incomes are declining, workers and other citizens may be subsidizing the nation's competitiveness. Any country can adopt labor market policies that reduce real wages so as to improve its position in world trade, but this practice does not involve genuine competitiveness.[11]

National competitiveness is not the same as the competitiveness of nationally owned firms. Multinational firms frequently place large amounts of their productivity-enhancing technologies in foreign locations so they can be internationally competitive without affecting the competitiveness of the home country. Indeed, encouraging foreign firms that use state-of-the-art design, production, and distribution technologies to locate in a country can enhance its competitiveness more than supporting domestic firms would do.[12]

A country does not need to be competitive in all industries to be competitive overall, but it *does* need to be competitive in a variety of industries. Countries that become overly specialized in the production of a small number of industrial goods tend to become overly

10. For a much lengthier discussion of the variables that explain competitiveness, see Michael Porter, *The Competitive Advantage of Nations* (New York: Free Press, 1990), chap. 3.

11. "Competitiveness is associated with rising living standards, and an upgrading of employment" (Cohen and Zysman, *Manufacturing Matters*, p. 61).

12. This issue is discussed in Jeffrey A. Hart and Laura Tyson, "Responding to the Challenge of HDTV," *California Management Review* 31 (Summer 1989): 132–45; Robert B. Reich, "Who Is Us?" *Harvard Business Review* 68 (January–February 1990): 53–64; and Laura Tyson, "They Are Not Us: Why American Ownership Still Matters," *American Prospect*, no. 4 (Winter 1991): 37–49.

vulnerable to external economic shocks such as disruptions in the supply of vital inputs, sudden changes in the demand for specialized products, and predatory behavior on the part of foreign producers in upstream or downstream markets. More important, some industries are economically strategic in the sense that their failure to be competitive makes it impossible for a country to be competitive in others in which participation is necessary to obtain access to generic technologies.[13]

MEASURING INTERNATIONAL COMPETITIVENESS

National competitiveness may be measured at economy-wide and industry-specific levels. In this book, the stress is on the latter, although there appears to be sufficient consistency across industries to suggest that the economy-wide approach can also be useful. The main reason to measure competitiveness at the level of specific industries is that data on them are easier to interpret than data on the economy as a whole. Interpreting economy-wide data on competitiveness is complicated by problems to be discussed below. In addition, it is impossible to test whether technological innovation and diffusion are important mediating variables (hypothesized in Figure 1) without looking at industry-specific data because technologies vary widely from industry to industry. The competitiveness of an entire country cannot be measured by focusing on a small set of specific industries but must take into account a judicious combination of industry-specific and economy-wide indicators.

Measuring Competitiveness at the Level of the Whole Economy

International competitiveness can be measured on an economy-wide basis using such indicators as trade balances, world export shares, rates of productivity growth, growth in real wages, and price elasticities of imports.[14] Increasing trade balances and world export shares, high rates of productivity growth, rapidly growing real wages, and decreasing price elasticities of imports all indicate increasing international

13. See Hart and Tyson, "Responding to the Challenge," pp. 37–39. For a contrasting view, see Porter, *Competitive Advantage,* pp. 6–11. Here Porter argues that national competitiveness is either meaningless or simply a proxy for productivity. Porter does not accept the idea that some industries may be economically strategic but notes that firms in any given nation tend to be competitive in clusters of related industries.

14. The logic behind this last measure is that low price elasticities of imports will indicate quality differentials between domestic products and imports. See *Global Competition,* p. 8; and Cohen and Zysman, *Manufacturing Matters,* pp. 61, 68.

competitiveness. Because productivity growth tends to be strongly correlated with growth in real income, and sustained growth in productivity requires constant upgrading of production techniques, productivity growth is the most fundamental and reliable way of measuring national competitiveness.[15]

All the economy-wide indicators are imperfect in some respect. Markets are often not free or fair. Trade balances and world export shares are subject to government manipulation of exchange rates and trade barriers. National production and export statistics usually do not reflect the ability of multinational firms to penetrate foreign markets through local production and licensing of technologies. Labor productivity grows rapidly during periods of massive layoffs; both labor and capital productivity increase sharply whenever aggregate demand surges. Nevertheless, the indicators listed above do a reasonably good job of measuring shifts in competitiveness over time.

A more accurate view of competitiveness is obtained by combining the separate indicators into a composite view. For example, a country that experiences growth in productivity, world export shares, and real wages (e.g., Japan) is clearly more competitive than one experiencing declining productivity, world export shares, and real wages (e.g., Britain).

Trade Balances and World Export Shares

Between 1980 and 1987, Japan and Germany experienced increasing global trade surpluses, while the United States and Britain suffered increasing deficits (see Figure 2).[16] France suffered from chronic but relatively smaller trade deficits than both the United States and Britain in the 1980s. World export shares in manufactured goods provide a similar picture. The United States and Britain both lost considerably in their shares of world manufactured exports between 1960 and 1982, although the United States started from a higher level. Japan's share rose rapidly during the same period, from around 6 percent of world exports to around 14 percent. Germany held steady at around 20 percent and France at around 10 percent.[17]

15. Porter, *Competitive Advantage*, p. 6.
16. The trade surplus from exports of petroleum in Britain (which ended in 1983) complicates using the trade surplus as a measure of British competitiveness.
17. Bruce R. Scott, "National Strategies: Key to International Competition," in Bruce R. Scott and George C. Lodge, eds., *U.S. Competitiveness in the World Economy* (Boston: Harvard Business School Press, 1985), p. 27.

Figure 2. Balance of trade of the five countries

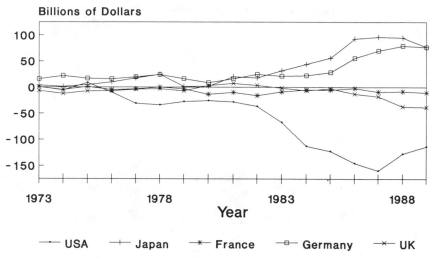

Billions of Dollars

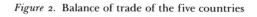

Source: International Monetary Fund, *International Financial Statistics Yearbook* (Washington, D.C., 1990), p. 140.

Productivity

Growth in productivity since 1960 has been most rapid in Japan and least rapid in the United States. From 1966 to 1973, Japanese total factor productivity grew at 6.3 percent per year. From 1960 to 1973, U.S. total factor productivity grew at 1.5 percent per year. French productivity growth has been somewhat more rapid than that of either Germany or Britain, but for all three it has been more rapid than for the United States (see Figure 3). Before the late 1960s, labor productivity in manufacturing in the United States grew at around 3 percent annually. Between 1973 and 1979, it grew at only 1 percent annually and increased to 3 percent between 1979 and 1986. But the authors of the MIT study *Made in America* warn against interpreting this as a return to economic health:

A significant fraction of the productivity gains in manufacturing were achieved by shutting down inefficient plants and by permanently laying off workers at others. Employment in U.S. manufacturing industry declined by 10 percent between 1979 and 1986, and that loss of jobs accounted for about 36 percent of the recorded improvement in labor productivity. Another reason for caution is that the productivity recovery spanned a deep recession; productivity growth always accelerates

Figure 3. Growth in productivity in the five countries, 1960–1988

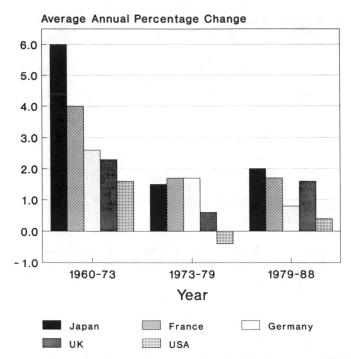

Average Annual Percentage Change

Year

■ Japan   ▨ France   □ Germany

▨ UK   ▦ USA

Source: Organization for Economic Cooperation and Development, *OECD Economic Outlook*, No. 48 (December 1990), p. 120.

following a recession as factories increase their output and take up the slack in the economy.[18]

Growth in Real Wages

Real wages rose steadily in all five countries between 1960 and 1989. The largest increases occurred in France and Britain (see Figure 4), the smallest in Germany and the United States, which started the period with higher absolute wages than the other three. That real wages in Japan and Germany grew slower than those in France and Britain, although the former two countries outperformed the others in trade and productivity, suggests strongly that wage restraint was an important factor in their increased overall competitiveness. The slow growth of U.S. real wages combined with its poor trade, profits, and productivity

18. Michael L. Dertouzos, Richard K. Lester, Robert M. Solow, and the MIT Commission on Industrial Productivity, *Made in America: Regaining the Productive Edge* (Cambridge, Mass.: MIT Press, 1989), p. 31.

Figure 4. Growth in real wages in the five countries, 1960–1989

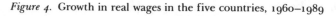

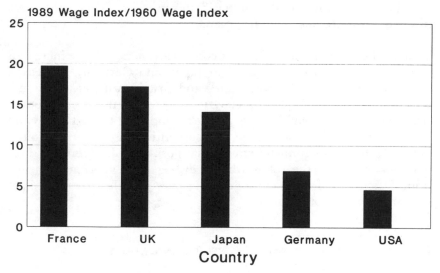

1989 Wage Index/1960 Wage Index

Country

Source: International Monetary Fund, *International Financial Statistics Yearbook* (Washington, D.C., 1990), pp. 112–13.

performance suggests a general decline in competitiveness. The British pattern, as usual, is the worst: bad trade and productivity performances and rapidly increasing real wages.

Price Elasticity of Imports

The price elasticity of imports in the United States increased in the 1970s and 1980s, as U.S. buyers no longer were willing to pay a premium for U.S.-made products because of perceived differences in quality.[19] Price elasticity of imports has never been particularly high in Japan because of a generally low propensity to import (which is related to the Japanese distribution system). Nevertheless, as Japanese consumers became more affluent in the 1980s they began to buy consumer products from abroad: luxury goods from Europe and low-end standardized products from Asian developing countries. Increased importation from Asia was partly the result of perceptions of decreasing quality differentials, that from Europe the result of continued perceptions of quality differentials in favor of European goods. With a few

19. Cohen and Zysman, *Manufacturing Matters,* p. 67, citing Elizabeth Kremp and Jacques Mistral, "Commerce extérieur american: D'où vient, où va le deficit?" *Economie prospective internationale* 22 (1985): 5–41.

exceptions, Japanese buyers remained convinced of the superiority of Japanese producer goods. Consumers in Britain and France have behaved more like those in the United States in recent years, consumers in Germany more like those in Japan.

In sum, the economy-wide data on competitiveness indicate increased competitiveness across the board in Japan and Germany, decreased competitiveness in the United States and Britain, with France somewhere in the middle. Japan does particularly well in trade and productivity, but Germany remains a very close second. The United States and Britain have suffered a decline in competitiveness, but the United States started from a much better initial position. The French did remarkably well until the 1980s, when they began to experience chronic trade deficits and decreased productivity growth while wages remained on a steep upward trajectory.

Measuring Competitiveness in Specific Industries

National competitiveness in specific industries may be measured by growth in national shares of global production, in employment of production workers, and in revenues and profits of firms in the industry and by the frequency of industrial crises. In a specific industry, a country that is increasing its share of global production, increasing (or decreasing relatively slowly) its level of employment, increasing its revenues and profits, and experiencing very few industrial crises relative to other countries has increased its international competitiveness. Although it is impossible to present statistical evidence for all these indicators, it will be possible to show that the available industry-specific data reinforce the message conveyed by the economy-wide data; that is, that Japan and Germany have increased their international competitiveness relative to the United States and Britain, while France lies somewhere in between.

Production Shares

Global production of steel was 313 million metric tons in 1956 and by 1985 had increased to 793 million metric tons. The average annual growth of steel production by volume during that period was 3.4 percent. The share of U.S. production in this total dropped from 37 percent to 11 percent (see Figure 5). The absolute level of U.S. production remained near the 1956 level through the beginning of the 1980s, averaging around 120 million metric tons. The mid-1950s were

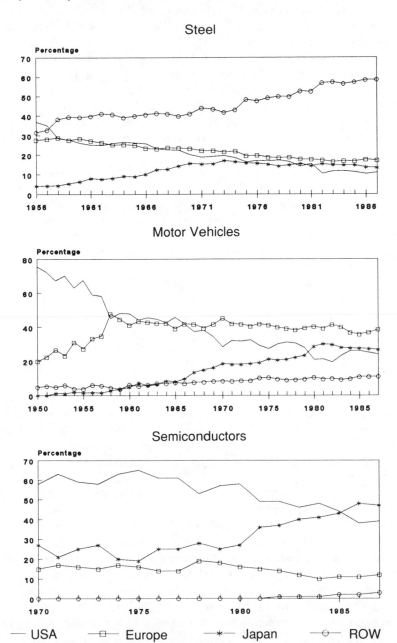

Figure 5. World production shares in steel, motor vehicles, and semiconductors

Source: American Iron and Steel Institute, *Annual Statistical Report* (Washington, D.C., various years); Motor Vehicle Manufacturers Association, *Motor Vehicle Facts and Figures* (Detroit, various years); and Dataquest.

Note: ROW stands for "rest of the world." Dataquest statistics for semiconductor production include estimates of captive production of semiconductors by large firms like IBM and AT&T.

a relatively high point in the U.S. share of global production because of the sales of iron and steel to Europe, which was not fully recovered from the damages sustained in World War II, and because the U.S. defense industry had grown enormously during the Korean War.

The European share of global steel production rose from the mid-1950s to the early 1970s, finally overtaking U.S. production in 1968, and then dropped off to a plateau of 130–140 million metric tons. The Japanese, also recovering from World War II, increased their share of global production from 4 percent in 1956 to around 15 percent in the late 1970s. Japanese steel production surpassed that of the United States in 1980, but the gross national product (GNP) of Japan was then about half that of the United States. Japanese production levels hovered around 115 million metric tons after 1975. U.S. production, in contrast, never regained its high point of 151 million metric tons (in 1973) but sank to below 90 million metric tons by the mid-1980s.

Global motor vehicle production grew rapidly after the 1950s, increasing at an average annual rate of 5.1 percent between 1956 and 1985. The number of motor vehicles produced doubled from 10 million in the early 1950s to 20 million in the mid-1960s and doubled again to 40 million in the late 1970s. The U.S. share of global production dropped from 75 percent in 1950 to 26 percent in 1985. Europe increased its share from about 20 percent in 1950 to almost 50 percent in the late 1960s but fell back to less than 40 percent by the end of the 1970s. Japan increased its share from virtually zero in 1950 to more than 30 percent by 1981. Even though Europe remained the largest producing region, Japan became the largest producing country, taking the lead away from the United States in 1980. From a peak of 12.9 million motor vehicles produced in 1978, U.S. production declined to 7.0 million in 1982 (lower than the production level of 1962), recovering to 11.7 million in 1985.

In 1987, world production of semiconductors was worth around $39 billion and of integrated circuits (semiconductor devices that contain entire electronic circuits on a single chip) around $29 billion. Between 1970 and 1987, world production of semiconductors grew at an average annual rate of 18.8 percent. The share of discrete devices (devices that are *not* integrated circuits) in the overall market for semiconductors has been declining steadily since the invention of integrated circuits in 1958. Integrated circuits made up slightly over 30 percent of world production of semiconductors in 1970; by the 1980s, this figure was over 70 percent.

In 1975, the United States accounted for 65 percent of world production of semiconductors and 76 percent of integrated circuits. The corresponding figures for 1987 were 39 and 41 percent, respectively.

Japan's share of world semiconductor production increased from less than 20 percent in 1975 to 47 percent in 1987. Its share of world integrated circuit production increased from 14 percent in 1975 to 48 percent in 1987. In 1986 Japanese production of both semiconductors and integrated circuits surpassed that of the United States.

The increase in the Japanese share of world production is remarkable, but perhaps more important is its domination of markets for the more advanced integrated circuits and especially complementary metal oxide silicon (CMOS) devices and the latest generation of random access memories (RAMs). By the end of 1979, Japanese firms controlled 43 percent of the U.S. market for 16-kilobit (16K) dynamic RAM (DRAM) devices.[20] By the end of 1981, they supplied almost 70 percent of 64K DRAMs in the open part of the U.S. market.[21] In 1984, Japanese firms introduced 256K DRAMs before major U.S. firms did so and replicated that feat in 1987 with 1-megabit DRAMs. Japanese firms controlled over 90 percent of both 256K and 1-megabit DRAM markets after 1986 and, on average, 75 percent of total DRAM markets between 1985 and 1987.[22]

Employment

Employment in the British steel industry fell from over 270,000 in 1972 to around 52,000 in 1981. This was the largest percentage drop in steel employment in the five countries, but the largest absolute decline occurred in the United States, where it dropped from 478,000 in 1974 to 170,000 in 1988. Although there were major reductions in the number of jobs in the Japanese and German steel industries after 1973, they were not as large as in the United States and Britain (see Figure 6).[23]

Employment in the British auto industry fell from 184,000 in 1972 (a peak year) to 78,000 in 1985 (see Figure 6). U.S. auto employment dropped from 304,000 in 1978 to 194,000 in 1982 but rose to around 250,000 in 1984 and 1985 because of the recovery of the U.S. economy and the voluntary export restraint (VER) agreement with Japan. The French and German auto industries created new jobs in the 1960s and

20. Michael Borrus, James Millstein, and John Zysman, *International Competition in Advanced Industrial Sectors: Trade and Development in the Semiconductor Industry* (Washington, D.C.: Joint Economic Committee of Congress, 1982), p. 106.

21. Gene Bylinsky, "Japan's Ominous Chip Victory," *Fortune*, December 14, 1981, p. 55.

22. Dataquest data presented by Andrew A. Procasssini, president of the Semiconductor Industry Association, at Stanford University, October 21, 1988.

23. All data cited in this paragraph are from the *U.S. Industrial Outlook* (Washington, D.C.: U.S. Government Printing Office, 1988 and 1989).

Figure 6. Employment in steel and motor vehicles

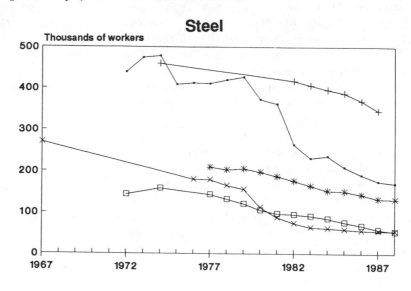

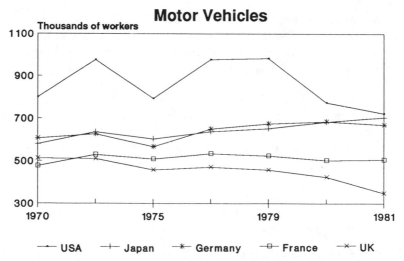

Sources: Louka Tsoukalis and Robert Strauss, "Crisis and Adjustment in European Steel: Beyond Laisser-Faire," in Yves Mény and Vincent Wright, eds., *The Politics of Steel: Western Europe and the Steel Industry in the Crisis Years* (New York: Walter de Gruyter, 1986), p. 208; Statistical Office of the European Community, *Iron and Steel Yearbook* (Luxembourg: Eurostat, 1989), p. 24; *U.S. Industrial Outlook* (Washington, D.C.: U.S. Government Printing Office, various years); and Alan Altshuler, Martin Anderson, Daniel Jones, Daniel Roos, and James Womack, *The Future of the Automobile: The Report of MIT's International Automobile Program* (Cambridge, Mass.: MIT Press, 1984), p. 201.

1970s, but the French industry began to shed jobs in the 1980s. German employment in automobile production stabilized during the 1980s, possibly at the expense of needed rationalization.

Accurate and fully comparable statistical data on employment in the semiconductor industry are hard to find; most countries have only recently begun to report figures on employment in this industry. Several lump these data together with data on employment in electronics or data processing. My findings take these caveats into account.

Employment in semiconductor production in the United States rose from 234,000 in 1972 to 375,000 in 1984 and then fell to around 320,000 in 1986–87.[24] Employment in electronics in Japan was exceedingly buoyant from the early 1970s on, increasing from 948,000 workers in 1982 to 1,212,000 workers in 1986.[25] In the production of monolithic integrated circuits employment remained stable at around 50,000 workers in France, Britain, and Germany between 1983 and 1989. In Germany employment in hybrid integrated circuits increased from 58,000 to 103,000 workers and in France from 80,000 to over 150,000 workers during the same period; in Britain employment in this area declined slightly from 182,000 to 164,000 workers.[26]

Profitability

Data on the profitability of domestically owned firms in each industry are presented in the chapters on each country. I will not attempt to present a statistical overview because wide variations in the degree of vertical integration of firms in the five countries and major differences in accounting methods make comparisons difficult. Nevertheless, some summary judgments can be made about industry-specific profitability.

Firms in all five countries experienced financial difficulties during global recessions, but Japanese and German firms tended to do better during these periods and to emerge from them in better shape than American, British, and French firms. Both Japanese and German steel firms suffered financially when demand for steel stabilized after 1973. In contrast, the larger automobile firms of both countries did remarkably well financially during the entire period. There were exceptions, of course, such as the financial problems of Mazda and Volkswagen in

24. Ibid.

25. MITI data from the census of manufacturers as cited in *Facts and Figures on the Japanese Electronics Industry* (Tokyo: Electronic Industries Association of Japan, 1988), p. 29. These figures include employment in the manufacturing of all types of electronic components and systems and not just in semiconductor manufacturing.

26. Eurostat, *Industrial Production: Quarterly Statistics* (Luxembourg: Eurostat, Third Quarter 1990), p. 173.

the mid-1970s, but these were generally short-lived. Smaller firms that had financial problems were either acquired by or became linked to larger firms through various cooperative agreements. The Japanese semiconductor industry has made excellent profits, especially since 1986, whereas those of the semiconductor operations of Siemens, Germany's largest producer, have been relatively small compared with its main source of profits: large central-office switches for public telecommunications networks.

French firms did less well financially than the German and Japanese firms, especially during the 1980s, after steady growth in revenues and profits in the 1960s and 1970s. The French steel firms were unprofitable from the late 1970s until the late 1980s (see Figure 11 in Chapter 3). The two main French auto firms suffered losses from 1980 until 1986–87, although Renault's losses were deeper and longer lasting than Peugeot's (see Figure 12 in Chapter 3). The only major French producer of semiconductors, Thomson, did not make much money from that business during the 1980s.

British financial performance mirrored the stop-and-go pattern of the British economy, but profits took a turn for the worse in the 1970s and 1980s. British Steel Corporation and British Leyland, the national champions in steel and automobiles, suffered deep and prolonged losses in the 1970s and 1980s, even during periods of economic recovery (see Figures 14 and 15 in Chapter 4). British semiconductor firms were marginally profitable, but profits were contingent on the continued funding of defense programs which provided the main source of demand in Britain for application-specific integrated circuits. With the exception of the small Inmos Company, British firms did not produce high-volume, standardized semiconductor devices.

American financial performance was reasonably strong in all three industries until the 1970s. The profits of the American auto industry generally depended on domestic demand and thus were cyclical. The huge losses of Chrysler and the lower profitability of Ford and General Motors (GM) beginning in the late 1970s were ended artificially when a voluntary export restraint with Japan was negotiated in 1981 (see Figure 22 in Chapter 6). The semiconductor industry seemed recession-proof until the global slump of 1985 (see Figure 23 in Chapter 6). Firms such as Intel and Motorola sprang back quickly when demand increased again, but others such as AMD and National Semiconductor never fully recovered.

Thus profitability data reinforce the notion that Germany and Japan experienced increased international competitiveness during the period and the United States and Britain suffered from competitive decline. The French experience was mixed: profits were generally up until 1980, and the losses of the mid-1980s were followed by a turnaround in the late 1980s.

Industrial Crises

Table 1 lists forty-seven industrial crises the five countries' steel, automobile, and semiconductor industries experienced between 1960 and 1989. The main criterion for considering an event a crisis is the perception of the potential for financial collapse of a firm or industry and possible consequences in increased national or regional unemployment and negative effects for important downstream industries.[27] Each crisis also involves a combination of government, business, and labor responses and a variety of outcomes, including bankruptcies, liquidations, acquisitions and mergers, and government rescues.

Japan experienced the fewest industrial crises during the period and only one after 1973. Most of its crises were limited in scope, dealt with quickly, and did not recur. Britain and France suffered the most crises, but those in Britain were deeper and more prone to recur. French crises were often provoked by the breakdown of bargaining between business interests and the state and thus are not always good indicators of changes in competitiveness of firms or industries. Even though the United States suffered relatively few industrial crises, those that occurred tended to be industry-wide and were more likely to be responded to by government imposition of trade barriers than in the other four countries (see Chapter 6).

One surprise in Table 1 is the frequency of industrial crises in Germany. The most serious of these were in steel, and the others were relatively limited in scope and time. The German system was able to manage most of its crises without resort to government intervention. Indeed, the federal government's avoidance of industry-specific interventions is a key factor in the generation of German industrial crises (see Chapter 5).

Industry-specific measures show that Japan and Germany have become more competitive and Britain and the United States have become less so. Industry-specific competitiveness in France rose until the late 1970s and declined in the 1980s. Although some anomalies exist in specific indicators, the general pattern is clear and is highly consistent with that suggested by the economy-wide indicators discussed above.

27. For a more complete description and analysis of these data, see Jeffrey A. Hart, "Crisis Management and the Institutionalization of Corporatist Bargaining Mechanisms," paper delivered at the Conference of Europeanists of the Council for European Studies, Washington, D.C., October 18–20, 1985.

Table 1. Industrial crises since 1960 in the five industrial countries in steel, autos, and electronics

Country	Steel	Autos	Electronics
U.S.A.	1968 1977 1981	1970 Chrysler 1979 Chrysler 1980	1985 semiconductors
Japan	1964	1966 Prince 1968 Isuzu, Mitsubishi 1977 Toyo Kogyo (Mazda)	
Germany	1962 1977 Saar 1982 Ruhr	1965 Auto Union 1967 BMW 1969 NSU 1974 VW	1980 AEG-Telefunken 1982 AEG-Telefunken
France	1965 1976 1983 Creusot	1963 Simca 1974 Citroen 1978 Chrysler 1980 Renault 1984 Citroen	1964 Bull 1968 CSF 1970 Bull/GE 1975 CII 1977 Sescosem
Britain	1967 1977 BSC 1982 BSC	1964 Rootes 1967 Triumph, Talbot 1974 Chrysler 1977 Chrysler 1981 BL 1982 Delorean 1986 BL/Rover	1964 ICL 1980 ICL 1984 Inmos 1989 Inmos

Source: Jeffrey A. Hart, "Crisis Management and the Institutionalization of Corporatist Bargaining Mechanisms," paper delivered at the Conference of Europeanists of the Council for European Studies, Washington, D.C., October 18–20, 1985.

Note: Each crisis is identified by its initial year. If no specific firm or region is mentioned after that date, the crisis affected the whole industry in all regions.

Technological Innovation and Diffusion in Competitiveness

Technological innovation was central in determining which firms and countries would come out on top of international competition. State-societal arrangements played a key role in the creation and diffusion of the necessary technologies and therefore had a major effect on international competitiveness.

The Steel Industry

The most important technologies introduced into the steel industry after World War II were basic-oxygen furnaces and continuous casting. Basic-oxygen furnaces first replaced other types on a major scale in Japan, spread quickly to Germany, and diffused more slowly to the rest of Europe and the United States. In 1960, 11.9 percent of Japanese production was basic oxygen, compared with 3.4 percent in the United States. In 1970, 79.1 percent of Japanese production was basic oxygen, while U.S. production was still only 48.2 percent basic oxygen.[28] The larger German companies were also quicker to adopt basic-oxygen furnaces than most U.S., French, and British firms.

The basic-oxygen technology was invented in Austria. The Japanese firms licensed the necessary patents from Canadian firms and encouraged the major Japanese firms to adopt this technology in part to lower their dependence on imported scrap iron and steel, a dependence that had been present in U.S.-Japanese relations in the years before the attack on Pearl Harbor.[29] The firms were motivated to their dependence on imported scrap because large U.S. firms set the prices just high enough to discourage competition.

The basic-oxygen technology was risky because it was unproven at the size required to have cost advantages over the Bessemer technology. In the 1950s, when U.S. producers made major investments to upgrade their facilities, they did not convert, either because they did not see the future of the basic-oxygen technology or because their major investors were unwilling to assume the risks involved in adopting the new technology.[30]

Bad management or risk-averse financial institutions may have slowed the adoption of basic oxygen technology in France, Britain, and the United States, but one reason for its slow diffusion in the United States was that investments were made in the 1950s in the now obsolete older technologies. Nevertheless, by the mid-1970s, the U.S. industry had caught up with the rest of the world in the adoption of oxygen furnaces (see Figure 7).

U.S. industry remained far behind Japan and Europe in the adoption of continuous casting. Before its introduction, steel ingots or slabs were cast in separate plants and then reheated in another location so that they could be formed or rolled into their final shapes. With continuous casting, the molten steel is poured from the steelmaking furnace directly onto a processing line that produces the required shapes.

28. Leonard H. Lynn, *How Japan Innovates: A Comparison with the United States in the Case of Oxygen Steelmaking* (Boulder, Colo.: Westview, 1982), p. 23.

29. Together with Britain and the Netherlands, the United States imposed an embargo on iron ore and scrap exports to Japan in July 1941 after the takeover of Indochina. See Paul Kennedy, *The Rise and Fall of the Great Powers* (New York: Random House, 1987), p. 303.

30. I conducted personal interviews with representatives of governments, businesses, and labor unions over several years. Unless otherwise noted these interviews were carried out under a guarantee of confidentiality in order to elicit necessary information. I tried to verify information obtained in interviews with documentary materials whenever that was possible. This source is referred to hereafter as "Interview materials."

Figure 7. Diffusion of new production technologies

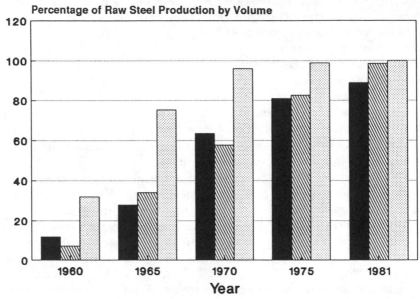

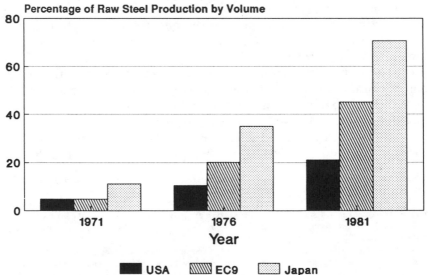

Source: Donald Barnett and Louis Schorsch, *Steel: Upheaval in a Basic Industry* (Cambridge, Mass.: Ballinger, 1983), p. 55.

Substantial savings are realized in the energy required to reheat the cooled steel ingots and slabs and in processing time and handling. Continuous casting requires relatively sophisticated scheduling, however, which has become easier with the introduction of computer-controlled production lines.

In adopting continuous casting the Japanese had the advantage that many of their plants built in the 1960s were "greenfield" plants (on sites where no previous facility had existed) as opposed to the "brownfield" plants (modernized or renovated facilities) of the United States and Europe.[31] Nevertheless, some new integrated plants with continuous casters were built in the United States and Europe. The steel plants of Britain, France, the Saar Valley in Germany, and the United States, however, were predominantly in traditional steel-producing regions where there was little room for plant expansion or where the costs of building greenfield plants were so high as to discourage the required investment. Higher labor costs and environmental restrictions were minor compared with the obstacles to upgrading production technologies.

Chapters 3, 4, and 6 will describe major mistakes in France, Britain, and the United States that delayed the phasing out of obsolete production facilities. In Britain, when steel production in modern plants expanded in the 1970s, obsolete plants should have been shut down. The British paid a high price for not doing so, as did France and the United States in similar situations.

When demand for steel fell following the oil price increases of 1973, no national steel industry was in a strong financial position. By the early 1980s, even the traditionally strong firms of the Ruhr Valley in Germany were experiencing financial losses because of depressed prices in a European market glutted with excess production. Nippon Steel also experienced lower than average rates of profitability and began to redeploy its idle workers by loaning them to other firms. The German and Japanese firms, however, weathered the recessions better than did the firms of the other three countries; employment in steel decreased in Germany and Japan but not as much as in the other three countries.

The Auto Industry

Technology played a vital role in the rise of the Japanese automobile industry as well. Both product and process innovations were

31. See Ira C. Magaziner and Robert B. Reich, *Minding America's Business: The Decline and Rise of the American Economy* (New York: Vintage Books, 1983), chap. 13.

important. In the 1950s and 1960s, the Japanese firms worked at catching up to U.S. and European product and process technologies. Initially, the Japanese firms imported new product technologies through licensing and co-production agreements with Western firms. By the mid-1960s, they began to produce their own car models and to compete intensively among themselves for domestic market shares.

Toyota invented an entirely new way to produce motor vehicles. The assembly process was redesigned to reduce the time required to produce a single unit. This redesign included the shift to *kanban*, or just-in-time production, wherein minimal inventories of components and parts were kept and suppliers were required to make early morning deliveries of only the parts needed for the day's production schedule. Suppliers had to locate near the main factory for this system to be feasible, in marked contrast with the wide distribution of suppliers in both the U.S. and European systems.[32]

By the 1970s, the Japanese auto firms began to respond to increasing domestic wage rates by automating production and assembly with increased use of robots, computer-controlled machine tools, and computerized assembly lines. These new process technologies allowed Japanese firms to increase worker productivity in the face of increased wages and also to improve the quality of vehicles produced. Products were redesigned to make the new processes work more efficiently and to make the products more reliable. The resulting new models were able to compete overseas with the generally higher-quality vehicles produced in the United States and Europe. Computerized automation reduced downtime for retooling for the annual changes in models, resulting in major efficiency gains for Japanese firms.

The innovations pioneered by the Japanese might not have resulted in such dramatic increases in exports had not the increased oil prices created a demand for small cars—especially in the huge North American market. Had U.S. producers matched Japanese innovations in small car production, Japan's opportunities in that market would have been greatly diminished. Chapter 6 will take up the question of why the U.S. auto industry did not respond rapidly enough to the Japanese challenge and will provide an answer in terms of state-societal arrangements.

U.S. product and process technology lagged seriously behind that of Japan, especially in small cars, and European technology followed at a somewhat shorter lag. European production was aimed to meet demand for small cars, and many of the product innovations introduced in Japanese models either originated in Europe or were quickly copied there. Some European firms were slower than others in this regard, of

32. See note 61 in Chapter 2.

course. British Leyland (now called the Rover Group) suffered the most from its inability to match Japanese innovations, a suffering accentuated by its overmanning with high-wage labor. French and Italian producers were lulled into a false sense of security by traditional tariff and nontariff barriers and, in the case of France, the availability of less expensive North African and Turkish workers. Even Volkswagen suffered diminished export demand as a result of intensified competition from Japan and problems in making the transition to multi-model production in the mid-1970s.

European firms responded to the Japanese challenge by accelerating the diffusion of computerized automation. Volkswagen, Renault, and Fiat rapidly introduced new flexible manufacturing systems that allowed them to produce more than one model on a single production line. Automation was also used as a tool of management by eliminating workers from processes that were particularly vulnerable to work stoppages.[33] Both European and U.S. manufacturers moved some production to lower-wage countries.

The issue of offshoring of production comes up again in the case of semiconductors. Japanese auto and semiconductor producers acted as if they did not have the option of locating labor-intensive production processes overseas, thus forcing themselves to use automation to compensate for increasing wages. U.S. and European firms, in marked contrast, used a combination of offshoring and less expensive foreign workers to compete with Japanese firms. Even after Japanese wage rates began to increase in the 1960s and 1970s, most U.S. and European firms continued to believe that differences in wage rates were the most important reason for the lower prices of Japanese cars. Only when those firms began to perceive that Japanese innovations in process technology were compensating for rising labor costs did they make the necessary investments in production technology. By and large, the Europeans and the European subsidiaries of U.S. firms were faster in doing this than the North American subsidiaries of U.S. firms.

The Semiconductor Industry

From the invention of the transistor in the late 1940s, the semiconductor industry was characterized by very rapid rates of technological innovation. The jump from integrated circuits to large-scale integrated (LSI) circuits in the mid-1970s was made possible by the invention of a new process in which photographically produced masks created an

33. See, for example, Wolfgang Streeck and Andreas Hoff, "Industrial Relations and Structural Change in the International Automobile Industry," working paper, International Institute of Management, Berlin, August 1981.

electronic circuit of thousands of transistors, resistors, and capacitors on a small portion (chip) of a wafer of silicon. This process made possible a series of product innovations, including the calculator chips that were responsible for the rapid rise in the fortunes of companies like Texas Instruments and National Semiconductor. The next generation, very-large-scale integrated (VLSI) products, in the late 1970s was made possible by another process innovation—the wafer stepper. Wafer steppers allowed manufacturers to etch hundreds of copies of a single circuit design on a silicon wafer.

Photolithography and wafer steppers alone were not responsible for the move from one generation of integrated circuits to another. They had to be supplemented with a variety of new technologies to produce wafers with fewer and fewer impurities and very smooth surfaces so that smaller and smaller line widths could be etched on the silicon. A variety of chemical baths evolved to make the etching process cheaper and more reliable. Clean-room technology also evolved to make the chip yields per wafer high enough that new generation products were price competitive with older generation products. Finally, the processes by which circuit designs were converted into masks had to be improved as line widths got smaller. But the transition from generation to generation would have been impossible without advances in photolithography and the introduction of wafer steppers.[34]

Japanese firms were not competitive with U.S. firms in integrated circuits until the transition from LSI to VLSI circuits. Previously, by the time the Japanese firms' manufacturing costs reached U.S. levels, the U.S. firms had begun to produce the next generation of circuits. U.S. firms were driven to innovate in semiconductors first by the rapid growth of demand from the military and space programs and later by the enormous growth of the computer industry. The innovative potential of Japanese firms was limited by their having to supply the demand for consumer electronics circuitry.

In the transition to VLSI, however, both the major firms and the Japanese government were committed to beating the Americans in process technology so as not to be dealt out of the competition in VLSI products. The government also believed that overtaking the United States in semiconductors was the key to improving Japanese competitiveness in all major downstream industries such as consumer electron-

34. See Ernest Braun and Stuart Macdonald, *Revolution in Miniature: The History and Impact of Semiconductor Electronics*, 2d ed. (New York: Cambridge University Press, 1982); Michael Borrus, *Competing for Control: America's Stake in Microelectronics* (Cambridge, Mass.: Ballinger, 1988); and George Gilder, *Microcosm: The Quantum Revolution in Economics and Technology* (New York: Simon and Schuster, 1989). Gilder provides an excellent bibliography on this subject on pp. 385–402.

ics, computers, and telecommunications equipment. Thus in the transition from LSI to VLSI in semiconductors, the connection between state-societal arrangements and technological innovation was extremely clear.

Technological innovations were very important, in some cases crucial, in explaining the rise in the international competitiveness of Japanese firms in steel, automobiles, and semiconductors and the continued or enhanced competitiveness of German steel and automobile firms. Almost every decline in competitiveness in the three industries can be traced to a failure either to invent or to incorporate a new product or process technology. The technological explanation does not explain all cases of rises and declines in competitiveness, of course, but as a general explanation it is superior to its main competitors.

ALTERNATIVE EXPLANATIONS OF CHANGES IN INTERNATIONAL COMPETITIVENESS

Five main approaches besides the state-societal approach outlined above have been put forward to explain changes in competitiveness: the macroeconomic, culturalist, statist, neocorporatist, and coalitional approaches. All of these have severe shortcomings, which is why a new one is needed. Some of these approaches are more parsimonious than the state-societal arrangements approach, but none fits the data as well.

Macroeconomic Explanations

The macroeconomic approach to explaining changes in competitiveness focuses on variables connected with factor prices, aggregate demand, the rate of savings and investment, and international currency exchange rates. It is parsimonious because it focuses only on underlying economic conditions, which are often assumed to be determined primarily by market forces and to be only marginally affected by government policies. Thus the macroeconomic approach appears at first glance to dispense with the need to consider government policies, business strategy, or institutional variations across countries. But behind almost any given macroeconomic explanation is a deeper set of causal factors that operate at the level of state-societal arrangements.

The prices of factors of production—land, labor, and capital—are considered in classical and neoclassical trade theory to be crucial in determining the comparative advantages of nations. If international trade is open and free, a country with a relative abundance of capital and relative scarcity of labor will specialize in the production of capital-intensive goods and exchange those goods for labor-intensive products from abroad. A country with a relative abundance of labor but a relative scarcity of capital will specialize in the production of labor-intensive goods and will trade them for capital-intensive products from abroad. Both countries will be better off as a result because both will gain from the collectively more efficient allocation of resources.[35]

Wage and interest rates are sometimes taken as rough indicators of the relative scarcity of labor and capital, and analysts often claim that countries with low wage rates (and high interest rates) should specialize in the production of labor-intensive goods and countries with high wage rates (and low interest rates) should specialize in the production of capital-intensive goods. Similarly, it is claimed that if wage rates are rising, as they are in almost all industrialized nations, there will be a natural tendency for countries to disinvest from labor-intensive production and shift investment to capital-intensive areas.

If one wants to remain competitive in the production of labor-intensive goods, one must accept lower wages in that industry. If wages are "sticky" because of labor-management contracting or minimum wage laws, either unemployment will increase or there will be labor shortages in other industries. Either will be harmful to the economy as a whole. The use of protectionist policies (tariffs and nontariff barriers) to preserve jobs in labor-intensive industries will not succeed in the long run and will place a difficult and unnecessary burden (in the form of higher costs) on other domestic industries that use the outputs of those industries as inputs.[36]

This is an elegant and highly useful logical structure for understanding basic forces in international trade. Yet it has serious shortcomings for understanding trade among the industrialized countries and therefore as an explanation for shifts in competitiveness. Trade among rich countries is not as easily categorized as based on either labor- or capital-intensive production as is trade between rich and poor countries. With the notable exception of Japan, trade among the rich countries is mostly intraindustry trade, that is, an exchange of goods in

35. For more complete summaries of the results of neoclassical trade theories, see Edward Leamer, *Sources of International Comparative Advantage: Theory and Evidence* (Cambridge, Mass.: MIT Press, 1984), chaps. 1–2; and Elhanan Helpman and Paul R. Krugman, *Market Structure and Foreign Trade: Increasing Returns, Imperfect Competition, and the International Economy* (Cambridge, Mass.: MIT Press, 1985), chap. 1.

36. See, for example, J. Peter Neary, "Intersectoral Capital Mobility, Wage Stickiness, and the Case for Adjustment Assistance," in Jagdish N. Bhagwati, ed., *Import Competition and Response* (Chicago: University of Chicago Press, 1982); and David G. Tarr and Morris E. Morkre, *Aggregate Costs to the United States of Tariffs and Quotas on Imports* (Washington, D.C.: Federal Trade Commission, 1984).

almost all industrial categories without specializing in goods for which factors are relatively abundant.[37]

Japan and Germany, which have increasing real wage rates and are increasingly competitive internationally, have not diversified out of labor-intensive production as is predicted by neoclassical trade theory. Rather, they have automated production in labor-intensive goods and shifted investment toward capital- and knowledge-intensive industries so as to remain competitive in a broad variety of industries. They are producing more technologically advanced and higher-priced labor-intensive goods to compensate for higher relative wage and capital costs. Although there has been some offshoring of production by Japanese and German firms in low-wage countries through contracting the direct foreign investment, this option has been exercised less frequently than it has by firms in the United States and Britain.[38]

The key problem with applying the factor prices approach to competition among the industrialized countries seems to be the great importance of technology and education to compensate for resource and factor scarcities and for high or increasing labor costs. Education produces knowledge and skills that ease the creation and diffusion of new technologies. Education also seems to affect tastes, often accentuating national differences in countries that have achieved a certain level of affluence, which provides an important advantage for firms that understand national differences in tastes.

Other macroeconomic approaches to competitiveness stress the growth of aggregate demand and the level of savings and investment as key to understanding shifts in international competitiveness, especially among the industrialized countries. This approach also has a compelling logic. Faster growth in aggregate demand creates more capital for investment than does slower growth. Countries experiencing rapid growth will invest at higher rates and have the advantage of lower capital costs over countries experiencing slow growth. Regardless of the rate of growth, a country with a high rate of savings will have more money available for investment, and hence lower capital costs, than a country with a low rate of savings.[39] Governments can encourage individual saving in a variety of ways. The tax structure can be designed to penalize consumption and to reward savings and investment. Reducing the government budget deficit, if it is financed by borrowing, frees

37. For a review of the literature on intraindustry trade, see Elhanan Helpman, "Increasing Returns, Imperfect Markets, and Trade Theory," in Ronald W. Jones and Peter B. Kenen, eds., *Handbook of International Economics* (Amsterdam: North-Holland, 1982).

38. See industry studies A through H in Dertouzos, Lester, and Solow, *Made in America.*

39. Ibid., pp. 35–39. The authors argue that macroeconomic factors alone cannot explain shifts in competitiveness.

up funds for investment in more productive areas. Financial institutions can make it easier and safer to invest one's savings. The combination of fast growth in aggregate demand and a high investment rate, therefore, should be an unbeatable combination.

The two countries that experienced large increases in international competitiveness after World War II, Germany and Japan, also experienced long periods of rapid growth and high savings, whereas the countries experiencing declining competitiveness, the United States and Britain, grew slower and saved less than the other three. France experienced rapid growth in the 1960s and 1970s and a moderate level of savings and investment throughout the period. Thus it appears that this macroeconomic approach to explaining shifts in competitiveness has much validity. This approach, however, does not explain why firms and governments in Japan and Germany implemented savings and investment-inducing policies which were opposed or ignored in the United States and Britain. Luck played a small part, but the continued strength of Japan and Germany and the steady decline of the United States and Britain belie an explanation based solely on chance.

A final macroeconomic explanation of competitiveness centers on exchange rates.[40] Advocates of this view suggest that wrongly valued exchange rates tend to produce structural trade and payments imbalances that can be quickly corrected by adjusting the rates. This explanation received a great deal of attention from U.S. policy makers in the 1980s because it presented the possibility of fixing the trade deficit problem by devaluing the dollar relative to the currencies of trade-surplus countries.

The appreciation of the dollar in the early 1980s clearly contributed to the subsequent rapid growth of U.S. trade deficits (see Figure 2 above) and forced the United States to raise interest rates to attract foreign investment (much of which took the form of Japanese purchases of U.S. Treasury Bonds). It is not likely that further depreciation of the dollar will bring trade and the balance of payments back into equilibrium. The authors of *Made in America* explain why: "The trade balance of 1980 will not be achieved if the dollar falls to its 1980 level. One reason that trade cannot bounce all the way back is that foreign industry has continued to gain in relative productivity. Another reason is that producers abroad are willing to accept lower profit margins rather than give up their foothold in the U.S. market. . . . Nevertheless, depreciating the dollar is one way to balance the foreign trade account."[41]

40. See, for example, C. Fred Bergsten and William R. Cline, *The United States–Japan Economic Problem* (1985; rev. ed. Washington, D.C.: Institute for International Economics, 1987).
41. Dertouzos, Lester, and Solow, *Made in America*, p. 34.

They point out that depreciating the dollar would produce a balance in the trade account but result in a major recession and therefore would not contribute to U.S. competitiveness.

Culturalist Explanations

Among those who assert that the ultimate sources of changes in international competitiveness are cultural are George Lodge and Ezra Vogel, who believe that ideology, or "the collection of ideas that a community uses to make values explicit in some relevant context," has a strong effect on competitiveness.[42] The major dimension along which ideologies vary, again according to Lodge and Vogel, is individualism versus communitarianism. After examining the ideological orientations of nine major capitalist countries, they conclude: "Those countries with a coherent communitarian ideology have been able to best adapt to this international competitive economic system."[43]

The main problem with the culturalist view is that culture is presumed to be relatively fixed even though many of the variables it is supposed to explain change over time. For example, Japan and the newly industrializing countries (NICs) had communitarian ideologies long before they began their rapid economic growth. Similarly, culturalists often neglect to consider the possibility that cultural or ideological factors may be a response to changes in material conditions or to shifts in the balance of domestic political power. Ideologies have been known to change rapidly in response to major social upheavals. Political and economic elites have tried to mold ideologies to their interests. Thus, viewing culture and ideology as exogenous variables that explain shifts in economic competitiveness seems historically naive.

Statist Explanations

Believers in statist explanations assume that the governments of industrialized countries are relatively autonomous from civil society, that is, that the interests of the country differ from those of specific groups or even coalitions. Moreover, statists assume that conflicts between the state and civil groups over the definition of national interests are often won by the state. Thus explaining the decisions of governments requires a careful examination of internal politics but not of the actions

42. George C. Lodge, "Introduction: Ideology and Country Analysis," in George C. Lodge and Ezra Vogel, eds., *Ideology and National Competitiveness* (Boston: Harvard Business School Press, 1987), pp. 2–3.
43. Ezra F. Vogel, "Conclusion," ibid., p. 305.

of groups in civil society except those that directly affect the deliberations of the state.[44]

Some statists believe that government policies of countries with centralized industrial policy-making institutions result in greater international competitiveness. One of the best examples is Chalmers Johnson's
MITI and the Japanese Miracle. Johnson argues that the Japanese state
had a developmental orientation (as opposed to the regulatory orientation of the U.S. government) and that it was "plan rational" rather
than "market rational" (again the comparison was with the United
States). This meant that the Japanese state possessed the policy instruments necessary to reallocate resources across industries, while the
U.S. state did not. According to Johnson, Japan located many of these
instruments in a single agency, the Ministry of International Trade and
Industry or MITI. As to the effect of MITI policies on Japanese economic performance, Johnson says, "the government was the inspira-
tion and the cause of the movement to heavy and chemical industries
that took place during the 1950's. . . . This shift of 'industrial structure'
was the operative mechanism of the economic miracle."[45]

One does not have to argue that industrial policies directly affect
macroeconomic performance, however, to say that they are important
for international competitiveness. Statists often suggest that industrial
policies permit states to make payoffs to political opponents of adjustment strategies that are vital for the pursuit of intelligent and effective
macroeconomic policies. They may also help the state to change the
comparative advantages of the country in international trade over time
by altering the level of investment in physical and human capital.[46]

Criticism of statist works emphasize the limited autonomy of the
state vis-à-vis other societal actors in reallocating resources across industries and in determining the success of specific industries in international competition: "The state appears as a network of institutions,
deeply embedded within a constellation of ancillary institutions associated with society and the economic system. Contemporary states do
not seem to be as autonomous from societal influence as state-centric
theories imply."[47] Even in Japan, the state must confer extensively with

44. A useful discussion of statist approaches can be found in G. John Ikenberry, David
A. Lake, and Michael Mastanduno, "Introduction: Approaches to Explaining American
Foreign Economic Policy," in Ikenberry, Lake, and Mastanduno, eds., *The State and For-
eign Economic Policy,* pp. 9–14.

45. Chalmers Johnson, *MITI and the Japanese Miracle: The Growth of Industrial Policy,
1925–1975* (Stanford, Calif.: Stanford University Press, 1982), p. 31.

46. For an example, see John Zysman and Laura Tyson, "American Industry in International Competition," in Zysman and Tyson, eds., *American Industry in International
Competition* (Ithaca, N.Y.: Cornell University Press, 1983).

47. Hall, *Governing the Economy,* p. 17.

other societal actors before making changes in industrial policies[48] and needs their cooperation to implement new policies. Thus government policy alone does not explain changes in competitiveness.

A purely statist approach does not fully explain the competitive success of Japan and Germany. Japan is considered to have a strong state, while the federal government of Germany is comparatively weak. Why do strong states in Japan and France produce different results? It is clear that state strength, capacity, or autonomy cannot explain changes in competitiveness.

Corporatist Explanations

Neocorporatism occurs when a partially autonomous state helps certain social groups in civil society gain privileged access to it. The state here is not the heroic individualist of the pure statist model, but it still has substantial control over structuring its domestic social environment. The literature on neocorporatism does not explain changes in competitiveness but rather criticizes liberal or pluralist ideals for democracy in light of empirical observations about state-societal arrangements in industrialized capitalist countries. Nevertheless, it is possible to infer that neocorporatism is good for economic problem solving, including the problem of increasing international competitiveness.[49]

The principal problem with the literature on neocorporatism is its focus on the issue of whether a given country is or is not neocorporatist, asking whether there are institutions for concertation of the state with privileged social groups and where these institutions (which are necessarily parastatal in nature) are the key determinants of policy decision making and implementation in a wide variety of issue areas. By these restrictive criteria, only a few small industrial countries qualify as fully neocorporatist. Large industrial countries rarely give wide-ranging decision-making authority to tripartite concertative bodies. Therefore, this way of applying the neocorporatist approach does not help much in explaining changes in competitiveness in large industrial countries.

Despite the limitations of the neocorporatist approach, the examination of neocorporatist institutions is subsumed within the state-societal arrangements approach. Neocorporatist mechanisms can be an important way of bridging the gap between the state and groups in

48. See, for example, Richard Samuels, *The Business of the Japanese State: Energy Markets in Comparative and Historical Perspective* (Ithaca, N.Y.: Cornell University Press, 1987), p. 8; Johnson, *MITI and the Japanese Economic Miracle*, p. 312.

49. See, for example, Peter Katzenstein, *Small States in World Markets: Industrial Policy in Europe* (Ithaca, N.Y.: Cornell University Press, 1985), chaps. 3–4.

civil society. Even in countries relatively hostile to neocorporatist institutions such as the United States and Britain, important examples of the application of neocorporatist principles can be found. Indeed, the irony of the U.S. and British cases is that a failure to address problems of competitiveness often leads to the neocorporatism of the large-scale industrial bailout.[50]

Coalitional Explanations

The coalition approach starts from the assumption that the policies of the state are determined by bargaining among influential and autonomous societal groups. The state becomes the agent of a coalition of social groups, which may change from issue to issue but shares perceptions of long-term interests. The state is not an independent actor because its goals are determined externally. The Marxist variant of the coalition approach focuses exclusively on classes as social actors; the pluralist variant focuses exclusively on interest groups. More recent approaches define societal actors on the basis of the abundance or scarcity of factors of production—for example, groups in capital-intensive versus labor-intensive industries or groups in capital-abundant versus labor-abundant countries—to explain changes in coalitions that determine government policies.[51]

The approach used here differs from the coalitional approach in making the state a potential party to national bargaining and explicitly examining the role of institutions that link state and society. In the coalitional approach, the state is usually not a party to the bargaining, and state-societal linkages do not matter. In short, I agree with John Ikenberry when he says, "It is not enough to delineate the preferences of social groups and government officials themselves. Those preferences will be constrained, and perhaps even shaped, by the larger institutional setting in which they are situated."[52]

50. See Hart, "Crisis Management."
51. All of the following works use the coalitional approach: Peter Alexis Gourevitch, *Politics in Hard Times: Comparative Responses to International Economic Crises* (Ithaca, N.Y.: Cornell University Press, 1986); Rogowski, *Commerce and Coalitions;* Thomas Ferguson, "From Normalcy to New Deal: Industrial Structure, Party Competition, and American Public Policy in the Great Depression," *International Organization* 38 (Winter 1984): 41–94; and Jeffry Frieden, "Sectoral Conflict and U.S. Foreign Economic Policy," in Ikenberry, Lake, and Mastanduno, eds., *The State and American Foreign Policy.* The coalitional approach is implicit in Theda Skocpol, *States and Social Revolutions: A Comparative Analysis of France, Russia, and China* (New York: Cambridge University Press, 1979), but because Skocpol includes the state as an actor along with groups in civil society, her approach is more consistent with the state-societal approach used here.
52. Ikenberry, "Conclusion," p. 223. The state-societal arrangements approach is similar to the institutional approach that Ikenberry advocates but differs in its focus on the distribution of power among the state and two specific social groups—business and or-

In the first part of this chapter measures of competitiveness were suggested at the levels of whole economies and of specific industries. A fairly consistent pattern emerged of increasing competitiveness in Japan and Germany, declining competitiveness in the United States and Britain, with France in the middle. It is not necessary or advisable to deny the usefulness of macroeconomic, cultural, statist, neocorporatist, or coalitional approaches for explaining changes in international competitiveness. Indeed, it would be silly to exclude such important macroeconomic variables as productivity and exchange rates in any serious treatment of international competitiveness. Macroeconomic approaches are elegant and parsimonious and often explain many important macroeconomic outcomes, but they do not explain changes in competitiveness in the five countries. Similar problems of fitting the data exist for the other four approaches.

The creation and diffusion of new technologies are vital in explaining shifts in competitiveness among the five countries in specific industries. New technology is easy to create and diffuse in a fast-growing economy with extensive cooperation between government and business, but the case of Germany shows how it can be done even with slow and moderate growth in a country that lacks centralized industrial policy-making institutions or an Asian-style communitarian ideology. The cases of the United States and Britain show that it is possible to create new technologies without necessarily being able to apply them rapidly and broadly. An understanding of state-societal arrangements is necessary, in short, to explain changes in competitiveness. I turn, accordingly, to the task of describing state-societal arrangements in each of the five countries together with government policies, business strategies, and competitive outcomes in the steel, auto, and semiconductor industries.

---

ganized labor—as a key to understanding state-societal institutions. In this respect, the state-societal arrangements approach is an attempt to build on the strengths of the statist, neocorporatist, coalitional, and institutional approaches without inheriting their weaknesses.

Two

Japan

This chapter discusses the evolution of Japanese industrial policy, including specific government policies toward the steel, auto, and semiconductor industries. It begins with a summary of the main issues and an outline of the institutional arrangements that underpin industrial policy and then describes policies toward the three industries in recent years. The next five chapters follow the same format, presenting general issues, institutional arrangements, and specific policies. Readers familiar with the major institutional arrangements of a country may want to skim lightly through that section and go directly to the descriptions of industry-specific policies and outcomes.

KEY ISSUES

The performance of the Japanese economy from the 1950s to the present has been impressive both in aggregate economic terms and in specific industrial sectors. Growth rates, although higher before 1973 than after, have remained faster than those in the other four large industrial countries. Japanese unemployment remained less than 3 percent into the 1980s when all other major industrial countries experienced rapid increases in unemployment. Inflation has been low, with the exception of a short period following the oil price increases of 1973.

In Chapter 1, the great successes of the Japanese steel, automotive, and semiconductor industries were described with aggregate data. This chapter shows how state-societal arrangements in Japan led to the rapid adoption and diffusion of technological innovations and the adjustment of the industrial structure as domestic wages increased and competition from lower-wage Asian countries intensified. The chapter also touches upon some of the alternative ways of thinking about Japan which appear in the voluminous literature on Japanese political economy.

One of the least useful ways of thinking about Japan is embodied in the idea of "Japan, Inc." This idea, which has a popular currency in the United States, suggests an image of unbreachable solidarity between business and government. In the words of Yasusake Murakami: "This once popular notion asserts that the Japanese cultural tradition is most clearly manifested in the way Japanese society is controlled as a whole. According to this notion, Japanese society is monolithic and tightly regulated and thus resembles a single corporation run by a group of clever leaders, who mobilized the postwar Japanese populace for the sake of economic growth. Any closer examination, however, shows this to be a crude and simplistic stereotype."[1] Almost no one who has written seriously on Japan believes that such an arrangement ever existed there—or, for that matter, in any other country. It is impossible to reach such a high degree of harmony of interests among private groups or between private groups and the government that an entire nation can be compared to a corporation. Nevertheless, Japan emerged from its military defeat in World War II with a strong societal consensus to build a robust domestic economic base, and Japanese society has a strong tendency toward group-oriented activities and communitarian values.

Within the small group of scholars who write about Japan, a split exists between those who see the role of the Japanese state as central to recent economic successes and those who believe it to be peripheral.[2] If the role of the state is peripheral, then the economic success must be attributable mainly to market forces. The dichotomy between state and market implicit in this debate does not leave room for subtler influences available both to the state and to key private economic actors.

1. Yasusuke Murakami, "The Japanese Model of Political Economy," in Kozo Yamamura and Yasukichi Yasuba, eds., *The Political Economy of Japan*, vol. 1: *The Domestic Transformation* (Stanford, Calif.: Stanford University Press, 1987), p. 39. See further discussion in J. A. A. Stockwin, *Japan: Divided Politics in a Growth Economy*, 2d ed. (New York: Norton, 1982), pp. 137–38; Chalmers Johnson, *MITI and the Japanese Miracle: The Growth of Industrial Policy, 1925–1975* (Stanford, Calif.: Stanford University Press, 1982), p. 8.

2. See the summary of the views of the two sides in Marie Anchordoguy, "Mastering the Market: Japanese Government Targeting of the Computer Industry," *International Organization* 42 (Summer 1988): 509-44. See also Gregory Noble, "The Japanese Industrial Policy Debate," in Stephan Haggard and Chung-in Moon, eds., *Pacific Dynamics: The International Politics of Industrial Change* (Boulder, Colo.: Westview Press, 1989). Within the group of those who acknowledge the importance of state policies, there are differences between those who think that only macroeconomic policies made a difference and those who think industrial (meso- and microeconomic) policies were also crucial.

Accordingly, in recent years, a third view has appeared: that the government and business, state and market, are in a reciprocal and interdependent relationship and that the politics of Japan, as Richard J. Samuels has stated, is a politics of reciprocal consent: "By 'reciprocity' I imply that jurisdiction can belong to private firms as well as to the state. Control is mutually constrained. In exchange for the use of public resources, private industry grants the state some jurisdiction over industrial structure in the 'national interest.' Business enjoys privilege, systematic inclusion in the policy process, access to public goods, and rights of self-regulation. It reciprocates by agreeing to state jurisdiction in the definitions of market structure and by participating in the distribution of benefits."[3]

Although these theoretical issues are not the central concern of this chapter, a theoretical approach allows for empirical observation of the goal-setting and goal-seeking behavior over time on the part of government and private actors. Accordingly, the analysis is premised on the relative autonomy of the state and key social actors, which varies over time and from issue to issue. Only in this way can we trace the impact of state-societal arrangements (and the societal institutions behind them) on the adoption and diffusion of new technologies.

THE INSTITUTIONAL FRAMEWORK FOR JAPANESE INDUSTRIAL POLICY

Organization of the State

All discussions of Japanese industrial policy focus on the role of three major state agencies: the Ministry of International Trade and Industry (MITI), the Ministry of Finance (MOF), and the Bank of Japan (BOJ). The evolution of the powers and competencies of these agencies, especially MITI, is the cause of controversy, especially in recent years, because those who argue for the importance of the state in explaining Japanese economic performance base their arguments on the power of these agencies.

MITI

MITI has extensive powers, even in comparison with such powerful agencies as the Ministry of Research and Industry in France. MITI influences tax incentives, credit allocation, trade policy, the enforcement of antitrust laws, and, in the case of officially designated "recession car-

---

3. Richard J. Samuels, *The Business of the Japanese State: Energy Markets in Comparative and Historical Perspective* (Ithaca, N.Y.: Cornell University Press, 1987), p. 9.

tels," whatever it deems necessary to stabilize a failing industry or firm or to promote a growing one.

The recruitment of officials for MITI resembles the Confucian ideal. MITI recruits the top graduates of the most prestigious universities in Japan, especially the Tokyo Imperial University or Todai. Applicants for positions in MITI have to pass the very difficult higher civil service entrance examinations. But there is a fast-track system that favors those who pass the class A civil service examinations and who graduate from the most prestigious faculty of Todai, its law school. Once recruited into MITI, individuals retain social links with other graduates of elite universities to further their advancement within the bureaucracy. The high status accorded government bureaucrats makes competition for entrance to Tokyo University very intense. Business elites are also recruited from these elite universities, but it is generally recognized that the most talented go to the state bureaucracies. After a long period of service in the government, typically when they reach the age of fifty, Japanese bureaucrats have to "descend from heaven" (*amakudari*) into a lucrative job in business to make room for new recruits.[4]

MITI is organized internally into horizontal and vertical bureaus. The horizontal bureaus deal with broad issues of international trade, industrial policy, development, and environment and safety. The vertical bureaus are divided by industrial sectors. Some observers have stressed the importance of the vertical divisions as organizers of industry-specific coalitions and the potential for fragmentary and incoherent national policies in the absence of intersectoral bargaining. How much of this intersectoral bargaining is done within MITI itself is controversial. Clearly MITI maintains a key role for itself in intersectoral disputes in part through its monopoly over the negotiation of foreign trade agreements.

Along with the members of its advisory board, the Industry Structure Council, MITI is responsible for producing overviews of the structure of industry which are embodied in highly influential documents called "visions." The most recent vision—"Industrial Policy Vision of the 1980s"—called for a major shift in government policies away from the promotion of heavy manufacturing and toward information technologies. These visions provide an official stamp of approval to a shifting consensus between the bureaucracy and the private sector about the desired direction of national industrial policy. But much more important than the vision documents are the day-to-day monitoring and

4. See Johnson, *MITI and the Japanese Miracle*, pp. 59–68. There is a close parallel between the elite bureaucracies in Japan and France.

supervision of industrial sectors conducted by members of the relatively small but elite staff (only about twenty-five hundred persons).

The Ministry of Finance and the Bank of Japan

The Ministry of Finance influences industrial policy primarily through its control over monetary policy (it has some power to direct the actions of the Bank of Japan) and financial regulation. Japanese companies are more dependent on debt financing than U.S. or European firms, and their capital costs are directly affected by the policies of the Ministry of Finance and the Bank of Japan. The Ministry of Finance strives for low interest rates and a stable dollar/yen exchange rate to ensure a rapid rate of growth and a strong international position for Japanese firms in world export markets.

Until the early 1970s, the Bank of Japan controlled the growth of the country's money supply by allocating public investment funds to private banks. According to the *Economist:* "The supply of money was controlled by quantity, not price, by lowering or raising the amounts of credit made available by the Bank of Japan to private financial institutions, a powerful lever as the banks relied heavily on the central bank for funds. If that was not enough, the Bank of Japan 'asked' the private banks to lower or raise their level of lending to companies, a technique of moral suasion it called 'window guidance.' "[5]

The Ministry of Finance and the Bank of Japan try to keep interest rates low through a system of "voluntary interest rate regulation." Yasusuke Murakami described the system in 1987: "A bank lending at an interest rate higher than the BOJ advised would have faced serious inconveniences when it tried to borrow money at the BOJ's window or to get licenses to open new branches. . . . In this way, the MOF and BOJ could effectively control the interest level as well as the direction of fund flows."[6] MITI and the Economic Planning Agency set guidelines for the Bank of Japan, which are followed for the most part, even though the Bank of Japan and MITI sometimes differ over the allocation of lower-interest-bearing loans financed by public financial institutions. In the 1950s, for example, the Bank of Japan wanted preferential treatment for light, export-oriented industries, whereas MITI pushed for low-interest loans to basic and high-technology industries.[7]

5. "Limbering Up: A Survey of Japanese Finance and Banking," *Economist*, December 8, 1984, p. 25.

6. Murakami, "Japanese Model," p. 48.

7. See John Zysman, *Governments, Markets, and Growth: Financial Systems and the Politics of Industrial Change* (Ithaca, N.Y.: Cornell University Press, 1983), pp. 234–50; Hiroya Ueno, "The Conception and Evaluation of Japanese Industrial Policy," in Kasuo Sato, ed., *Industry and Business in Japan* (White Plains, N.Y.: Sharpe, 1980).

Organization of Business

Business interests in Japan can be articulated by (1) an individual firm; (2) a *shitauke* (a major firm and its circle of smaller suppliers and subcontractors); (3) a *keiretsu* (an industrial group of large firms associated with one of the major banks); (4) a sector-specific industry association (such as the Japanese Iron and Steel Federation); (5) a major peak association[8] (such as the Keidanren, the Keizai Doyukai, the Nikkeiren, and the Chamber of Commerce and Industry); or (6) an informal business group (such as the *Zaikai*, literally meaning "financial circle" but actually a club made up of the chief executive officers (CEOs) of major companies with close ties to the leaders of the Liberal Democratic party).[9] The Zaikai and the Keidanren speak with greater influence on questions of national policy than the narrower groups, but the latter often are more influential in the making of industry-specific policies.

The Keidanren, the most important business peak association, was founded in 1946. It is a federation of more than 110 leading industrial associations and includes in its membership the Japanese Iron and Steel Federation, the Japanese Automobile Manufacturers Association, and the Electronic Industries Association of Japan. Private financial institutions as well as manufacturing firms belong. The president of Keidanren is always also the head of the Zaikai and a chief executive officer of one of Japan's largest firms.

The Nikkeiren, the Japan Federation of Employers' Association, bargains for Japanese industrial management in the annual Spring Offensives (see the discussion of this institution below). The Nikkeiren was founded in 1948 to act as a political counterweight to the socialist- and communist-dominated trade unions that formed under the American occupation. The Nikkeiren played an important role in breaking the power of the nascent union movements in key strikes at Hitachi, Toshiba, and Nissan Motors in the late 1940s and early 1950s.

The Keizai Doyukai, the Japanese Committee for Economic Development, is analogous to the American Committee for Economic Development in that it focuses on long-term economic issues and the

8. A business peak association is one that aspires to represent all businesses in a given society and not a specific industry or sector of the economy. Examples outside Japan include the U.S. Chamber of Commerce, the Confederation of British Industries, and the Bundesverein der Deutschen Industrie.

9. The distinction between *shitauke* and *keiretsu* was suggested by Ronald Dore in *Flexible Rigidities* (Stanford, Calif.: Stanford University Press, 1986), p. 79, but Dore calls them *keiretsu* and *gurupu*, respectively. *Keiretsu* is used in common parlance to mean a group of any sort and *gurupu* is a Japanization of the English word *group*. A *shitauke* is literally a supplier. The terms *keiretsu* and *shitauke* are used here as they are in Murakami, "Japanese Model."

social responsibilities of business. It is less antilabor in tone than the Nikkeiren and less important in a political sense than the Keidanren and the Zaikai but plays an important role in commissioning private sector studies on industrial structure, internationalization, financial liberalization, and similar issues.

The Japanese Chamber of Commerce and Industry (JCCI), founded in 1878 during the Meiji period but dormant before, during, and after World War II, represented the interests of the smaller firms in the Japanese economy. In 1970, Nagano Shigeo, the former chairman of Nippon Steel, became president of the JCCI and reorganized it to make it more representative of the smaller cities and regions in Japan. This reorganization, together with other reforms, raised the political visibility of the organization and gave it greater access to the bureaucracy.[10]

The politics of Japanese business, as in other industrialized countries, involves the continual making and breaking of coalitions. The *keiretsu* and *shitauke* are particularly important because of the long-term interfirm relationships in the Japanese economic and social system. The *keiretsu* are the successors of the older tradition of the zaibatsu, large industrial groups such as Mitsui, Mitsubishi, and Sumitomo, linked by their dependence on the family-based banks that dominated the Japanese economy until the 1920s.

The dominance of the *zaibatsu* was first challenged between World Wars I and II, when the military government tried to establish its own state-dependent *zaibatsu*. One of the important firms that arose from these efforts was Nissan Motors. Some firms operate outside the clubbish environment of the *keiretsu*, for example, mavericks Honda and Sony, which have their own *shitauke* but do not have strong ties to any of the larger industrial families.

In 1977, the six largest *keiretsu*—Mitsui, Mitsubishi, Sumitomo, Fuyo, Sanwa, and Daiichi Kangin—accounted for 16 percent of all sales in Japan, 27 percent of all profits, and 6 percent of employment.[11] The relative power of these groups has waned in recent years with the rapid growth of the Japanese economy. Individual firms are less dependent on financing from a single bank or industrial group than they were in the 1950s and 1960s. Rapid export growth has enabled the automobile and electronics firms to finance more of their investments from retained earnings. The increasing liberalization of Japanese capital markets and the natural tendency of banks and other financial institutions

10. See Charles J. McMillan, *The Japanese Industrial System* (New York: Walter de Gruyter, 1984), pp. 56–60; and Leonard H. Lynn and Timothy J. McKeown, *Organizing Business: Trade Associations in America and Japan* (Washington, D.C.: American Enterprise Institute, 1988), pp. 13–15.
11. Dore, *Flexible Rigidities*, p. 79.

Table 2. The large financial institutions of Japan, assets or deposits as of the end of the 1987–1988 fiscal year

Type	Examples	
		Assets (billion yen)
Government	Bank of Japan (the central bank)	35,433
	Japan Development Bank	8,146
	Small Business Finance Corporation	—
		Deposits ($ billion)
	Postal Savings Bank	789.7
"City Banks"	Dai-Ichi Kangyo	275.3
	Sumitomo	257.6
	Fuji	249.4
	Mitsubishi	242.2
	Sanwa	238.2
	Tokai	167.2
	Mitsui	149.4
	Taiyo Kobe	129.4
	Daiwa	124.1
	Bank of Tokyo	113.5
	Kyowa	69.7
	Saitama	61.1
	Hokkaido Takushoku	46.5
	Total, "city banks"	1,848.3
Long-term credit banks	Industrial Bank of Japan	206.1
	Long-term Credit Bank	117.1
	Nippon Credit Bank	77.6
		Assets (billion yen)
Trust banks	Mitsubishi	25,027
	Mitsui	23,405
	Sumitomo	16,585
	Nippon	12,617
	Yasuda	9,237
	Toyo	6,523
	Chuo	4,122
		Securities in custody (billion yen)
Securities firms	Daiwa	1,348
	Yamaichi	846
	Nomura	828
	Nikko	823

Sources: Nathaniel Nash, "Japan's Banks: Top 10 in Deposits," *New York Times,* July 20, 1988, p. C1; "When $2.3 Trillion Looks for a New Japanese Home," *Economist,* February 20, 1988, p. 83; Jonas B. Blank and Constance A. Gustke, "The 100 Biggest Banks," *Fortune,* August 1, 1988, p. D41; and *Moody's International Manual* (New York: Moody's Investors Service, Inc., 1989).

Note: Securities firms are not allowed to accept deposits. They just invest other people's money directly into securities.

Table 3. *Keiretsu* memberships of Japanese firms in the steel, auto, and semiconductor industries

Industry	Sumi-tomo	Mitsui	Mitsu-bishi	Fuyo	Sanwa	Daiichi Kangin
Steel						
Nippon Steel	A	A		A	A	
Nippon Kokan						A
Kobe Steel					A	A
Kawasaki Steel						A
Sumitomo Metal	F					
Automobiles						
Toyota		A				
Nissan				A		
Mitsubishi			F			
Honda			A			
Mazda	A					
Isuzu						A
Daihatsu					A	
Fuji Heavy				A		
Semiconductors						
NEC	F					
Toshiba		A				
Matsushita	A					
Hitachi				A	A	
Fujitsu				A		A
Mitsubishi Electric			F			
Oki				F		

Sources: Naoto Sasaki, *Management and Industrial Structure in Japan* (New York: Pergamon Press, 1981); Michael Gerlach, *Alliance Capitalism: The Social Organization of Japanese Business Networks* (Berkeley: University of California Press, 1989); and interview materials.

Note: F = companies that are full members of the *keiretsu*. A = companies affiliated with the *keiretsu* through a long-term relationship with the lead bank of the group or through membership in the President's Council of the group. Nippon Steel, Fuji Heavy Industries, and Nissan are linked to the Industrial Bank of Japan, a long-term credit bank that is independent of the *keiretsu*. Nissan and Hitachi are tied historically through their common origin in the 1930s under the same holding company. Hitachi is the main supplier of automotive electronics to Nissan. Nissan and Hitachi, Toyota and Fujitsu, are linked to one another through mutual purchasing arrangements.

to diversify their holdings to reduce risk have also weakened the bonds that used to bind firms to the *keiretsu*.[12] Nevertheless, large Japanese firms continued to cluster in groups for competitive reasons so as to have secure sources of supply for vital components and secure markets for strategic products.

12. This argument is made most forcefully in James C. Abegglen and George Stalk, Jr., *Kaisha: The Japanese Corporation* (New York: Basic Books, 1985).

Table 3 shows that the *keiretsu* generally avoid having a stake in more than one firm in a given industry. This tendency is called "one-setism." Exceptions sometimes occur when the *keiretsu* support firms that are not directly competing. A good example is the membership of the Nippon Electric Company (NEC) and Matsushita in the Sumitomo group. Nippon Electric is primarily a manufacturer of heavy electrical and telecommunications equipment, whereas Matsushita mainly produces consumer electronic goods. Another example is the membership of both Honda and Mitsubishi in the Mitsubishi group. Both of these firms are specialty producers, but Honda makes higher-priced models mainly for export, and Mitsubishi makes only lower-priced models and sells a large portion of its output abroad via its partnership with Chrysler.

Table 3 also illustrates that there are some differences in *keiretsu* linkages across industries that are a function of the historical evolution of the Japanese economy. The old *zaibatsu* had ties to iron and steel firms that were disrupted by World War II and the U.S. occupation. The old zaibatsu lost their steelworks in China and Korea at the end of the war. Mitsubishi, in particular, emerged from the occupation without a linkage to a major steel firm. Increased state intervention in the 1930s and 1940s allowed some firms to grow without being associated with a private zaibatsu; some emerged after the occupation that were either independent or part of a quasi-governmental keiretsu such as that associated with the Industrial Bank of Japan. Finally, the newcomer keiretsu—Sanwa, Fuyo, and Daiichi Kangin—were more likely than the successors to the old *zaibatsu* to deviate from the pattern of one-setism. The reason was simply that they tended to be financially linked to newer firms that had not established as strong a market presence and supported more than one firm as a way of diversifying their portfolios to reduce risk.

Organization of Labor

Because of the extreme fragmentation of organized labor in Japan, labor interests have been much less represented than others in the formulation and implementation of industrial policies. Most unions in Japan are organized at the enterprise level. They often associate the interests of their members with those of the firms that employ them. Occasionally, the unions and firms differ on important matters, but the system of wage bargaining has developed in such a way that wages are rarely the main source of labor management friction. A few weeks in March and April, called the Spring Offensive, are set aside each year to arrive at national and firm-specific norms for wage increases.

Bargaining during the Spring Offensive is highly ritualized, taking the form primarily of choreographed demonstrations, one-day work stoppages, media exchanges between management and union leaders, and technical exchanges of data on productivity and profitability. Japanese unions, like those in Germany, often cooperate with the firms to restrain wage increases during times of recession and restructuring.[13]

The trade union federation that covers the bulk of private industry is the Domei. Because most of its members are enterprise unions, the Domei takes a more moderate stance politically than other labor federations. The Domei is most closely aligned with the Democratic Social party. The Sohyo, the federation of public sector unions, is most closely associated with the Socialist party. Three other opposition parties— the New Liberal Club, the Communist party, and the Komeito—also represent the interests of some parts of the labor force, but they have no ties to the large labor federations.[14] The fractured nature of the leftist opposition to the dominant Liberal Democratic party therefore partly reflects the fragmentation of organized labor in Japan.[15]

The combination of strong centralized bureaucratic control of industrial policy with strong domestic business interests and relatively weak labor interests led some observers to call the Japanese system "corporatism without labor."[16] Japan and France are strikingly similar in this respect. In both cases, the institutional weakness of labor in national politics occasionally resulted in periods of high labor militancy and even widespread violence. The main differences between Japan and France are that Japanese business is stronger than French business and the Japanese state and business have been able to win greater wage restraints from the workers, especially during long periods of rapid economic growth, by avoiding layoffs and upgrading skills.

POLICIES FOR THE STEEL INDUSTRY

The Japanese succeeded in building an internationally competitive steel industry after World War II because they chose to use the basic

13. See the excellent discussion of this system in Dore, *Flexible Rigidities*, pp. 101–7.
14. See ibid., pp. 20–22 and chap. 4.
15. For a good summary of recent efforts to unite the efforts of Domei and Sohyo into a single organization called Rengo, see Koji Taira, "Labor Confederation in Japan," *Current History*, April 1988, p. 161.
16. See T. J. Pempel and K. Tsunekawa, "Corporatism without Labor? The Japanese Anomaly," in Philippe Schmitter and Gerhard Lehmbruch, eds., *Trends toward Corporatist Intermediation* (Beverly Hills, Calif.: Sage, 1979).

oxygen furnace (BOF) technology for a large proportion of the new plants built in the 1950s; a competitive industrial structure in the steel industry emerged after World War II; the costs of two major imported inputs (coking coal and iron ore) and of transporting finished steel products to foreign markets declined rapidly; and a series of major strikes in the United States, beginning in 1965, opened that market for the first time to Japanese exports. Only the first factor was a consequence of explicit government policies. Although the other three were largely outside the control of the Japanese government and firms, both reacted quickly and positively to the new opportunities. The case for the positive effect of industrial policies, and more broadly for the effect of Japanese state-societal arrangements, rests primarily on the effects of those arrangements on the rapid diffusion of new steelmaking technologies.

After 1973, the stagnation of demand for steel and the rise of competition from Asian developing countries created pressure to reduce excess capacity. A series of "recession cartels" was organized for the steel industry to slow the growth of foreign imports rather than to reduce excess capacity. Japanese firms were able to introduce technological improvements such as continuous casting to compensate for the rapid increase in energy prices and wage rates and thus maintained and even increased their international competitive advantage through the end of the 1970s. Japanese industrial policies for steel worked better during the period of expansion than during the stagnation and retrenchment following 1973. Nevertheless, state-societal arrangements were important in easing the transition from high growth to stagnant demand.

The Diffusion of Basic-Oxygen Furnace Technology

The choice of the BOF technology was strongly influenced by Japanese experience before and during World War II. Between 1920 and 1950 the Japanese steel industry was heavily dependent on imports of scrap iron and steel for its open-hearth furnaces. Because of the U.S. embargo on exports of scrap iron to Japan after 1937, the Japanese industry suffered from very high costs and eventually had to reduce production by the open-hearth method. The use of other steelmaking processes (most notably the Thomas converter system) resulted in costly and very low-quality steel. After the end of the U.S. occupation, Japanese authorities sought ways to avoid dependence on imported scrap.

Figure 8. Crude steel production of major Japanese firms

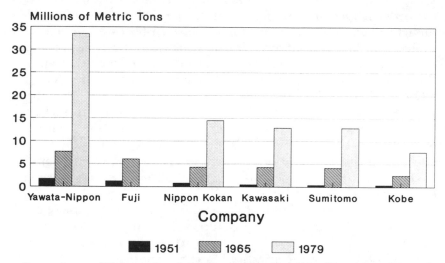

Sources: Leonard H. Lynn, *How Japan Innovates* (Boulder, Colo.: Westview, 1982), p. 58; and David Dale Martin, "The Iron and Steel Industry: Transnational Control without Transnational Corporations," unpublished manuscript, Indiana University, 1983.
   Note: Yawata and Fuji were merged into Nippon Steel in 1970.

The Breakup of Nippon Steel

In 1950 the giant steel complex Nippon Steel, formed by the military government in 1934 by merging five independent steel companies with the government-owned Yawata works, was broken up into two firms—Yawata Steel and Fuji Steel. Yawata Steel was an integrated steel producer with weaknesses in the production of pig iron; Fuji produced primarily pig iron. After the split, Yawata made major investments in blast furnaces so as not to be dependent on Fuji for pig iron, and Fuji invested in steelmaking plants and rolling mills so as not to have to sell its pig iron to Yawata. Competition between the two major firms intensified, and both became integrated steel producers.[17]

The First and Second Modernization Programs

After 1946, MITI controlled the allocation of imported coking coal and scrap iron and access to low-interest public loans. Although it did not use this control directly, it could use subtle "administrative guid-

17. Interview with Takeo Tanai, employee of Nippon Steel, at the center for International Affairs, Harvard University, March 23, 1983.

ance" to influence the investments made by Japanese steel firms.[18] Under MITI's guidance, the Japanese steel firms replaced their Thomas and Bessemer converters with BOFs more rapidly than U.S. firms and at roughly the same rate as the West German firms. BOF production increased from virtually nothing in the early 1950s to 17.6 million metric tons in 1964, over 40 percent of Japanese total raw steel production.[19]

In the First Modernization Program of 1951–55 direct investment subsidies, accelerated depreciation, and other incentives (such as reductions in property taxes), mostly to the larger firms, were used to encourage investments that would reduce production costs in the industry. Over five years, 128 million yen were invested, 88 percent by the top six firms: Yawata, Fuji, Nippon Kokan, Kawasaki, Kobe Steel, and Sumitomo Metal Industries. Because relatively small amounts were invested, only one new plant was constructed, the Chiba works of Kawasaki Steel. Most of the money went into updating equipment in existing plants. Modest decreases in production costs resulted from the program, and the concentration of ownership in the industry increased.[20]

Another important goal of the First Modernization Program was to reduce the cost of coking coal, a key input to the steelmaking process. The price of domestic coal was high mainly because of the continuation of prewar cartel arrangements protecting the interests of *zaibatsu*-owned coal mining firms.[21] The *zaibatsu* had lost control over the steel industry at the end of the war because most of their production had been located in Manchuria, but they retained ownership of their coal mines in Japan. There was, therefore, an important conflict of interest between the *zaibatsu* and the government over coal prices, which, when coupled with the desire of the U.S. occupation authorities to break up the *zaibatsu*, might have ended in a major defeat for the *zaibatsu*.

The two largest steel firms, Yawata and Fuji, were largely dependent on public investment funds from the Industrial Bank of Japan, the Long-Term Credit Bank, and the Japan Development Bank. These firms joined the government in pressing for lower coal prices, but the *zaibatsu* were still strong enough to prevent a breakup of the coal cartel.

18. Johnson, *MITI and the Japanese Miracle*, p. 87, notes the close historical ties between Yawata and the Ministry of Commerce and Industry (and later MITI). The sales offices of the Yawata firm in Tokyo were located in the MCI building until 1934. By 1957, MITI was pushing BOF actively in the publications of its iron and steel production section. See *Tekkogyo no genkyo to mondaiten* (Tokyo: MITI, 1957) as cited in Leonard Lynn, *How Japan Innovates* (Boulder, Colo.: Westview, 1982), p. 112.
19. Lynn, *How Japan Innovates*, p. 27; Kiyoshi Kawahito, *The Japanese Steel Industry* (New York: Praeger, 1972), chap. 1.
20. Kawahito, *Japanese Steel Industry*, p. 26.
21. Samuels, *Business of the Japanese State*, chap. 3.

The First Modernization Program, perhaps unintentionally, resulted in the steel industry becoming more dependent on the government than on *zaibatsu* or *keiretsu* ties.[22]

The Second Modernization Program of 1956–60 was more ambitious than the first. In 1955, the government had to limit steel exports so that domestic demand could be met. Most of the integrated steel-works in Japan used open-hearth or electric furnaces. Scrap iron, which had been cheap and plentiful after World War II, became increasingly scarce and expensive. Recalling the U.S. embargo on scrap iron after 1937, Japanese public officials and managers focused the Second Modernization Program on reducing dependency on imported scrap by encouraging the building of integrated plants with basic-oxygen furnaces. Scrap imports as a percentage of domestic consumption declined steadily from a high of 29 percent in 1960 to less than 10 percent in 1974 as a result of these policies.[23]

New blast furnaces were built to increase the supply of pig iron, but a more stable source of iron ore and coking coal was needed. In 1955, Japan imported 85 percent of its total consumption of iron ore and 40 percent of its coking coal. Some effort had been made under the First Modernization Program to negotiate long-term agreements with overseas suppliers and to develop new mines in Malaya, the Philippines, and India. Under the Second Modernization Program, plans were made to construct giant ore- and coal-carrying ships to reduce the transportation costs connected with importing ore and coal.

The new integrated steel plants constructed during the second program were at seaside locations because of the reliance on imported raw materials (see Table 4). Many of these new plants used BOF technology. The expenditure of approximately 533 million yen between 1954 and 1961 for capital investments enabled Japanese steel firms to match the raw material input costs of their foreign competitors by the beginning of the 1960s.[24] By the mid-1960s, because of low input costs and low wage rates in the steel industry, the Japanese firms were underpricing their competitors in international trade. They then outpaced their foreign competitors by scaling up plant sizes to take advantage of the lower average production costs connected with BOF technology.

Recession Cartels in the 1960s

The key policy instrument in the 1960s, once the new productive capacity came on line, was MITI's power to organize recession cartels by

22. Kawahito, *Japanese Steel Industry,* pp. 22–28.
23. Tsutomu Kawasaki, *Japan's Steel Industry* (Tokyo: Tekko Shimbun Sha, 1985), p. 430.
24. Kawahito, *Japanese Steel Industry,* pp. 35–47.

Table 4. Major steel plants in Japan constructed after World War II

Date of construction	Firm	Location	1958 capacity (million tons/year)
1951	Kawasaki	Chiba	6
1958	Fuji Steel	Nagoya	7
1959	Yawata Steel	Yawata	12
1960	Sumitomo	Wakayama	9
1961	Kawasaki	Mizushima	10
1965	Yawata Steel	Kimitsu	11
1965	Nippon Kokan	Fukuyama	16
1967	Sumitomo	Kashima	10
1968	Kobe Steel	Kakogawa	10
1971	Nippon Steel	Oita	12
1975	Nippon Kokan	Ohgishima	20

Sources: James C. Abegglen and George Stalk, Jr., *Kaisha: The Japanese Corporation* (New York: Basic Books, 1985), p. 74; and Tsutomu Kawasaki, *Japan's Steel Industry* (Tokyo: Tekko Shimbun Sha, 1985), pp. 252–56.

establishing production quotas during short-run price declines, thereby stabilizing prices. These cartels made it possible for the larger firms to continue to operate their new plants close enough to full capacity that they could benefit from economies of scale. The recession cartels for steel in the 1960s did not result in reduced capacity.[25]

In the recessions of 1962–63 and 1965–66, the pricing system set up by MITI and the steelmakers to "avoid mutually destructive price competition" failed to prevent a collapse in prices. During these two recessions, MITI resorted to administrative guidance, which in this case meant freezing inventories, purchasing low-priced products in the market, and negotiating reductions in production.[26] In the 1965–66 recession, believing that there was overproduction in steel, MITI ordered an across-the-board cut of 10 percent.[27] Sumitomo, alone of the "big six" steel firms, refused to go along. It claimed that, in forcing all firms to absorb production cuts, MITI was not taking into account Sumitomo's superior export performance and management.

In rebelling against MITI, Sumitomo was expressing a common perception among the smaller steel firms that MITI tended to favor Fuji and Yawata. There was, of course, some truth to this because Fuji and Yawata were more heavily dependent on public investments than Sumitomo (a member of the Sumitomo *keiretsu*) and had been more willing

25. Dore, *Flexible Rigidities*, pp. 142–44.
26. Kawahito, *Japanese Steel Industry*, p. 106.
27. There was a basis for this belief in the shakeout that resulted in the bankruptcy of Japan Specialty Steel Company in December 1964 and the Sanyo Specialty Steel Company in March 1968. See Johnson, *MITI and the Japanese Miracle*, p. 264.

to follow MITI's guidance on the diffusion of BOF technology. MITI responded by both promising support for a new steelworks and threatening restrictions on licenses for Sumitomo to import coking coal. When the story leaked to the press, the public supported Sumitomo as an underdog, and MITI was embarrassed by assertions that it had favored firms in which its former officials served in management positions (Sumitomo had no such persons.) A compromise was worked out whereby Sumitomo got an increased export quota in exchange for implementing the production cuts. Sumitomo asked a former MITI official to join its board of directors in 1969.[28]

The Merger of Fuji and Yawata

The success of the Japanese steel industry in the 1960s brought on intense domestic price competition. In April 1968, price competition in heavy plate steel forced Otani Steel to join the Yawata group; a downturn in the sales of steel bars forced Osaka Steel to join Yawata and Tosa Denki and Nisshin Steel to join the Nippon Kokan group.[29] Government policy was to limit competition by encouraging mergers.

In the late 1960s, MITI pushed for the merger of Fuji and Yawata in the hope that the resulting firm would act as a price leader and stabilize prices. The merger, which took place in March 1970, was authorized by the Fair Trade Commission even though the combined market share of the two firms was well over the legally sanctioned limit of 30 percent. The merger was kept secret from the public until April 1978, when a story appeared in the newspapers about it. A public outcry arose, and the Fair Trade Commission responded by requiring Fuji and Yawata to sell one plant each to Nippon Kokan and Kobe Steel, respectively.[30]

The merger of Fuji and Yawata illustrates the importance of long-term relationships between firms and their employees. For many years after the merger, people within the new Nippon Steel (so named in 1978, when the merger was made public) continued to distinguish between those who had worked for Fuji and those who had worked for Yawata. Because of the informal ties among managers and workers within the two firms, the management of Fuji and Yawata remained separate for many years, thus delaying some needed rationalization of facilities.[31]

28. Ibid., pp. 269–71.
29. Kawasaki, *Japanese Steel Industry,* p. 172.
30. Johnson, *MITI and the Japanese Miracle,* pp. 277–83.
31. Interview materials; Dore, *Flexible Rigidities,* p. 62.

Fortuitous Events beyond the Control of the Government

Iron ore prices declined primarily because of the exploitation of newly discovered deposits in Brazil, Venezuela, Malaysia, and India. The Western Australian provincial governments were not permitted to develop their iron ore deposits until the mid-1950s. In addition, the development of "pelletization" of iron ore made it possible to use lower grades of ore than previously. Thus the supply of iron ore expanded relative to demand, and global iron ore prices dropped, thereby reducing the advantages of national steel industries that had access to cheaper domestic iron ores.

In addition, a major round of building of ore and coking coal carriers resulted in markedly reduced freight costs for shipping those two crucial imputs. Thus the new Japanese plants built on the coasts near major urban markets were able to combine superior technology (BOF and, later, computerized continuous-casting processes) with lower input and labor costs to produce steel at internationally competitive prices. When the United Steelworkers went on strike in the United States in 1965, Japanese firms won a significant foothold in the U.S. market by offering high-quality steel at competitive prices. Japanese production costs per ton were at least $100 less than those of the average U.S. firm.

Post-1973 Policies

In the 1970s demand for steel was stagnant worldwide. The Japanese industry, like those in Europe and the United States, had expected domestic and world demand to expand and by the early 1970s had the capacity to produce roughly 150 million metric tons annually. But between 1972 and 1983, annual production never exceeded 120 million tons, averaging slightly more than 100 million tons.

MITI was slow to recognize the decrease in demand. An interim report written by MITI for the Industry Structure Council, published in November 1973 under the title *Steel Industry in the 1970s,* projected 8 to 10 percent annual growth in domestic demand for steel and 3.5 percent growth in demand for exports. This, of course, was at the height of the world economic boom before the oil price increases of 1973. By 1975, optimistic projections of total demand (domestic plus export) of 162 million tons by 1980 were revised downward to 151 million tons, but this new estimate was still too optimistic by about 50 million tons.[32]

MITI's policies for the steel industry in the early 1970s focused on building new and larger blast furnaces and putting more continuous

32. Kawasaki, *Japanese Steel Industry,* p. 186.

casters in steelworks. Firms were challenged to build blast furnaces with a capacity of four thousand cubic meters. The object was to increase the scale of the integrated works so that they could take better advantage of static economies of scale. Seventy-two new continuous casters were installed between 1970 and 1975, in addition to the pre-existing thirty-nine, and MITI encouraged even the smaller electric-furnace and open-hearth furnace plants to install them.[33]

After 1975, however, MITI began to encourage steel firms to shut down underused blast furnaces. The remaining open-hearth plants were encouraged to convert their operations to electric-furnace technology or to close. In February 1977, MITI recommended a cap on investments in new electric furnaces. Financial problems among the electric-furnace and minimill operators resulted in private bailouts by the larger integrated firms and incorporation of the smaller firms into the larger industrial groups. Nippon Steel, for example, consolidated the operations of two of its affiliates, Osaka Steel and Otani Heavy Industry, into a new firm called Godo Steel.

In May 1978, the government passed the Law for Special Measures to deal with particular depressed industries, aimed at artificial fibers, aluminum smelting, shipbuilding, and open-hearth and electric-furnace steelmaking, but it was extended later to cover ammonia, urea, spinning, ferro-silicon, corrugated cardboard, and wet-process acid-making. All of the industries affected were highly dependent on energy and therefore badly hurt by the energy price increases of the 1970s. This law became the basis for the establishment of temporary recession cartels that were meant to be succeeded quickly by major reductions in capacity through scrapping or mothballing.[34] In the steel industry a reduction of 3.3 million tons in open-hearth and electric-furnace production (about 16 percent of total capacity) was called for. Participating firms were given access to a Credit Insurance Fund, jointly funded by the government and the industry (each contributing to 350 million yen).[35] In October 1982, the government ruled that the steel industry was eligible for aid to retrain or relocate employees.

The government's policies eventually had the desired effect of reducing productive capacity. The number of blast furnaces declined from a high of seventy-two in 1976 to fifty-four in 1987, sixteen of which were idle that year.[36] MITI formulated a plan in 1987 to reduce

33. Ibid., pp. 203–5.
34. Dore, *Flexible Rigidities*, pp. 140–41.
35. Gary Saxonhouse, "Industrial Restructuring in Japan," *Journal of Japanese Studies* 5 (1979): 295–314.
36. John Burgess, "FYI [For Your Information] Pittsburgh: Japan's Steel Industry Is Sick Too," *Washington Post National Weekly Edition*, February 16, 1987, p. 20.

the number of blast furnaces to twenty-eight by 1990.[37] The policy to encourage the installation of continuous casters remained in place and was given greater urgency because of the energy-saving nature of that technology.

Wages in Japan increased more rapidly than in the other industrialized countries, and the Japanese wage-cost advantage was considerably reduced. One necessary response to higher wages and stagnant demand was to reduce the work force, which was made possible by the higher worker productivity that resulted from investments in new process technologies. Employment was reduced from a peak of 459,000 in 1974 to 345,000 in 1987,[38] much of it through attrition (not hiring new workers when older ones retired), granting early pensions, or shifting workers to new businesses within the company. Some firms loaned workers to auto producers: for example, Nippon Kokan to Toyota and Kawasaki Steel to a small auto company. Another common practice was to transfer workers from obsolete plants to new plants located nearby.[39] Reductions continued well into the 1980s: for example, Nippon Steel announced a reorganization plan in February 1987 to reduce its work force from 65,000 to 46,000 by March 1991.[40]

In the late 1970s and early 1980s, the reduction in steel employment was carried out in ways consistent with the postwar Japanese avoidance of layoffs and with the so-called "lifetime employment" guarantees. In December 1986, however, Kawasaki Steel sent 2,000 workers home for two-day furloughs at 70 percent of their normal wages. Nippon Steel did the same thing with about 30,000 workers. A senior manager of Kawasaki said: "Things have reached the point where traditional labor practices no longer work."[41]

Profits, already low in the Japanese steel industry, declined further, and some large companies began to suffer major losses. In the fiscal year ending in March 1984, the five biggest Japanese firms lost $425 million (Nippon and Kawasaki remained profitable).[42] In fiscal 1987, the industry lost $2.7 billion.[43]

37. "Steel: How South Korea Scares Japan," *Economist*, May 14, 1988, p. 68.
38. Everett M. Kassalow, "Crisis in the World Steel Industry: Union-Management Responses in Four Countries," paper delivered at the annual meeting of the Industrial Relations Research Association, Dallas, Texas, December 28–30, 1984, p. 2.
39. Steve Lohr, "Critical Shift for Japan's Steel," *New York Times*, March 20, 1984, p. 31; Leonard Lynn, "The Political Process of National Policy-Making in the Steel Sector: Japan," paper delivered at a conference on sectoral crisis management, Friedrich Ebert Stiftung, Bonn, June 1984, p. 6.
40. Susan Chira, "Nippon Steel's Job Cuts Reflect Industry's Woes," *New York Times*, February 14, 1987, p. 17.
41. Burgess, "FYI Pittsburgh," p. 20.
42. "Is Steel Over the Hump—Or Over the Hill?" *Economist*, July 14, 1984, p. 65.
43. Burgess, "FYI Pittsburgh," p. 20.

Major reductions in the steelmaking capacity of the larger integrated firms did not occur until the appreciation of the yen (*endaka*) after March 1985, which further reduced Japan's labor and raw material input cost advantages in export markets. According to Toshio Chiba, vice-president of the Japanese Federation of Iron and Steel Workers' Unions, "The high yen is almost destroying what we have planned in order to fight back the advancement of the newly industrializing countries. . . . It is a huge handicap."[44]

Trade Policies toward the NICs

The recession cartels and the traditional relationship between Japanese firms and steel distributors may have played an important role in reducing the rate of increase in imports from NIC steel producers. According to Ronald Dore,

> Brazil and Korea can now land some kinds of steel in Japan more cheaply than Japanese producers can supply it. But very little Brazilian or Korean steel is sold there. . . . None of the major trading companies would touch Brazilian or Korean steel, especially now that things are going so badly for their customers, the Japanese steel companies. Small importers are willing to handle modest lots. But they will insist on their being landed at backwater warehouses, away from any shipping point for domestic steel, so that the incoming steel is not seen by a Japanese steel company employee. If it were seen, the trucks carrying the imported steel might be followed to their destination, and the purchaser, if he turned out to be a disloyal customer, would be marked down for less than friendly treatment next time a boom brings a seller's market.[45]

Despite the continued insulation of domestic markets, the larger firms began reacting to increased competition from the NICs and to the appreciation of the yen by investing in overseas production and diversifying out of steel.

The Japanese steel industry grew rapidly in the 1960s and early 1970s as a result of government policies of the late 1950s to speed the adoption and diffusion of key technologies. But if the firms had been less dependent on government investment funds during the period, the government might have been less successful in imposing its will.

44. Susan Chira, "Japanese Steel's Darkest Days," *New York Times*, August 3, 1986, p. F4.
45. Ronald Dore, "Goodwill and the Spirit of Market Capitalism," in Daniel Okimoto and Thomas P. Rohlen, eds., *Inside the Japanese System* (Stanford, Calif.: Stanford University Press, 1988), pp. 96–97.

MITI's recession cartels and export promotion policies in the 1960s allowed the new giant integrated steel plants to operate efficiently despite fluctuations in domestic demand. When demand stagnated after 1973, MITI reacted by establishing a series of new recession cartels to reduce production by open-hearth and electric-furnace producers. MITI also acted to speed the diffusion of continuous-casting technology during this period. Japanese firms reduced the adjustment costs for workers by avoiding layoffs and firings. The avoidance of layoffs was a general feature of Japanese labor-management relations, thanks to state-societal arrangements in this sphere. MITI's recession cartels of the 1970s decreased the rate of penetration of imports from the newly industrializing countries and protected the profit margins of the major firms by preventing excessive price competition. Japanese state-societal arrangements allowed both government and firms to adjust to changes in the market to take advantage rapidly of changes when they were favorable and to reduce the pain of adjustment when they were not.

POLICIES FOR THE AUTOMOBILE INDUSTRY

The Japanese automobile industry enjoyed rapid expansion after the late 1950s. Automobile production after World War II was virtually nonexistent. By 1962, 1 million motor vehicles (buses, trucks, and passenger cars) were being produced. By the early 1980s, this figure had increased to over 11 million units. This amazing growth stemmed from a combination of intelligent strategies pursued by Japanese firms, a favorable environment for expansion that resulted from well-chosen public policies, and the failure of American auto producers to respond rapidly to the increase in the demand for small fuel-efficient cars after the oil price increases of the 1970s.

The Japanese government's control over inward foreign investment and limiting imports of large vehicles gave Japanese producers a sheltered domestic market from 1933 until the 1970s. Japanese firms specialized in the production of very small cars because they were all most Japanese consumers could afford. The only potential external competitors in the small car market were European firms, which were excluded from the Japanese market by restrictions on inward investment and a series of export-restraint agreements negotiated in the 1950s.[46]

46. I am indebted here and elsewhere in this section to the history of the Japanese auto industry contained in C. S. Chang, *The Japanese Auto Industry and the U.S. Market* (New York: Praeger, 1981).

The Japanese Auto Industry before World War II

The Japanese government first became involved with the automobile industry at the end of World War I. In 1918, the army sponsored a law to provide subsidies to manufacturers and users of vehicles that were certified by military inspectors. The legislation authorized three local firms to produce trucks, but demand was so low that they all failed to turn the subsidies into actual production. The Tokyo earthquake of 1923 destroyed railways and trolley networks, thereby stimulating demand for trucks and automobiles that was met primarily by imports.

Ford and GM controlled more than 90 percent of the Japanese market until 1934. Strong sales in Japan encouraged Ford to establish a subsidiary, Ford Motor Company of Japan, in Yokohama in 1925. GM established a subsidiary, GM Japan, in Osaka in 1927. Both operated assembly plants in these cities.[47]

In 1926, the Ministry of Commerce and Industry (MCI) formed the Japanese Industry Promotion Committee. In September 1929, this committee published a study titled "Policy for Establishing the Motor Vehicle Industry." In June 1931, another MCI committee recommended the joint production of a single model by Japanese firms. Following the Manchurian incident in 1931, after which the military took effective control of Japan, the government urged the three largest *zaibatsu* (Mitsui, Sumitomo, and Mitsubishi) to enter the motor vehicle business. Mitsubishi responded but limited its activities to the construction of trucks. None of these policies reduced the dominance of the U.S. firms.

The Japanese military government decided to force out the American firms. In the early 1930s, GM proposed that GM-Japan merge with three smaller Japanese firms, with GM retaining 51 percent ownership. The opposition of the Japanese government, however, resulted in the cession of majority ownership to Nissan on April 18, 1934. Nissan had been founded in 1933 out of the remnants of DAT Jidusha Seizo Company, producer of Datsun cars and itself the successor to a firm founded in 1911, Kaishinsha Motor Car Works.[48] When the military government later blocked GM from repatriating profits under the Exchange Control Order, the merger agreement was suspended. When in 1936 GM proposed a link with Toyota, which had only begun to pro-

47. Michael A. Cusumano, *The Japanese Automobile Industry: Technology and Management at Nissan and Toyota* (Cambridge, Mass.: Harvard University Press, 1985), pp. 15–16.
48. John Bell Rae, *Nissan/Datsun: A History of Nissan Motor Corporation in the USA, 1960–1980* (New York: McGraw Hill, 1982), pp. 6–7; Cusumano, *Japanese Automobile Industry*, p. 33.

duce automobile engines in 1931 and assembled its first car in 1935, Kiichiro Toyoda, its founder, rejected the offer, thus leaving GM with no other option but to quit the Japanese market.

Ford tried to maintain a presence in Japan by proposing that its vehicles be produced with 100 percent local content, while keeping majority control over the Japanese subsidiary. But this deal depended on Ford's ability to build a new plant at Yokohama, which the Japanese army strongly opposed. The cabinet of the military government issued the Motor Vehicle Manufacturing Business Act on May 29, 1936, which decreed that all motor vehicle manufacturers had to be licensed by the government. The U.S. embassy to Japan asked that GM and Ford be licensed under the law, and the Japanese government complied. But the denial of the permit to build the Ford plant at Yokohama and restrictions on GM's ability to repatriate funds, plus a substantial increase in tariffs, convinced both companies to suspend all assembly operations in Japan in 1939.[49]

The two main Japanese firms licensed under the 1936 act were Nissan and Toyota. They are still the dominant firms in the Japanese market (see Figure 9). Toyota was developed by the Toyoda family, based on capital produced by selling patents for automatic looms to a British firm. After 1936, Toyota received most of its funding from the Mitsui banks. By 1942, the firm was still producing only slightly more than sixteen thousand vehicles per year. Nissan was not a family-run firm like Toyota and had no ties to the old *zaibatsu*. It was closely linked with a government-owned bank and the military. Its main source of investment funds after World War II was the Industrial Bank of Japan, a long-term credit bank with close ties to MITI and the Ministry of Finance. By 1942, Nissan produced fewer than twenty thousand vehicles per year, most of them for the military. Thus, though the military government's policies excluded the U.S. firms, they did not create a thriving indigenous industry. Quality-control problems and dissatisfaction with production rates resulted in the establishment of a military-controlled monopoly in October 1943 under the War Plant Law.[50]

Early Postwar Policies

After World War II, until the end of the occupation in 1952, the Japanese auto industry was unable to do major rebuilding, first because of

49. Chang, *Japanese Auto Industry*, pp. 11–24.
50. Ibid., pp. 25–34.

Figure 9. Automobile production of Japanese firms

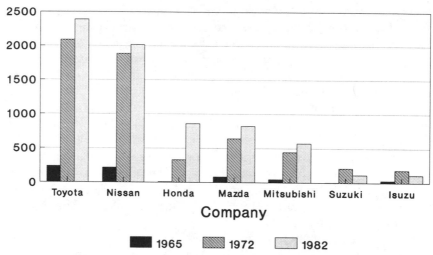

Sources: For 1965: P. Baynes, *Japan: Its Motor Industry and Market* (London: Her Majesty's Stationery Office, 1971), p. 134; for 1972: *The U.S. Automobile Industry, 1980: Report to the President from the Secretary of Transportation* (Washington, D.C., March 1981), p. 54; Alan Altshuler, Martin Anderson, Daniel Jones, Daniel Roos, and James Womack, *The Future of the Automobile; The Report of MIT's International Automobile Program* (Cambridge, Mass.: MIT Press, 1984), p. 124.

limits on production and then by the general austerity imposed by the Dodge Line.[51] Major strikes occurred at Toyota when wages were cut by 10 percent and 23 percent of the workers were laid off. The firm was rescued from bankruptcy in 1949 when the Bank of Japan organized a consortium of banks under the leadership of Mitsui to provide new funds. The Bank of Japan was reluctant to help Toyota because it was not convinced that Japan could ever have a competitive automotive industry.[52] MITI disagreed with the Bank of Japan and the Ministry of Transport, arguing that rather than wasting resources, the development of an automobile industry would stimulate other sectors, especially steel and metal machinery. Huge orders for trucks from the U.S. army during the Korean War put these arguments to an end, in MITI's favor.[53]

51. The Dodge Line was a set of deflationary economic policies mandated by a U.S. commission headed by Joseph Dodge, a Detroit banker. See Mikiso Hane, *Modern Japan: A Historical Survey* (Boulder, Colo.: Westview, 1986), p. 354.

52. See Cusumano, *Japanese Automobile Industry*, p. 124.

53. See Ira C. Magaziner and Thomas M. Hout, *Japanese Industrial Policy* (London: Policy Studies Institute, 1980), p. 55; Cusumano, *Japanese Automobile Industry*, pp. 19–20.

MITI published its "Basic Policy for the Introduction of Foreign Investment in Japan's Car Industry" in 1952, which, contrary to its title, restricted inward foreign investment, limited repatriation of profits, and authorized the government to screen joint-venture arrangements. Approximately 9 percent of all investments in manufacturing between 1951 and 1955 were made by automotive firms and were financed primarily by reconstruction loans from the Japan Development Bank. Firms were allowed to depreciate their equipment at accelerated rates as high as 50 percent in the first year.

Joint Ventures with Foreign Firms

A few new firms began to produce automobiles in the 1950s. Isuzu was formed in 1949 out of the wreckage of Diesel Motors, a truck producer. Hino, a producer of heavy trucks, separated from Isuzu in 1952 and began to produce automobiles in the early 1950s. But Nissan and Toyota continued to dominate the market. The government promoted joint ventures with European firms to manufacture foreign-designed models in Japan. Nissan concluded an agreement in 1952 with Austin Motor Company of Britain for the assembly and eventually the building of Austin models in Japan. In 1953, Isuzu signed up with Rootes of Britain to produce Hillmans; Hino teamed up with Renault of France to produce the Renault 4CV model; and Mitsubishi joined with Willys-Overland of the United States to produce Jeeps. Toyota decided to develop product and process technologies on its own and emerged in the 1950s as a stronger competitor than its chief rival, Nissan.[54]

After import restrictions were lifted, imports of European cars began to increase in 1952, accounting for 31.1 percent of domestic demand that year.[55] In 1954, however, foreign exchange shortages were used to justify a cabinet statement restricting imports, which remained in effect until the general liberalization of trade in the early 1960s.

Loans from the Japan Development Bank to the auto firms totaled 1.5 billion yen ($4.2 million) between 1951 and 1955 and about 14 percent of fixed investments by the firms between 1956 and 1965. As Michael Cusumano has written:

MITI combined low-interest loans with tax privileges, such as special depreciation allowances for new machinery instituted for original-equipment

54. See Rae, *Nissan/Datsun*, p. 10; Gilbert R. Winham and Ikuo Kabashima, "The Politics of U.S.-Japanese Auto Trade," in I. M. Destler and Hideo Sato, eds., *Coping with U.S.-Japanese Economic Conflicts* (Lexington, Mass.: D.C. Heath, 1982), pp. 77–78; Julian Gresser, *Partners in Prosperity: Strategic Industries for the U.S. and Japan* (New York: McGraw-Hill, 1984), pp. 110–11; and Cusumano, *Japanese Automobile Industry*, p. 9.
55. Chang, *Japanese Auto Industry*, p. 92.

manufacturers in 1951 and for parts suppliers in 1956. Beginning in 1956, MITI also exempted companies from import duties on machinery and tools purchased abroad . . . and allowed firms to deduct as income any revenues obtained from export sales. Japan had to abandon this latter practice when it joined the General Agreement on Tariffs and Trade (GATT) in 1964 as a full member, but the government subsequently permitted automakers to establish tax-free reserves for expenditures related to overseas marketing and to adopt depreciation schedules tied to export performance."[56]

The Strikes of 1950 and 1953

One major goal of the democratization program of the U.S. occupation was to establish free and independent labor unions. Unions had been suppressed under the military government so it was not difficult to find issues to mobilize workers after the war. The All-Japan Automobile Industry Labor Union (or Zenji) came into existence in 1947. Zenji aspired to be an industrial union, not an enterprise union. It was linked to other industrial unions through the Sohyo. A series of strikes occurred at both Nissan and Toyota, some acrimonious. The bank-led rescue of Toyota in 1949 required that surplus workers be laid off, and in April 1950 the management presented its plan to lay off sixteen hundred workers. This plan sparked a series of protests, strikes, and work stoppages that lasted over two months and resulted in the resignation of Kiichiro Toyoda from the presidency of the firm as well as the promise of lifetime employment for workers who supported the firm in its dispute with the union.[57]

In 1953, Zenji called for a unified strike at Nissan, Toyota, and Isuzu. After several months of short strikes and negotiations, the Toyota and Isuzu workers settled with management, but the Nissan negotiations remained deadlocked. The Nissan management encouraged the white-collar members of the Nissan union to form a second union in exchange for pay increases and promises of future promotions. When the strike fund ran out and a sufficient number of workers had defected to the second union, Zenji admitted defeat and ended the strike. Zenji was dissolved in 1954, leaving only enterprise unions in the auto industry. These unions all cut their ties to the Sohyo, opting instead to associate with the Domei.

The outcome of the auto strikes of the late 1940s and early 1950s established a clear precedent for the next forty years for enterprise

56. Cusumano, *Japanese Automobile Industry*, p. 20.
57. See Eiji Toyoda, *Toyota: Fifty Years in Motion* (Tokyo: Kodansha, 1987), pp. 103–4; Cusumano, *Japanese Automobile Industry*, p. 182.

unions in manufacturing. Tactical errors by industrial unions like Zenji and political errors by radical labor federations like the Sohyo were important factors in the rise of enterprise unions. But in addition, the settlement of these strikes through the organization of company-affiliated unions committed the managements to avoid layoffs and to other aspects of labor-management relations that would later prove difficult to keep.

Policies for the Components Industry

In the 1950s, government policies favored improving the automotive components industry in Japan to provide a base for the expansion of the industry as a whole. According to Professor Konosuke Odaka of Hitotsubashi University, "The government decided that a strong parts industry was necessary to build a strong auto industry. However, MITI had scarce resources, so it was forced to select a limited number of important suppliers for direct assistance. Suppliers were able to apply for capital, and then some of the applications were granted. Although the amount of capital which was supplied solely by the government was minimal, it was worthwhile for the suppliers to receive this capital because it could be used as leverage to get other loans from the private sector."[58]

The Japan Development Bank and the Small Business Finance Corporation extended $50 million to low-interest loans to suppliers between 1956 and 1966. One result of this program was to increase the concentration of ownership in components markets and to decrease average production costs. Components production remained relatively unconcentrated, however, with most firms specializing in only one or two products. MITI had hoped that larger and more horizontally integrated components producers would improve Japanese auto firms' competitive position. Thus from MITI's perspective, the program was only partly successful.[59] But the fragmented and highly competitive nature of the components market made possible the "just-in-time" (or *kanban*) system.

Kanban, Zero Defects, and the Toyota Production System

Kanban, meaning card, referred to the paper cards (later, plastic plates) used by the Toyota Corporation to provide information about

58. Quoted from Alan M. Webber, Mark Fuller, David Dyer, and Malcolm Salter, "The Wreck of the Japanese Auto Industry," manuscript, Harvard Business School, January 18, 1983, p. 8.
59. See Magaziner and Hout, *Japanese Industrial Policy*, pp. 58–59; and Cusumano, *Japanese Automobile Industry*, p. 245.

parts inventories to workers at each production station. There were three main types of *kanban:* withdrawal, in-house production, and subcontractor production. When a certain lot of parts had been used, a worker would send back the basket containing those parts to the workers at the next workstation upline, together with a withdrawal *kanban.* When a sufficient number of withdrawal *kanban* accumulated at a stocking point, the worker there would send an in-house production *kanban* to the appropriate production center if the part in question was made in-house. If not, the worker would send a subcontractor production *kanban* to the subcontractor to restock that part.[60]

The general principle behind the *kanban* system was to keep inventories to an absolute minimum so as to reduce inventory costs and keep production turnaround time at a minimum. Large parts inventories were used traditionally as a form of insurance to keep the assembly line functioning smoothly in case of delivery problems or malfunctioning parts. The *kanban* system compelled managers to think of a major assembly plant as being linked to its suppliers by invisible assembly lines, forcing them to optimize production at all points. This meant working closely with suppliers to prevent problems in the scheduling of deliveries and to maximize the quality and reliability of components.

Besides the just-in-time system, Japanese auto producers adopted other processes that later helped reduce production costs. One was a defect-reduction approach that assigned responsibility for quality control to production workers instead of supervisors. Another was the quality circle, an idea invented in the United States but more widely used in Japan, whereby production workers were asked for their advice about how to improve products and production processes and given bonuses based on the usefulness of their advice.

But as important as the just-in-time system was the concentration of production facilities in a single location, or only a few, with the main engine-building, body-construction, and assembly plants ringed by dozens of independent components producers. The point of this concentration was to reduce transportation costs, minimize delays in deliveries of components to the main plants, and minimize the time between the beginning of assembly of a given vehicle and the moment it rolled off the assembly line. The best example was Toyota City near Nagoya. Even though it was impossible to build components plants directly adjacent to the main assembly plants of Nissan in Tokyo, suppliers were close enough that Nissan could match Toyota in just-in-time production methods. The physical concentration of plants and the fragmentation of the components market made just-in-time practices

60. Cusumano, *Japanese Automobile Industry,* chap. 5.

possible. Until the introduction in the 1970s of robots and automation in factories, there were no other major differences between the organization of auto production in Japan and that in Europe and the United States.[61]

MITI Promotes Mergers

The growth of the Japanese auto industry began to take off in the 1960s, after the Ikeda government adopted a policy of expanding the domestic economy. Nissan, for example, built four plants during the 1960s and added 3,800 new employees.[62] Toyota and Nissan remained the two largest producers, but Isuzu, Hino, Daihatsu, and Prince were producing automobiles in the 1950s, and in 1960 three new firms entered the market: Mitsubishi, Fuji, and Mazda (Suzuki and Honda did not enter the market until somewhat later). The combined domestic market share of Toyota and Nissan dropped from around 75 percent in 1960 to under 50 percent in 1962. This was worrisome to MITI, which believed that there were too many firms in Japan to take advantage of static scale economies in the industry. The smaller firms believed that they could match the production costs of the larger firms, especially if they could make major inroads in export markets. MITI remained skeptical about the prospects for increasing exports and began to push for a restructuring and reconcentration of auto production.

At the 1961 meeting of the Industry Structure Council, MITI proposed that the passenger car producers be organized into three groups based on basic design types: regular passenger cars, minicars, and specialty cars (including sports cars). Each firm would be allowed to produce only one type and must produce a minimum volume within three years or it might not be allowed to remain in the market. The obvious result of such a policy would be to eliminate small producers. Toyota and Nissan were not opposed to these proposals because they were likely to benefit from decreased competition from the smaller firms.

MITI's proposal in 1963 for a special measures law was the result of the discussion in 1961. It was partially motivated by MITI's concern

61. For further discussion of the Toyota innovations, see James P. Womack, Daniel T. Jones, and Daniel Roos, *The Machine That Changed the World* (New York: Macmillan, 1990), chap. 3; William J. Abernathy, Kim B. Clark, and Alan M. Kantrow, *Industrial Renaissance: Producing a Competitive Future for America* (New York: Basic Books, 1983), chapters 5–6; Richard J. Schonberger, *Japanese Manufacturing Techniques: Nine Hidden Lessons in Simplicity* (New York: Free Press, 1982); and Yasuhiro Monden, *Toyota Production System* (Norcross, Ga.: Industrial Engineering and Management Press, Institute of Industrial Engineers, 1983). The last is an English-language summary of Taichi Ohno, *Toyota seisan hohshiki* (Tokyo: Daiyamondo, 1978).

62. Chang, *Japanese Auto Industry*, p. 70.

about underconcentration in the auto industry. The law was not enacted, partly because of opposition from the automotive industry. The small producers—especially Mazda, Mitsubishi, Fuji, and Daihatsu—were gaining market share and making profits. These firms were part of the political alliance that defeated the special measures law. But MITI remained worried about the structure of the industry because, in the mid-1960s, only Toyota and Nissan appeared to be potentially competitive in international markets. MITI therefore began to propose mergers on a case-by-case basis as smaller producers ran into trouble.

The first such merger was between Nissan and Prince in 1966. MITI helped the two companies get financial assistance (only $15 million) from the Japan Development Bank. Later the same year, another government-sponsored loan was made to encourage the merger of Hino with Toyota. Nissan became the major shareholder in Fuji Heavy Industries, manufacturers of Subaru automobiles, in 1968. Attempts by MITI between 1966 and 1968 to bring about mergers between Isuzu and Nissan, Isuzu and Fuji, Isuzu and Mitsubishi, and Fuji and Mitsubishi all failed.[63]

The Mitsubishi-Chrysler Deal

On May 12, 1969, Mitsubishi announced a 65/35 percent joint venture with Chrysler. The Japanese government (not just MITI) opposed this move. The cabinet initially tried to liberalize capital markets to make it easier for Japanese firms to merge with one another, but the deal went through anyway. A similar arrangement between Isuzu and GM and a linkup between Suzuki and GM followed. Mitsubishi became the number three producer in Japan, displacing Mazda in the mid-1970s. Mitsubishi produced the Dodge Colt for Chrysler, a model that helped Chrysler winter the storms that overtook that firm in the late 1970s.

MITI's defenders saw these new ventures as vindicating the merger-promotion policies of the 1960s; critics cited them as examples of the limits of MITI's foresight and power. But the real story was how Mitsubishi, a member of the Mitsubishi *keiretsu*, and the other small auto firms forced MITI to abandon its policies favoring Toyota and Nissan. It was no coincidence that Toyota and Nissan owed their market dominance to the interwar policies of the Japanese military government or that Nissan was affiliated with the government through the Industrial Bank of Japan and Toyota was affiliated with the Mitsui *keiretsu*. Upstarts like Mitsubishi, Mazda and Honda now had a chance to carve out a niche for themselves in the auto market. MITI's failure to force con-

63. Magaziner and Hout, *Japanese Industrial Policy,* pp. 62–63.

solidation increased competition within Japan, which strengthened all the firms in their later efforts to penetrate world markets by further accelerating innovation in products and processes. The failure of its merger-promotion efforts was a shock to MITI and helped to produce a consensus for a change in the agency's stragegy that eventually became the basis for Naohiro Amaya's Vision for the 1970s.[64]

Import Barriers and Export Promotion

Japanese firms began to test their chances in world export markets in the 1960s. They were generally unsuccessful except in relatively small and specialized markets, including some in the developing world. In the largest potential market, the United States, Japanese exports suffered from insufficiently developed dealer networks, the poor image of Japanese workmanship, models that did not appeal to the average American consumer, and competition from Volkswagen and other European firms. The firms learned their lessons quickly and developed dealer networks, designed new models, and worked to improve their image among American consumers. But their great opportunity for expansion in the U.S. market came in the 1970s, when oil prices increased, creating a demand for small, fuel-efficient cars and U.S. and European firms failed to produce cars to meet this demand.

The role of the Japanese government during this period was primarily to facilitate the expansion of exports and limit the growth of imports, despite the so-called liberalization of 1967. In September 1960, the government announced that it was lifting import restrictions on small cars. But the definition of a small car was changed from a vehicle with an engine displacement of less than fifteen hundred cubic centimeters to one with an engine displacement of less than two thousand cubic centimeters. Larger vehicles would continue to be subject to import duties of over 30 percent. No U.S. firms and only a few European firms manufactured cars that met the new definitions, and the European manufacturers that did were still bound by voluntary export restraints negotiated in the 1950s. Toyota and Nissan knew that they had to make cars in the fifteen-hundred-to-two-thouand-cubic-centimeter range if they were to penetrate the U.S. market so the redefinition of smallness was clearly in their interest.

Import duties on larger cars were reduced to 28 percent in 1968 and then to 17.5 percent in 1969. Import duties on smaller cars remained at 20 percent after 1970. By this time, Japanese manufacturers no

---

64. MITI works with the Industry Structure Council to produce a Vision document for each decade, a sort of road map for structural change in the Japanese economy. See Johnson, *MITI and the Japanese Miracle*, pp. 267–68.

longer needed tariff barriers to protect them from international competition. Continuing complaints from foreign producers and the recognition of Japanese strengths resulted in a cut in tariffs on all cars to 8 percent in 1972 and zero in 1978. Imported autos as a percentage of sales never rose above 2 percent in Japan and actually dipped below 1 percent in the early 1980s.[65]

The Rescue of Mazda

Only one firm, Toyo Kogyo (now called Mazda Motors), experienced difficulties during this period. Toyo Kogyo had marketed a rotary-engine model, based on a revolutionary engine design originally developed in Germany. The engine was remarkable in its reliability and performance, but it was not fuel-efficient. Worldwide sales declined by 19 percent in 1974 after the oil price increases. U.S. sales dropped by 44 percent. The management of Toyo Kogyo was slow to respond to the decline in profitability that resulted from the precipitous drop in sales. Toyo Kogyo's operations were concentrated in Hiroshima, and the possible collapse of the firm became an important regional issue. Nevertheless, the Japanese government did not get involved in the crisis.

In October 1974, the lead bank of Toyo Kogyo's *keiretsu*, Sumitomo Bank, placed two of its senior officers on the managing board of Toyo Kogyo. On January 1, 1975, a $114 million loan was announced to finance inventory and to help defray costs of laying off workers. Over the next two years, more Sumitomo officers were added to the board of Toyo Kogyo, and a series of loans were made to restructure the operations of the firm. The firm C. Itoh was charged with marketing Toyo Kogyo vehicles in the United States. The previous CEO, Kohei Matsuda, was kicked upstairs. Three new products were planned and successfully introduced: the GLC (1977), the 626 (1978), and the sporty RX-7 (1979). Ford Motors was sold a 25 percent equity interest in the firm in exchange for purchasing new stock issues for approximately $135 million and relinquishing its Yokohama landholdings. Finally, and perhaps most important, production in the firm was rationalized, eliminating excess labor, new models were produced with more standardized components, and some of the components operations of the firm were contracted out. Most of the laid-off workers were retrained as salesmen and sent to Tokyo and Osaka to sell cars door to door. By 1981, the firm was out of the red and heading toward very respectable profits.

65. Cusumano, *Japanese Automobile Industry,* pp. 24–25.

All this would have been impossible without the Sumitomo Bank, whose large asssets made it possible to bail out the firm without seeking funds from the government. Members of the Sumitomo *keiretsu* purchased newly issued stock in Toyo Kogyo and sold real estate to finance these purchases. They also promoted sales of Mazda cars whenever they had the opportunity, buying Mazdas for their own fleets as well.[66]

Managing the Trade Dispute

The Japanese government remained aloof from the affairs of the auto industry until the end of the 1970s. In 1979, the rapid increase in Japanese imports into the United States following the second oil price increase created a trade dispute that required the government's attention. The dispute led to the adoption of a voluntary export restraint agreement that limited the number of vehicles Japan could export to the United States.

The VER forced MITI to play the role of involuntary cartel organizer, establishing quotas for each Japanese firm so that the overall quota could be met. Each firm received an export allowance equal to its proportion of Japanese exports to the United States for the previous three years times the total quota. The objective was to freeze the export shares of each firm in the U.S. market. This system was uniformly unpopular. Toyota and Nissan believed that without quotas they would have been able to increase their U.S. shares relative to their competitors. The smaller firms, such as Honda and Mazda, experienced rapid growth in demand for their models and thus wanted their quotas increased. In addition, the big three U.S. firms had come to depend on imports from Japanese firms in which they had an equity share: GM had purchased 34.2 percent of Isuzu in 1971 and 5.3 percent of Suzuki in 1979; Ford owned 25 percent of Toyo Kogyo; and Chrysler had a deal with Mitsubishi, negotiated in June 1981, to market Mitsubishi models in the United States. The U.S. firms, especially GM, were put in the strange position of lobbying for higher export quotas for Japan so that they could market a sufficient number of small Japanese-built models under their own labels.[67]

In administering the quota system, MITI achieved some leverage over the auto firms, despite the use of the previous three years' export

66. See James P. Womack, "Public Policy for a Mature Industrial Sector: The Auto Case" (Ph.D., Massachusetts Institute of Technology, 1982), pp. 233–45.

67. "Nissan Shifts Gear," *Economist*, October 29, 1983, p. 88; Mary Saso, *Japanese Industry* (London: Economist Intelligence Unit, 1981), p. 94; "Why Carmakers Will Mourn If Export Quotas Die," *Business Week*, February 18, 1985, p. 46; and Amal Nag, "GM Seeks Higher Japanese-Import Quotas So That It Can Sell Affiliates' Cars in U.S.," *Wall Street Journal*, September 12, 1983, p. 17.

performance to determine export shares. If a firm failed to sell the cars allotted to it under its quota, the unsold cars could be apportioned among the remaining firms. MITI used its limited discretionary power to encourage Japanese firms to adopt a variety of strategies to reduce the underlying trade tensions. It limited export quotas of Toyota and Nissan as an inducement for them to consider alternatives to exports in meeting U.S. demand. MITI particularly approved of joint ventures for producing Japanese models in the United States (as in the GM-Toyota joint venture in Fremont, California) and for setting up assembly and production facilities in general (as in Nissan's truck plant in Smyrna, Tennessee, and Mazda's plant in Flat Rock, Michigan).[68]

The remarkable shift in Japanese firms' attitudes toward producing vehicles in the United States was the result of a combination of factors: pressure on the U.S. government by the unions and firms to establish export restraints; the threat that Congress would pass a local content law (the bill originally introduced in 1980 was reintroduced several times in the 1980s); MITI's increased power over the Japanese industry during the VER period through its administration of the export quota system; and the increased perception of Japanese firms that they could establish labor-management and component-supplier systems similar to those available to them in Japan.

The tactical errors of industrial unions in the late 1940s and early 1950s in the development of the Japanese auto industry contributed to the institutionalization of enterprise unions and employer guarantees of lifetime employment. It would not have occurred, however, had there not been a widespread consensus on the need to strengthen Japanese industry in international competition, starting with certain key industries like steel and autos. Without such a consensus, workers would not have supported enterprise unions and wage restraints.

The institutionalization of the *keiretsu*, or industrial families, was equally important and was manifested in the auto industry by the growth of rivals to Toyota and Nissan in the 1950s and 1960s. The Toyo Kogyo rescue of 1974–75, in which the Sumitomo *keiretsu* was crucial, illustrates the importance of the *keiretsu* in the Japanese system. The government was not involved in the rescue because the Sumitomo *keiretsu* possessed sufficient resources of its own. Both the *keiretsu* and the government preferred that the crisis be handled in this way. The parallels between the Japanese mode of resolving this crisis and the German mode—most notably in the cases of AEG and Volkswagen—will become evident in Chapter 5.

68. See Susan Chira, "For Mazda, a U.S. Car Plant," *New York Times*, December 1, 1984, p. 21.

Government policy was crucial for the successes of the Japanese auto industry. The industry got its start behind investment barriers established in the 1930s and was shattered by trade and investment barriers through the 1960s. Government subsidies for the auto firms in the 1950s helped raise production volumes to meet the growth in demand that began during the Korean War and continued afterward.

But after the mid-1950s, direct subsidies to the auto assemblers played no role in the success of the industry. Government programs to develop the machine tool and automobile components industries were more important from the mid-1950s through the 1970s because they helped Japanese firms to become international least-cost producers, while maintaining quality and reliability standards equal to or better than those of other countries. Without a base of suppliers and subcontractors, the Japanese firms could not have implemented the *kanban* innovations successfully.

The heavy domestic competition among the Japanese firms was partly a consequence of the *keiretsu* system. Domestic competition hastened the diffusion of new product and process technologies. Toyota and Nissan led in the creation and introduction of new technologies. Toyota aggressively sought answers to key technological and business problems; its most important innovation was the *kanban* production system. Nissan rapidly adapted technology imported from abroad, starting with the trucks it built in the 1930s for the military and continuing after the war with its extensive use of automation and robotics. Matching Toyota's innovations in product and process technologies, Nissan transcended its earlier dependence on foreign technology. Later on, Honda and Mazda were innovative in product technology and in new forms of overseas investment and production. The government in the 1970s created a stable economic environment as a base for innovation.

Other analysts of the role of industrial policy in the success of the auto industry have placed too much stress on the failure of MITI to impose its will on the firms in the 1960s.[69] MITI mistakenly thought that it was necessary to increase the concentration of ownership in the industry to match that in other industrial regions. MITI was unsuccessful in reducing the number of firms in the 1960s partly because the *keiretsus'* desire to back their own auto firms prevailed against MITI's desire to rationalize the industry. MITI adapted quickly to the growth

69. See, for example, John O. Haley, "Administrative Guidance versus Formal Regulation: Resolving the Paradox of Industrial Policy," in Gary R. Saxonhouse and Kozo Yamamura, eds., *Law and Trade Issues in the Japanese Economy* (Seattle: University of Washington Press, 1986), esp. pp. 121–23; and Philip H. Tresize, "Industrial Policy Is Not the Major Reason for Japan's Success," *Brookings Review* 1 (1983): 13–18.

of export markets in the 1970s, just as it had adapted quickly to the growth in domestic demand in the early 1950s. MITI's overall strategy changed in response to its own analyses of what it had done wrong in dealing with the auto industry in the 1960s.

The tremendous success of the Japanese auto industry gave it unusual autonomy from the powerful, centralized industrial policy instruments of the government in the 1960s but ironically led to a reduction of autonomy under MITI's administration of the "voluntary" export restraints in the 1980s. When the state was unable to influence the industry in the 1960s, it wanted greater concentration in ownership; but when it finally got some leverage over the firms in the 1980s, it used that leverage to reduce the concentration of ownership and to force its former champions, Toyota and Nissan, to invest in overseas production. The importance of the *keiretsu* in the automotive sector constrained the government's power over the industry, but those constraints increased rather than reduced the international competitiveness of the industry.

Policies toward the Semiconductor Industry

Whereas the growth of the steel and auto industries depended on government policies that fostered innovation in production techniques and the diffusion of existing technologies, the success of the semiconductor industry was the result of conscious efforts by the state, working together with the major firms, to create new technologies.[70] The key difference between semiconductors, on one hand, and steel and autos, on the other, was that for the former the state had to finance research and development directly.

The Japanese government knew that Japan needed to acquire the latest information technology to realize its goals for the 1970s and 1980s in the face of higher prices for imported energy sources and growing competition from the developing countries. In pursuit of its goals, the Japanese government invented new policy instruments: for

70. The main sources for this section are Julian Gresser, *Partners in Prosperity* (New York: McGraw-Hill, 1984), chap. 5; Ezra F. Vogel, *Comeback, Case by Case: Building the Resurgence of American Business* (New York: Simon & Schuster, 1985), chap. 5; Michael Borrus, *Competing for Control* (Cambridge, Mass.: Ballinger, 1988); Michael Borrus with James Millstein and John Zysman, *Responses to the Japanese Challenge in High Technology: Innovation, Maturity and U.S.-Japanese Competition in Microelectronics* (Berkeley, Calif.: Berkeley Roundtable on the International Economy, 1983); Daniel I. Okimoto, Takuo Sugano, and Franklin B. Weinstein, eds., *Competitive Edge: The Semiconductor Industry in the U.S. and Japan* (Stanford, Calif.: Stanford University Press, 1984); and Anchordoguy, "Mastering the Market."

research and development (R&D), means for procuring technology, leasing arrangements for expensive electronic systems, and the formation of R&D consortia. MITI usually avoided administrative guidance and recession cartels in dealing with its clients in the electronics industry. But it continued to restrict imports and inward foreign investment so as to enhance the environment for the growth of Japanese firms.

Policies toward the Computer Industry

Japan, like Europe, was far behind when it began to catch up to the technological leader, the United States. The Japanese government early perceived the need to avoid importing large computer systems. Early government policies, therefore, were oriented primarily toward the computer industry and were largely unsuccessful. The early successes of Japanese consumer electronics firms in incorporating semiconductor technology into products and the rapid technological change in semiconductor component technology pushed both firms and government to change their emphasis in research and development from computers to basic semiconductor technology. The Europeans were somewhat slower in focusing on the centrality of semiconductor components to the new information industries because their electronics industry was not as open to international competition as were those of the United States and Japan. The Europeans' slowness in this area put them behind Japan and the United States in information technology in the 1970s and 1980s.

Most of the research on computer technology in the 1950s took place in the laboratories of universities and Nippon Telegraph and Telephone (NTT). American computer exports started to arrive in Japan in 1954. The clear superiority of U.S. products led MITI to organize a research committee in 1955 to determine how to make Japanese computer manufacturing competitive. The committee concluded that imports of foreign computers should be limited and attempts should be made to acquire access to foreign (i.e., U.S.) technology. The Electronics Industry Provisional Development Act, made law in 1957, authorized research cartels exempted from the Antimonopoly Law, direct subsidies, low-interest loans, tax incentives, and R&D tax credits. Between 1957 and 1961, the industry received only $1 million in direct subsidies and approximately $25 million in indirect subsidies (mostly from the Japan Development Bank). A new electronics division was established within MITI's Heavy Industry Bureau, and an Electronics Industry Deliberation Council was formed as a government-industry forum.

Import Barriers and Restrictions on Inward Investment

In 1960, foreign computer manufacturers dominated at least 70 percent of the domestic market. IBM and Sperry were the two most important firms, with IBM far in the lead. In 1960, the Japanese government raised tariffs on computers from 15 to 25 percent and restricted allocations of foreign exchange to firms that wanted to import computers (Nippon Electric Company and Hitachi had introduced some small business machines in the late 1950s). MITI used the import licensing requirements to pressure firms to buy computers from Japanese producers, a form of administrative guidance the firms resented.[71] In addition, IBM's manufacturing activities and profit repatriations were limited by the government.

MITI permitted IBM to establish a wholly owned subsidiary in Japan in 1960 to manufacture its popular 1401 small business computer and to repatriate profits in the form of royalties up to a limit of 10 percent of sales, an exception to the general rules regarding repatriation of profits. In return, IBM agreed to make its patents available for licensing to Japanese manufacturing, a right U.S. manufacturers had gained under a 1956 court decree. The Japanese government wanted IBM to conclude a joint-venture agreement with a Japanese firm, but IBM resisted, and MITI eventually relented. But the head of MITI's Heavy Industries Bureau politely warned IBM: "Japanese makers are mosquitoes, IBM is an elephant. I would appreciate it if IBM does not do anything to crush the mosquito under its feet."[72]

MITI tried to reduce the impact of IBM's decision by limiting the types of machines IBM-Japan could produce and the volume it exported. MITI particularly did not want IBM to produce small and medium-sized machines so Japanese firms could build their sales in that area. IBM patents were transferred to Japanese firms in January 1961, but IBM-Japan was not permitted to start production until 1963.[73] Even though IBM-Japan came to resemble Japanese firms in many ways, including its recruitment of the top graduates of Tokyo University, the firm was excluded from Japanese government programs such as the Japan Electronics Computer Corporation.

All other U.S. computer firms were prohibited from establishing wholly owned subsidiaries in Japan. Instead, they were forced to conclude joint-venture arrangements with Japanese firms: Hitachi with RCA (1961), Mitsubishi with TRW (1962), NEC with Honeywell (1962), Oki with Sperry (1963), and Toshiba with GE (1964). The only

71. Anchordoguy, "Mastering the Market," p. 513.
72. Ibid., p. 515.
73. Ibid., p. 516.

Japanese firm that did not enter a joint venture was Fujitsu. The fear of IBM dominance was uppermost in the mind of firms and government officials in the negotiation of these alliances. In Europe such alliances had failed to keep domestic firms on the technological frontier. They were not much more helpful in Japan.

But the high tariff and investment barriers had the desired result of decreasing dependence on imports. Imports as a percentage of total consumption declined from 80 percent in 1959 to 20 percent in 1968. Sales of foreign computers declined from 93 percent in 1958 to 42.5 percent in 1969. Tariff barriers were not removed until after 1975, but by that time Japanese firms had developed mainframes and small business computers that were competitive with IBM products.[74]

The JECC

In 1961, MITI approved the formation of the Japan Electronics Computer Corporation (JECC) financed by several firms and the Japan Development Bank. A former vice-minister of MITI was put in charge. The JECC purchased computers from Japanese firms and leased them to Japanese users. IBM leased its models to users so they did not have to bear the costs of scrapping obsolete equipment.

Even though fifteen companies had been given access to IBM's patents in 1960, only six firms joined JECC: Hitachi, Fujitsu, NEC, Mitsubishi, Toshiba, and Oki. MITI had decided that, because of the large amount of capital needed to develop advanced systems, only six firms would be allowed to enter the industry. Table 5 shows that the six firms included representatives of all the major *keiretsu*. The JECC served not only as a leasing device but also as a funnel for government subsidies to the firms. The low-interest government loans for leasing freed up capital the firms would have used for financing rentals. Instead of receiving payments over time from renters, the firms received an immediate lump-sum payment from JECC. Marie Anchordoguy has estimated that the firms received payments of $269 million during 1961–69 and $495 million during 1970–81 from this source.[75]

When IBM introduced the system 360 in 1964, it became evident that previous policies were insufficient to deal with the company's technological strength. In 1964, MITI's Electronic Industry Deliberative Council recommended that the government strengthen the JECC, subsidize the development of supercomputers, rationalize the production of computer peripherals, and make efforts to increase the supply of

74. Ibid.
75. Ibid., p. 521.

computer technical personnel. MITI then urged the firms and JECC to establish a private clearinghouse for information on the computer industry, which was to be called the Japan Information Processing Developing Center. The Keidanren also formed its own computer policy review committee.

Between 1966 and 1975, MITI sponsored a 10-billion-yen program to develop a super high-performance computer at the Electro-Technical Laboratory (ETL). Hitachi was chosen as the lead firm in this program. Hitachi, Fujitsu, and NEC were responsible for developing mainframe hardware; Toshiba, Oki, and Mitsubishi were to develop optical-character-recognition hardware, *kanji* displays, and high-quality cathode ray tubes (necessary for displaying the more complex *kanji* characters); Hitachi and Fujitsu were to develop new disk drives; a software consortium of major computer firms, the Japan Software Company, was to develop software.

In 1968, NTT began a project called the Denden Information Processing System (DIPS) in collaboration with Fujitsu, Hitachi, and NEC. The principal goal of this project was to create a system for interconnecting computer systems via digital telephone exchanges. By 1973, NTT announced its first DIPS product. Fujitsu then marketed several successors. Thus DIPS helped subsidize the development of data networks by Japanese firms.

In 1971, MITI initiated the Pattern Information Processing System (PIPS), which lasted until 1980 and was designed to produce hardware and software for high-speed computer systems that could integrate the processing of *kanji* characters, human speech recognition, and three-dimensional graphics capabilities. The total budget for PIPS was 35 billion yen. The PIPS project bore fruit in the 1980s, when Japanese computer firms were able to beat IBM in introducing products using *kanji* characters to business and small-computer customers.

The ETL computer project was the first to recognize that U.S.-based computer firms, particularly IBM, had advantages because of their superior components. In that project, Tokyo University was given funds to begin research on advanced components. Texas Instruments (TI) was the main supplier of advanced semiconductor components to IBM. In the 1960s, TI had applied for a wholly owned subsidiary in Japan. When the government countered with an offer to permit a minority-share joint venture, TI refused. As Julian Gresser has written:

> NEC and the other firms' sublicensees were in fact producing ICs [integrated circuits] based on technology developed by TI and Fairchild through an NEC-Fairchild licensing agreement. However, because the TI-Fairchild licensing agreement explicitly excluded Japan, these Japanese

firms were not protected, as Fairchild licensees in Europe were, against patent-infringement suits brought by TI. The Japanese government delayed its approval of TI's patent application in Japan. This action helped NEC and the other firms to catch up, and forced TI to negotiate for quicker access. After the Japanese government restrained Japanese exports of IC-based systems to the United States when TI threatened an infringement action, a compromise was finally reached. TI got a 50 percent share of a joint venture with Sony, and in return TI agreed to license its IC patents to NEC, Hitachi, Mitsubishi, Toshiba, and Sony, and to limit its future share of the Japanese semiconductor market to no more than 10 percent. TI bought Sony's share of the joint venture in 1972, and through 1980 remained the only U.S. semiconductor firm with a wholly owned manufacturing subsidiary in Japan.[76]

The Policy Shifts toward a Focus on Semiconductors

The release of the IBM 370 in 1975 demonstrated once again that concentrating on computer hardware without dealing with the revolution in semiconductor components would leave Japanese computer firms far behind in international competition. In addition, the strength of Japanese firms in consumer electronics products such as calculators, TVs, and radios had given them an incentive to develop circuits that were low in power consumption but not necessarily suited to performing the functions required of integrated circuits for large computers. Out of a total of $252 million in semiconductor production in Japan in 1968, only $24 million was in integrated circuits.[77] The Japanese were particularly weak in the production of memory devices and microprocessors, the two main components needed for computer systems.

The principal semiconductor producers in the 1970s were large electronics concerns: NEC, Fujitsu, Hitachi, Toshiba, Mitsubishi Electric, and Oki Electric. NTT, a government-owned corporation, also played a crucial role in the development of the semiconductor industry. NTT was founded in 1952 as a state enterprise under the supervision of the Ministry of Posts and Telecommunications. It held a legal monopoly over domestic public telephony and telegraphy (another firm—Kokusai Denshin Denwa—was formed in 1953 for international telecommunications) until it was privatized in 1985. NTT designs its own infrastructure, conducts basic research on telecommunications technology, and contracts out much of its equipment construction to members of a group of favored suppliers called the *Denden*, which

76. Gresser, *Partners in Prosperity*, pp. 122–23.
77. Borrus, *Competing for Control*, p. 117.

Table 5. Major Japanese semiconductor producers

Firm	Date founded	Principal lines of business (other than semiconductors)	1979 Semiconductor sales as percentage of total revenues
Fujitsu	1935	comuters, telecommunications	6.7
Hitachi	1910	heavy machinery, consumer goods, telecommunications, computers	4.1
Matsushita	1918	consumer electronics	2.3
Mitsubishi	1921	heavy electrical machinery, computers, consumer goods	3.8
NEC	1899	computers, telecommunications	17.8
Oki	1881	telecommunications	9.8
Sanyo	1950	consumer electronics	4.8
Sharp	1967	consumer electronics	4.3
Toshiba	1879	heavy electrical machinery, consumer goods	5.5

Sources: Julian Gresser, *Partners in Prosperity: Strategic Industries for the U.S. and Japan* (New York: McGraw-Hill, 1984), pp. 113–15; Michael Borrus, James Millstein, and John Zysman, "Trade and Development in the Semiconductor Industry: Japanese Challenge and American Response," in John Zysman and Laura Tyson, eds., *American Industry in International Competition* (Ithaca, N.Y.: Cornell University Press, 1983), p. 188; and Rob van Tulder and Eric van Empel, "European Multinationals in the Semiconductor Industry," University of Amsterdam, October 1984, p. 24.

Note: Semiconductor sales as percentage of revenues for Matsushita, Sanyo, and Oki are 1981 figures.

includes NEC, Fujitsu, Hitachi, and Oki. Table 5 provides some historical background on these firms. None of them depended on semiconductor production for more than 18 percent of its revenues in 1979.

IBM's rapid pace of innovation in computer systems forced the Japanese firms to build "plug compatible machines" (PCMs). PCMs may be simply plugged into an existing IBM system without requiring major changes in software or peripherals. MITI encouraged computer manufacturers to team up to meet their international competition. NEC was paired with Toshiba, Hitachi with Fujitsu. The NEC-Toshiba partnership worked better than the Hitachi-Fujitsu one. In 1971, Fujitsu rescued a failing U.S. firm called Amdahl (named after its founder, Gene Amdahl), which had been one of the most successful U.S. PCM manufacturers, so that it could pursue a PCM strategy. Fujitsu produced and marketed Amdahl-designed PCM mainframes, and Amdahl marketed Fujitsu's supercomputers and non-PCM computers in the United States. By the late 1970s, NEC and Fujitsu emerged as the two major mainframe computer manufacturers in Japan; both had adopted a PCM strategy. Fujitsu's sales of mainframes in Japan surpassed those of IBM-Japan in the late 1970s. According to Michael Borrus: "Through 1970, direct Japanese government subsidization of advanced IC and production technology R&D by Japanese firms was not significant, although significant basic research was carried out in government and especially NTT laboratories. Moreover, private company funding of R&D was not at all competitive with U.S. firm spending. Indeed in the early 1970s, combined spending by Fujitsu, Hitachi, and NEC on semiconductor and computer R&D ws less than TI's R&D budget."[78]

In 1970–71, MITI began to pay closer attention to the semiconductor industry in its efforts to beat IBM at incorporating large-scale integrated circuitry in mainframe computers. The 1971 Law for Provision Measures to Promote Specific Electronic and Machinery Industries focused on the development of LSI product and process technologies. This law split the responsibility for administering funding for electronics between MITI and NTT: MITI was to finance R&D and rationalize production, NTT to handle product and process development. Also in 1971, MITI encouraged the formation of three pairs of firms—Fujitsu-Hitachi, NEC-Toshiba, and Mitsubishi-Oki—to force specialization of development efforts and segmentation of the computer market.

By the early 1970s, Japanese firms' growing strength in LSI circuitry helped them to become major suppliers of components for the rapidly growing calculator business. But heavy price competition in 1974 from Texas Instruments and Hewlett-Packard shrank the Japanese share of this market. The Japanese firms responded by outspending U.S. firms in capital investments to expand production of calculator chips. They chose to sacrifice profit margins for a larger share of the market. They later made the same choice in the much larger markets for metal oxide silicon (MOS) memories.[79]

The VLSI Project

In the mid-1970s, the Japanese expected that by the end of the decade IBM would introduce a new generation of computers based on very large-scale integrated circuits. The government was authorized to make sure that Japanese firms developed VLSI components at least as rapidly as U.S. firms did. In 1975, NTT formed a VLSI group with Hitachi, Fujitsu, and NEC at a cost of 20 billion yen to assure that VLSI devices would be available for the Japanese telecommunications system. Shortly after, MITI proposed consolidation of the NTT effort with its own research at the Electro-Technical Laboratory. Initially, NTT was opposed, but on July 15, 1975, NTT and MITI agreed to establish a joint program.

78. Ibid., p. 122.
79. Ibid., p. 124.

The VLSI Project began in March 1976 and extended to 1979. The government contributed 29 billion yen, and the private firms contributed 43 billion yen (a total of approximately $300 million). Oki was excluded at first because it was not strong enough technologically, in MITI's view, to produce the required results. A VLSI Technology Research Association was organized, and a laboratory was set up in a wing of the NEC central lab in Kawasaki. Advanced manufacturing and testing equipment was purchased from the United States. Most of the early effort was focused on constructing 64K DRAM devices, although the real test of VLSI capability would be in building 256K DRAMs.

The VLSI Project focused on wafer fabrication technology. The firms had spent much of their research money in the early 1970s on developing equipment for automating the assembly of integrated circuits. They had been able to catch up with U.S. firms in the production of LSI circuits and later lengthened their lead in VLSI circuits, but further investments in automated assembly needed to be supplemented with basic research on VLSI process technology if the Japanese firms were to match or overtake U.S. firms in the next generation of devices. They had learned this lesson from their failures in the computer competition.

The VLSI Project was successful in speeding the development of state-of-the-art memory circuits, but, more important, it put Japan on the leading edge of process technology. Japanese firms were the first to deliver both 64K DRAMs (in 1978) and 256K DRAMs (in 1982) from their factories to customers.[80] Toshiba was the first firm in the world to ship 1-megabit DRAMs (in 1985). NTT helped to promote the production of advanced integrated circuits by transferring its designs for DRAMs and other circuits to the firms and by purchasing devices for use in the telecommunications system.[81] Until 1978, Japan had a trade deficit in integrated circuits. That year the deficit became a

80. The early lead in 64K DRAMs was not based on superior product technology. See ibid., p. 144: "Japanese firms chose, essentially, a straightforward scale-up to 64K of their 16K DRAM, based on U.S. merchant Mostek's industry-standard 16K design. They accomplished this through incremental improvement of older photolithographic techniques—proximity aligners, which few U.S. firms believed capable of reaching the 2–3 micron design rules of the 64K device."

81. The importance of NTT is underlined in Michael Borrus, Laura D'Andrea Tyson, and John Zysman, *Creating Advantage: How Government Policies Shape High Technology Trade* (Berkeley, Calif.: Berkeley Roundtable on the International Economy, 1984), pp. 68–70. For an interesting account of the limits to cooperation among Japanese semiconductor firms, see Glenn R. Fong, "State Capacity, Industrial Structure and Industrial Policy: American and Japanese Experiences in Microelectronics," paper delivered at the annual meeting of the American Political Science Association, Washington, D.C., August 30–September 2, 1984.

surplus and grew rapidly until 1984, when it peaked at around 550 billion yen.[82]

The main benefits to the firms in the VLSI Project were the pooling of research efforts in wafer fabrication and the subsequent freeing of resources for investments in plant and equipment. MITI's involvement in the VLSI Project meant that the Japanese government was committed to helping the firms obtain a preeminent global position in the production of integrated circuits. Japanese firms, accordingly, made very large investments in plant and equipment between 1978 and 1987. They invested an average of 40 percent of sales in research and capital equipment during the early and middle 1980s. These investments increased from less than $500 million in 1976 to over $4 billion in 1984.[83]

Although U.S. firms matched Japanese investment until the downturn of demand for semiconductors in 1985, their total pool of research and capital investment funds had declined. The merchant U.S. firms, in particular, were hard-pressed to match the "deep pockets" and "patient capital" of the more integrated Japanese firms. In addition, the Japanese firms began to build much larger production facilities for MOS memory than any that had existed before to take advantage of the large and relatively steady demand for memories in their computer, telecommunications, and consumer electronic equipment operations.

In 1979, IBM was manufacturing its new generation of computers, the 4300 series. Because of a shortfall of production of 16K DRAMs in the United States, IBM purchased a significant number of these devices from Japanese manufacturers. The Japanese firms obtained a 40 percent share of the U.S. market for 16K DRAMs in 1979. The sudden presence of the Japanese firms in these markets came as a shock to U.S. manufacturers. By 1982, the Japanese firms controlled 70 percent of the market for 64K DRAMs. Motorola and Texas Instruments were able to keep up with the Japanese firms in production and pricing, but Intel was forced to withdraw from the market, Mostek had to redesign its device, and National Semiconductor ended up licensing technology from Oki. Japanese firms controlled 90 percent of the market for 256K DRAMs in 1986.[84] By 1988, Japanese firms controlled over 90 percent

82. Ministry of Finance Statistics, as cited in *Japanese Electronics Almanac, 1989* (Tokyo: Dempa, 1989), p. 305.

83. Thomas R Howell, William A. Noellert, Janet H. MacLaughlin, and Alan William Wolff, *The Microelectronics Race: The Impact of Government Policy on International Competition* (Boulder, Colo.: Westview, 1988), p. 37.

84. Borrus, *Competing for Control*, p. 173.

of the market for 1-megabit DRAMs, and there were only two U.S. firms left in the market for DRAMs: Texas Instruments and Micron Technology.[85]

The Semiconductor Slump of 1985 and the U.S.-Japanese Trade Dispute

After the downturn in demand for semiconductors in 1985, Japanese manufacturers were under pressure to cut back production. Total losses in the industry were around $4 billion in that year, compared with the $2 billion loss in the U.S. semiconductor industry. Despite enormous losses, however, Japanese firms did not cut back productive capacity as did U.S. firms; rather, they slightly increased their capacity and dumped semiconductors on international markets. DRAM prices dropped precipitously in 1985. Some U.S. firms claimed that Japanese firms were selling their 256K DRAMs for less than the cost of the ceramic package that enclosed the chips.[86] This blatant dumping led to the filing of antidumping and unfair trade petitions by some U.S. firms and the Semiconductor Industry Association.

After the U.S.-Japanese Semiconductor Trade Agreement was signed in September 1986 to end dumping by Japanese firms in all world markets and improve access to the Japanese market for U.S. firms, Japanese firms continued to offer DRAMs in third-country markets below the fair market value (FMV) established under the agreement. Dumping stopped only after the U.S. government imposed sanctions amounting to a total of $300 million in additional duties on laptop computers, power tools, and a few other items in April 1987.

The U.S. government had insisted on the FMV system because it wanted prices to reflect relative efficiencies in semiconductor production. Because Japanese firms' production costs varied, MITI had opposed the FMV system, preferring instead a floor-price system that would have allowed both efficient and inefficient Japanese producers of DRAMs to stay in business. In taking this position, MITI continued to provide opportunities for the weaker firms associated with major *keiretsu*. The major beneficiaries at this point were Toshiba and Oki, which, unlike NEC and Hitachi, had not been able to bring their 256K DRAMs to market fast enough to compete in world markets. MITI had insisted that the market access part of the semiconductor agreement

85. See Vogel, *Comeback,* pp. 145–46; and "Chips: The War of Tomorrow's Worlds," *Economist,* August 24, 1985, p. 67. All market share figures cited here exclude the "captive production" of semiconductors by large U.S. integrated firms such as IBM and AT&T because these devices are not traded on the open market.

86. Clyde Prestowitz, *Trading Places: How We Allowed Japan to Take the Lead* (New York: Basic Books, 1988), p. 57; and interview materials.

remain secret. It failed to get floor prices but succeeded in keeping the market access agreement secret.

The major semiconductor producers were extremely unhappy about the negotiation of the 1986 trade agreement. They felt that they were being punished unfairly by the United States for their successful commercialization of DRAMs. They also resented the intrusion of MITI in industry affairs. To induce the firms to adhere to the government position on trade negotiations, MITI tried to get an agreement that would result in increased profit margins for all. Hence MITI favored floor prices (as in the steel dispute of 1977). MITI also tried to get an agreement that was uneforceable (hence, the secret "side letter" on market access). In the end, news of continued discounting by major firms at the height of tensions over semiconductors was used as a political club to get the firms in line.

Even though MITI failed to get the U.S. government to agree to a floor-price system, it achieved more or less the same result when, in March 1987, it called for a 10 percent across-the-board cutback in production of DRAMs. The subsequent shortage of 256K DRAMs drove up prices. By mid-1988, 256K DRAM prices were about two times higher than FMV levels, and there were long delays between orders and deliveries in both 256K DRAMs and 1-megabit DRAMs. Japanese firms got faster delivery and possibly lower prices than did foreign customers. U.S. computer and electronics firms became very unhappy with the trade agreement, blaming it for their problems in competing with Japanese producers. Profit margins for all the major Japanese firms increased dramatically. They benefited not only as semiconductor producers but also as sellers of downstream products.

The trade dispute with the United States over semiconductors, like that over automobiles, strengthened MITI's position in making policy for the industry. Until the trade dispute began in 1985, MITI had shared authority with NTT and the Ministry of Posts and Telecommunications. After the conclusion of the semiconductor trade agreement, MITI's power over the industry increased because its role in enforcing the FMV pricing system and in establishing a production cartel for DRAMs.

Japanese policy toward the semiconductor industry is again illustrative of the success of the government in fostering growth and international competitiveness. As in the case of automobiles, the increasing strength of Japanese firms in international markets eventually enabled them to resist the efforts of MITI and other government agencies to influence their strategies because they no longer relied heavily on government help to meet international competition. The best example is the resistance of semiconductor firms to continuing joint research within the VLSI Project after 1979. But again as in the case of automobiles, the increasing strength of the Japanese semiconductor industry created trade frictions with the United States, which led to the reinvolvement of MITI in industry affairs. This on-again, off-again pattern seems to be a necessary result of the efforts of MITI and other government agencies to create many champions in high-technology industries.

The semiconductor case also illustrates the importance of the *keiretsu* system in the Japanese political economy. Differences in the structure of the semiconductor industries in Japan and the United States—particularly the *keiretsu* system in Japan—help explain the inability of U.S. merchant firms to make the large capital investments required to compete with the more integrated Japanese firms during the transition of VLSI circuitry. In the United States many small merchant firms could establish themselves independently of the larger consumer, computer, and telecommunications systems firms, which was inconceivable in Japan. The smaller U.S. merchant firms could not match the huge investments of integrated Japanese firms.

The Japanese government helped Japanese firms pool their R&D investment expenditures so they could catch up with and overtake their U.S. competitors in process technology. It tried to assure that at least one successful semiconductor firm was associated with each *keiretsu*. MITI had learned a valuable lesson from its run-in with the automobile producers in the 1960s. It no longer insisted on a concentration of ownership and production to allow firms to take advantage of static scale economies. It learned that specialization in high-growth market niches, combined with strong export performance based on high-volume, standardized production, using patient *keiretsu* capital, can produce excellent results.

CONCLUSIONS

This chapter began with a discussion of controversies in the literature on Japanese industrial policy. It is only fitting that it conclude by reexamining those controversies in light of the discussion of policies toward steel, autos, and semiconductors. The Japanese government has been an important agent in the transformation of the country's economy since World War II. Direct subsidies, the organization of cartels, and the use of sometimes heavy-handed administrative guidance by MITI to accomplish state goals have greatly declined in recent years, but new instruments of influence—generally subtler ones—have taken their places. These instruments include the use of R&D subsidies and government procurement, the organization of R&D and leasing consortia, combined with trade and inward investment policies designed to shelter domestic firms initially from international competition and to reduce risk so that the firms can make major investments in new product and process technologies.

Industrial policy for steel, autos, and semiconductors generally helped those industries to grow. In the 1950s and 1960s the Japanese government helped the steel industry increase production and select the best technology for its expansion. The merger of Yawata and Fuji into Nippon Steel in 1970 reduced price competition so that the industry could continue to invest in new plants without worrying about profits. The government helped the industry adjust to slackened demand in the late 1970s and 1980s, shifting many of the adjustment costs onto workers (as elsewhere) but reducing those costs by responding more quickly to the decline. In autos, the government played a major role in the 1930s by expelling the dominant U.S. multinationals and keeping them out until the late 1960s. In the years of rapid growth, the government lost its influence over the industry, but when the industry became so strong internationally that it encountered threats of foreign market closures, MITI stepped in to negotiate and enforce export restraints. In semiconductors, the government played a key role in the late 1970s in bringing the firms up to internationally competitive standards in technology and prices by subsidizing R&D and organizing R&D consortia. In the late 1980s, after the increased competitiveness of Japanese semiconductor firms sparked a major trade dispute between Japan and the United States, MITI helped to negotiate the U.S.-Japanese Semiconductor Trade Agreement and organize a DRAM production cartel.

But an analysis of the reasons why Japanese firms became more internationally competitive in the three industries is incomplete unless the *keiretsu* system is taken into account. In steel, the government initially favored Yawata and Fuji over their smaller competitors because it tried to create national champions by insisting on concentrating production. Nippon Steel was a member of a government *keiretsu* because of its dependence on financing from the Industrial Bank of Japan. The tenacity of the private *keiretsu* in pushing for their own integrated steel manufacturing capability was manifested in the struggles of Kawasaki and Sumitomo Metal to establish a niche for themselves despite the government's sponsorship of Nippon Steel. The *keiretsu* system guaranteed that there would be competition in the steel industry for Nippon Steel. It created incentives for firms to adopt the latest technologies beyond those created by MITI. But it also guaranteed that when productive capacity needed to be cut back, it would be done slowly. The *keiretsu* had a great deal to do with the resistance of auto firms to the merger and consolidation policies of MITI in the 1960s. Similarly, in semiconductors, the existence of the *keiretsu* made it easier for the government to assist the firms to realize dynamic scale economies through segmentation of markets and pooling of R&D investments. Yet the *keiretsu* made it difficult to organize long-term research consortia or to enforce the trade agreement of 1986. The Japanese government appears to have learned its lesson from the auto industry battles of the 1960s. It took great care to allow each major *keiretsu* to maintain a presence in microelectronics markets and proposed no mergers across *keiretsu* lines.

Analysts of the importance of Japanese industrial policy on economic outcomes make the mistake of focusing on the ability of MITI to win in conflicts with firms. This distracts attention from the much more common role of MITI and the rest of the Japanese government in building an industry-government consensus. MITI's role is not to lord it over the firms but to work with them to ensure that they will be able to invest in product and process technologies that will bring them to a "world-class" status. The *keiretsu* system maintains intense domestic competition even when the government erects temporary trade and investment barriers to reduce uncertainty for private investors.

THREE

France

France is the Western nation that most closely parallels the centralized bureaucratic approach to industrial policy used in Japan. Like Japan, France wanted to become an industrial power after World War II. The French approach, like that of Japan, combined centralized public administration of industrial policy with extensive regulation of financial markets and a highly elitist system of recruitment for state bureaucracies. But the ambitious French government policy was in sharp contrast to its timid private business sector. It lacked an equivalent of the Japanese *keiretsu* system that guaranteed intense domestic competition, a lack that impeded the creation and rapid diffusion of new technologies. The narrow elitism of the higher educational system, the low level of investment in training workers, and the generally hostile relations between management and labor in the French system all contributed to the slow diffusion of key technologies.

Like the Japanese, the French were successful in catching up to the other industrial states following World War II, at least until the early 1970s, in basic industries such as steel and consumer durables such as automobiles. After that, they ran into problems because their "national champions" were not, for the most part, internationally competitive. Like the other Europeans, with the exception of Germany, they failed until rather late to see the importance of building international competitiveness on the basis of world-class technology and transcending the limitations imposed by sheltering firms within national market boundaries.

The French have not been able to foster internationally oriented and fiercely competitive firms such as developed in both the Japanese and German systems. The Japanese approach was distinctive mainly for its combination of temporary but effective sheltering of domestic industries from international competition and the incentives for rapid diffusion of technology that came from strong domestic competition. The distinctiveness of the German system is its reliance on private banks to make the necessary investments in new technologies and a highly skilled work force to integrate them quickly on the factory floor. Domestic competition in Germany, as in Japan, is strong. The French, in contrast, have tended to shelter their favored domestic firms from both external and domestic competition, often with bad results.

The national champions approach has increasingly been criticized by French intellectuals and the public at large. It has been replaced by an approach in which the national champions are encouraged to make alliances with foreign firms and to invest in overseas production, especially in the rest of Europe and in the United States. Thus the national champions are no longer as French as they once were.

THE EFFECTS OF RECENT POLITICAL CHANGES ON STATE-SOCIETAL ARRANGEMENTS

One of the most important controversies in the literature on French state-societal arrangements concerns the impact of political change. The most important political change since the presidency of Charles de Gaulle was the election of a leftist government in 1981. Much of the analysis of the early years of the presidency of François Mitterrand has focused on the nationalizations of 1982. The privatizations implemented after 1986 by the government of Jacques Chirac during the unprecedented "cohabitation" of a centrist prime minister (Chirac) with a socialist president (Mitterrand) are frequently portrayed as the returning swing of a political pendulum.[1] I will argue that these important political changes produced only marginal changes in state-societal arrangements, particularly in those connected with industrial policies and strategies.

THE INSTITUTIONAL FRAMEWORK FOR FRENCH INDUSTRIAL POLICY

The Grandes Ecoles

Top bureaucrats who set industrial policy were recruited from elite schools—*grandes écoles,* A system that originated in the efforts of the

1. See, for example, George Ross, "Introduction," in George Ross, Stanley Hoffmann, and Sylvia Malzacher, eds., *The Mitterrand Experiment: Continuity and Change in Modern France* (New York: Oxford University Press, 1987).

French monarchy to establish its political supremacy vis-à-vis the aristocracy by building public works with public revenues. A class of civil servants, wholly dependent on the monarchy for its existence, was trained in the Ecole des Ponts-et-Chaussées, the Ecole des Mines, and the Ecole du Génie Militaire de Mézieres. In 1794, shortly after the Revolution, the Ecole Polytechnique took over the training of military officers and became the prototype for the postrevolutionary *grandes écoles*. Napoleon envisioned the *grandes écoles* as a state monopoly on higher education. He therefore established state schools for physicians, lawyers, and other professionals to supplement the existing schools for engineers and military tacticians. After World War II, the Ecole Nationale d'Administration was founded to end the monopolization of state agencies by alumni of the older *grandes écoles*. Instead, it simply added another source of graduates for recruitment into those agencies.

The *grandes écoles*, unlike the French universities, are highly selective in their admissions. To enter a *grande école*, a student must pass a series of examinations much more difficult than those required for university entrance. Once accepted, however, students are guaranteed high-paying and influential posts within the government. The smallness of the *grandes écoles* relative to the demand for the technical skills they provide guarantees that their graduates will always be in demand. But because the French educational system does not provide adequately for the training of engineers and technicians outside the *grandes écoles* and because of the highly theoretical nature of the studies offered in the *grandes écoles*, French government agencies and private firms always need to provide extensive on-the-job training of both managers and staff.[2]

Organization of the State

The most important state agencies for industrial policy are the Finance Ministry, the Ministry of Industry, the Commissariat Général du Plan (CGP), and the semiautonomous development funds and interministerial committees.[3] The Finance Ministry and the Treasury are

2. J. Nicholas Ziegler, "The Hare and the Tortoise Revisited: Political Strategies for Technological Advance in the French and West German Semiconductor Industries, 1972–1985," manuscript, Department of Government, Harvard University, December 12, 1987. Also see Ezra Suleiman, *Politics, Power, and Bureaucracy* (Princeton, N.J.: Princeton University Press, 1974); Ezra Suleiman, *Elites in French Society* (Princeton, N.J.: Princeton University Press, 1978); and Michel Crozier, *The Stalled Society* (New York: Viking, 1973).

3. The offices of the president and the prime minister often resolve disputes among the heads of agencies. The recent tendency for ministers to appeal to the president when their preferred policies are rejected by the prime minister is discussed in Thierry Pfister,

the primary industrial policy makers because they control the allocation of public credit. The Ministry of Industry and Research plays the important role of monitoring events in specific industries and providing staffing for the Finance Ministry during industrial crises. The CGP played a major role until 1968 and especially during the administration of the Marshall Plan in France. It was eclipsed by the Finance Ministry after 1968. Much of French industrial policy is carried out by smaller interagency committees and delegations and funded by special trust funds.

The Ministry of Finance

The Finance Ministry is the main focus of macroeconomic and industrial policy making in France. The Treasury (Trésor) is "the temple within the temple" of the Finance Ministry. It has three main divisions: International, Money and Finance (MF), and Investments and Participations (IP). MF sets targets for monetary policy, regulates the securities industry, manages the public debt, and handles a system of credit allocation called the *encadrement de crédit*. IP is responsible for intervening in specific firms and industries, primarily export-oriented and energy-related ones, and supervising financial institutions that channel capital to industry: official financial intermediaries such as the Crédit National and the Caisse Nationale du Crédit Agricole (CNCA, the national agricultural bank), the fifteen regional development societies, and the Instituts de Participations (offices that raise local capital for industrial investment). IP is also the general secretariat for three of the more important interministerial committees: FSAI (the Special Fund for Industrial Adaptation) CIDISE (the Interministerial Committee for the Development of Investments and Maintenance of Employment, CODIS (the Interministerial Committee for the Development of Strategic Industries). Finally, the IP is directly responsible for the management of the Electricité de France, SNCF (the national railway system), and the Paris Metropolitan Transport System.

The *encadrement du crédit* was the system by which the Finance Ministry through the MF controlled the rate of credit growth in the French economy from 1972 to 1987. Each financial institution was allocated a target each month for growth in lending and was penalized severely for either exceeding or dropping below that target. This system applied to listed commercial banks, business banks, and the CNCA (from 1979 to 1987). Only relatively minor amounts of credit, primarily trade credits,

---

La vie quotidienne à Matignon au temps de l'union de la gauche (Paris: Hachette, 1985), pp. 122–32.

escaped regulation under this system. The system effectively froze market shares for financial institutions and thus had, in the words of Stephen S. Cohen, James Galbraith, and John Zysman, a "paralytic effect on interbank competition for new lending."[4] Banks could be exempted from penalties if they did what the Treasury wanted or if they agreed to give priority to loans in specific areas. The discretionary power given the Treasury in administering the system gave it significant leverage over firms and other borrowers. The system encouraged exports by excluding export credits from the targets.[5]

The *encadrement de crédit* was begun in 1972 to replace a system in which credit was allocated through state-controlled financial intermediaries. Pierre Bérégovoy, the second finance minister of the Mitterrand government, announced in November 1984 that the *encadrement de crédit* would be replaced by a system of interest rate targets in the hope of liberalizing the French financial system.[6] But efforts made during the Barre, Fabius, and Chirac governments to liberalize the financial system failed to reduce the power of the Finance Ministry over the allocation of credit.

Thus the two divisions of the Treasury (IP and MF) within the Ministry of Finance exercised substantial power in setting monetary and industrial policy during the entire post–World War II period. It was rivaled by the Commissariat Général du Plan only during its early years under Jean Monnet. After 1968, the Ministry of Finance had the final word on industrial policy matters. It used the Ministry of Industry as a source of expertise and advice on central decisions and left day-to-day administrative matters to the industrial specialists in that ministry.

The Ministry of Industry

The Ministry of Industry, in the words of John Zysman, "monitors the primary communication lines to the business community."[7] According to one French planning official, "Whenever the industry

4. Stephen S. Cohen, James Galbraith, and John Zysman, "Rehabbing the Labyrinth: The Financial System and Industrial Policy in France," in Stephen S. Cohen and Peter Gourevitch, eds., *France in the Troubled World Economy* (Boston: Butterworths, 1982), p. 54.
5. Arnold J. Heidenheimer, Hugh Heclo, and Carolyn Adams, *Comparative Public Policy* (New York: St. Martin's Press, 1983), p. 137.
6. "France Gives More Credit to the Market," *Economist*, November 2, 1984, p. 91.
7. The Ministry of Industry became the Ministry of Research and Industry in 1981 when the Mauroy government merged the new Ministry of Research into the old Ministry of Industry. It was renamed the Ministry of Industrial Redeployment in 1986. I refer to this agency throughout as the Ministry of Industry. John Zysman, *Governments, Markets, and Growth: Financial Systems and the Politics of Industrial Change* (Ithaca, N.Y.: Cornell University Press, 1983), p. 113.

minister comes into a meeting we can hear big business outside the door."[8] Like many other ministries of industry, it is organized along sectoral lines. The vertical directorates represent specific industries; horizontal ones deal with internal coordination and administration.

Some vertical directorates such as that for steel are stronger than others. Michel Crozier and Erhard Friedberg believe this is because some industries are more oligopolistic than others, the less concentrated industries tend not to be inclined to express their interests through the Ministry of Industry, and the ministry's bureaucrats like to focus their attention on concentrated industries that are easier to understand and manipulate. In any case, attempts to coordinate across vertical directorates are usually unsuccessful. Each vertical directorate is jealous of its territory and defends itself immediately when threatened by horizontal coordination. Crozier and Friedberg conclude that the Ministry of Industry "is not an organ of the state capable of bringing about an autonomous mediation between the means and end of industrial action: it is not even the site where such mediation can take place."[9]

The influence of the Ministry of Industry is highly dependent on the relationship between the minister and the president and on the minister's role in national politics. Raymond Barre gave his ministers of industry, René Monory and André Giraud, rather than the CGP, the task of carrying out his industrial policies. Jean-Pierre Chevènement, the leader of the Centre d'Etudes de Recherches et d'Education Socialiste faction in the Socialist party, had more influence than most while in office. Laurent Fabius, his replacement, was considered a caretaker and agreed not to oppose the policies of Jacques Delors, the minister of finance, or dictate policies to the heads of the state-owned firms.

The Finance Ministry cannot handle the burdens its central role in economic and industrial policy making place on it so the Ministry of Industry serves as a staffing and research arm of the Finance Ministry and the Office of the President. The most important means of control the Ministry of Industry has are its input to interministerial committees controlling state-subsidized loan funds, its responsibility for managing state enterprises, especially the steel industry after 1966 (see the section on steel policy, below), and its discretionary powers in the administration of a variety of programs that affect the competitiveness of individual firms.

8. Sol Estrin and Peter Holmes, *French Planning in Theory and Practice* (London: Allen & Unwin, 1983), p. 98.

9. Michel Crozier and Erhard Friedberg, *Actors and Systems: The Politics of Collective Action,* trans. Arthur Goldhammer (Chicago: University of Chicago Press, 1980), pp. 90–96; quotation p. 90.

The Commissariat Général du Plan

The CGP was created in 1946 as a small but elite body of planners and researchers. In 1979, it had only about 140 white-collar employees, including secretaries. Its main job is, in the words of Sol Estrin and Peter Holmes, "to orchestrate the process of consultation and deliberation on national problems and priorities which leads up to the drafting of a five-year plan."[10] Preparing the plan takes about two years and the participation of thousands of government officials and business representatives in a series of meetings of "modernization commissions."

The head of the CGP, the *commissaire du plan*, is a senior civil servant, usually with a technocratic orientation. The first *commissaire*, Jean Monnet, was indubitably the most powerful of them all. Not only was he a personal friend of General Charles de Gaulle, but his CGP worked closely with the Marshall Plan administrators to carry out plans for the reconstruction of French industry.

Collaboration was close but wary between the CGP and the Ministry of Finance during that period. The CGP's data on economic sectors were collected by the Finance Ministry and the National Statistical Institute, as they are today. The Finance Ministry has never fully accepted the need for a plan or for the CGP and has fought a long-term and largely successful battle to downgrade the CGP while returning itself to a position of primacy in macroeconomic policy making within the bureaucracy.

In recent years the CGP settled into a role of shepherding several small research agencies entrusted with projecting future developments: Centre d'Etudes Prospectives d'Economic Mathématique Appliquées a la Planification (application of mathematical methods to planning), Centre d'Etudes des Revenus et des Couts (gathering data on households and income distribution), and Centre d'Etudes Prospectives et d'Informations Internationales (investigating changes in the world economy).[11] The plan and therefore the planning process have declined in importance. The Mitterrand government tried unsuccessfully to revive the importance of the plan.[12]

The Interministerial Committees and Special Funds

On November 28, 1974, the Interministerial Committee for the Restructuring of Industries (CIASI) was created by the French government

10. Estrin and Holmes, *French Planning*, p. 91. The definitive work on French planning is Stephen Cohen, *Modern Capitalist Planning: The French Model*, rev. ed. (Berkeley: University of California Press, 1977).

11. Estrin and Holmes, *French Planning*, p. 94.

12. Peter Hall, *Governing the Economy: The Politics of State Intervention in Britain and France* (New York: Oxford University Press, 1986), chap. 5 and pp. 213–14.

to arrange financing for firms in difficulty. It rescued small to medium-sized firms in regions that were particularly dependent on them. CIASI has been a relatively minor instrument of the state, although it did participate in several important deals involving the restructuring of the French auto industry in the late 1970s (see the section on auto policies, below).

In September 1978, the Special Fund for Industrial Reconversion was set up within the older Economic and Social Development Fund (FDES) to deal with special problems of adjustment to international competition. The 1979 budget of the FDES was 474.3 million francs. Ninety percent of the funding for CIASI came from FDES, 10 percent from the Ministry of Industry. CIASI spent about a half billion francs per year until 1981. In 1980, FSAI lent approximately 3 billion francs ($750 million), mostly for the reconversion of the steel and shipbuilding industries.[13]

In 1978, the National Agency for the Application of Research (ANVAR) was founded. In the first term of the Mitterrand presidency this agency became the focus of efforts to raise French R&D spending to 2.5 percent of gross domestic product by 1988. Its main activity was to lend money to private firms for R&D investments. In 1983, for example, ANVAR spent around 900 million francs, mainly for these loans.[14] In July 1979, the Interministerial Committee for the Development of Investments and Employment was established, followed a few months later by the the Interministerial Committee for the Development of Strategic Industries. CIDISE, a branch of the Ministry of Economy and Finance, was designed to promote small business activities in high-technology industries. Its budget in 1979 was roughly 500 million francs, used mainly for the restructuring (shrinking and concentration) of the textile industry.[15]

CODIS was specifically designed to fund projects undertaken by large firms in advanced technologies. It designated six strategic technologies in 1979–80: bioengineering, marine industries, robots, office automation, consumer electronics, and alternative energy production.[16] Its main function was to help cut government red tape, which had at times impeded the growth of smaller and more innovative firms. During the

13. French Embassy to the United States, Press and Information Division, "Industry and the State," no. 36, 1980, p. 4.

14. Hall, *Governing the Economy*, p. 208.

15. Lynn Mytelka, "In Search of a Partner: The State and the Textile Industry in France," in Cohen and Gourevitch, eds., *France in the Troubled World Economy*, p. 143.

16. Cohen, Galbraith, and Zysman, "Rehabbing the Labyrinth," pp. 61–62; François DeWitt, "French Industrial Policy from 1945 to 1981: An Assessment," in F. Gerard Adams and Lawrence Klein, eds., *Industrial Policies for Growth and Competitiveness* (Lexington, Mass.: Lexington Books, 1983), p. 229; and Christian Stoffäes, "Les reorientations de la politique industrielle," *Revue d'Economie Industrielle* 14 (1980): 219–32.

first term of the Mitterrand presidency, CODIS was replaced by the Industrial Modernization Fund (FMI). In 1983, FMI spent 3 billion francs appropriated from the Caisse des Dépôts et Consignations. In 1984, it spent 5 billion francs using funds raised by a new savings bond, the Account for Industrial Development, on which interest was tax-free for three years.[17]

In 1982, the Interministerial Committee for the Reconstruction of Industry (CIRI) replaced the CIASI. Chaired by Finance Minister Jacques Delors, it was to speed up the process of refinancing failing firms and to delegate some arrangements to regional committees. Typically CIRI was approached by the lead bank in the group of creditors of a specific firm. CIRI had the power to waive taxes and social security payments and thus could considerably ease the pain of putting together a refinancing deal. Like many institutions aimed at industrial rescues in other countries, CIRI did not provide for the representation of foreign creditors in rescue negotiations.

The most important regional policy-making institution in the French government was the General Delegation for Land Management and Regional Action, an interministerial body with a staff of forty experts. One of its main functions in recent years has been to encourage foreign investment in the less developed regions of France.

Science and technology policy was made most notably through CODIS, FDES, FSAI, ANVAR, and the Ministry of Research and Industry. Several special units were set up to deal with specific problems. The Compagnie Internationale de l'Informatique (CII) was a joint venture founded by the state in 1966 to help France compete against the giant (mostly U.S.-based) multinationals in the computer industry (see the section on semiconductors below). It was monitored by a state agency called the Delegation for Informatics, which was dissolved in 1974 when CII was purchased by Honeywell-Bull.

A state agency called the General Delegation for Scientific and Technical Research was established in the 1960s to improve French computing and data processing. Between 1966 and 1977, this agency spent less than 1 billion francs, of which approximately one-fourth went to electronics.[18] The National Center for Scientific Research was funded by the state to conduct basic and applied research. Also in the 1960s, the state established the National Center for Telecommunication Studies, which has conducted basic research in telecommunications technology but, more important, established standards for the French telecommunications industry. In 1979, the Agency for the Development of

17. Hall, *Governing the Economy*, p. 207.
18. John Zysman, *Political Strategies for Industrial Order* (Berkeley: University of California Press, 1977), p. 96.

Informatics was set up to find new ways of promoting technological development and the diffusion of technology in the computer industry.[19]

The budgetary outlays for most of these R&D efforts are fairly minor, especially compared with state-subsidized loans. In 1983, for example, the outstanding amount of long-term subsidized loans was 46 billion francs, of which 26 billion were accounted for by loans from the Crédit National. The Finance Ministry, therefore, had much greater control over the state's financial resources than any other agency, eclipsing the resources of the various funds and interministerial committees. Bad experiences with the promotion of the computer industry made subsequent governments wary of putting too much stress on direct state promotion of high technology. Instead, the state relied more on indirect assistance through long-term support of large national champion firms.

Organization of Business

One of the most distinctive features of the organization of French business has been heavy penetration of the state into the financial sector. The banking system is divided into two main categories: the commercial banks and the parapublic financial institutions. The Banque Nationale de Paris, the Société Générale, and the Crédit Lyonnais were commercial banks until they were nationalized in 1945. These three accounted for about 75 percent of all deposits in France in the early 1980s. In 1981, the Mitterrand government nationalized thirty-six private banks and two investment groups—Paribas and Suez—bringing the nationalized share of deposits to over 95 percent.

The parapublic financial institutions were all either created or dominated by the government. Some have even been staffed by officials of the Ministry of Finance. The most important of these institutions is the Crédit National, a financial intermediary for long-term loans to industry. The Caisse des Dépôts et Consignations is the repository for funds that flow in from the public savings network. It is used primarily for infrastructural and housing loans. A third important parapublic institution is the Crédit Agricole, which serves as a vehicle for pooling rural savings for reinvestment in rural and small-town areas. All together, the parapublics account for about one-third of all credit in the system.

Together with state ownership and control over public and parapublic financial institutions, the state's ability to allocate credit to priority areas through the *encadrement du crédit* has made private businesses very dependent on it for their loan capital. French firms, like those in Japan,

19. Stoffäes, "Les reorientations," p. 231.

tend to be highly debt-leveraged. Only a few French industrial firms make sufficient profits to finance a major share of their investments.

The efforts of the state to transform France from an agricultural to an industrial nation after World War II required a "divide and conquer" posture toward traditional industries. John Zysman argues that the state used a variety of means, including its foreign economic policy of promoting competition in domestic markets through membership in the European Community, to reduce the power of the older sector-specific industrial groups such as the Syndical Chamber of the French Steel Industry (CSSF).[20] But even without such manipulation, the general financial dependency of firms on the state makes them extremely anxious to avoid confrontations with it and reduces the influence of business peak associations relative to that of industry-specific trade associations in setting national policies. Industry-specific trade associations worry about the tendency of larger firms to negotiate directly with the government—but that is true in other industrial countries as well. The state and business work together to pursue industry-specific policies, developed during extensive consultations between the government office that has jurisdiction (*tutelle*) over the industry in question and the representatives of that industry. Often the participants in these consultations are graduates of the same *grande école*.

Macroeconomic and labor market policies are the concern of peak associations such as the National Council of French Employers (CNPF).[21] But the CNPF played the limited role during the Gaullist period of preventing the passage of progressive labor laws. After the turmoil of May–June 1968, the CNPF temporarily took a conciliatory approach to labor-management relations, which failed for reasons discussed below. The state does not hesitate to enlist the CNPF to resolve problems that cannot be solved at the sectoral level.

Organization of Labor

French organized labor is fragmented into three main confederations: the Communist Confédération Générale du Travail (CGT), the Socialist Confédération Française Démocratique du Travail (CFDT), and the reformist CGT-Force Ouvrière. Competition between the Communist and Socialist parties for membership and influence in the

20. Zysman, *Government, Markets and Growth*, p. 137.
21. The most important work on the CNPF is Henry W. Ehrmann, *Organized Business in France* (Princeton, N.J.: Princeton University Press, 1957). More recent discussions of the CNPF are in Jack Hayward, *The State and the Market Economy: Industrial Patriotism and Economic Intervention in France* (Brighton, Eng.: Harvester Press, 1986), chaps. 3–4; Martin Rhodes, "Labour and Industry: The Demise of Traditional Unionism," in Sonia Mazey and Michael Newman, eds., *Mitterrand's France* (London: Croom Helm, 1987).

workplace guarantees that French labor cannot speak with a single voice in national politics. The French legal system contributes to this fragmentation by excluding unions from participation in economic decision making, thus ensuring that workers' militancy will be expressed through national partisan politics rather than shop-floor politics. Except for a brief period from 1972 to 1975, there has been no tripartite corporatist bargaining in France among government officials, firm managements, and union representatives.[22]

In 1963, the *commissaire du plan*, Pierre Massé, tried to end a coal miners' strike by establishing a tripartite bargaining arrangement, an experiment in "incomes policy." But the CGT rejected the arrangement as compromising its role as the chief instrument of social revolution on behalf of the workers. It did not help that the government had passed anti-strike legislation in July and had adopted deflationary macroeconomic policies in September. Similarly, after the events of May–June 1968, the government adopted the Grenelle Agreements to establish a system of tripartite national wage bargaining. But the Grenelle Agreements were undercut by the devaluation of the franc, and they ended with the dismissal of the Chaban-Delmas government.[23]

The CGT remains ever wary of concertative and corporative mechanisms, which it sees as diversions from the main task of defeating capitalism. The CFDT is more willing to discuss such arrangements but can do little as long as the CNPF and managers of individual firms oppose them. In the words of Jack Hayward: "Trade union leaders remain outsiders committed by ideology, political conviction, and concern to retain the support of their membership in the conflicts that bring them into more or less brutal collision with employers and agents of the state, to resist integration."[24]

The difficulties of adjusting to the higher energy prices of 1973 reduced the tendency toward factionalism in leftist politics. The Socialists and Communists united politically in 1978 to promote the political success of the Left around a set of ideas embodied in the 1972 Common Program, which called for a Keynesian reflation of the economy, a reform of workplace rules, an increased reliance on local and regional governments to make and implement policies (federalism), and the nationalization of strategic firms and industries. But partisan conflict

22. See Peter Lange, George Ross, and Maurizio Vannicelli, *Unions, Change and Crisis: French and Italian Strategy and the Political Economy, 1945–1980* (London: Allen & Unwin, 1982), chap. 1; Martin Rhodes, "Organized Interests and Industrial Crisis Management: Restructuring the Steel Industry in West Germany, Italy, and France," in Alan Cawson, ed., *Organized Interests and the State* (Beverly Hills: Sage, 1985), pp. 206–9; and Rhodes, "Labour and Industry," pp. 57–60.

23. See Hall, *Governing the Economy*, p. 247.

24. Hayward, *The State and the Market Economy*, p. 61.

split the two groups before the election and victory went again to the Right-Center. In the 1981 election, only the astute political maneuverings of Mitterrand prevented another Socialist-Communist split from again ruining the electoral chances of the Left.[25]

The election of Mitterrand in 1981 was somewhat of a surprise for all concerned. One unexpected element was the revelation during the election campaign that Giscard d'Estaing had undergone psychoanalysis. Giscard had alienated some of his supporters with his quasi-monarchical manner of governing. More important, the Giscard government had tried to open the French economy to international trade and investment without easing the adjustment costs for French capitalists and workers. Mitterrand had done well in 1974, receiving 49.5 percent of the vote. In 1981 he assured the electorate that replacing the Center-Right with a leftist government would be good both for the French democratic system and the economy. It would demonstrate the ability of the constitution to withstand a period of leftist rule and provide alternatives to the liberal internationalism of the Giscardists.

After the election, policies were adopted to address the ideological concerns of both the Socialists and Communists in the governing coalition. Many of these policies—such as the nationalizations of banks and strategic industries—had appeared in the 1972 Common Program. The Socialists wanted to promote faster growth of the economy. They preferred democratic planning over nationalization, strengthening the powers of local and regional governments over centralization of power in the national government, and worker self-management (*autogestion*) over union- or firm-mandated workplace rules. The Communists took the position that "genuine democracy" would occur only after changes in basic structures of accumulation (through nationalizations and centralization of control over the economy in the hands of a leftist government). These two very different visions were bound to collide.

The French Finance Ministry and Treasury played the central (though not undisputed) role in the determination of both industrial and monetary policies. Only in specific industries such as steel has the Ministry of Industry exercised significant authority over industrial policies, and even those decisions have to be approved by the Treasury. Only for a brief period after World War II did the Commissariat Général du Plan exercise similar authority. Much of the work of industrial policy making has been carried out within interministerial committees and special

25. See Patrick McCarthy, "Victory in 1981: The Long March of the Socialists," in McCarthy ed., *The French Socialists in Power, 1981–1986* (Westport, Conn.: Greenwood Press, 1987), pp. 18–19.

funds. Regional policy has not been a major concern of the French government, nor have science and research been major priorities until recent years.

French policy toward specific industries has tended to be consistent with its overall economic and industrial policies because of the centralized nature of decision making. The tendency of economic policies to focus on the promotion of strategic industries strengthens the role of industry-specific business associations relative to that of peak associations. Nevertheless, peak associations play a significant role in representing business interests with respect to macroeconomic and labor market policies of the government.

French unions are weak and fragmented; therefore, they are partisan. The close association of the two largest unions—the CGT and CFDT—with the Communist and Socialist parties, respectively, resulted from laws governing labor-management relations which are highly unfavorable to the workers and their representatives. Because unions lacked the power to affect conditions in the workplace, workers have had no alternative but to support unions with a broad political agenda. Until 1981, labor interests were unrepresented in economic policy making. Since then, the fragmentation of the Left and the shallow electoral support for leftist economic alternatives have caused a series of twists and turns in policy that have undermined the ability of French firms to adjust to growing international competition.

POLICIES FOR THE STEEL INDUSTRY

French policies for the steel industry have shown not only the central role played by the state in the industry but also the dangers of pursuing a policy of promoting national champions. Initially, state policies were extremely successful in increasing the productive capacity of the industry and modernizing its plant and equipment. After 1958, a key policy was an effort to reduce the number of companies so that French firms would be large enough to compete with the huge concerns of other industrial nations. France now has only a single large steel firm—Usinor-Sacilor—formed from the merger of two national champion firms in 1986. Not only did the uncompetitive structure of the industry domestically hurt its chances for international competitiveness, but state interventions were poorly timed, especially after 1973. The state directly funded or guaranteed large investments to modernize and increase productive capacity just at the time when capacity needed to be reduced. The state and the firms did not recognize early enough the need to match the technological innovations of the German and Japanese steel industries. In the late 1970s, restructuring was further delayed by the terrible state of labor-management relations in the industry. The steel industry had become a large drain on government: between 1978 and 1986 around 60 billion francs in public funds had been spent to finance the operations of Usinor and Sacilor.[26] Ironically, it was left to a Socialist government to impose major reductions in the work force.

There have been at least five major turning points in French steel policies since the end of World War II: the beginning of the Monnet Plan in 1945, entry into the European Coal and Steel Community (ECSC) in 1951, the General Convention between the state and the private steel firms in 1966, the initiation of large-scale state-financed building projects in Lorraine and at Dunkerque and Fos in the 1970s, and the crisis and restructuring of the industry in 1977–78.[27]

The State and Steel before World War II

Before World War II the French steel industry was dominated by private industrialists, families such as the Schneiders and De Wendels, who were referred to as *maîtres de forges*. The first Wendel bought a forge in Hayange in 1704. His sons founded Creusot, which was expropriated during the French Revolution but returned to the family in 1803. In 1864, the Comité des Forges was founded under the presidency of Eugène Schneider, who then headed Le Creusot. Jacques Ferry, who went on to become the executive secretary of the Chambre Syndicale de la Sidérurgie Française in 1964, said of the Comité des Forges in the 1930s: "It was the great institution representative a certain liberal order and of financial orthodoxy. I had the feeling—a little owing, I admit, to my age at the time—that I had joined the holy of holies of 'la grande industrie.' "[28]

Its association with French military capability gave the steel industry a certain cachet that other industries lacked. Large public contracts were awarded to the Wendels in Lorraine and the Schneiders at Le Creusot during the nineteenth century. French investors, always overly cautious, required the enactment of high trade barriers before they would invest in steel. Exclusive iron-mining and coal-mining concessions issued by the state in the 1810 Mining Code favored entrepreneurs "selected by the state." The French steel industry was therefore, to some extent, a hothouse product from its origins. It suffered in

26. Hall, *Governing the Economy*, p. 298.
27. Cohen, Galbraith, and Zysman, "Rehabbing the Labyrinth," p. 70.
28. Jean G. Padioleau, *Quand la France s'enferre* (Paris: Presses Universitaires de France, 1981), pp. 10–12, 19.

international competition because of the lack of domestic mineral resources, especially coal, which had to be imported.[29] Plants tended to be smaller than minimum-scale economies required. The location of the Wendel factories in Lorraine made them vulnerable to seizure during the world wars, and in 1914 they were dismantled by the German occupying forces. Nevertheless, the Wendels played a major role in French steel for almost three centuries, most recently through their 50 percent equity in one of the two largest firms in France, Wendel-Sidelor.

The Comité de Forges

The heads of the steel industry in France have never been known for their enlightened views toward labor. The Comité de Forges opposed a law in the Chamber of Deputies in 1912 to limit the workday to ten hours. The close association between the steel industrialists and the state fostered the popular myth of the Comité de Forges as a "state within the state." The Comité de Forges was a highly effective lobbying organization, but its reputation was severely injured during World War II. Production had sunk to an all-time low of 2 million tons per year by 1945. The Comité de Forges had not been sufficiently anti-Nazi during the years before 1939 and had not met the challenge posed by the German steel industry in the interwar years, despite the repossession of Alsace and Lorraine and the occupation of former German territory in the demilitarized zone after World War I. The Comité de Forges was reorganized as the Chambre Syndicale de la Sidérurgie Française in 1946. Little changed other than the name, and the CSSF continued to occupy the same building on Rue de Madrid as the Comité de Forges. But the commitment of the French state after World War II to industrialize France and the financial weakness of the industry fundamentally changed the relationship between the state and the industry.[30]

The Monnet Plan

After World War II and until France entered the European Coal and Steel Community in 1953, the Commissariat Général du Plan made French steel policy. On November 23, 1946, Jean Monnet launched the Plan of Modernization (later called the Monnet Plan). The Commission of Modernization published its objectives in 1947: to bring French steel production up to 6 million tons per year immediately, to increase it to 10 million tons within three years, and eventually to obtain a pro-

29. See Christian Stoffäes and Pierre Gadonneix, "Steel and the State in France," *Annalen der Gemeinwirtschaft* 49 (October–December 1980): 407–8.
30. Jean Baumier, *Le fin des mâitres de forges* (Paris: Plon, 1981), pp. 64, 73.

ductive capacity of 12 million tons. Marshall Plan funds were used to rebuild productive capacity in two major producing regions: the North and Lorraine. The plants in Lorraine were older and smaller than those in the North. The major firms in the Lorraine region were Sidelor and Sollac, founded in 1947–48, and De Wendel, founded in 1950–51. The major firm in the North was Usinor, founded in 1947–48.[31]

Entry into the ECSC

France's entry into the ECSC in 1953 required adjustment to increased international competition, mainly from Germany. The Marshall Plan aid tapered off, and the French steel industry began to modernize and expand on the assumption of the continued need to compete with the Germans. Unfortunately, state promotional policies in steel conflicted with those for industry in general. During the years 1949–55, state-imposed price controls on steel products, designed to keep input costs low for downstream manufacturers, reduced the profitability of the steel industry. State subsidies continued, however, and the industry failed to make major new investments to preserve its competitiveness.

The General Convention on Steel

In 1963, a general financial crisis occurred. Between 1960 and 1965, gross profits in the steel industry dropped from 1.29 billion francs to 0.56 billion; debt increased from 46 percent of sales to 69 percent. On October 14, 1964, Prime Minister Georges Pompidou appealed to the Ministry of Finance, suggesting that further capital investments should be linked to wage arrangements in the steel industry. The Commissariat Général du Plan assigned a working group that included experts from the Ministry of Finance to discuss problems with industry representatives. In 1964–65, the industry was invited to submit plans for state financing to the Steel Office of the CGP. On February 17, 1965, the ministers of industry and finance sent a letter to the CSSF suggesting that there should be more concentration of ownership in the industry, greater sharing of production facilities, and a general rationalization of employment (in other words, layoffs). In exchange for these concessions on the part of the industry, the state would issue new loans of around 300 million francs.[32]

31. See Padioleau, *Quand la France s'enferre*, p. 12; Stoffäes and Gadonneix, "Steel and the State in France," p. 411; Baumier, *Le fin des maîtres de forges*, p. 73; and Domenico Moro, *Crisi e ristrutturazione dell'industria siderurgica italiana* (Varese: Giuffre, 1984), p. 70.
32. Padioleau, *Quand la France s'enferre*, pp. 48–51.

Figure 10. FDES steel investments, 1953–1977

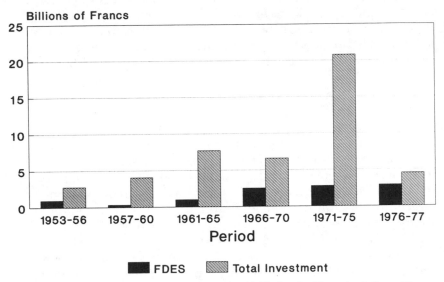

Source: Domenico Moro, *Crisi e ristrutturazione dell'industria siderurgica italiana* (Varese: Giuffre, 1984), p. 78.

Out of the bargaining during this period emerged the General Convention on Steel, adopted by the French Council of Ministers on July 23, 1966. Under this convention, the state agreed to make 2.7 billion francs in loans available under the Economic and Social Development Fund at favorable interest rates in exchange for restructuring of the industry (see Figure 10). The restructuring arrangements include the absorption of Lorraine-Escaut (a small northeastern firm) by Usinor; the merger of De Wendel, Sidelor, and Mosellane to form Wendel-Sidelor, later renamed Sacilor; the consolidation of the plants of Sacilor and Sollac; and the elimination of fifteen thousand jobs. As incorporated into the Fifth Plan, this agreement also decreased tariffs on coking coal imported from the United States and gave rebates on social security payments. Six billion francs were eventually made available by the state for loans to finance the purchasing of coke and coal and for the transportation costs of the industry. The industry agreed to increase production to 25 million tons per year. The Commissariat Général du Plan was to chair a consultative committee to implement the convention.[33]

33. See ibid., pp. 23 and 54–56; Andrew Shonfield, *Modern Capitalism* (New York: Oxford University Press, 1965), p. 139; Stoffäes and Gadonneix, "Steel and the State in France," p. 411.

The Plants at Fos and Dunkerque

Between 1966 and 1971 investment and production increased significantly, and both industry and government projected a sharp rise in domestic demand for steel. About 10 billion francs were invested during this period, 30 percent of which was provided by the Trésor. The Trésor and the Crédit National provided loans for building two new modern plants at Dunkerque and For-sur-Mer. The productive capacity of the Usinor plant at Dunkerque was doubled from 1.5 to 3 million tons per year. Increases in productive capacity nationwide cost 31 billion francs between 1971 and 1974.[34]

The plant at Fos, called Solmer, was an equally shared venture between Sacilor and Usinor. It was planned to have a capacity of 6 million tons per year. The Fos and Dunkerque plants were built on the coasts—modeled after the Japanese coastal plants of the same period—to take advantage of the lower cost of ocean shipping of both inputs and final products. They were to use the latest steelmaking technologies, including basic oxygen processes and continuous casting.

Usinor, the stronger of the two national champions, eventually agreed to help finance the plant at Fos after being permitted to acquire Lorraine-Escaut and receiving a fresh infusion of capital from the state. Usinor had wanted to diversify into long products and steel plate, which was precisely what Lorraine-Escaut produced. But the state still needed Usinor to help Sacilor finance the plant at Fos.[35]

Ownership in the industry became much more concentrated. In 1965, the major industrial groups accounted for 44 percent of sales; by 1970, they accounted for 75 percent.[36] The state had adopted a form of national champions policy, favoring the two firms most beholden to it, Usinor and Sacilor. Creusot and Empain-Schneider, the two private firms that were relatively independent of the state, were encouraged to increase their market shares in specialty steels and mechanical engineering. Creusot diversified into nuclear power plants (through its Framatome subsidiary) and machinery.

Jean-Jacques Servan-Schreiber, remarking on the poor state of the industry in 1969, compared it to the more successful and innovative

34. Pierre Dacier, Jean-Louis Levet, and Jean-Claude Tourret, *Les dossiers noirs de l'industrie française* (Paris: Fayard, 1985), p. 183.

35. Initially, the German steel firm Thyssen was to be a partner in the joint venture creating Solmer, but it dropped out because it was unsure of the potential profitability of the venture. The minister of finance opposed the entry of a German firm into the French market and exerted pressure on Sacilor and Usinor to finance the plant by themselves. See Padioleau, *Quand la France s'enferre*, p. 38; and Patrick Messerlin, *The European Industrial Adjustment Policies: The Steel Industry Case* (Brighton: Sussex European Research Center, 1981), pp. f2–f4.

36. Baumier, *Le fin des mâitres de forges*, p. 80.

consumer goods firms: "L'Oreal yes, de Wendel no. One must change industrial patriotism." Jacques Ferry, general secretary of the CSSF, responded with an indignant putdown of the cosmetics industry: "The French steel industry will not be content with a policy of whipped cream and cosmetics."[37] *Le Figaro*, which published the exchange, apologized to its readers for the polemical nature of the dispute. Nevertheless, Servan-Schreiber had sensed the beginning of a change in the previously unbroachable support for the industry from the state and the general public.[38]

The Industry after 1973

Unfortunately, the modern plants at Fos and Dunkerque were not used at full capacity. The stagnation of domestic demand after 1973 and delays in closing inefficient plants and implementing layoffs eventually created pressures for reducing the work force and capacity. The work force decreased from 158,000 in 1960 to 143,000 in 1972[39] but did not keep up with the pace of rationalization set by Germany and Japan.

After 1973, demand for steel dropped because of a recession in Organization of Economic Cooperation and Development economies and the substitution of less expensive metals and plastic for steel in many downstream products. Productive capacity continued to increase, however, and the French industry did not diversify sufficiently to capture the increased demand for specialty steel products. Government policy was to protect productive capacity by pushing exports of French steel, but exports did not improve the financial picture: in 1975–76, losses exceeded 4 billion francs. In 1976, 12.4 percent of sales went to repay debts (compared to 3.6 percent for the rest of the industry in the European Community [EC]). Thus in 1977, another rescue plan was prepared for the steel industry, but this time without the usual extensive consultations between the state ministries and Sacilor and Usinor.[40]

The Rescue Plan of 1977

The 1977 plan, announced on September 20, 1978, had seven points. The debt claims of the FDES, the Crédit National, and the various consortia of private lenders would be converted into special par-

---

37. Servan-Schreiber and Ferry quoted from Hayward, *The State and the Market Economy*, p. 68.
38. See Padioleau, *Quand la France s'enderre*, p. 39.
39. Stoffäes and Gadonneix, "Steel and the State in France," pp. 412–13.
40. See Baumier, *Le fin des maîtres de forges*, pp. 163 and 168–69.

ticipatory loans (a form of equity participation). A Steel Sinking Fund would be established and maintained by the Treasury to service some of the debt so as to guarantee repayment of small-denomination bonds issued in the early 1970s. Two finance companies were to be created with a combined capital of 2 billion francs, which would hold a majority of total equity in the industry (with percentage shares apportioned as follows: banks, 30 percent, FDES, 15 percent, Steel Industry Group, 15 percent, Caisse des Dépôts, 30 percent, and Crédit National, 10 percent. Payment of steel paper held by foreign banks was guaranteed, and the major steel groups would be restructured, mainly by closing obsolete plants, reducing growth in overall capacity, and placing greater emphasis on production of specialty steels. Finally, new managers would replace the heads of Sacilor and Usinor, and twenty to forty thousand workers would be laid off.[41]

The plan was mostly implemented by April 1979, but the industry still suffered from depressed demand and overcapacity. The political battles between the Center and Left resulted in increased state subsidies for the industry to maintain the steelworkers' allegiance to the Center.[42] Between 1977 and 1981, fifty thousand jobs were lost to downstream specialization and integration agreements.[43]

Riots in the Steel Regions

On February 23, 1979, the chamber of commerce of the steel industry in Longwy, the site of a major steel plant in Lorraine, was assaulted by a mob of angry workers and their supporters. This action was precipitated by a series of small plant closures and announcements of further cuts in production and employment. On March 1, violent protests spread to Valenciennes, Denain, Chier, and Anzin. At the Sacilor plant at Homecourt, the management office was occupied by workers. Despite efforts of the union, dominated by the CGT, to restrain the violence, the size and unruliness of the demonstrations grew. On March 6, the minister of labor, Robert Boulin, met with the representatives of the five main labor unions. On March 16, a general strike was called, and the plant at Longwy was shut down. The frontier with Belgium was blocked by steelworkers, and a huge

41. See Stoffäes and Gadonneix, "Steel and the State in France," pp. 419–20; Cohen, Galbraith, and Zysman, "Rehabbing the Labyrinth," pp. 69–72.

42. See Josef Esser, "Sozialisierung als beschäftigungspolitisches Instrument? Ehrfahrungen mit der verstaatlichten Stahlindustrie in Europe," *Gewerkschaftliche Monatshefte* 31 (July 1980): 450.

43. See Christian Stoffäes, "Industrial Policy in France: Changes and Continuity," *Lo Spettatore Internazionale* 17 (April–June 1982): 162.

steel ingot was placed in the main square of Longwy as a symbol of the workers' discontent.[44]

The state tried to mollify the workers with a series of belated adjustment programs. Between 1977 and 1981, 3.5 billion francs were injected into the industry, mostly by state agencies. A special Loan Fund for the Steel Industry (Caisse d'Amortissement pour l'Acier) was created. The work force declined by only eight-five hundred rather than the twenty to forty thousand projected in the 1977 rescue plan.[45] Nevertheless, feelings continued to run strong concerning the closing of plants in Lorraine. When Usinor announced an additional four thousand layoffs for 1979, a forty-year-old steelworker of Lorraine, René Delamotte, was quoted as saying: "I feel stabbed a second time. I do not ask for pity. Only a little understanding. If they let me go, it will be for me, my wife, and three kids, the equivalent of deportation."[46] When François Mitterrand visited Lorraine in 1979, he was so impressed with the workers' sentiments that he pledged to try to preserve jobs in the steel industry in the absence of alternative sources of employment in any future leftist government. He even promised to build new steelworks in Denain and Longwy. He was not able to keep these promises.

The Steel Policies of the Mitterrand Presidency

By the early 1980s, continued weakness in demand for steel and steel products and insufficient reduction of production capacity again created financial pressures on French firms. A new medium-term steel plan was unveiled by the leftist government in June 1982. Despite a series of studies indicating that annual demand for steel was likely to remain flat at 20 million tons or less, the cabinet agreed to try to maintain a productive capacity of 24 million tons. Usinor and Sacilor had lost around 6 billion francs in 1981 (see Figure 11). The government, perhaps overly influenced by optimistic projections of increased demand circulated by the CSSF, seemed to be set on a disastrous course. The EC Commission set a deadline of September 1982 for member states to submit proposals for reducing productive capacity. All such reductions were to be completed by 1985.

The French government's 1982 steel plan called for a reduction of employment in the industry of ten to twelve thousand jobs. An effort was made to keep Mitterrand's pledge to Lorraine by encouraging early retirement and reducing the workweek. By April 1984, this approach had proved just as unsuccessful as previous ones. Not enough

44. Baumier, *Le fin des maîtres de forges,* pp. 12–15.
45. Stoffäes and Gadonneix, "Steel and the State in France," p. 421.
46. Baumier, *Le fin des maîtres de forges,* p. 11.

Figure 11. Net income of Sacilor and Usinor

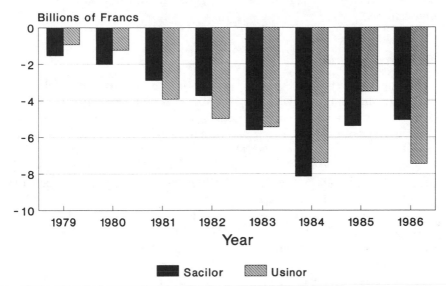

Source: French Company Handbook (Paris: International Business Development SARL, 1985 and 1987).

jobs could be saved by reducing the workweek from forty to thirty-five hours, and older workers resisted the imposition of early retirement. Mitterrand admitted at a press conference on April 4 that a more drastic reduction in steel production was required. He admitted that errors in forecasting had been made and gave special powers to the minister of industry to preside over a major redeployment out of the industry.[47]

The Restructuring Plan of 1984

In March 1984, yet another steel restructuring plan was implemented. The financial losses of Sacilor and Usinor cost the treasury 10 billion francs in 1983, 15 billion in 1984, and 9 billion in 1985. Pierre Mauroy, the prime minister, and Jacques Delors, the minister of the economy and finance, decided on a rapid series of plant closings, against the advice of the industry minister, Laurent Fabius. Two new corporate entities, Ascometal and Unimetal, were created to deal with the restructuring of the most depressed segment of the market: slabs and steel for construction. Ascometal and Unimetal were 51–49 joint ventures of Sacilor and Usinor. It was also decided not to

47. Dacier, Levet, and Tourret, *Les dossiers noirs*, pp. 192–93.

build a new factory at Fos-sur-Mer and to allocate 30 billion francs between 1984 and 1987 for retiring accumulated debt and for new investments.[48]

The Merger of Sacilor and Usinor

The operations of Sacilor and Usinor were merged on September 4, 1986. On that date, the Chirac government replaced the presidents of both firms with a single chief executive, Francis Mer, formerly of Saint Gobain. Although this move was not officially acknowledged as a merger until later, it was indeed a merger. Usinor-Sacilor became the largest steel producer in Europe, second only to Nippon Steel in global production. The main reason for the merger was to reduce the size of government subsidies to the steel industry.

A key element in the merger was a major restructuring of the capital of the two firms. Restructuring involved three stages. First, capital was reduced to zero so accumulated losses could be audited. Then, new shares were offered to the general public to recapitalize the firms. Finally, old shares were exchanged for new at a fixed rate. The main losers were the private shareholders; after vocal protests, the government agreed to compensate them partially for their losses. After the financial restructuring, Francis Mer pursued a strategy of returning to profitability by focusing on core steelmaking activities, upgrading existing facilities, and reducing the size of the work force. Whereas combined operations lost 4 billion francs in 1986, profits had risen to 7.9 billion francs by 1989.

Demand for steel in France increased from 14.5 million tons in 1986 to 16.8 million in 1988, and prices stabilized, thanks largely of the absence of the usual bitter competition between Sacilor and Usinor. The Longwy and Denain plants were closed, as was the Marais plant near Saint Etienne. Major new investments increased the preparation of steel produced by continuous casting to 93 percent in 1987. The work force was reduced from 124,000 at the end of 1984 to 62,000 at the end of 1989.

In 1989, Usinor-Sacilor purchased 70 percent of the shares in Saarstahl of Germany. Apparently, the heroic rationalization efforts of Saarstahl had begun to pay off by the late 1980s, thus adding to Usinor-Sacilor's profits in a major way. Cooperation agreements were arranged with Mannesmann in the production of steel tubes and with Thyssen in the area of thin-slab technology. In April 1990, Usinor-

48. Ibid. pp. 194–99.

Sacilor acquired Jones and Laughlin Specialty Products Corporation, an American steel firm, for $570 million. Thus while other steel firms in Europe were disinvesting or diversifying, Usinor-Sacilor was becoming a specialized producer with a major presence in Germany and the United States.

After the successes of the immediate postwar period in building a French steel industry, the policy of the French state favored the concentration of integrated steelmaking in two national champion firms—Sacilor and Usinor. Because of the extensive intervention of the state in the most important decisions of these firms, but also because of bad management, the industry modernized without closing down obsolete production facilities. Thus it was not able to take advantage of the increased productivity resulting from innovations in steelmaking technology at the newer plants. Major investments were made in the 1970s, just when both domestic and international demand for steel was declining.

France's inability to capitalize on large investments in modern steel plants in the 1970s is related to the state's reluctance to close down obsolete facilities. The desire of both French industrialists and government authorities to avoid giving politically marginalized and hence militant labor organizations an issue that could increase their political power is at the heart of the matter. In France, as in both the United States and Britain, the weakness of labor impedes the adoption of new technologies.

In addition, the state's insistence on a division of labor between the publicly owned integrated steelworks and the privately held specialty and mechanical engineering firms meant that neither group could use vertical integration as a survival tactic. Downstream diversification—particularly into mechanical engineering—was used successfully by both German and Japanese firms to keep profits higher during periods of low prices for steel. This strategy was not available to French firms.

The overcapacity in European steelmaking in the late 1970s, accentuated by the global recession of the early 1980s, created a political crisis. Under strong pressure from other members of the European Community the Mitterrand government rapidly reduced production and employment in the least efficient plants. By the late 1980s, the creation of Usinor-Sacilor and the closing of many inefficient plants made it possible for the state to approve the purchases of Saarstahl and Jones and Laughlin, making the French steel industry considerably less French.

Policies for the Automobile Industry

The French government had less influence in the auto industry than in steel before World War II because the auto industry financed most of its investments from retained earnings. Immediately after World War II, the nationalization of Renault combined with the ambitious state goals for postwar industrialization gave the state greater leverage over industry investments. As growth accelerated in the 1950s and 1960s, however, the French auto industry again became relatively independent of state authority. The state's key role before 1973 was to prevent inflows of foreign investment, especially that aimed at acquiring failing French firms. When financial problems developed later in the 1970s, however, the state stepped in to facilitate mergers, loans for new investments, and reductions in the work force. Intervention increased in the early and middle 1980s as French firms became less able to keep up with their competitors in Europe. By 1987, however, both Renault and Peugeot were making profits following major restructuring.

The Auto Industry before World War II

The French auto industry got off to a very good start, with production increasing from 1,850 in 1898 to 45,000 in 1914. The number of member firms in the Syndical Chamber of the Automobile Industry increased from 190 in 1908 to 230 in 1913.[49] In the 1920s, however, the French, like most other industrialized countries, were unable to compete with the new giant U.S. firms, Ford and GM, on price. In 1913, Ford established a company in France; in 1919 GM tried, unsuccessfully, to acquire Citroën. Ford increased its presence in France during the 1920s by building an assembly plant at Asnières. In 1938, Ford built a large plant at Poissy, but this venture was unsuccessful and Simca purchased the plant in 1954.[50]

The French expected mass-produced American automobiles to penetrate their domestic market. In 1906, a French journalist warned of "the American peril": "You will see when the Americans invade Europe with cheap cars produced by mass production [*fabriques en serie*]. . . . It begins in Germany where the people don't like to buy expensive things. . . . I pose for myself this problem: suppose the American factories try to produce 10,000 cars using the same type of

49. Patrick Fridenson, *Histoire des usines Renault* (Paris: Seuil, 1972), pp. 26–27.
50. Daniel T. Jones, *Maturity and Crisis in the European Car Industry* (Brighton: Sussex European Research Center, 1981), p. 111.

body, consequently of very low price. Once finished, they will feel the necessity of selling these outside their native country."

After World War I, France adopted a relatively protectionist trade regime to shelter domestic firms from international competition. This strategy was only partly successful. Many smaller firms went out of business as a result of the combined pressure from the Americans and the three largest French firms: Renault, Citroën, and Peugeot. The three French firms controlled 48 percent of the domestic market in 1919, 56 percent in 1925, and 63 percent in 1926. They went through a period of drastic rationalization of production, but in 1927, French productively lagged way behind American: to build one vehicle required seventy man-days in the United States, two hundred in France.[51]

Peugeot was the market leader in the 1920s and early and middle 1930s but was overtaken by Renault in the late 1930s. Both firms emulated American production techniques by standardizing parts, speeding up the production line, and increasing the number of vehicles produced per worker. Renault made key investments in the early 1930s, during the height of the Great Depression, to modernize its plants and by the mid-1930s was well positioned to take market share away from Peugeot by underpricing, although at a political cost.

The Auto Industry after World War II

After the war, Renault was nationalized for political reasons: the management's collaboration with the occupying Nazi powers and, in the words of Daniel Jones, "the harsh treatment of trade unions by Louis Renault" in the 1930s.[52] Nationalization made Renault a *régie nationale*, like the Paris urban transport authority, which meant that its financial status was permanently guaranteed by the state.[53] Renault's strong position in the domestic market, the result of policies of the interwar years, insulated it from excessive interference from state officials, even after its nationalization.

In the post–World War II period renewed challenges came from abroad. The state continued to exclude foreign competitors from domestic production (with the exceptions of Ford, which had gotten in early enough to escape this fate, and Chrysler, which purchased a controlling interest in Simca in 1963). Ford and GM proposed building assembly plants in Strasbourg in 1964, but the government blocked this plan. Ford built its new plant in Saarlouis in Germany; GM

51. Fridenson, *Histoire des usines Renault*, pp. 34–35, 163, 165.
52. Jones, *Maturity and Crisis*, p. 36.
53. Paul Betts, "Restructuring Programme Pays Off," *Financial Times*, September 29, 1988, Special survey on France, p. 6.

constructed new facilities in Belgium. In 1968, Fiat acquired a 15 percent stake in Citroën. When it tried to purchase a controlling interest in 1969, it was permitted only a 49 percent interest. Fiat sold its interest in Citroën in 1973.

Bosch, a German auto components firm, tried to enter the French market but was not allowed to. In 1978, Lucas, a British components firm, put in a bid to take over Ducellier (a maker of electrical components for automobiles). Instead, the French government insisted on the establishment of a joint venture between Lucas and Ferodo (the favored domestic electronic components firm).[54]

The State Encourages the Pooling of Resources

During the 1960s the French government tried to make French auto firms more competitive by encouraging joint ventures and the pooling of research. The firms responded favorably. In 1966, Renault and Peugeot agreed to pool patents. Later, they began to standardize components so they could be produced jointly. In 1979, Renault and Peugeot put forth plans for the construction of a common components plant in Lorraine, a region that was suffering from declining employment in the steel industry.[55]

The government was asked to provide subsidies for research and development in the late 1970s, which led to the funding of the Eve and Vera projects in 1979 under the Ministry of Industry. The firms matched the 14-million-franc contribution of the ministry for these two programs, which were designed to subsidize the construction of prototypes of more fuel-efficient vehicles. By 1981, the prototypes were ready, and two additional projects were begun. The goal of the 1981 projects was to produce a new model, based on the Renault R-5, that could get seventy-five miles to a gallon of gasoline. The Mitterrand government contributed 200 million francs for this purpose, adding two more goals: improved safety and facilitating the production of automobiles with advanced automation techniques.[56]

The Rescue of Citroën

Fiat's 1973 sale of its interest in Citroën was a harbinger of financial problems for the French company. The government loaned 1 billion francs to Citroën in 1975 through FDES at 9.75 percent interest (the

54. Jones, *Maturity and Crisis*, pp. 112–13.
55. Ibid.
56. James P. Womack, "Public Policy for a Mature Industrial Sector: The Auto Case" (Ph.D. diss., Massachusetts Institute of Technology, 1982), pp. 175–77.

market rate was around 11 percent at the time) for fifteen years. In 1976, Peugeot purchased a 90 percent interest in Citroën. The loan, followed by the absorption, was part of a plan worked out between the state and Peugeot in 1974, when it first became clear that Citroën was in trouble.

Until 1974, Peugeot, the largest private auto producer in France, had never asked the state for assistance. In 1977, Peugeot tried to accommodate the state by promoting Jean-Paul Parayre to be chief executive officer. Parayre was a graduate of a grande école, The Ecole des Ponts et Chaussées, and had been an elite bureaucrat in various government ministries from 1963 to 1974, when he left to become an employee of Peugeot. Parayre was an aggressive manager who believed that Peugeot could be become one of the largest European auto firms with the help of the state. According to Daniel Jones, "Once a very secretive, private company located well away from Paris, with as little contact with the government as possible, [Peugeot had] now taken on a new role."[57] In 1978, this new role became evident when Chrysler's financial crisis spread to its European subsidiaries.

Chrysler's International Crisis Hits France

The Chrysler subsidiary in France had done well at first. The plant at Poissy worked better for Chrysler than it had for Ford or Simca. In addition, investments in Spain in the early 1970s allowed Chrysler to continue to compete with other major firms in Europe, even though its plants in Britain and France were no longer competitive. Chrysler's financial difficulties in the U.S. market became so great by the late 1970s that it seemed that its relatively unprofitable operations in Europe would have to go as part of a global restructuring. In 1978, therefore, Peugeot, with the approval of the French government, offered to purchase Chrysler-Europe.

According to the deal agreed to in August 1978, Chrysler was to be paid $230 million in cash and 15 percent of Peugeot's stock (then worth around $200 million) and Peugeot would assume the debt of Chrysler's European operations (around $400 million). Chrysler-Europe then became known as Talbot, and the new combination of Peugeot, Citroën, and Talbot was renamed PSA (for Peugeot Société Anonyme), although I will continue to refer to it as Peugeot. The cash payment to Chrysler came mostly from Peugeot's reserves. But the deal required negotiation with the state because it was clear that Peugeot would have to engage in some rationalization of its new plants in France, Belgium, and Britain, and the state would be sure to push for cutting jobs outside France.

57. Jones, *Maturity and Crisis*, p. 40.

Figure 12. Net income of Renault and Peugeot

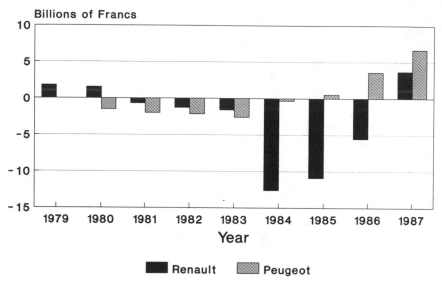

Sources: French Company Handbook (Paris: International Business Development SARL, 1983, 1985, and 1987); and recent business press reports.

The Rescue of Peugeot

Peugeot was now the biggest auto firm in Europe, selling 2.2 million vehicles per year, worth around $1.2 billion.[58] The firm planned to reduce employment by fifty-five thousand after acquiring Chrysler-Europe, but pressure from the new Socialist government reduced that number. The Talbot plants in Belgium and Britain were eventually closed, but the plant at Poissy remained in operation. Peugeot had losses of about 8.6 billion francs between 1980 and 1985 (see Figure 12). Despite the successful introduction of two new models—the 205 Supermini and the Citroën BX—losses mounted.

Peugeot's domestic market share dropped from 43 percent in 1979 to 30 percent in 1982.[59] In 1982, the Peugeot family asked Jacques Calvet, previously the head of the state-owned Banque Nationale de Paris, to be their financial adviser. In September 1984, Calvet replaced Parayre as head of the firm after an interim period in which Parayre remained chairman but Calvet made most of the crucial decisions. Calvet had graduated from the prestigious Ecole Nationale d'Administra-

58. Michael Moritz and Barrett Seaman, *Going for Broke: The Chrysler Story* (New York: Doubleday, 1981), pp. 191–92.
59. "Peugeot: Job Cuts, Not Bailouts," *Economist,* July 13, 1983, p. 56.

tion and had worked for Valery Giscard d'Estaing in the Ministry of Finance in the 1970s. He was brought in to rein in the expansion of the firm and to secure the government's agreement to rationalizations that would reduce employment at key plants. Thus Calvet was likely to work even more closely with the state than Parayre had. His own understanding of how to do this was reflected in a statement made in the summer of 1983: "I never negotiate with the state. I explain very clearly what I want to do, why I want to do it, and what the consequences of not doing it will be. Then I wait for the government to decide."[60]

Calvet was much less committed to expanding the firm than Parayre was. He was willing to cut the losses in the Talbot and Citroën divisions and concentrate efforts on a smaller number of products. In the summer of 1983, Calvet announced plans for the elimination of twelve thousand jobs, six thousand in Citroën. The aim was for a work force of forty-three to forty-six thousand in 1984. The work force at the Talbot plant in Poissy was to be reduced from seventeen thousand to thirteen thousand. In October 1983, the government authorized elimination of forty-five hundred workers by early retirement but withheld authority to dismiss twenty-eight hundred additional workers.[61]

Citroën asked thirty-five hundred workers aged fifty-five to sixty to accept early retirement and offered financial assistance for foreign workers who wanted to leave France to return to their home countries. The CGT (despite internal splits between representatives of French and North African workers) vigorously protested the projected cuts, especially the plans for assisting foreign workers to leave France. In January 1984, the CFDT led a strike of Talbot immigrant workers at Poissy demanding no cuts at all. But both the CGT and the CFDT eventually had to back down.[62]

The 1984 Strikes at Citroën and Talbot Plants

The CGT struck several major Citroën plants in May 1984 to protest further cuts. The union suggested that instead of importing cars manufactured in Spain, Citroën should increase production in France. But Talbot had already cut its Spanish labor force by nine thousand (60 percent). A further twenty-thousand jobs were lost in Britain when the Talbot plants there were closed. The CFDT called for no job cuts until

60. Quoted from Paul Lewis, "Peugeot Chief Fights State's Embrace," *New York Times*, November 4, 1984, p. F6.

61. "French Government Authorizes Peugeot to Cut 4,500 Jobs," *Wall Street Journal*, October 13, 1983, p. 38.

62. Roger Rickles, "Citroën Seeks to Lower Employment by 3,500: Renault Mulls Job Cuts," *Wall Street Journal*, June 21, 1983, p. 40.

adoption of a thirty-five-hour week. The government mediated the dispute, helping to negotiate a compromise.

In August 1984, Peugeot laid off two thousand workers at the Talbot plant in Poissy. There were work stoppages at the Poissy plant and at several Citroën plants. In mid-August, the firm again asked the state for approval to lay off workers at Citroën. The main long-term need was to improve productivity. Peugeot was losing its ability to compete with other low-cost European producers such as Fiat. Fiat produced twenty-six cars per worker per year, but Peugeot produced only ten. The difference in labor productivity had an obvious effect on profitability and competitiveness. To reduce the gap in productivity, Peugeot would have to make large and continuous investments in its plants. Because of the huge debts incurred to stay in operation during the early 1980s, Peugeot would be able to make these additional investments only if it had the backing of the French state.

Thus in approximately ten years Peugeot had gone from a position of high autonomy to one of intense dependence. Through a combination of good management and skillful collaboration with the state, Peugeot returned to profitability in 1985. Thanks to strong demand for its new models, production and profits increased through 1988. The crisis of the mid-1980s was brought on by the firms' slowness to adopt the productivity-enhancing technologies used by German, Japanese, and Italian firms. Part of its slowness was attributable to bad management, but the weakness of French labor and its hostility to the introduction of labor-saving technologies are also to blame. The French government's policy of limiting both domestic and international competition reduced the pressure on management and labor to adopt the productivity-enhancing technologies used elsewhere.

Renault Begins to Slide

As a state-owned firm, Renault had benefited from access to state financial assistance. Unlike Peugeot, it did not have to learn how to extract resources from the state. But that advantage was eroded by delays in developing new models to replace the highly successful R-5 model. In addition, Renault's management failed to recognize the problems caused by depending on inexpensive immigrant labor rather than investing in new process technology to keep production costs low. Renault's management engaged in an ambitious diversification policy in the 1970s, from which it had to retreat in the 1980s. An extra burden was placed on the firm by the Mauroy government's efforts to turn it into a model of labor-management relations for all French firms. The heavy-handed efforts of Jean-Pierre Chevènement to micromanage the affairs of Renault from the Ministry of Industry illustrated the necessity of limiting the authority of the state over its own enterprises.

In 1974, the government loaned the firm 450 million francs to purchase Berliet (the truck-producing arm of Citroën) as part of a general restructuring of the industry. In 1978, Renault purchased a 22.5 percent stake in American Motors Corporation (AMC) out of its cash reserves. In January 1979, Renault concluded an agreement with AMC to distribute Renault vehicles in the United States. In March 1979, the FSAI and CIASI helped, with a government loan of 550 million francs, to finance the purchase of 20 percent stake in Mack Trucks. In 1980, Renault acquired a 20 percent stake in Volvo.[63] Renault increased its stake in AMC to 46.4 percent in January 1982 at a cost of $40 million. It raised its share of Mack Trucks from 20 to 45 percent in May 1983 at a cost of $100 million. It nearly doubled its Spanish production from 182,000 vehicles in 1973 to 325,000 in 1980. It planned to build a new engine plant in Mexico at a cost of $400 million. A sum of $1.7 billion was to be allocated over the 1982–86 period for the development of new models.[64] Thus Renault had become larger and more internationaliz by the early 1980s. Its international strategy had shifted from exporting to foreign markets to a greater stress on local production, emulating firms like VW and Honda.[65]

Renault was relatively successful in keeping up with technological changes in the industry. By the early 1980s, it was the leading producer in the EC of industrial robots. In 1978, Renault had established a joint venture with Bendix Corporation to produce electronic components for motor vehicles. In 1980, Renault and Thomson-Brandt signed a deal to produce electronic components.

Despite increased size, greater internationalization, and efforts to incorporate changes in product and process technologies, the firm did poorly financially. After a long series of profitable years, including a profit of 1.547 billion francs in 1980, Renault began to lose larger and larger sums (see Figure 12). In addition, its domestic market share dropped from 39 percent in 1982 to 35 percent in 1983 and 31 percent in 1984. The main competition in the domestic market came from imports, especially Volkswagen, Fiat, and Ford, but Japanese models manufactured in Europe were becoming noticeable. Renault's declining

63. George Maxcy, *The Multinational Motor Industry* (London: Croom Helm, 1981), p. 147.

64. Ben Dankbaar, "Is the International Car Industry Moving South? Trade, Foreign Investment and Relocation in the Passenger Car Industry," Industrial Policy Discussion Paper, International Institute for Management, Berlin, February 1983, Tables 4 and 13; "Le defi français," *Economist*, September 15, 1984, p. 73.

65. "Local production" means producing goods inside foreign countries rather than exporting to them.

market share was largely attributable to its failure to develop a successor to its R-5 model. Renault's overseas automobile operations were generally profitable, with the notable exception of its American subsidiary, AMC. Renault lost $600 million in the United States between 1980 and 1983. The two main AMC models—Alliance and Encore—did not fare well against their competitors in North America.[66]

Renault invested 450 million francs to design a new model, the Super Cinq, to follow the R-5. The Super Cinq was supposed to be bigger, lighter, and more powerful. But Renault not only had to compete with Peugeot in this section of the market but also with Fiat (Uno), Opel (Corsa), VW (Polo), Ford (Fiesta), and Austin (Metro). Cost reductions in the Super Cinq plant at Le Mans initially helped minimize losses, but the wage settlement that ended the September 1984 strike at that plant sharply increased Renault's labor costs. The head of Renault, Bernard Hanon, was harshly criticized by the Socialists for making bad decisions. Not only did they dislike his wage settlement, but they were unhappy with the timing of the redesign of the R-5 (too little, too late) and with his overly ambitious program for internationalization of the firm.

In January 1985, Hanon resigned, following leaked press reports that he was about to be dismissed. The French cabinet approved Georges Besse as the new chairman of Renault on January 25. Besse planned to reduce production from 2 million vehicles to 1.6 million and the work force from ninety-four thousand to seventy-seven thousand by the end of 1985. Besse sold off some of Renault's real estate holdings, including its head office in suburban Paris, to raise cash. In addition, he began to build up the AMC affiliate in the United States so that it could become an important part of Renault's international strategy rather than a fiscal drag. In June, Besse was forced to sell Renault's equity in a subsidiary called Renix, which was a 51-49 joint venture with Bendix Corporation, to Bendix's new parent, Allied Corporation. The reduction of French jobs and production—which were negotiated with and approved by the minister of finance, Pierre Bérégovoy—made Besse very unpopular among the extreme Left, and he was assassinated by terrorists in November 1986. His successor, Raymond Levy, quickly sold Renault's 46 percent share of AMC to Chrysler.

The Chirac government would have liked to privatize Renault, along with the other major firms on its list, but the firm's heavy debt and low profitability through 1986 made that prospect unlikely. Instead, the government proposed to alter its legal status from a *régie nationale* to a regular state enterprise. In 1987, the firm returned to profitability and reduced its debt from 56 billion to 46 billion francs, partly through the

66. Dacier, Levet, and Tourret, *Les dossiers noirs*, p. 233.

sale of AMC to Chrysler. It adopted a just-in-time production system as part of a larger effort to improve its manufacturing processes. But Renault was more vulnerable than ever to work stoppages, and it had lost a good part of its technological thrust by selling its stake in Renix.

The French government played a key role in the postwar development of the auto industry by restricting the inflow of foreign investment and creating a favorable environment for the expansion of the auto firms by its industrial policies in upstream industries. The two main firms, Renault and Peugeot, kept up with international competitors through the early 1970s but then began to face difficulties in matching the product and process technological innovations of the German, Italian, and Japanese firms. Whereas Volkswagen faced the challenge of Japanese production techniques in the mid-1970s, the French firms did not do so until the mid-1980s. The availability of cheap immigrant labor and the success of new models like the R-5 had given French firms the illusion but not the reality of international competitiveness in the 1970s. The resistance of organized labor (both CGT and CFDT and their allies in the Mauroy government) to the modernization of plants and the insulated nature of the French domestic market also worked against the firms.

Although Renault and Peugeot emerged from their financial difficulties in the 1980s, the relative autonomy from the state that they had enjoyed for decades had rapidly eroded. The Fabius government was encouraging the firms to reduce employment and, in the case of Peugeot, productive capacity. For a government that was supposed to promote the interests of the working class, this was a source of confusion and embarrassment. The inability of the Chirac government to privatize Renault and to effect a rapid turnaround in the auto industry was an embarrassment for the Right. The fluctuations in policy from Barre to Mauroy to Fabius to Chirac were not the root causes of the rapid downturn and slow recovery of the French industry, but they contributed to a general environment of uncertainty that made adjustments more difficult.

POLICIES FOR THE SEMICONDUCTOR INDUSTRY

Until 1982 French policy toward semiconductors was subordinated to the promotion of downstream businesses: computers, military electronics, consumer electronics, and telecommunications. Most important for the politics of industrial policy in this area was the French attitude toward the domination of domestic markets by foreign firms:

IBM in computers, International Telephone and Telegraph (ITT) in telecommunications, Texas Instruments and others in semiconductors. French electronics firms developed strengths in some electronics markets. Thomson emerged from a long string of mergers and acquisitions as the most important consumer electronics firm in France and a major player in world markets. After Giscard decided to develop an alternative to ITT for supplying the national telecommunications network, Compagnie Générale d'Electricité (CGE) became a major producer of telecommunications equipment. Thomson and Matra were competitors in markets for military electronics. Bull, a firm much less internationally competitive than Thomson, CGE, and Matra, became a national champion in computers.

These four large firms were bound to play an important role in the state's efforts to increase technological strength in the rest of electronics, especially in semiconductors. Because high state officials did not understand the dynamics of the electronics complex, French government policy often impeded the developments it was supposed to promote. The resulting frustrations led to French support for European cooperative schemes such as the European Strategic Program for Research and Development in Information Technologies (ESPRIT), Research and Development in Advanced Communications Technologies for Europe, and European Research Coordination Agency (EUREKA).[67]

Policies designed to establish a French presence in computers were developed in 1967, the year the Plan Calcul was initiated. Between 1967 and 1970, 91.5 million francs were spent on developing a French semiconductor company. Most of this went to SESCOSEM, a member of the Thomson group of companies, which was formed in 1968 through the state-sponsored merger of SESCO (Thomson) and COSEM (Compagnie Génerale de Télégraphic sans Fil, (CSF).[68] But France did not have a specific program for promoting the semiconductor industry until 1977: the so-called Plan Composants of the Giscard-Barre era. The approximately 400 million francs devoted to Plan Composants between 1978 and 1982 was not close to the amount allocated by the Japanese government (the equivalent of 800 million francs) to the VLSI Project in the same period.[69] In 1982, the Mauroy government made the semiconductor industry a major priority and planned to spend 5.6 billion francs on it—3.4 billion for R&D and 2.2 billion for industrial invest-

67. Wayne Sandholtz, *High-Tech Europe* (Berkeley: University of California Press, 1992).

68. Giovanni Dosi, *Technical Change and Survival: Europe's Semiconductor Industry* (Brighton: Sussex European Research Center, 1981), p. 27.

69. Dacier, Levet, and Tourret, *Les dossiers noirs*, p. 387.

ments. This grandiose scheme had to be abandoned when austerity measures were adopted in 1983.

De Gaulle's Effort to Build a French Computer Industry

At the end of the Algerian war in 1963, de Gaulle launched his "crusade for national independence" through the development of an independent French military capability. In attempting to develop an independent nuclear deterrent, France needed to purchase the most powerful computers then available. Speculation that the U.S. government would block the development of a French nuclear force fueled French desires to promote their own computing capabilities. In fact, the U.S. government did not inhibit sales of computers to France. Research for the French nuclear program was carried out on computers purchased from Control Data by the Société d'Etudes et de mathématiques Appliqués.[70] But the French did not want to remain dependent on the United States as their sole source of advanced computers, especially because at least one French firm was capable of producing such machines, Compagnie des Machines Bull. According to John Zysman, "The notion of national self-sufficiency and technological glory was, by the time the choice was made, an unquestioned value."[71]

Bull was named after Frederik Bull, a Norwegian engineer who invented a method to encode data on punched cards. In 1931, a Swiss company called Egli-Bull was founded in Zurich with Belgian and Swiss capital. Its name was changed to Compagnie des Machines Bull in 1932 and its headquarters moved to Paris. The new French financiers of the company were the Caillies family, owners of paper factories in Aussedat and allies of the Michelin family. By 1963, the firm employed eighteen thousand workers and was producing advanced machines, including the Gamma 60, that were competitive with products sold by firms like IBM. Nevertheless, the main customers of computers in France, the SNCF (the national railroad) and other state agencies, preferred to lease computers from IBM. The first sign that Bull was in trouble came when 650 workers were laid off in July 1963.

Bull Goes to GE

Seeking capital, Bull approached investors in Europe outside France. Because of the involvement of foreign investors, the Ministry of Finance under the command of Valery Giscard d'Estaing refused to

70. Jacques Jublin and Jean Michel Quatrepoint, *French Ordinateurs* (Paris: Alain Moreau, 1976), pp. 17, 28–29.
71. Zysman, *Political Strategies*, p. 74.

authorize the issue of new securities by Bull. The ministry was afraid that this would eventuate in American control of the firm, as in Chrysler's purchase of Simca in 1963.

There was some justification for this fear because Bull had approached General Electric. Joseph Caillies had proposed that GE purchase some equity in Bull (limited to 20 percent) and provide Bull with access to U.S. markets. Under this agreement, Bull would have shared its research results with GE. Giscard, believing that the proposal for a new capitalization of Bull would lead to GE's eventual purchase of a majority share of Bull, pushed for a new agreement under which the French bank Paribas would rescue the company and replace Joseph Caillies with its own manager, Roger Schulz. This agreement was embodied in a protocol signed by the relevant parties on February 15, 1964.

The approval of Bull's smaller shareholders had to be gained. But at a meeting on April 14, 1964, at which the terms of the arrangement were revealed to the shareholders, there appeared to be an escape clause at the end of the text, which said that the government would accept participation by Americans (GE) if all else failed. This produced a furor that eventually spread to the press (with headlines like "The Government Was Fooled," "Bull: Giscard Is Gored," and "General Electric Forced Our General to Retreat") and then to the trade unions. The CGT and the French Communist party demanded the nationalization of Bull.

The deal had to be renegotiated so representatives of GE were asked to return to the bargaining table. A new agreement was signed on July 22, 1964, with a new escape clause: in case of disagreement, any participant could sell or repurchase its share of the firm at a price it designated. Three new societies were formed: the Société Industrielle Bull–General Electric, the Compagnie Bull–General Electric, and the Société de Promotion Commerciale Bull. GE had a majority share in only the second of these, but it acquired control over Bull's commercial network overseas, which accounted for 60 percent of Bull's sales.

Unfortunately for Bull, GE's participation failed to help develop its technological base. One of Bull's midsized systems, the Bull 140, was dropped from the line, and Bull-GE was to distribute the GE 400 model. Because of the rapid success of GE's small computer models, GE 55 and GE 58, Bull-GE was not permitted to develop any small models. After the discontinuation of Bull 140, many of Bull's best engineers defected to CII.[72]

72. Elie Cohen and Michel Bauer, *Les grandes manoeuvres industrielles* (Paris: Pierre Belfond, 1985), p. 38.

The Plan Calcul

Electronics was an important part of the efforts of the Pompidou government after 1965 to create national champions—especially in industries with links to national security concerns. The label given to these efforts was the Plan Calcul. The Plan Calcul was directed by a new government agency (actually a very small office) called the Delegation à l'Informatique. The government tried to create an independent French computer firm through a joint venture called the Compagnie Internationale de l'Informatique. In addition, it facilitated the merger of the two largest producers of electronic components, Thomson-Brandt and CSF, which was officially announced at the end of 1968. These moves were motivated by the desire to build a national presence in electronics, with national security concerns—not international competition—as the main purpose.

The new environment created by the Plan Calcul led to the "nonaggression pact" between Paul Richard of Thomson and Ambroise Roux of CGE in 1969 in which the two firms temporarily called a halt to competition in heavy electrical equipment, telecommunications equipment, and consumer electronics. Thomson's shares in Alsthom (heavy electrical and telecommunications equipment) were transferred to CGE, which transferred its control of Compagnie Continentale Edison (radios and televisions) to Thomson.

CII initially was a joint venture between CSF, CGE, and Schneider. Schneider dropped out soon after the formation of CII, and CSF was replaced by Thomson when they merged in 1968. Thomson and CGE both hoped to diversify into computers and related electronics industries so their mutual suspicion prevented them from fully funding the computer activities of CII. CII was given the task of producing a mainframe computer competitive but not compatible with the computers of IBM, Control Data Corporation (CDC), and Bull- GE for use in French research and development projects. The government heavily subsidized CII's R&D investments and assured that large research computers would be purchased for government laboratories. CII, under the leadership of Jean-Pierre Brulé, pursued its own research agenda, probably too broad and ambitious, to develop a whole line of computers from micros to mainframes. Unfortunately, CII was never given the personnel or financial resources to do this, and it was in financial trouble, despite state subsidies, in a few years.

CII's Merger with Honeywell-Bull and the Failure of Unidata

In 1968, the head of CII, Michel Barré, attempting to free himself from the constraints imposed by the company's French owners, visited the headquarters of Siemens, Philips, Olivetti, and International Computers Limited in search of a European solution to his problems. Barré had sown a seed that was to be harvested five years later. The idea of a European effort in computers caught on when Siemens, which had teamed up earlier with RCA, had to deal with the withdrawal of RCA from the computer business in August 1971. Philips, of the Netherlands, was also looking for European partners so that it could enter the computer business. In the spring of 1970, GE decided to get out of the computer business and sold all its computer facilities, including Bull-GE, to Honeywell. Despite the efforts of Barré of CII to get the government to purchase Bull-GE from Honeywell and to merge CII with Bull-GE, the government permitted the transfer to Honeywell to go through on July 29, 1970.

CII's efforts to become European so as to escape the constraints imposed by its French owners finally culminated in Unidata—a joint venture of CII, Siemens, and Philips that went into effect with the signing of a joint-venture agreement on July 4, 1973. This deal came under fire immediately from CGE and Honeywell-Bull. CGE was concerned that Philips would enter the French minicomputer markets it had begun to develop and that Thomson would acquire entry into French telecommunications markets. Honeywell-Bull perceived the threat to be mainly to its French computer markets. Ambroise Roux of CGE and Jean-Pierre Brulé of Honeywell-Bull worked together to sabotage Unidata by promoting a merger between CII and Honeywell-Bull.

When Giscard d'Estaing took office in 1974, CII and the Delegation à l'Informatique favored the Unidata approach because it avoided a linkage with an American firm, whereas Michel D'Ornano, Giscard's new minister of industry, favored the CII-HB merger because CII would be the weak partner in the Unidata venture and an alliance with an American firm was probably inevitable. Giscard sided with the latter, and it was announced on May 12, 1975, that the CII-HB deal would go through.

The government created a new office called La Mission à l'Informatique to encourage the diffusion of technology created by CII-HB, and it announced 1.2 billion francs in subsidies for the 1976–80 period and 4 billion in guaranteed public procurements. Philips eventually allowed the Unidata arrangement with Siemens to lapse because it felt that it had gained the technological capability to go it alone. Thus was the first attempt to establish an independent European presence in the computer industry abandoned. Philips and Siemens remembered the incident for a long time. It would return to haunt the French when they sought cooperation with the Dutch and the Germans in the late 1980s in the development of new semiconductor technologies.[73]

The Components Plan of 1979

The government was beginning to realize that French computer firms were too dependent on foreign electronic components. CII machines, for example, were designed to use Texas Instruments components. There was no independent French producer of advanced semiconductors and integrated circuits. In 1968, as part of the overall merger deal between Thomson and CSF, the government had sponsored the creation of an independent components firm by means of a merger between their components subsidiaries: SESCO and COSEM. The resulting firm, SESCOSEM, became a second source for Texas Instruments components. In 1970, a new firm, Société pour l'Etude et la Fabrication des Circuits Integrés Speciaux (EFCIS), was created by the government as a 50-50 joint venture between Thomson and the Commissariat à l'Energie Atomique. EFCIS produced components under a licensing arrangement with Motorola.

In 1976, the government tried to arrange a merger between SESCOSEM and Radiotechnique, the French subsidiary of Philips. But Philips rejected this idea, remembering the bad experience with Unidata.[74] Both SESCOSEM and EFCIS remained weak. In 1977, Thomson-CSF purchased SESCOSEM which was on the brink of collapse, having lost $21 million in 1976. Because of the problems of SESCOSEM and the French components industry, the Giscard-Barre government came up with a new plan, the Plan Circuits Intergrés, to run from 1978 to 1983 with a budget of 600 million francs. Under this plan, which was announced by Giscard in September 1979, there was to be a major restructuring of the industry.

Three joint-venture arrangements were made with foreign firms to promote local production of state-of-the-art components: Saint-Gobain and National Semiconductor formed a 51-49 joint venture called Eurotechnique, to produce NMOS (N-channel metal oxide silicon) integrated circuits; Matra (a French arms manufacturer) formed another 51-49 joint venture with Harris to produce CMOS (complementary

73. The description of the Unidata episode in taken mainly from Jublin and Quatrepoint, *French Ordinateurs;* Joseph Grieco, "Technological Knowledge, Rational Exchange, and International Cooperation: The Cases of Airbus Industrie and the Unidata Computer consortium," paper delivered at the annual meeting of the American Political Science Association, Chicago, September 1–4, 1983; Cohen and Bauer, *Les grands manoeuvres,* pp. 40–43; Dacier, Levet, and Tourret, *Les dossiers noirs,* pp. 299–300.
74. Dacier, Levet, and Tourret, *Les dossiers noirs,* p. 386.

metal oxide silicon) products, mostly for telecommunications applications; and Radiotechnique and EFCIS were jointly to produce bipolar integrated circuits for the French market. Despite the neat division of labor between NMOS and CMOS, Matra announced at the beginning of 1981 that it was planning to begin production of NMOS circuits. Eurotechnique responded by announcing its future production of CMOS circuits. This skirmish between the two most important components producers ended went the Left came to power in 1981.[75]

The semiconductor and integrated circuits programs of the French government were administered jointly by the Ministry of Industry, the Direction Générale des Télécommunications (DGT), and the Ministry of Defense. The importance of advanced components for communications and national security interests of the state necessitated this sharing of power. The office in charge of these programs in the Ministry of Industry was the Direction des Industries Electroniques et de l'Informatique. By the mid-1980s, only two French firms were involved in advanced semiconductor devices: Thomson and Matra.

In the production of computers, the struggle between CGE and CII-HB continued. The head of CII-HB, Jean-Pierre Brulé, decided to enter the small business computer market by purchasing the Hermes-Olympia subsidiary of Algemeine Elektricitäts Gesellschaft (AEG). The head of CGE, Ambroise Roux, opposed the purchase and made his wishes known to the directors of Honeywell, who turned down the agreement with AEG. Brulé then opened negotiations to amend the technical agreements with Honeywell, not only because of losing the Hermes-Olympia deal but also because he believed Honeywell had evaded its agreement to share technical data with CII-HB. Ambroise Roux then attempted to discredit Brulé in French official circles and to argue for his dismissal. Brulé tried to convince Giscard that CGE should not be a shareholder of CII-HB and that CII-HB's capital should be reduced by arguing that large firms such as GE and RCA had failed where smaller and more focused firms such as Digital Equipment Corporation and Apple had succeeded. Giscard was not convinced and decided instead to ask Saint Gobain (a manufacturer of glass products with some experience in managing high-technology businesses) to replace CGE as a major shareholder in CII-HB.

Saint Gobain apparently had no intention of investing its own money in the computer business. In April 1980, Saint Gobain purchased a substantial portion of the shares of Olivetti with financial assistance from Carlo de Benedetti (Olivetti's head). This assistance had a price, however, for at the end of April, de Benedetti insisted on receiving a 40

---

75. Ibid., p. 388.

Figure 13. Net income of major French electronics firms

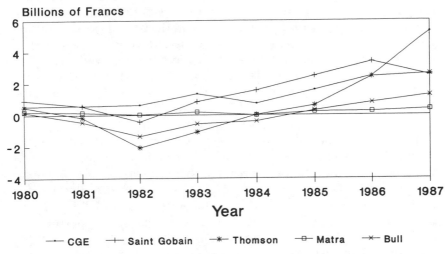

Sources: *French Company Handbook* (Paris: International Business Development SARL, various years); and Reuters Dataline database.

percent share of a new subsidiary of CII-HB called R2E, which would specialize in the production of microcomputers. Olivetti was using Saint Gobain as an entry into the French computer market. Giscard was fully in accord with this scheme and brushed aside objections from Brulé.[76]

The Components Plan of 1982

When the Left took power in 1981, Thomson, Matra, Saint Gobain, CGE, and CII-HB were all nationalized. Saint Gobain was relieved of the responsibility for developing the French computer industry when the state purchased its shares of CII-HB. Jacques Stern was installed as the new head of CII-HB, which was renamed Bull, and Alain Gomez became the new head of Thomson. In 1982, Bull had a net loss of 1.4 billion francs and a consolidated debt of 6.2 billion francs. Stern negotiated distribution agreements with Nippon Electric Company for mainframe computers and with the U.S. firms Ridge and Convergent for minicomputers. Bull returned to profitability in 1985 (see Figure 13).

In July 1982, the state announced the formation of the Programme d'Action Filière Electronique (Action Program for the Electronics Industry) under which 140 billion francs (around $21.3 billion) would be spent over five years to promote the French electronics industry as a

76. Cohen and Bauer, *Les grands manoeuvres*, pp. 48–53.

whole, with 5.6 billion francs going to semiconductors. Designed to match the efforts of Japan in the VLSI Project and the United States in the Very High-Speed Integrated Circuits (VHSIC) Program, the French semiconductor program focused on the fabrication of wafers and the development of VLSI circuits and wafer-scale technology. The last of these was implemented by Thomson in a joint venture with other European firms and Gene Amdahl in a new firm called Trilogy, which ended in failure in 1984. In addition to providing R&D subsidies, the French government reserved DGT and Ministry of Defense procurements of components for French producers.

The new government decided to reallocate responsibilities for semiconductor production among the nationalized firms. Eurotechnique was transferred to Thomson when Saint Gobain was nationalized. Thomson received a large proportion of the 3 billion francs allocated for R&D contracts. National Semiconductor was forced to sell its 49 percent share of Eurotechnique to Thomson so that a new partnership could be formed between Thomson and Motorola. The Matra-Harris venture was shored up by a technology-sharing arrangement with Intel.[77] Thus the two main French semiconductor producers got a new lease on life in certain product lines, notably microprocessors, by state-sponsored alliances with stronger U.S. firms. It is no coincidence that by the early 1980s, the battle in the microprocessor markets was between Motorola (whose 68000 chip was the microprocessor in Apple Computer's Lisa and Macintosh models) and Intel (whose 8086 and 8088 chips were the microprocessors in the first generation of IBM-PCs).

The Thomson-Grundig Deal

Thomson attempted to increase its share of the European consumer electronics market by buying out other EC firms. In 1983, Thomson made a bid for Grundig, a privately owned German firm that controlled 50 percent of the German video and TV market. Thomson had already pruchased three other German firms: Nordmende (TVs), Saba (TVs), and Dual (stereo equipment). The bid created a serious problem for the German government because Grundig had been a major customer of semiconductor components made by Siemens. It was assumed that if Grundig was purchased by Thomson, that firm would supply its semiconductors. The Germans were also concerned that a merger would reduce compitition because Grundig was the largest German consumer electronics firm.

77. Organization of Economic Cooperation and Development, Director for Science, Technology and Industry, "Trade in High-Technology Products: Industrial Structure and Government Policies," Paris, February 2, 1984, second draft, pp. 83–85.

The German government rejected the proposed merger through the Federal Cartel Office (Bundeskartellamt), but not simply to preserve competition. The Germans were concerned about the effect on Siemens and on competition in consumer electronics, but Thomson had gained a reputation in Germany as a "job-killer" because it had rapidly reduced the work force of Saba and Nordmende after purchasing those two firms. In addition, the German government was still angry about the treatment of Siemens in the Unidata incident.[78]

The German government suggested that Thomson make a bid for Telefunken Fernseh und Rundfunk, the consumer electronics division of AEG. Telefunken had been losing money. A 75-25 joint venture called Thomson-Telefunken was created by an agreement signed in March 1983. Thomson agreed to this deal at least partly because one division of Telefunken, Telefunken Electronik, was a joint venture between AEG and United Technologies and the acquisition would enable Thomson to compete with Siemens in the EC market for dynamic memory devices. Thomson paid $28 million for its share of Thomson-Telefunken. Some French sources suggested that the Cartel Office did Thomson a great favor by forcing it to buy a less expensive German firm.[79]

The Battle of Poitiers

In 1982–83, fears about the fate of Thomson caused the so-called Battle of Poitiers. Just before the Christmas buying frenzy in 1982, the French government required that all imported videocassette recorders (VCRs) be shipped to an undermanned customs office in Poitiers, which is in the interior of the country and therefore inconvenient for ocean shipping. In case the Japanese exporting firms failed to get the message, television pictures were broadcast of a lonely agent at Poitiers slowly stamping import documents. Much was made of the symbolism of the move: Poitiers was where the famous French medieval hero Charles Martel had successfully repulsed the Saracens. The Japanese government immediately protested this blatant act of protectionism, but the act was not undone until after the shopping season was over.

France's trade deficit in electronics generally was increasing sharply. Some members of the government were trying to make more concrete their earlier promises concerning the "reconquest of the domestic market." But the government was primarily concerned about the possibly

78. Interview materials; "Auf schlimmes gefasset," *Manager Magazin*, January 1983, pp. 24–27.
79. Interview materials.

disastrous effect of even greater losses at Thomson resulting from intense competition of the Japanese in consumer items like VCRs.

This trade conflict was resolved by a deal between JVC (Japan Victor Corporation, one of Japan's most important VCR producers), Thorn-EMI of Britain, and Thomson by which Thomson would produce VCR subassemblies and eventually entire VCRs in France for the French market. Philips may have felt somewhat miffed by Thomson's turn-around, which may have made the Dutch more amenable to an entente with AT&T and Olivetti. In any case, the French state had once again demonstrated its power, in collaboration with major firms, to win concessions from foreign exporters by threatening to close the domestic market.

Semiconductor Policies after the U-Turn

By 1983–84, the French government and semiconductor industry appeared to realize the need to collaborate with Japanese and U.S. firms. The continued weakness of the French computer industry was underlined in 1984 when Bull and Honeywell-U.S. signed a ten-year agreement with NEC to market Japanese mainframe computers. The trade minister, Edith Cresson, visited Tokyo in the fall of 1984 to urge more Japanese investment in France. Sony had just announced its decision to build a cassette tape factory in Bayonne/Dax. Following Cresson's visit, Pioneer would build stereo equipment in Bordeaux, Clarion in Pompey, and Akai in Honfleur. In addition, Sumitomo Rubber would take over a failing Dunlop-France plant in Montluçon, thereby saving thirty-eight hundred jobs.

Besides demonstrations of continued strength (especially by the CGE) in telecommunications and a more open attitude toward Japanese investment, the French government had some small successes in the field of semiconductors. Thomson signed a contract with IBM to supply IBM-France with 64K DRAMS and 256K DRAMS from its Eurotechnique plant in Rousset. In doubling the capacity of this plant, Thomson got assistance from Oki to help it begin producing five-inch wafers. IBM had previously relied on Siemens as its prime European source of dynamic memories. It switched in 1984 to Thomson and Societá Generale Semiconduttori (SGS) of Italy.

In 1985, Thomson purchased Mostek (of the United States) from United Technologies for $70 million, hoping to use it as a North American base for production of advanced circuits. But Mostek was a sick company when Thomson bought it, and 1985 was a very bad year for the industry. To reduce losses caused by the slump in demand, Thomson sold some of Mostek's production lines to TRW and scheduled some plant shutdowns. After abandoning its unprofitable DRAM markets, Thomson-Mostek diversified into semi-custom circuits such as gate arrays and into microprocessors (Thomson had a second-source agreement with Motorola), microcontrollers, and communications circuits.

Thomson's long-term relationship with Motorola ran into trouble in 1985, when Motorola delayed documentation and tooling for its 68020 microprocessors. Apparently, Motorola had decided to switch to Toshiba as its main second source for the 68020 chip. Thomson sought another partner to help it broaden its line of products and particularly to reduce its dependency on Motorola and brought a 3.2 million franc breach-of-contract suit against Motorola in the French Tribunal of Commerce in May 1987.

Matra

Only one other French semiconductor producer besides Thomson had hopes of becoming internationally competitive in the 1980s—Matra. Matra's joint venture with Harris Corporation, Matra-Harris Semiconductors (MHS), had diversified in 1980 into the production of bipolar integrated circuits from its original focus on CMOS circuitry. MHS later concluded agreements with Intel to produce CMOS versions of Intel's NMOS circuit designs and formed a joint venture with Intel called CIMATEL (Circuits Integrés Matra-Intel) to provide special design and support services for applications of Intel circuits in automotive electronics and telecommunications.

The French government, and particularly the Ministry of Defense, was critical of the partnership between Matra and Intel. At one point, the Ministry of Industry asked Intel to invest $40 million in France as the price of entry into the French market, which Intel refused to do. The ministry of Defense decided that because only 51 percent of Matra had been acquired in the nationalizations of 1982, MHS (51 percent of which was owned by Matra) would not qualify for military procurement and R&D projects.[80] Despite the absence of military sales and R&D, MHS did fairly well through 1975. Sales doubled between 1983 and 1984, and MHS made a profit of 8.4 million francs in 1984 after a loss of 18.9 million francs in 1983.[81]

On January 18, 1988, the Chirac government announced its intention to sell the government's 51 percent stake in Matra, which it had postponed after the stock market crash of October 1987. Matra's 1987

80. Ziegler, "The Hare and the Tortoise Revisited," p. 33.

81. "Le defi français," *Economist*, September 15, 1984, p. 73; and Eugene DiMaria, "Matra-Harris Bringing on 1.6 Micron CMOS Process," *Electronic News*, October 29, 1984, p. 59.

profits moved up to around 200 million francs from 27 million in 1986. Among the core group of the new owners of the firm would be Daimler Benz. In October 1989, the semiconductor subsidiary of AEG, Telefunken Electronik GmbH, replaced Harris as the joint venture partner of MHS.

Thomson's Merger with SGS

On April 29, 1987, Thomson merged its nonmilitary semiconductor business with Italy's SGS Microelettronica by creating a 50-50 joint venture called SGS-Thomson. Together the two firms controlled 3 percent of world semiconductor markets and had around $800 million in annual revenues. The merger made SGS-Thomson the second largest semiconductor firm in Europe, after Siemens, and the twelfth largest in the world. According to Alain Gomez, head of Thomson, the deal was necessary to achieve a "critical mass" in semiconductors.[82]

The SGS-Thomson merger was one of the fruits of a series of efforts to meet competition from outside the EC through cooperation among European firms. Both Thomson and SGS had participated in a variety of ESPRIT projects. In December 1986, they began working together on the development of 4-megabit EPROMs (erasable programmable read only memories) under the EUREKA umbrella. That collaboration had apparently gone well enough to encourage the two firms to merge their activities on a broader front.

ESPRIT, the Mega Project, and JESSI

Thomson became increasingly aware that its strategy of specializing in the production of application-specific integrated circuits was making it vulnerable to competition from firms with a broader technological base in semiconductors. Thomson had to buy all its DRAMs from other firms, and its licensing arrangement for microprocessors had proven to be less permanent than it had hoped. Accordingly, Thomson began to show much greater interest than it had before in cooperating with other large European firms to develop basic semiconductor technologies.

Thomson had participated in a variety of ESPRIT and EUREKA programs, but it had not participated in the effort begun in 1985 to develop 1-megabit DRAMs, the so-called Mega Project, created by Siemens and Philips and co-funded by the German and Dutch governments. There was still some bad feeling left over from the Unidata experiment.

82. "Thomson: A World Force in Electronics," *Fortune*, January 18, 1988, French advertising section, p. 4.

But more important, Thomson did not agree with Siemens and Philips that it was necessary to make massive investments to stay at the technological frontier in semiconductor production. By early 1988, Thomson had asked to become a partner in the Joint European Submicron Silicon Initiative (JESSI). Philips and Siemens objected that Thomson would benefit from the work they had done in the Megaproject through its participation in JESSI without paying for it. Though they were inclined to let Thomson "stew in its own juices," SGS-Thomson was allowed to participate in JESSI in the spirit of European unity.[83]

French industrial policy toward the electronics industry underwent major changes between the beginning of the Plan Calcul in 1965 and the 1980s. Attempts to create a completely independent French computer firm were abandoned when CII was allowed to merge with Honeywell-Bull. With American and Japanese partners (Honeywell and NEC), Bull became a national champion of dubious nationality. National champions also emerged in consumer electronics (Thomson), military electronics (Thomson and Matra), and telecommunications equipment (CGE's Alcatel). The French government played a crucial role in creating market conditions that allowed these firms to grow and prosper. In consumer electronics, unrestricted merger and acquisition activity allowed Thomson to become a giant, not just in France but in all of Europe. Giscard's policy of promoting French telecommunications was the underpinning of the growth of Alcatel. Standard military R&D and procurement policies were behind the military successes of Thomson and Matra.

It was not until 1982 that the French government recognized that weakness in semiconductors was a key problem in building strength in electronics. The Mauroy government tried to build up a semiconductor industry through massive investment of public funds in nationalized electronics firms. That policy had to be abandoned when austerity measures were introduced in 1983. After 1983, government policy combined R&D subsidies, industry restructuring, and the fostering of joint ventures with foreign firms to shore up the strengths and reduce the weaknesses of the national champions. Toward the end of the 1980s, the French government and firms tended to favor ties with the rest of Europe over partnerships with American firms. This decision was brought on by a change in the second-sourcing strategy of the two giants in microprocessing technology: Motorola and Intel. The shift in

83. Guy de Jonquieres, "European Chips Plan Clouded by Siemens, SGS-Thomson Dispute," *Financial Times*, April 5, 1988, p. 1; and interviews conducted by the author in Europe, June 1988.

Motorola's and Intel's strategies was itself brought on by the growing strength of Japanese semiconductor producers.

Of all the French electronics companies, only Thomson and Matra had a chance to be come internationally competitive in semiconductors. Thomson was a much larger firm with a more diversified set of electronics markets and had a better chance than Matra, but both were late, compared to European competitors Philips and Siemens, in recognizing Europe's weakness in basic semiconductor technology. Once Thomson recognized the problem, it enlisted the state to get it into JESSI and other European collaborative R&D efforts.

The results of French efforts to build a semiconductor industry have not been awesome (as were the Japanese), but neither have they been unimpressive. France has a respectable presence in semiconductors, consumer electronics, and telecommunications equipment. Some policies were ill-advised. There has been a tendency toward overconcentration and a failure to encourage small start-up firms. Nevertheless, the basic national champions approach has a flexibility that resulted in limited successes where a more doctrinaire strategy would have failed. The nationalizations of 1982, and by extension the privatizations of 1986–87, were simply an ideological diversion. They did not change the underlying policy of promoting national champions, nor did they alter the crucial role of the state in structuring and restructuring domestic competition.

CONCLUSIONS

France's international competitiveness has been both helped and hurt by its state-societal pattern of strong government, weak business, and weak labor. Strong governments can defend domestic firms against international predation, but they cannot make them internationally competitive. In the absence of strong business, strong governments, especially in smaller countries, may rely on large firms to be national champions. The resulting reduction in domestic competition removes incentives for rapid adoption and diffusion of new technologies.

Government policy toward industries in France has been characterized by centralization of bureaucratic authority (mainly in the Treasury); government control over the allocation of credit; the promotion of large national champion firms; and government control over foreign firms' access to the French domestic market. Obviously, the French government has a great deal of discretionary power in industrial matters.

Because French industrial policy has been made in a centralized and explicit manner, it has been more consistent across sectors than in other industrialized countries, with the possible exception of Japan. But it has been markedly less successful than the Japanese case, mainly because the French were unable to structure domestic markets so as to ensure high levels of domestic competition. France has no *keiretsu* system to guarantee competition in the face of state efforts to limit it. The state has frequently accentuated this problem through its own capital allocation and merger policies.

The dependence of most French firms on the state may have reduced their ability to adapt to changes in international markets. In the steel industry in particular, the state encouraged producers to invest massively at a time of stagnating demand and to delay downstream diversification. In autos, the state has been less obtrusive, at least until the 1970s, when the firms met increased competition from Italian, German, and Japanese producers. The internationalization strategies of Renault and Peugeot put them in a position of less autonomy because they needed to obtain state approval and subsidized loans for foreign acquisitions and direct investments in production. French electronics firms have been strongly dependent on the state both as a source of financing and as a customer for advanced products. Firms like CGE, Thomson, and Saint Gobain occasionally can resist the mandates of the state. But in the long run, all French firms must accommodate themselves to the state's policies.

In all three industries, the weakness of French organized labor and the resulting militancy of unions impeded the adoption and diffusion of new technologies. Fear of political repercussions delayed the closing of obsolete steel plants. Labor militancy slowed the closing of inefficient auto plants and probably delayed adoption of the production methods used successfully in Japan. Labor did not directly determine the fate of the French semiconductor industry but affected it indirectly by slowing down the adoption of microelectronics-based technologies in other industries. The marginalization of the work force results in the continued political weakness of labor and the consequent resistance to innovations at the workplace.

The effects of political changes on industrial policies have been important but have not altered the most essential aspects of state-societal arrangements. The nationalizations of 1982 were in many respects irrelevant because they simply made explicit the tutelary relationship between national champion firms and the state. Once the firms were nationalized, it was easier to transfer public capital into them, which would have been necessary in any case. The privatizations during and after 1986 were possible only because the injection of public capital between 1982 and 1986 allowed the nationalized champions to weather the financial storms of the 1980s. Newly privatized firms quickly resumed their prenationalization tutelary relationship with the state. After 1986, however, the national champions lost some of their national character as the state and the firms turned increasingly toward Japan and the rest of Europe to build France's international competitiveness.

The French case shows somewhat more variation over time than the other four analyzed in this book. The French steel and automobile industries grew rapidly from the early 1950s until the early 1970s. From the late 1970s through the mid-1980s, however, all three industries encountered major difficulties. More recently, the larger French firms in all three industries have shown signs of renewed vitality, albeit in somewhat different markets than the state originally intended. France has done better than both the United States and Britain in meeting the challenges from Japan and Germany because it has a strong state that adapts relatively quickly to changes in international markets. It cannot match the performance of Japan and Germany because it lacks the Japanese *keiretsu* system, which maintains high levels of domestic competition, or the highly skilled work force of Germany, which helps German competitiveness by reducing resistance to the introduction of new technologies.

Four

The United Kingdom

The British approach to industrial policy combines liberal, free market doctrine with poorly executed attempts at state-led and negotiated adjustment within an overall framework of misconceived macroeconomic policies. The steadily increasing weakness of British manufacturing in international competition after World War II is a key to understanding the higher than average level of state intervention even under Conservative governments. Institutions left over from the industrial revolution and the building of an empire are the primary sources of this weakness. The British state is unable to adopt either the Japanese combination of centralized industrial policy making with *keiretsu* competition or the German combination of bank-led industrial policy making with cooperation between business management and a highly skilled work force. Instead, the British have muddled along with halfhearted efforts at both bureaucratic centralization and neocorporatism.

Britain's macroeconomic performance after World War II was unimpressive, to say the least. Average annual growth in real gross domestic product was 2.8 percent between 1954 and the beginning of 1973 but only 1.9 percent from 1973 to 1986. Unemployment rose from 1.4 percent in 1954 to over 11 percent in 1982 and remained in the double digits into the middle and late 1980s. Inflation rose from an annual average of 4.0 percent between 1954 and 1973 to 12.1 percent between 1973 and 1986.[1] Although there was some dampening of inflation rates during the Thatcher administration, unemployment stayed high and growth remained low.

1. Calculations based on statistics reported in *Economic Report of the President* (Washington, D.C.: U.S. Government Printing Office, 1988 and previous years).

The generally ad hoc or reactive nature of industrial policy has made it unable to compensate for a poor macroeconomic environment. Britain's share of world exports of manufactures dropped from 25.5 percent in 1951 to 10.2 percent in 1980. Imports as a percent of domestic demand for manufactured goods rose from 6 percent in 1955 to 21 percent in 1976.[2] British industry has continued its decline in world markets. For example, British Steel Corporation's share of the domestic market dropped from 70 percent in 1971 to 54 percent in 1978.[3] Imports accounted for only 5 percent of domestic consumption of automobiles in 1966 but by 1984 had risen to 57.5 percent.[4] General Electric Company and Ferranti's combined share of the British market for semiconductors declined from 12 percent in 1962 to 7 percent in 1977.[5] The weakness of British manufacturing has made it very difficult for the British economy to generate employment and has reinforced the tendency of consumers to buy more imported goods more during times of economic prosperity, thus accentuating the relationship between economic growth and trade deficits.

As a result, the state became more interventionist than anyone except the most ardent socialists ever intended. Even Prime Minister Margaret Thatcher had to accept the necessity of continuing state intervention in specific industries, despite her belief in the benefits of unregulated competitive markets. The United States of Ronald Reagan and the Britain of Margaret Thatcher have differed in practice, not in mythology. British practice (as distinct from the free market doctrine so dear to Thatcherites) has primarily been the result of the system's belated and mostly ineffectual response to declining international competitiveness.

Key Issues

Britain responded poorly to the challenges of international competition in large part because of institutions and doctrines inherited from the past. David Marquand, for example, points out that in the seventeenth and eighteenth centuries Britain led the world into the industrial age and began to form a global empire:

Having made one cultural revolution in the seventeenth and eighteenth centuries . . . Britain has been unable to make another in the twentieth. In

2. Karel Williams, John Williams, and Dennis Thomas, *Why Are the British Bad at Manufacturing?* (London: Routledge & Kegan Paul, 1983), pp. 116–17, 122–23.
3. Iron and Steel Trades Confederation, *New Deal for Steel* (London, 1980), p. 58.
4. Motor Vehicle Manufacturers Association, *World Motor Vehicle Data* (Detroit, 1986).
5. Giovanni Dosi, *Technical Change and Survival: Europe's Semiconductor Industry* (Brighton, Engl.: Sussex European Research Center, 1981), p. 75.

the age of the industrial laboratory, the chemical plant, and later of the computer, she stuck to the mental furniture of the age of steam. . . . British entrepreneurs failed to compete with the Germans and Americans in the new technologies of the late nineteenth and early twentieth centuries because, in the short term, they could survive and prosper by selling more of their existing products in their traditional markets in Latin America and the colonies.[6]

In the literature on British industrial policy, one of the items under dispute is the degree of continuity or discontinuity in government policies over time. Some scholars argue that a major turning point came in 1979, with the election of Margaret Thatcher. That argument focuses on the irreversibility of the Thatcher government's privatization campaign. Others argue that a more important turning point was in 1972, when the Conservative government of Edward Heath adopted the Industry Act creating new institutions for industrial policy making. Still others stress the underlying continuities that transcended the institutional changes begun in 1972 and 1979. My argument emphasizes the continuities rather than the discontinuities, but I will describe the attempts at institutional changes over time, both successful and unsuccessful as they have affected the instruments available to the state for making industrial policies.

THE INSTITUTIONAL FRAMEWORK FOR BRITISH INDUSTRIAL POLICY

Organization of the State

The British government seems well equipped with formal institutions to create and implement industrial policies, but the power for making economic and industrial policies is widely distributed among conflicting agencies. The most important actors are the prime minister and the cabinet, the chancellor of the exchequer (known as the Treasury), the Department of Trade and Industry, the National Economic Development Council (NEDC) and related agencies, and the British Technology Group (and its predecessors the Industrial Reorganization Corporation and the National Enterprise Board). The Monopolies and Mergers Commission (MMC) is responsible for administering competition law and would, in most other industrial countries, have a strong voice in industrial policy. In Britain, however, competition law is vague and weakly enforced, and the MMC plays a minor role.

6. David Marquand, *The Unprincipled Society: New Demands and Old Politics* (London: Jonathan Cape, 1988), pp. 8–9.

The Prime Minister and the Cabinet

The prime minister, often with the consent and cooperation of the cabinet, sets the overall direction for British government policy. Changes in governments, especially when they involve major shifts in doctrine, tend to result in changes in policies and attempts at institutional change. The most important such changes in government after World War II occurred in 1945, 1951, 1964, and 1979. In 1951 and 1964, Labour governments with a socialist or social democratic program replaced Conservative governments. They used nationalization and direct state intervention to deal with specific industrial crises. They flirted with economic planning but abandoned these experiments because their priorities were elsewhere. In 1951, a Conservative government was elected which reversed some of the perceived excesses of the Labour government elected in 1945, focusing particularly on the nationalization of basic industries. In 1979, a Conservative government came into power determined to undo the interventionist experiments of preceding governments, both Labour and Conservative.

Other than these global changes in policy directions, the prime minister and the cabinet monitor the activities of government agencies. The cabinet makers major decisions on issues that cut across the department boundaries and create differences within the government over the desired direction of policy. Even decisions made within a single agency can come to the cabinet's attention if they raise larger issues of policy and doctrine.

Between 1971 and 1983 the cabinet was assisted by an in-house "think tank" called the Central Policy Review Staff (CPRS), the British equivalent of the domestic policy staff of the president of the United States. The members of the CPRS were "policy intellectuals," most of whom had earned Ph.D.'s from elite universities. The CPRS produced reports on a variety of policy topics, most of them highly controversial, but it was dissolved by Margaret Thatcher in 1983 after producing a particularly insightful piece on the government pensions system.[7]

The Treasury

The Treasury is connected with the Bank of England, making it authoritative on questions of government financing of industrial projects. In the 1975 reorganization of the Treasury, an Industrial Policy Group

7. Tessa Blackstone and William Plowden, *Inside the Think Tank: Advising the Cabinet* (London: Heinemann, 1988); Dennis Kavanagh, *Thatcherism and British Politics: The End of Consensus?* 2d ed. (New York: Oxford University Press, 1990), pp. 252–54; and "Of Policy and Pedigree," *Economist*, May 6, 1989, p. 52.

was formed, headed by the under secretary of treasury. Although this group survived the change in government in 1979, it was not much used by Sir Geoffrey Howe, the first chancellor of the exchequer in the Thatcher administration. Its main function has always been to monitor the expenditures of the Department of Trade and Industry. The Industrial Strategy Staff Group, an interministerial committee, is chaired by the representative from the Treasury and includes representatives of other ministries, the Confederation of British Industries (CBI), the Trades Union Congress (TUC), and the National Economic Development Council. This main function of this group is to discuss the industrial consequences of government regulations.[8]

The Department of Trade and Industry

In 1964, the Labour government created the Department of Economic Affairs with an industrial policy division to formulate the implement a national plan and the Ministry of Technology to deal with what Harold Wilson called the "white heat" of the technological revolution in industry. When the National Plan was abolished in 1966, the Ministry of Technology was upgraded and the Department of Economic Affairs downgraded. In 1969, the Ministry of Technology absorbed the Ministry of Power and took over some of the responsibilities of the Board of Trade. In 1970, the Conservative government merged the Board of Trade and the Ministry of Technology into the Department of Trade and Industry. After the election of 1974, the Wilson government divided the Department of Trade and Industry into the Department of Trade and the Department of Industry. The Thatcher government reunited the two departments in June 1983.

The Department of Trade and Industry is organized primarily along sectoral lines, employing experts in each major branch of industry to monitor developments, to administer aid programs, and to provide the minister with proposals for policy initiatives. It is a highly politicized agency and serves as an important conduit through which the interests of manufacturing firms and unions are passed to the government.[9]

At the peak of British interventionism in the late 1970s, the Department of Industry was responsible for managing the government

8. Wyn Grant, *The Political Economy of Industrial Policy* (Woburn, Mass.: Butterworths, 1982), p. 28. See also Henry Roseveare, *The Treasury: The Evolution of a British Institution* (New York: Columbia University Press, 1969), chap. 9; Hugh Heclo and Aaron Wildavsky, *The Private Government of Public Money* (London: Macmillan, 1974); and Wyn Grant and Shiv Nath, *The Politics of Economic Policymaking* (Oxford: Basil Blackwell, 1984), pp. 26–27.

9. Grant, *Political Economy*, p. 29; and Stephen Wilks, "Liberal State and Party Competition: Britain," in Kenneth H. F. Dyson and Stephen Wilks, eds., *Industrial Crisis: A Comparative Study of State and Industry* (New York: St. Martin's Press, 1983), p. 135.

interests in British Steel, the Post Office (and later British Telecom), British Leyland,[10] Rolls-Royce, British Aerospace, and the National Enterprise Board. It has therefore been the locus of many important industrial policy decisions. Nevertheless, it is generally subordinate to the Department of the Treasury in overall economic policy making and is often challenged and overruled by other agencies. The Conservative government merged the ministries of Industry and Trade in 1983 to give the Department of Industry a broader, and possibly less protectionist, perspective.[11]

The National Economic Development Council

The NEDC was established in 1962, a period of slow economic growth, by the Conservative government. It has a complex organization. The council itself is a broad, overarching body to summarize and reconcile the work of the ten economic development committees and the thirty sector working parties (SWPs) with the help of the secretariatlike National Economic Development Office (NEDO). The SWPS (also called "little Neddies") produce periodic documents summarizing the status of their particular sector and recommending government policies to improve that status. The SWPs represent firms that account for roughly 40 percent of total manufacturing production.[12] At every level of NEDC (except the NEDO), there are representatives of the government, the trade unions, and business management. At the council level, the trade unions are represented by the Trades Union Congress and business by the Confederation of British Industries. These are the most important national union and business organizations. The main animus behind the NEDC-NEDO-SWP complex is the belief that there is a value to getting government representatives, union leaders, and business managers together periodically to exchange views.

Andrew Shonfield believes the government through the NEDC has put itself on a too equal level with management and labor. "It behaved," he said, "as if it were an interest group arguing its case with equal partners who were expected to have other interests." Gerald Dorfman called the NEDC the "institutional re-creation of pluralistic stagnation."[13]

10. British Leyland was renamed the Rover Group in July 1986. To avoid confusion in the text, the firm will be called British Leyland (or BL) throughout this chapter.

11. Grant, *Political Economy*, pp. 31–35.

12. Michael Davenport, "Industrial Policy in the United Kingdom," in F. Gerard Adams and Lawrence R. Klein, eds., *Industrial Policies for Growth and Competitiveness* (Lexington, Mass.: Lexington Books, 1983), p. 341.

13. Andrew Shonfield, *Modern Capitalism: The Changing Balance of Public and Private Power* (New York: Oxford University Press, 1969), pp. 151–52. Dorfman quoted from Stephen Blank, "Britain: The Politics of Foreign Economic Policy, the Domestic Econ-

The NEDC is one of several concertative arrangements set up by the British state to provide access to industrial policy making for labor and management.

As Stephen Wilks argues, "[British] governments in practice have been reluctant to abolish the 'talking shop' of the NEDC, which supplies one of the few arenas for consensus generation."[14] In addition to consensus building, the NEDC provides an alternative way of obtaining information about industries, compared to the more traditional bureaucratic model provided by the Department of Trade and Industry. It is also more suited to industrial lobbying because of the direct role taken by industrial representatives on SWPs and the NEDC itself.

The National Enterprise Board and the British Technology Group

The British Technology Group is the latest in a series of quasi-governmental entities designed by the British government to promote the growth of high-technology concerns. It was preceded by the Industrial Reorganization Corporation (IRC), which was set up in 1966 with an initial capital fund of 150 million pounds. The IRC was active in the 1960s but was abolished by the Conservative government after the 1970 elections in its so-called "u-turn over industrial policy."[15]

In 1975, the Labour government established the National Enterprise Board as a state-owned holding company that would manage state-owned enterprises. Members of the board were to be appointed by the secretary of state for industry, and a chairman and reporting chairman would be selected from the private sector. There were to be eight or nine other members, four of which were to come from the trade unions. The initial borrowing authority of the NEB was 1 billion pounds. The authorizing statute for the NEB was the 1975 Industry Act, which instructed the NEB to promote "industrial democracy" and to achieve a high (15–20 percent) return on its investments. It was not able to do either but focused primarily on promoting the growth of high-technology firms that had difficulty getting private financing. It inherited from the Department of Industry the task of managing the government's interests in British Leyland, which distracted it

---

omy, and the Problem of Pluralistic Stagnation," in Peter Katzenstein, ed., *Between Power and Plenty* (Madison: University of Wisconsin Press, 1978), pp. 98–99.

14. Wilks, "Liberal State," p. 137.

15. Martin Holmes, *Political Pressure and Economic Policy: British Government, 1970–1974* (Woburn, Mass.: Butterworths, 1982), p. 37; Grant, *Political Economy*, pp. 77–78; and John Zysman, *Governments, Markets, and Growth* (Ithaca, N.Y.: Cornell University Press, 1983), pp. 216–17.

somewhat from its other activities. Nevertheless, some of the NEB's firms did well, and it obtained a reasonable return on its investments, considering the atmosphere of recession and decline.[16]

The NEB's initial portfolio included 10.1 percent of the shares of British Leyland (BL), Britain's largest automobile firm, 50 percent of Ferranti, a Scottish electronics firm, and 25 percent of International Computers Limited (ICL). The NEB was responsible for setting up two high-technology firms in the late 1970s: Nexos and Inmos. Nexos was supposed to develop a line of office automation software; Inmos was to develop and produce advanced semiconductor devices. The Labour government also established the Advisory Council for Applied Research and Development (ACARD) to advise the cabinet on policies to promote research and development. One of ACARD's first major recommendations was that decision making regarding information technology be centralized. In 1980, the Thatcher government appointed a minister of state in the Department of Industry to deal with information technology.

The Thatcher government abolished both the IRC and the NEB in 1979 and replaced them with the British Technology Group (BTG). The 1981 Industry Act took management of BL away from the BTG and gave it back to the Department of Industry.[17] The Thatcher government announced a general policy of privatization, which meant selling state-owned shares of private companies. In 1979–80, the government sold 25 percent of the shares of ICL for 37 million pounds. In 1980–81, the government sold 50 percent of the shares of Ferranti for 54 million pounds. In 1987, most of the holdings of the National Enterprise Board had been sold.[18] A new minister for information technology was appointed to supervise government funding of research and development in microelectronics, fiber optics, and information and space technology. The funding for programs in this area increased from 50 million pounds in 1978–79 to 250 million pounds in 1983–84.[19]

The Monopolies and Mergers Commission

In the United Kingdom, as in most other large industrial countries, policies to foster competition are weakly enforced. The Monopolies

16. Grant, *Political Economy*, p. 105; and Michael Parr, "The National Enterprise Board," *National Westminster Bank*, February 1979, p. 55.

17. Grant, *Political Economy*, pp. 109–10.

18. See Yair Aharoni, "The United Kingdom: Transforming Attitudes," in Raymond Vernon, ed., *The Promise of Privatization* (New York: Council on Foreign Relations, 1988); Graham Thompson, *The Conservatives' Economic Policy* (London: Croom Helm, 1986).

19. Peter Hall, *Governing the Economy* (New York: Oxford University Press, 1986), p. 113.

and Mergers Commission is the main responsible agency, but many mergers have been actively promoted by the state (especially in the days of the IRC), and few large mergers have been referred to the MMC for rulings.

The commission was established under the 1948 Monopolies and Restrictive Practices Act. New legislation in 1956 strengthened the commission and established the Restrictive Practice Court. As a result, some preexisting cartel agreements were abandoned, but there was still too much room for anticompetitive practices, and in 1964 the Conservative government issued a White Paper with proposals for controlling mergers. These proposals were later incorporated in the 1965 Monopolies and Mergers Act, which James Fairburn has described as follows: "Mergers, like monopolies, were to be referred to the Commission by the relevant government department, at that time, the Board of Trade. The Commission would then have 6 months, or exceptionally up to 9 months, to ascertain whether the merger proposal would be expected to operate against the public interest, the vague standard set out in 1948. The Act provided the government with the means to halt a merger proposal while the investigation was underway (a provision absent in the preceding White Paper.)"[20]

The public interest criterion for assessing mergers contained from the start the notion that mergers could result in more internationally competitive firms. It was widely agreed that British firms were too small to compete internationally. Indeed, the Industrial Reorganization Corporation was established in 1966 to promote rationalization of British industry by encouraging mergers. The IRC sponsored approximately fifty mergers between 1966 and 1973, including the formation of British Leyland in 1968 and the mergers of General Electric Company (GEC) with Associated Electrical Industries (AEI) in 1967 and with English Electric in 1968. Thus even after attempts to tighten the law regarding competition in 1956 and 1964, it was still subordinated to the general desire to increase the average size of British firms.

Overt official encouragement of mergers ceased when the IRC was disbanded in 1971. For the next ten years merger activity was at a low level. The 1973 Fair Trading Act modified the market share and public interest criteria for competition law and established the Office of Fair Trading to protect consumers against restrictive trading practices. When the merger activity picked up again, however, only about 4 percent of the mergers qualifying under competition law between 1981

20. James A. Fairburn, "The Evolution of Merger Policy in Britain," in James A. Fairburn and John A. Kay, eds., *Mergers and Merger Policy* (Oxford: Oxford University Press, 1989), p. 195.

and 1986 were referred to the MMC, and about half of these cases were abandoned before the process was completed.[21]

Organization of Business

The Confederation of British Industries is the most important business peak association in the United Kingdom. It aggregates the views of industry-specific associations and tends to weigh those of the largest and most profitable firms most strongly. The CBI has traditionally represented the manufacturing industries and not the financial services, which are unusually strong in British politics because of Britain's former role as a key currency country for the world economy. Even though many financial institutions have joined the CBI since the 1970s, the financial firms have many alternative channels for making their views known. Conflicts within the CBI are not normally between manufacturing and services interests but more frequently are internal disputes among the smaller manufacturing firms that are unsatisfied with the dominance of the larger firms in the CBI.[22]

Another important business peak association is the Institute of Directors. Formed in 1906, it currently has around thirty thousand members, most of whom are chairmen or managing directors of companies. The Institute of Directors is the most vocal advocate of free enterprise in Britain because, in contrast to the CBI, it is not constrained by participation in concertative bodies such as the NEDC. The Institute of Directors has a small Policy Unit that maintains close ties with senior civil servants, political advisers in Whitehall, and the Policy Unit in 10 Downing Street (set up by Margaret Thatcher after the closure of the CPRS). The Institute of Directors has recommended reducing expenditures for social programs and lowering taxes.[23]

Britain's merchant banking system has prevented the emergence of bank-manufacturing alliances such as exist in Japan, France, and Germany. The British system lacks the personal contacts, close supervision of financial accounts, large shareholdings in specific firms, and bank memberships on supervisory boards of firms that typify the other three. The Bank of England plays a coordinating role in crises, and, increasingly, large banks such as Barclays and Midland participate in rescue operations as lead banks, but Britain falls far short of the so-called universal banking of Germany.[24]

---

21. Ibid., p. 209.
22. Grant and Nath, *Politics of Economic Policymaking*, p. 22.
23. Kavanagh, *Thatcherism and British Politics*, pp. 91–92.
24. Kenneth H. F. Dyson, "The Politics of Economic Management in West Germany," *West European Politics* 4 (May 1981): 60–61; Zysman, *Governments, Markets, and Growth*, chap. 4.

ORGANIZATION OF LABOR

Labor is relatively powerful in Britain with about the same influence in policy formation and implementation as labor has in Germany. Although union membership as a percentage of employment dropped from 58 percent in 1977 to 51 percent in 1985, most of the losses resulted from high unemployment after 1980, and the unions remained powerful despite losses.[25] The power of unions is expressed not simply at the level of national union leaderships but perhaps more importantly on the factory floor, through the British system of shop stewards. The attempts by the Thatcher government to weaken the shop-floor power of trade unionists have been only partially successful.[26]

The formal organization that aggregates labor interests in the Trades Union Congress, a confederation of 112 unions organized mostly along craft rather than industry lines. Connections between the TUC and the Labour party are close (as in the case of the Deutsche Gewerkschaftsbund and the Social Democratic party in Germany). The Labour party has consistently supported initiatives in the last two decades to institutionalize industrial policy making. In 1980, for example, the TUC–Labour Party Liaison Committee advocated an expanded industrial policy based on a combination of comprehensive planning, an upgraded NEB, establishment of a national investment bank, and greater use of import controls.[27]

Organized labor has lost some of its enthusiasm for such measures in recent years. The extreme weakness of British firms in international competition, combined with a policy of favoring inward foreign direct investment[28] and efforts to build from strength in military-oriented high-technology industries, has resulted in the growth of employment in some nonunionized enclaves (in Scotland and in the South) and in the growing influence of less adversarial unions such as the Electrical, Electronic, Telecommunications, and Plumbing Union. Unions have learned that the old patterns of labor-management relations are not necessarily in the interests of their members, and they have consequently accepted such innovations as more flexible work rules and single-union plants.[29] But trade unionists on the shop floor and in

25. Geoffrey Maynard, *The Economy under Mrs. Thatcher* (London: Basil Blackwell, 1988), p. 125.
26. Hall, *Governing the Economy*, pp. 83 and 132.
27. Ibid., p. 21.
28. Direct foreign investment is the investment of foreign capital directly into plants, facilities, offices, or branches in a host country, as opposed to indirect investment, which involves the purchase of stocks or bonds or the extension of loans through banks and other financial intermediaries.
29. For some concrete evidence, see Kevin Morgan and Andrew Sayer, *Microcircuits of*

national politics still remain more powerful than those in most other industrialized nations.

Business interests are relatively fragmented in Britain. A split between large and small firms in manufacturing and between manufacturing and the increasingly strong services sector accentuates the divisive tendencies of British business. In marked contrast, labor presents a relatively unified and powerful voice in British politics. Because labor is powerful, the state organization incorporates labor views in economic and industrial policy making but is insulated from too much labor influence in other areas (especially macroeconomic and trade policy). Business and labor interests have a great deal of control over the British state, and it has less autonomy vis-à-vis major social forces than the states of other major industrialized nations. Even though the British state is relatively fragmented in comparison with more centralized and powerful states such as those in France and Japan, it has important instruments of power vis-à-vis other social actors. Direct state intervention in the economy through nationalizations and state subsidies increased rapidly in the 1970s, followed by a major reversal of this trend after 1979. To extricate the state from direct intervention in the economy, the Thatcher administration had to increase its power in other areas, often against the wishes of both business and labor interests.

Policies for Steel

British steel policies must be viewed in light of the general global overcapacity in steel production. Like many other countries, Britain's steelmaking capacity shrank, especially in the late 1970s and early 1980s, because of the recession, the decline in the demand for steel exports, and the reduced use of steel in manufacturing generally. The British steel industry in the middle and late 1970s was a greater disaster than that of other countries because a major push to increase capacity occurred just when demand took a downturn. British policies of the 1980s were much more realistic and effective than those of the 1970s. The overall story is one of painful learning.[30]

Trouble in the British steel industry began immediately after World War II. British steel plants had done yeoman service during the war,

---

Capital: "Sunrise" Industry and Uneven Development (Boulder, Colo.: Westview Press, 1988), esp. chaps. 8–13.

30. For another version of this story, see Heidrun Abromeit, *British Steel: An Industry between the State and the Private Sector* (New York: St. Martin's Press, 1986).

but they were increasingly becoming obsolete. Britain had a large number of relatively small steel firms, most with very old plants. The macroeconomic policies of British postwar governments in maintaining a high value of sterling relative to other currencies made British exports, less competitive, and the steel industry suffered with all the others. In addition, the management of the British steel industry was too conservative in adopting new technologies. When the Japanese and German steel industries were rapidly adopting new technologies, particularly basic oxygen furnaces and continuous casting, the British (like the Americans) stuck with open-hearth furnaces and delayed installation of continuous casters.[31]

Nationalization of the Steel Industry

Leftists in the Labour party considered the steel industry a key in socializing the economy. They nationalized the industry in 1950, but the Tories denationalized it in 1953. This early attempt must have discouraged private investment in the industry. After fourteen years of sluggish performance, the Labour government renationalized the industry in 1967, when Labour finally regained a majority in the House of Commons. Fourteen of the largest bulk steel producers were consolidated into a state enterprise called British Steel Corporation (BSC), which controlled 92 percent of British steel production and was at the time the third largest producer of steel in the world (by weight). BSC employed 270,000 people and produced 23.3 million tons of steel in its first year of operation.[32] There remained 210 private steel firms in the domestic market, most of which were quite small. Only two relatively large firms were left to compete with BSC: Guest, Keen, and Nettlefolds Ltd. and Johnson Firth Brown.[33]

In 1967, BSC used open-hearth furnaces to produce 57 percent of its raw steel (a high percentage compared to Germany and Japan but not too different from the United States). Subsidization of the industry began in earnest in 1968. BSC had inherited plants on more than sixty major sites. Many of these plants were in bad shape. Nevertheless, the first financial task was to pay for the nationalization. The BSC owed the former shareholders around 1.2 billion pounds. The British government helped to pay this debt by passing the 1969 Iron and Steel

31. See Jonathan Aylen, "Plant Size and Efficiency in the Steel Industry: An International Comparison," *National Institute Economic Review*, no. 100 (May 1982): 209–10.

32. Ibid., p. 73; Robert Lubar, "An American Leads British Steel Back from the Brink," *Fortune*, September 21, 1981, p. 89; and Anthony Cockerill, "Steel and the State in Great Britain," *Annalen der Gemeinwirtschaft* 49 (October–December 1980): 447.

33. Jonathan Aylen, "Innovation in the British Steel Industry," in Keith Pavitt, ed., *Technical Innovation and British Economic Performance* (London: Macmillan, 1980), p. 201.

Act, which wrote off some of BSC's debts and made up the difference with public revenue in the form of government loans. Subsidies subsequently took the form of a policy of forgiveness in repaying the dividends for those loans (called public dividend capital).

New Investments Create Overcapacity

In 1970, the newly elected Conservative government contemplated splitting BSC into two smaller firms but decided instead to undertake a careful study of the industry and BSC's prospects. This study resulted in a White Paper published in 1973, calling for a ten-year development strategy for steel. A 3-billion-pound expansion program was suggested to modernize old plants and construct five new modern facilities to raise steelmaking capacity to 30 million tons per year (about double the current level). All these facilities would use basic-oxygen processing. The Department of Trade and Industry staff recommended the expansion plan in the belief that demand for steel both domestically and in export markets was rising rapidly and that BSC had an excellent opportunity to profit from that increasing demand if it modernized and augmented its productive capacity.[34] Although BSC's profits had been low, the staff thought its early problems were more a result of price controls imposed by the Iron and Steel Board than of inherent deficiencies in the firm.

In retrospect, the stupidity of this plan is crystal clear. Yet the early 1970s were a time of economic boom and shortages of raw materials. When demand for steel slumped after the 1973 Organization of Petroleum Exporting Countries (OPEC) price increases (in the United Kingdom, demand dropped from 19.5 million tons in 1973–74 to 15 million tons in 1947–75), the foolishness of expansion become evident and the newly elected Labour government scaled it back. Unfortunately, the damage had already been done. BSC had begun to build major facilities at Scunthorpe and Lackenby in England, Ravenscraig in Scotland, and Llanwern and Port Talbot in South Wales. Once begun, this construction was hard to stop because important political constituencies for both parties had to be satisfied and the threat of devolution of Scotland and Wales was constantly in the minds of British leaders.

Because some of the new plants were on the coast, Britain could become less reliant on domestic ores and coking coals, which were more expensive than imports and of inferior quality. With the new facilities

---

34. Josef Esser, "Sozialisierung als beschäftigungspolitisches Instrument? Ehrfahrungen mit der verstaatlichen Stahlindustrie in Europa," *Gewerkschaftliche Monatshefte* 31 (July 1980): 448–51; Grant, *Political Economy,* p. 93; and Aylen, "Plant Size," p. 74.

Figure 14. Profits and losses of British Steel Corporation

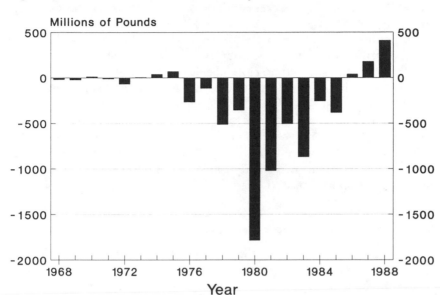

Millions of Pounds

Year

Sources: Iron and Steel Trades Confederation, *New Deal for Steel* (London: Iron and Steel Trades Confederation, 1980), p. 26; Keith Ovenden, *The Politics of Steel* (London: Macmillan, 1978), p. 170; and Anthony Cockerill, "Steel," in Peter Johnson, ed., *The Structure of British Industry,* 2d ed. (London: Unwin Hyman, 1988), p. 84.

BSC should have been able to take advantage of the economies of scale available to plants using the basic-oxygen process, but for political reasons, these plants were scaled down so they were too small to realize economies of scale. Nevertheless, the new plants were sure to result in greater productivity, lower energy costs, and more internationally competitive production.

Unfortunately, the stagnation of both domestic and export markets resulted in political pressure to keep the older and less efficient plants open, thus forcing the new plants to operate unprofitably at low levels of capacity. The older plants, of course, should have shut down, but it was politically difficult to do that because the entire effort had been originally sold as an expansion of capacity rather than a modernization of existing capacity. The unions opposed closing older plants, as did the communities in which they were located. Fourteen ministers in the Labour cabinet in 1976 represented constituencies threatened by plant closures.[35] BSC experienced heavy losses from 1975 through 1985 (see Figure 14). The share of imports in the British market in-

35. Aylen, "Plant Size," p. 227.

creased from 5 percent in 1970–71 to 20 percent in 1977–78. BSC's share of the domestic market declined from 70 to 55 percent during the same period.[36]

Government subsidies to BSC increased rapidly so that the firm could continue to meet its loan obligations. In 1977, BSC's chairman, Sir Charles Villiers, began to close obsolete plants and reduce capacity, but the firm still suffered large losses. In 1978, the minister of industry, Eric Varley, published a White Paper, *The Road to Viability*, which recommended that BSC make drastic cuts in investment and production.[37] Although the Labour government rejected these recommendations, BSC's work force was reduced by forty-four thousand between 1974 and 1979. BSC was near bankruptcy by the time the Thatcher government came to power in mid 1979.

The Thatcher Government Reduces Capacity

In June 1980, Sir Charles Villiers wrote to the minister of industry, Sir Keith Joseph, requesting an additional subsidy for BSC of 400 million pounds for the 1980–81 fiscal year. The disaster at BSC had been compounded by a major strike. Without the subsidy, the alternative, according to Villiers, was liquidation. Immediately after the strike was settled, the Thatcher government recruited Ian MacGregor, a partner of the firm of Lazard Freres in New York, to replace Villiers as the chairman of BSC. Despite the minister of industry's ideological objections to such a bailout, the subsidy request was granted in September 1980, followed by an additional 110 million pounds in November. Sir Keith Joseph must have felt that the new chairman would have to take a firmer position.

As soon as he took over in July 1980, MacGregor recommended further reducing the work force by 20,000 and reducing production by six hundred thousand tons per year.[38] At that point, BSC was losing about $4 million a day. Between January 1980 and May 1981, the work force was reduced by 62,000. MacGregor continued or accelerated reductions planned by Villiers. Between 1977 and 1981, fifteen midsize steelworks were closed, as were thirty-one of the forty-nine blast furnaces in the public sector.[39] The work force was eventually halved from 160,000 in 1980 to around 80,000 in 1981. The combination of layoffs and plant closings drastically increased the productivity of the remaining operations. BSC continued to sustain losses, but these too were reduced.

36. Iron and Steel Trades Confederation, *New Deal for Steel*, pp. 26 and 58.
37. Eric Varley, *The Road to Viability* (London: Her Majesty's Stationary Office, 1978).
38. Grant, *Political Economy*, pp. 93–94.
39. Aylen, "Innovation," pp. 68–69.

Furthermore, the 1981 Iron and Steel Act provided for a write-off of 3.5 billion pounds of BSC capital with a reserve of 1 billion for future purposes deemed fit by the chairman. MacGregor asserted that it would be possible to maintain production capacity at around 14.4 million tons, but there was some concern that low operating levels at the Ravenscraig plant would eventually lead to its closure.

The 1982 recession produced further losses for BSC, and the Labour party began to criticize the policies of MacGregor and the Thatcher government. One issue was that Lazard Freres was receiving compensation for MacGregor's services while he was on loan to BSC ($1.2 million as of July 1980, further payments depending on the length of employment, with a ceiling of $3.3 million).[40] Government subsidies rose again in fiscal 1983 to $871 million from $497 million the year before.[41] When it was announced that MacGregor would retire as BSC chairman in August 1983 to run the National Coal Board, the head of the British Mineworkers, Arthur Scargill, called him "the American butcher of British industry" and "a hatchet man." Nigel Lawson, chancellor of the exchequer, said that "hatchet men are a great deal cheaper than this." MacGregor himself said that he was not a "butcher" but "a plastic surgeon trying to redeem the features of aged properties which need some kind of face lift."[42]

Another tempest brewed when Ian MacGregor announced in April 1983 that BSC and U.S. Steel were contemplating an arrangement whereby BSC would sell U.S. Steel slabs made at the Ravenscraig plant in exchange for a $100 million investment by BSC in U.S. Steel's plant in Fairless, Pennsylvania. This move simultaneously angered the United Steelworkers, who objected to a concessionary wage arrangement that would have been part of the deal; Americans who were critical of subsidization of the British steel industry, including most of the Reagan administration; the Commission of the European Community, which saw the deal as possibly unraveling a larger deal made between the United States and Europe limiting European steel exports to the United States; and British citizens who were outraged by the spectacle of BSC making direct foreign investments in the United States with money that was largely a government subsidy. The economics of this deal looked good; the politics stank.[43]

40. Lubar, "An American," p. 88.

41. "British Steel Says Rivals Also Seek U.S. Steel Pact," *Wall Street Journal*, March 29, 1983, p. 3.

42. The quotes are from Robert L. Muller, "Britain Names Ian MacGregor Coal Board Chief," *Wall Street Journal*, April 6, 1983, p. 2.

43. Frederick Kempe and Thomas F. O'Boyle, "British Steel Says It May End Some Subsidies," *Wall Street Journal*, April 6, 1983, p. 2.

Previous governments had avoided adjustment because they were not sure it was necessary. The Thatcher government pursued a policy that shifted most of the adjustment costs onto the workers, although it retained some elements of the earlier approach. In March 1982, it announced that it had instructed BSC to keep all five of its integrated plants open for the next three years even though it had not allocated sufficient funds for this purpose.[44] When an attempt was made by BSC's management to close the Ravenscraig plant in the summer of 1983, before the elections, the government blocked it so as not to arouse discontent on the part of the Scottish nationalists.

British Steel Finally Turns Around

Eventually, the changes implemented by Ian MacGregor and his successor, Sir Robert Scholey, worked, and by 1986, BSC was again making profits. By 1988, profits rose to a respectable 410 million pounds. The work force was reduced from 180,000 in 1976 to 52,000 in 1988. The number of plants was reduced from thirty-two to five. Extensive investments were made in continuous-casting technology. The proportion of production that was continuously cast rose from 22 percent in 1981 to 82 percent by the end of 1988. Average per ton production costs by mid-1988 were around $415—less than the comparable cost in all the major industrialized countries and some newly industrialized countries. The number of man-hours required to make a ton of steel dropped from fourteen in 1982 to six in 1988. BSC's product mix was adjusted in the direction of higher value-added products such as coated steels and galvanized steel. Managers introduced new computer systems for communicating with major customers, and the firm began to look like a model for others in providing rapid service to customers.[45] BSC was privatized in December 1988, earlier than planned, thanks to its return to profitability.

British policies toward the steel industry have undergone dramatic changes since World War II and especially since 1979. BSC was nationalized twice and privatized twice, in 1953 and 1988. New steelmaking technologies such as basic-oxygen processing and continuous casting came very late to Britain. Inefficient and obsolete plants were closed

44. J. J. Richardson and G. F. Dudley, "Steel Policy in the UK: The Politics of Industrial Decline" (manuscript, Florence, Italy: European University Institute 1984).

45. Nick Garnett, "Roller Coaster Rider: Nick Garnett Talks to Sir Robert Scholey about the Revival of British Steel," *Financial Times*, October 22, 1988, p. 9; Steve Lohr, "A Case Study in Thatcherism," *New York Times*, December 5, 1988, p. C1; and "British Steel: Showing Its Mettle," *Economist*, July 2, 1988, p. 59.

too slowly. When these changes finally were made, they had a very salubrious effect on profits. But by that time the industry had shrunk substantially. Revenues remained almost flat during the 1980s, and about one hundred thousand workers lost their jobs. Approximately 8 billion pounds of public money were injected into the firm in the process of its revitalization. Such a performance is not consistent with the definition of increased international competitiveness provided in Chapter 1.

The declining international competitiveness of the British steel industry results from the pattern of state-societal arrangements in Britain: weak state, weak business, and strong labor. The state apparently was unable to speed the adoption and diffusion of new technologies even after the industry was nationalized. New BSC plants with basic-oxygen furnaces built in the 1970s could not be on a large enough scale because the state had to worry about the political repercussions of closing older facilities. Steel entrepreneurs lost considerable power after the nationalization of 1967, but they did not seem to have been particularly influential before then. Labor, in contrast, was able to block the closing of old factories and slow the introduction of new technologies.

POLICIES TOWARD THE AUTO INDUSTRY

The British auto industry grew up in the 1920s and 1930s under an imposing set of tariff barriers but with no restrictions on foreign direct investment. The two American giants, General Motors and Ford, began to manufacture in Britain in the 1920s. GM purchased Vauxhall in 1925. Ford's large plant at Dagenham was constructed in 1931.[46] In 1945, foreign exchange restrictions limited the ability of British firms to set up their own overseas manufacturing facilities. Thus, at that crucial time, they were imperfectly sheltered at home and effectively prevented from internationalizing. As a consequence, a large number of small British manufacturers became victims of later waves of internationalization and scale economizing in the global auto industry.

The first glimmering of what was to come was the merger of Austin and Morris in 1952 into the British Motor Corporation (BMC), prompted by increasing competition from Ford. Because of less than alert management, however, opportunities to rationalize production were overlooked, and the firm continued to produce in a wide variety of small and inefficient plants. The Austin Mini, Austin's innovative

46. For a detailed history of Ford in Britain, see Simon Reich, *The Fruits of Fascism: Postwar Prosperity in Historical Perspective* (Ithaca, N.Y.: Cornell University Press, 1990), chap. 3.

front-wheel-drive vehicle, was introduced in the late 1950s and was a technical but not a financial success. The larger domestic firms were barely able to hold on to their shares of the market, but profit margins deteriorated steadily. According to Peter Dunnett: "The boom of the early sixties created an overexpansion of the motor industry without a rationalization of industrial structure. This was particularly harmful for the UK motor industry in that, by 1965, the European motor industry experienced overcapacity, so intensifying international competition. The failure to rationalize meant that between 1965 and 1969 the UK motor industry consisted of manufacturers who were too small and failed to exploit potential economies of scales."[47] In addition, the government used the auto industry in the 1950s and early 1960s as a weapon in its fight against regional concentration of industry, encouraging the building of small and inefficient manufacturing facilities in underindustrialized areas.[48]

In 1965, BMC purchased Pressed Steel, the only large independent supplier of auto bodies in Britain. Smaller firms such as Rover and Jaguar realized that they would have to cooperate with BMC or other large firms if they were to survive. Leyland purchased Rover at the end of 1965, and BMC and Jaguar formed a joint venture called British Motor Holdings (BMH), which left Jaguar with considerable autonomy but guaranteed access to BMC's auto bodies. Thus by the end of 1965, there were only two major British-owned firms or groups, Leyland and BMH.

During the recession of 1967, the financial weaknesses of Standard-Triumph became apparent, and it was taken over by Leyland. Chrysler purchased 70 percent of the shares of Rootes in 1967, with the permission of the British government, and renamed it Chrysler-UK. The British government, through the IRC, purchased 15 percent of the shares of Rootes as part of the Chrysler deal. The remaining 15 percent was held by others. The Labour government approved the purchases because Rootes would have had to close if there had been no buyer, and only Chrysler, desperate for an outlet in Europe, was willing to purchase the firm. Chrysler bought all the outstanding shares in Chrysler-UK in 1973. (Ford had purchased 100 percent of Ford-UK in 1960.)

The Formation of British Leyland

In 1968, the continuing weaknesses of Leyland and BMC led the government to encourage them to merge to form the British Leyland

47. Peter J. S. Dunnett, *The Decline of the British Motor Industry* (London: Croom Helm, 1980), pp. 94–95.
48. Daniel T. Jones, *Maturity and Crisis in the European Car Industry* (Brighton, Eng.: Sussex European Research Center, 1981), p. 108; and Wilks, "Liberal State," p. 142.

Motor Company (BL). The IRC provided 25 million pounds in loans for retooling as an incentive. The traditionally independent-minded management of the auto firms was upset about this injection of government capital, and several executives resigned, but the head of Leyland, Don Stokes, was amenable to the arrangement and was rewarded by the Labour government with the deputy chairmanship of the IRC in 1969. British Leyland was thus freed from close supervision and scrutiny by the IRC.

In 1968, British Leyland was a very large firm. Its $1.9 billion in sales compared favorably with those of Volkswagen ($2.5 billion) and Fiat ($1.7 billion). But it was building too many models, and its output was low for the number of workers employed, 185,000. The same number of workers at Chrysler-U.S. produced $5.7 billion in sales. It has been suggested that the earlier mergers were partly to blame, that is, that Morris injected inefficiency into Austin in 1952 and BMC did the same to Leyland in 1968.[49]

The early 1970s were boom years for British Leyland and a period of relative nonintervention by the Tory government. This idyll was ended by two unforeseen catastrophes. BL decided to make a major investment (500 million pounds) to increase capacity in 1973, just before the OPEC-induced recession. In March 1974, Anthony Wedgewood-Benn became minister of industry. Because of BL's difficulties during this period the Ministry of Industry began discussions with Chrysler-UK about a merger between BL and Chrysler.[50] After the passage of the 1973 Industry Act, one of the first industries to receive financial assistance from the NEB was British Leyland. One of the first to be denied was Chrysler-UK.

Don Ryder, the first director of the NEB, issued a report in 1975 arguing that the government should be willing to provide BL with 2.8 billion pounds over eight years. The argument was premised on BL's remaining a mass producer of automobiles, which required both a rationalization of existing facilities and an expansion of capacity. According to John Barber, deputy chairman and managing director of BL, the firm did "not have the volume to compete with the real giants in the cheap end of the market." Harold Wilson agreed, accepted the Ryder report, stated: "The Government have decided that Britain must remain in the world league so far as a British-owned automobile industry is concerned."[51] In this way, BL became a state enterprise.

49. Dunnett, *Decline*, p. 101.
50. Wilks, "Liberal State," pp. 143–46.
51. Dunnett, *Decline*, p. 169; and George Maxcy, *The Multinational Motor Industry* (London: Croom Helm, 1981), pp. 228, 220.

Shortly after the Ryder report was issued and accepted, the Central Policy Review Staff published its own report on the auto industry, suggesting that British auto manufacturers needed to form linkages with other European firms to meet the challenges of international competition. The CPRS emphasized the difficulties created by having too many models and too many plants but pointed out that increasing production of fewer models would not solve the problems of British firms. Production needed to be increased to realize economies of scale but not by excessively reducing the number of models offered for sale (the CPRS correctly perceived the problems of Volkswagen). The CPRS report had a particularly important influence on later government policies toward Chrysler.

The Collapse of Chrysler-UK

Another important event in 1975 was the near collapse of Chrysler-UK. The crisis built for a long time, but the precipitating event was a message sent in October from the chairman of Chrysler-U.S., John Riccardo, to the British government announcing that Chrysler "would start liquidating Chrysler (UK) from the end of November . . . unless Her Majesty's government in the meantime took it over."[52] Chrysler-UK lost $35 million in 1974 and $71 million in 1975. Neither the NEB nor BL was interested in purchasing Chrysler-UK, and the Ministry of Industry initially favored liquidation if combined with important controls. The cabinet objected to import controls, and the Scottish Office strongly opposed the closing of the main Chrysler plant at Linwood. Concern over Scottish nationalism, the threat of devolution, and the threat to arms sales to Iran (Chrysler-UK had just completed an assembly plant there) led the cabinet to rescue Chrysler-UK with a 72.5-million-pound loan and 90 million pounds in loan guarantees.

In 1977, Chrysler-UK was taken over by Peugeot. Following the suggestions in the CPRS report of 1975, the government first promoted greater integration between Chrysler-UK and Chrysler-Europe (especially Chrysler-France). When Peugeot purchased Chrysler's European interests in 1977, the British government made no objection to the inclusion of Chrysler-UK. The Linwood plant, never cost-efficient since its construction in 1960–62 at the insistence of the Board of Trade, closed forever in June 1981, displacing five thousand workers (a

---

52. Michael Moritz and Barrett Seaman, *Going for Broke: The Chrysler Story* (New York: Doubleday, 1981), p. 187.

Figure 15. Profits and losses of British Leyland

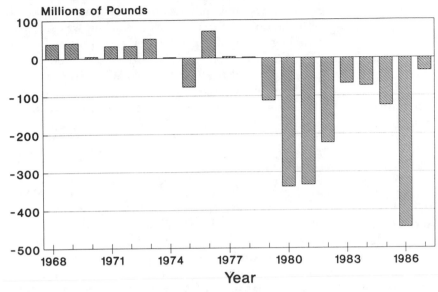

Sources: British Leyland annual reports, 1968–86; and Reuters Dataline database.

shadow of the original work force). Chrysler-Europe became Talbot under the direction of Peugeot. In 1982–83, Talbot-UK received 50 million pounds in loans from the British government.[53]

Continued Weakness at British Leyland

In 1975, BL experienced its first net loss since 1968 (Figure 15). Its share of the British market had declined rapidly. In 1968, it controlled 40.6 percent of the domestic market, in 1973, only 31.9 percent.[54] In the words of Peter Dunnett: "By 1979, Ford (UK), Vauxhall, and Chrysler (UK) had all become very much integrated into the European motor industry—a development encouraged by the Chrysler (UK) bail-out—whilst BL had become a secondary junior league producer."[55]

Don Stokes, the managing director of BL, was not a forceful individual and was replaced in late 1977 by Michael Edwardes, who immediately asked and received support for a major reduction in the size of the work force, the number of plants, and the degree of centralization

53. Wilks, "Liberal State," p. 147.
54. Maxcy, *Multinational Motor Industry*, p. 221.
55. Dunnett, *Decline*, p. 169.

of the firm's management. He also won greater managerial independence from the NEB and implemented a new policy of establishing performance targets for divisional managers. He began a round of tough bargaining with the unions for wage restraints and was successful, especially after the beginning of the Thatcher government, in getting a series of wage-restraint agreements.[56] In 1979, BL made a deal with Honda to co-produce a midsized car that would be sold in both Europe and Japan. This car would have a Honda engine, gearbox, and transmission with a BL body and other components. That same year, the government increased the flow of funds to BL to 1.205 billion pounds.

The Thatcher Government's Auto Policies

The Tories' electoral promise in 1979 to continue aiding BL helped them win in such important constituencies as Birmingham, Oxford, and Coventry. After the election, they still expressed willingness to support BL. In January 1981, Sir Keith Joseph announced that BL would receive 990 million pounds in aid to help launch a new model called the Minimetro. In addition the 1981 Industry Act increased the borrowing limit of the Department of Industry to cover its lending needs to BL after responsibility for BL was transferred from the NEB to the Department of Industry.[57]

Michael Edwardes took advantage of the political climate created by Margaret Thatcher's electoral victory by threatening to close plants—a threat that was intended to help push through reforms in work rules and to reduce the power of shop stewards. A corporate recovery program was presented to the government in July 1979, and the work force voted on it that autumn. The goal was to return BL to profitability by 1982 by introducing new models, automating production extensively, reducing overmanning, and reducing production by closing some of the smaller and more inefficient plants. Michael Edwardes described the last item as "shrinking the business to a level beyond which we believed it was not safe to go."[58]

A Triumph plant in Liverpool with the capacity to produce 100,000 cars annually was closed in 1978. Triumph's final assembly plant at Coventry was closed in 1980, and the decision was made to close an Austin-Morris assembly plant in Belgium as well. In 1981, Rover's recently built car plant at Solihull (Birmingham), with a capacity of 150,000 cars, was also closed. BL's final assembly operations, with the

56. Jones, *Maturity and Crisis*, pp. 48–49.
57. Grant, *Political Economy*, pp. 109–10.
58. Michael Edwardes, *Back from the Brink: An Apocalyptic Experience* (London: Collins, 1983), p. 95.

exception of the Jaguar plant in Coventry, were concentrated in two central plants: the old BMC factories at Longbridge (Birmingham) and at Cowley (Oxford). Rover production was transferred from Solihull to Cowley.[59]

The company decided to develop a compact model range centered on three new models: the Metro, the Maestro, and the Montego. All three were successfully introduced by 1984. The earlier cooperative arrangements with Honda were continued, and a new Rover model, the Rover 800, was introduced in the summer of 1986. British Leyland was renamed the Rover Group in July 1986.

The plants at Cowley and Longbridge were extensively retooled. The company spent 300 million pounds for two automated body lines used to produce the high-volume compact models. Sales were disappointing, however, and financial results remained poor through 1987 (see Figure 15).[60]

In July 1988, the Rover Group was sold to British Aerospace for 150 million pounds. The government contributed 550 million pounds in cash to retire the firm's debts. A week later, Graham Day, chairman and chief executive of the Rover Group, announced plans to close plants at Cowley South and Llanelli, reducing the work force by thirty-four hundred. British Aerospace netted around 45 million pounds from the sale of the property at Cowley and Llanelli. The closing and selling of these plants were loudly criticized by the Labour party, and British Aerospace was accused of "asset stripping."[61] The Rover Group returned a small profit in the first half of 1988 after a decade of annual losses.

British industrial policy in autos, as in steel, has been highly constrained by the weakness of the country's domestic firms. The government, including that of Margaret Thatcher, intervened extensively from the formation of British Leyland in 1968 up to the sale of the Rover Group to British Aerospace in 1988. A total of 3.5 billion pounds in state aid was pumped into the firm between 1979 and 1988. The political and economic necessity for state intervention bridged the ideological chasms separating the Labour government of Harold Wilson and the Conservative government of Margaret Thatcher. But the firm's problems remained unsolved despite large government subsidies, extensive efforts on the part of management to introduce new product and process technologies, and a major contraction of both pro-

59. Williams, Williams, and Thomas, *Why Are the British Bad at Manufacturing?* p. 262.
60. Karel Williams, John Williams, and Colin Haslam, *The Breakdown of Austin Rover: A Case-Study in the Failure of Business Strategy and Industrial Policy* (Leamington Spa: Berg, 1987), pp. 5–11.
61. "BAe Could Raise £560M by Property Sell-Offs," *Financial Times*, November 29, 1988, p. 18.

duction and the work force. British Leyland remained unprofitable. The necessary measures were taken too late and did not go far enough to meet the heavy competition from foreign firms.

One of the important consequences of the failure of government's policies concerning automobiles was that American and Japanese multinational auto firms became increasingly important in the British economy. The share of Ford-UK in the British market increased from 27.3 percent in 1968 to 30.7 percent in 1980; the share of British Leyland declined from 40.6 percent to 18.2 percent during the same period.[62] Japanese firms such as Honda and Nissan established an important presence in Britain—Honda in the joint venture with Rover and Nissan by building new factories in the late 1980s. The Japanese firms hoped that their British operations would give them a base from which to expand in Europe. As a result, Britain faced increasing conflict with its partners in the European Community over the rules governing inward foreign investment.

Policies for the Semiconductor Industry

Of the five largest industrial capitalist countries, the United States and Britain devote the most government research and development spending to defense.[63] Because of the extreme weakness of British computer and consumer electronics firms, the fates of British semiconductor producers like Plessey, Ferranti, Inmos, and GEC have been tied to government expenditures on R&D and procurement for military electronics. As in the United States, the increasing gap between the expensive and exotic forms of circuitry consumed by military electronics and those consumed by civilian electronics has prevented firms specializing heavily in military electronics from competing successfully in commercial markets. Thus there have been no successful British commercial semiconductor firms, with the possible exception of Inmos. Inmos was acquired by SGS-Thomson, an Italo-French concern, at the beginning of 1989.

Britain's policy toward semiconductors has been an offshoot of its policy toward computers and information technology. Like the French, Germans, and Japanese, the British did not recognize the importance

---

62. Maxcy, *Multinational Motor Industry*, p. 221; and Economic Research Associates, *EEC Protectionism: Present Practice and Future Trends* (Brussels: Economic Research Associates, 1982), p. 144.

63. Robert F. Wescott, "U.S. Approaches to Industrial Policy," in F. Gerard Adams and Lawrence Klein, eds., *Industrial Policies for Growth and Competitiveness* (Lexington, Mass.: Lexington Books, 1983), p. 110.

of semiconductors per se until the 1970s. When they did, they adopted an ambitious set of promotional schemes. But these were mostly too little, too late.

Policy toward Information Technology

The information technology industry in the United Kingdom grew at a rate of 12 percent annually between 1975 and 1985, which was slower than in the United States and Japan, and in the mid-1980s it controlled only about 4 percent of the world market in that field. The British domestic market is increasingly dominated by foreign-owned firms. In mainframe computers, for example, IBM is dominant (as it is in most of the rest of the world).[64] In semiconductors, the number one firm is Texas Instruments, followed by Philips (based in the Netherlands).[65]

The main British firms in the information technology industry are International Computers Limited, General Electric Company (it has only a faint connection with General Electric in the United States), Standard Telephone and Cables (STC), British Telecom, Racal-Vadic, Thorn-EMI, Ferranti, Plessey, and Inmos. ICL, which is now wholly owned by STC, is the only British-owned maker of mainframe computers. GEC, a highly diversified electrical and electronics manufacturer, owns what is left of the Marconi electronics businesses and controls a major part of the British light bulb market. GEC is the largest of the British information technology firms in revenues and profits (see Figure 16). British Telecom is the largest provider of telecommunications services in Britain. It was formed in 1984 after the privitation of the telecommunications services division of the Post Office. Racal-Vadic is a telecommunications equipment firm that grew from a base in modem production. Ferranti is a family-run Scottish firm that has specialized in high-technology factory automation and electronics businesses since World War II. Plessey specializes in semiconductors, military electronics, and telecommunications. Inmos, founded in 1978 with backing from the British government, is the youngest of the bunch. It was sold by the government in 1984 to Thorn-EMI, which sold it to SGS-Thomson in 1989.

Ferranti, ICL, British Telecom, and Inmos were all state-owned before 1979. Ferranti was the first to be privatized by the Thatcher

64. See M. Delapierre, L. A. Gerard-Varet, and J. B. Zimmerman, "The Computer and Data Processing Industry," in H. W. de Jong, ed., *The Structure of European Industry* (Amsterdam: Martinus Nijhoff, 1981), p. 269.
65. See Giovanni Dosi, *Technical Change and Survival: Europe's Semiconductor Industry* (Brighton, Eng.: Sussex European Research Center, 1981), p. 75.

Figure 16. Revenues and profits of U.K. electronics firms

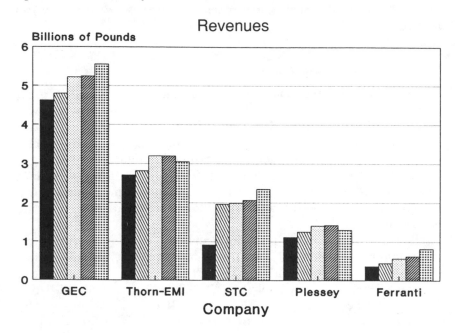

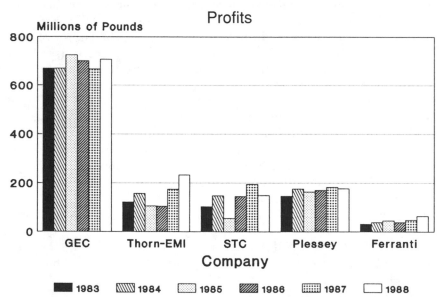

Sources: Reuters Dataline database; and *Moody's International Manual* (New York: various years).

government, in 1981. ICL was sold to STC and Inmos to Thorn-EMI in 1984. GEC, STC, Thorn-EMI, Plessey, and Ferranti are all now privately held, but GEC, Plessey, and Ferranti are all still highly dependent on British military contracts.

According to a study published by the Information Technology Economic Development Committee of the NEDC, "the U.K. information technology industry now has such a small share of world markets that it can no longer continue to invest adequately in product development, in marketing, or in production facilities." In 1983, the global revenues of IBM were more than sixteen times those of ICL and twenty-three times those of Plessey. By 1982–83, 54 percent of information technology products in Britain was imported.[66]

The Alvey Report and the Alvey Program

In 1982, the British government commissioned a report on the information technology industry (called the Alvey Report after the commission's leader, Sir John Alvey) which posed the problem as follows: "The issue before us is stark. We can either seek to be at the leading edge of these technologies; or we can aim to rely on imported technology; or we can opt out of the race. The latter we do not regard as a valid option. Nor is the reliance upon imported technology practical as a general strategy, though we cannot be completely self-sufficient either. . . . The only sensible option . . . is to share in the future growth and development of the world IT sector . . . in specific targetted priority areas."[67]

On April 23, 1983, the Thatcher government accepted the recommendations of the Alvey Report and the Electronics Components Sector Working Party that the government fund a research program for advanced information technology aimed at matching, at least on a small scale, the efforts of the United States and Japan. In September 1984, the Alvey Research Programme announced that thirty-four research projects had been funded at a total cost of around $83 million. About half of that amount would go to Plessey, GEC, and STC. The program was to run for five years with a total expenditure of 350 million pounds.[68] When the cash ran out in 1986, a committee chaired by Sir Austin Bide, chief executive of the Glaxo Corporation, recommended

66. James Fallon, "Says U.K. Losing Share of World Info. Tech. Market," *Electronic News*, September 10, 1984, p. 20.

67. Department of Industry, *A Programme for Advanced Information Technology* (London: Her Majesty's Stationery Office, 1982), p. 14.

68. *Alvey Programme: Annual Report 1984* (London: Institution of Electrical Engineers, 1984); and Department of Industry, *A Programme for Advanced Information Technology* (London: Her Majesty's Stationery Office, 1982).

that it be extended at a cost of 1 billion pounds, roughly half that amount going to research related to short-term commercialization of products.

The government at first failed to provide additional funds, claiming that the firms themselves should pay R&D expenses. In July 1987, however, the new minister of industry, Kenneth Clarke, endorsed the Bide Committee's recommendation and suggested a government contribution of 425 million pounds: 125 million for commercialization research and 300 million for basic research.

MISP and MAP

In 1978, the Electronics Components Sector Working Party in the National Economic Development Council complained to the government about its funding of Inmos, which was a new competitor in the semiconductor business. Ferranti, GEC, and Plessey were represented on this SWP. Shortly after receiving these complaints, the Labour government announced two new programs, the Microelectronics Industry Support Program (MISP) and Microprocessor Applications Project (MAP).[69]

MISP was designed to help domestic firms meet global standards in the manufacturing of integrated circuits. Only about 24 million pounds were allocated for 1978–83, but not that much was actually spent. The firms in the SWP questioned the emphasis on standardized (as opposed to customized) circuits implicit in the funding criteria.[70] The British government wanted its favored defense contractors to produce standardized components, and the funding of Inmos as well as of MISP and MAP was designed to pressure them to do so.

MAP was supposed to make British manufacturers more familiar with microelectronics technology so they could increase usage of that technology and thereby increase demand for domestic microelectronics and information technology products. A survey by the Department of Industry in 1977 had shown that only 5 percent of British firms were aware of developments in microelectronics. MAP offered training sessions for British industrialists that by 1982 had been attended by 133,000 persons.

After 1979, funding for MISP and MAP became much more uncertain, despite strong lobbying efforts on the part of British electronics firms. The Thatcher government saw these programs as yet another example of wasted money. Funds for MISP and MAP were temporarily

69. Grant, *Political Economy,* pp. 64–65.
70. Ibid., pp. 64, 86; and Dosi, *Technical Change,* p. 37.

suspended, then reauthorized at ridiculously low levels, despite extensive lobbying efforts on the part of the business members of the Electronic Components Economic Development Committee in NEDO.[71]

British government policy has strongly supported efforts to create new technologies but has done little to promote the diffusion of new technologies. Because of the strength of organized labor in the system and the low skill base of the British work force, it is difficult for British managers to introduce new technologies into the workplace. As a result, the demand for intermediate goods based on new technologies such as microelectronics is not as strong in Britain as in faster-moving countries like Japan and Germany. Most of the domestic demand for advanced circuitry comes from military electronics, which also provides the impetus for programs like MISP and MAP.

The Case of GEC

The GEC was formed in the late 1960s through the merger of the three leading British electrical engineering firms: General Electric Company, Associated Electrical Industries, and English Electric. The hostile takeover of AEI by GEC in 1967 was facilitated by the government's Industrial Reorganization Corporation, which supported GEC publicly and within the government. The IRC then supported the merger between GEC and English Electric in 1968. The short-lived Ministry of Technology, under Anthony Wedgewood-Benn, promoted the merger as well, and the Board of Trade, under Anthony Crosland, did not refer the merger to the Monopolies and Mergers Commission. Thus the government played an important role in the formation of the present GEC.

The mergers that created GEC were more successful financially than those that created British Leyland. GEC's profits have remained relatively strong since 1971 (see Figure 16). Real growth in revenues has been strongest in overseas subsidiaries, electronic systems, and power engineering. Between 1971 and 1981, there was a decline in revenues, after controlling for inflation, in components, heavy industrial products, and consumer electronics. GEC suffered particularly from intense competition from Japanese firms in consumer electronics and from European firms in home appliances. It responded by relocating production of those items elsewhere, mostly in Hong Kong.

Between the early 1960s and the early 1970s, despite its financial success, GEC lost its position of preeminence in the British semiconductor market. GEC had a joint venture with Mullard (the British

71. Interview materials.

subsidiary of Philips), called Associated Semiconductor Manufacturers, which once was the leading firm in the British market, but it yielded that lead in the early 1970s to Texas Instruments, which built its position in Britain by becoming the main supplier of semiconductors to the Ministry of Defense. Between 1968 and 1973, GEC became the largest single customer of Texas Instruments in the United Kingdom, larger even than the Ministry of Defense.

In 1978, GEC formed a joint venture with Fairchild, called GEC-Fairchild, to produce semiconductors. In 1979, the government provided 7 million pounds to permit GEC-Fairchild to build a new plant in Cheshire. Fairchild pulled out of the arrangement in July 1980, however, and GEC converted the Cheshire plant to the production of torpedoes.[72]

GEC continued to manufacture semiconductors through its Marconi Electronic Devices Limited (MEDL) subsidiary, which specialized in CMOS circuitry and silicon-on-sapphire devices. Although some of MEDL's CMOS production was useful for GEC's consumer electronics production, most of it went for military electronics applications. Silicon-on-sapphire is a process for manufacturing devices that are durable and reliable in very different operating conditions. Because of their high cost, these devices are used overwhelmingly in military applications. GEC became increasingly dependent on military work for profits and revenues in the late 1970s and early 1980s.[73] Overdependence on military clients, combined with fewer cost-plus contracting arrangements in the late 1980s, pushed GEC toward a series of diversification efforts, mainly through acquisitions. The case study of Plessey below shows the effects of this effort on another British electronics firm.

The Case of STC and ICL

The British computer industry, like that of the United States, had its roots in the development of digital computers for the decryption of enemy codes during World War II. The work of the British mathematician Alan Turing, first published in 1936, convinced mathematicians and scientists the world over of the feasibility of constructing a programmable computing machine. A large digital computing machine called Colossus was constructed in 1943 at Bletchley Park as part of the British effort to break enemy codes.[74]

72. John Williams, "GEC: An Outstanding Success?" in Williams, Williams, and Thomas, *Why Are the British Bad at Manufacturing?*
73. Interview materials.
74. See Kenneth Flamm, *Creating the Computer: Government, Industry, and High Technology* (Washington, D.C.: Brookings Institution, 1988), pp. 33, 136.

In the 1950s, the British government encouraged the domestic computer industry, primarily because its Atomic Energy Agency needed advanced computers. The National Research and Development Corporation (NRDC), established in 1949, was in charge of these efforts. The NRDC's contracts were focused on three firms: Ferranti, Elliott Brothers, and Electrical and Musical Industries. One of the first commercially sold digital computers in the world was the Ferranti Mark I, which was delivered to the University of Manchester in 1951.[75]

In 1954, the Development of Inventions Act extended the time the NRDC had to become self-supporting. In 1957, the NRDC initiated a project for the development of "supercomputers." The principal contractor was Ferranti, along with the Department of Electrical Engineering at Manchester University. Ferranti developed the Atlas model, which turned out to be more successful in the British market than IBM's STRETCH model, its main competitor.[76]

The British computing industry in the 1950s and 1960s was strongest in machines optimized for scientific or research applications. British firms were not able to adapt their products quickly for business users. Increased competition from U.S. firms in both business and scientific markets made it hard for many of the smaller British firms to maintain their technological edge.

In the 1960s, the Labour government, as part of its industrial strategy, increased government funding for research and development and encouraged a series of mergers that led to the formation of ICL. The IRC financed ICL initially with a loan of 3.5 million pounds. In 1968, ICL received an additional 13.5 million pounds and in 1972–73 another 40 million. Government purchasing policy favored computers from ICL. In 1967, the government started buying shares in ICL; by 1969, it owned 25 percent of the shares.[77]

As part of its overall policy of privatization, the Thatcher government instructed the British Technology Group (successor to the NEB) to look for private purchasers for its shares in ICL and Inmos. The NEB's shares in ICL were transferred to the BTG in 1979 in exchange for 150 million pounds. This was the end of a long and not very successful experiment in state entrepreneurship. The prospective privatizations of Inmos and ICL created a political controversy between the Conservative and Labour parties because of Labour's firm belief that

75. Ibid., pp. 139, 143.
76. P. Drath, M. Gibbons, and R. Johnston, "The Super-Computer Project: A Case Study of the Interaction of Science, Government, and Industry in the UK," *Research Policy* 6 (1977): 2–34.
77. Delapierre, Girard-Varet, and Zimmerman, "Computer and Data Processing Industry," p. 271.

the policies of 1967–79 had been responsible for maintaining some credible alternative to IBM (ICL) in computers and for allowing Britain to be the only country in Europe other than Italy with an independent, domestically owned producer (Inmos) of standardized integrated circuits. Peter Shore, Labour MP and shadow cabinet member, said that "to abandon public ownership now would be no more than ideological spite."[78]

Despite Labour objections, the Thatcher government proceeded with its plans. Kenneth Baker, the new minister of information technology, complained: "The previous government saw the NEB as a major interventionist instrument that could start up new ventures and buy companies that were about to collapse and save them. . . . [The problem is that] civil servants aren't very good at that sort of thing."[79] The irony of this statement is that the NEB and its predecessors had been set up in such a way as to minimize the influence of civil servants in industrial policy making. The members of the board of the NEB were primarily industrialists. It was perhaps the belated recognition of this fact that made it possible for the Thatcher government to replace the NEB with the BTG without abandoning the idea completely. But because the BTG was given the task of liquidating the assets of the NEB, the Thatcher government was apparently more reluctant than previous ones to use public funds as a form of risk capital.

Severe financial difficulties at ICL resulted in big losses beginning in December 1980 and continuing through 1981. In May 1981, when ICL was technically bankrupt, the Thatcher government replaced the managing director with Robb Wilmot (formerly the manager of Texas Instruments-UK). Wilmot arranged with Fujitsu to get access to its chips and to market Fujitsu IBM-compatible mainframes in Britain and Europe. The Fujitsu chips replaced chips previously supplied by Motorola. Wilmot secured new bank loans of 200 million pounds in exchange for government loan guarantees. He also raised money by issuing rights to loyal shareholders. Finally, Wilmot continued the restructuring and downsizing of the firm that began in 1980. The firm was again profitable in 1981–82.[80]

STC was founded in 1880 as an agency for the U.S. firm Western Electric. In 1925 it was acquired by ITT, which cut its stake in STC to 85 percent in 1979 and then to 35 percent in 1982. STC bought about 10 percent of the shares of ICL at the end of July 1984 in a "dawn raid"

78. Barnaby Feder, "Inmos: A Success for Britain," *New York Times,* July 4, 1984, p. 25.
79. Beth Karlin, "Britain's State-Run Microchip Maker Setting Plans to Seek Private Financing," *Wall Street Journal,* July 13, 1983, p. 34.
80. Letter by FAX from Robb Wilmot, July 19, 1989; Grant, *Political Economy,* p. 98; and Wilks, "Liberal State," pp. 148–55.

and then offered 350 million pounds for the rest of shares needed for control. ITT approved of the bid because it saw it as a necessary counterpart to the arrangement between IBM and Rolm (another computer/telecommunications linkup). The ITT holding in STC created some political opposition to the STC-ICL merger, but the Thatcher government approved the deal when ITT announced that it planned to reduce its share of STC from 35 to 25 percent (which meant a 26–27 percent share in the STC-ICL merged company).[81]

The merger mania of the summer of 1984 was a joint function of the desire of the Thatcher government to privatize rapidly and of the large cash holdings accumulated by the more dynamic British firms during the recovery of 1983–84. The wisdom of selling off government equity holdings so rapidly was questionable. The government could have obtained greater value for its investments and would have introduced less uncertainty into national capital markets if, like France and Japan, it had sold its shares on the open market more slowly.

The purchase of ICL nearly doubled the revenues of STC to 921 million pounds in 1984, and ICL's profits contributed measurably to STC's profit base. But STC did not make any important new investments in the computer area until the late 1980s. In November 1988, STC purchased Computer Consoles, a U.S. telecommunications equipment firm, for $168 million. In December 1988, for $90 million, STC purchased National Semiconductor's Datachecker subsidiary, a firm that specialized in electronic point-of-sale systems. According the chairman of ICL, Peter Bonfield, "the new combined organization will have a scale of operation capable of succeeding on the world stage, increased focus on the retail market, and a greater depth of product capability."[82] ICL was apparently hoping that the two U.S. acquisitions would help it to capture commercial and government markets in the United States. STC would remain highly dependent on external sources of both componentry and systems integration. Thus when STC sold 80 percent of the shares of ICL to Fujitsu in August 1990 for 742 million pounds, no one was surprised.

The Case of Thorn-EMI and Inmos

The year 1978 was particularly important for policy initiatives in the semiconductor industry. The NEB, in one of its last major transactions, purchased 75 percent of the shares in the new microelectron-

---

81. James Fallon, "ITT to Reduce Ownership in STC to Less than 25%," *Electronic News*, September 10, 1964, p. 27.
82. Quoted from Louise Kehoe, "STC to Pay $90m for National Semi Unit," *Financial Times*, December 14, 1988, p. 22.

ics firm Inmos, which had been founded by Iann Barron and two Americans, Richard Petritz and Paul Schroeder. These three each held 5 percent of the shares of the firm. Petritz, a former executive at Intel, saw opportunities for a start-up firm to produce static RAMs and fast microprocessor chips (later called transputers). Inmos's founders approached the NEB with their ideas and secured the support of the Labour government.

Petritz became the chief executive officer of the firm. It was decided to build two plants: one in South Wales near Bristol to produce 64K DRAMs and transputers, the other in Colorado to produce 16K static RAMs and 64K DRAMs. The building of the facility in South Wales was delayed by disagreements between the firm's management and the government over the location of the plant. British officials insisted that the plant be built in an officially designated depressed area; the managers wanted it next to their new laboratory in Bristol. The Wales site was a compromise. By 1984, there were 844 employees in the United States and 544 in the United Kingdom.[83]

The BTG dismissed Richard Petritz as CEO of Inmos in July 1983 and replaced him with Sir Malcolm Wilcox. Soon after its deregulation in the United States, AT&T had purchased a 25 percent stake in Olivetti. It wanted the Inmos plant in South Wales to assure access to EC markets and to avoid the 17.5 percent tariff on microelectronic imports. AT&T offered $69 million dollars in February 1984 for 60 percent of Inmos's shares, as well as additional $96.6 million for retooling the plant in South Wales, and said it would transfer the seventy-person Inmos design team, which was working on the transputer, to the control of ICL. Robb Wilmot later said that he had suggested this arrangement to AT&T so that ICL could get access to the transputer design team.[84]

The British government was not pleased with this offer because it had already invested over $140 million in Inmos and wanted to recover at least that sum from the sale. Inmos itself was opposed to the sale, as were the BTG and the inventor Sir Clive Sinclair (pioneer in the production of inexpensive microcomputers), all of whom wanted Inmos to remain in British hands. Peter Shore of the Labour party called the deal "technological treason," and David Owen of the Social Democratic party called it "little short of lunacy."[85] The bid was soon rejected for

83. Feder, "Inmos," p. 25; James Fallon, "U.K. Unit Hits Inmos for Investment in U.S.," *Electronic News*, May 21, 1984, p. 73; Mick McLean and Tom Rowland, *The Inmos Saga* (Westport, Conn.: Quorum Books, 1985).
84. Letter by FAX from Robb Wilmot, July 19, 1989.
85. "AT&T Technology Offers $80M for 2 Inmos Plants: We Invest $96M in Wales Unit," *Electronic News*, June 25, 1984, p. 1.

being too low. Merrill Lynch had estimated that a public offering of Inmos shares would bring in around $270 million.[86]

The firm had lost around $78 million by the end of 1983, and substantial sentiment could be found in the Thatcher government to sell it. A parliamentary debate in June 1984 resulted in the passage of an amendment endorsing privatization of the firm. Soon afterward, Thorn-EMI offered 13.8 million pounds for slightly less than 10 percent of Inmos's shares. Inmos and the BTG welcomed the offer as a gesture of support that would help counter offers from foreign firms such as AT&T. Also in June, Inmos was approached by a consortium of Dutch interests that wanted to finance the building of a new chip-making facility in Limburg for about $69 million. Although this would help Inmos, it conflicted with the company's plans to build another plant in Britain. In any case, the BTG had the right to veto the arrangement.

In 1984, Thorn-EMI offered to buy the BTG's 75 percent of Inmos's shares for $124 million. It was expected to purchase the remaining shares for around $39 million, but the offer to the BTG was not contingent on its doing so. Thorn had just unsuccessfully bid around $1.12 billion for British Aerospace. A merger of Thorn and British Aerospace would have created a firm with $6.95 billion in annual sales. GEC also offered to purchase British Aerospace, which would have created a military-industrial giant with $11 billion in annual sales, accounting for about 25 percent of the expenditures of the British Defense Ministry. When British Aerospace rejected the bid from Thorn-EMI, GEC announced that it might not submit its bid because of possible objections from the Monopolies and Mergers Commission.[87] It was rumored that Ferranti and Plessey would push for the commission to hold a hearing if the deal went through.[88] When Thorn-EMI upped its bid for Inmos to $165 million in August, Inmos accepted and the merger took place.

Inmos's profits were too low to justify investments that would keep the firm internationally competitive. Inmos's three main product lines were problematic. The transputer microprocessor suffered from competition from the less powerful but also less expensive microprocessors sold by Intel and Motorola. Transputer sales remained low but profitable. Inmos's static RAMs suffered from heavy competition from both

86. "Thorn-EMI Will Buy a 76% Share in Inmos," *New York Times*, July 13, 1984, p. 26.
87. James Fallon, "British Aerospace Rejects Thorn-EMI's $1B Bid," *Electronic News*, June 18, 1984, p. 64.
88. Barnaby J. Feder, "A Partner for British Aerospace," *New York Times*, June 18, 1984, p. 32.

U.S. and Japanese firms. Inmos's share of the world market in SRAMs dropped from 40 percent in 1983–84 to less than 15 percent in 1988. Low demand for DRAMS in the global semiconductor recession of 1985 forced Inmos to close its production facility in Colorado, which had been a major source of profits. Only the plant in South Wales remained in operation. Accumulated losses at Inmos between 1984 and the end of 1987 were 260 million pounds. Thorn-EMI's main businesses were light bulbs, musical recordings, and electronics rentals. The diversification into semiconductors was probably a bad decision from the start. Thus Thorn-EMI began to look for a purchaser for Inmos as early as 1985. According to Inmos's former CEO, Doug Stephenson, "Thorn would have given Inmos away with Green Shield stamps."[89]

Inmos was sold in March 1989 to SGS-Thomson in exchange for 10 percent of the latter's shares. In addition, Thorn-EMI paid SGS-Thomson 10 million (5.8 million pounds) for a $100 million rights issue. Thorn-EMI hoped to generate at least $30 million over the next five years in revenues from licensing Inmos patents to SGS-Thomson. SGS-Thomson seems likely to make the major investments needed to keep Inmos competitive in transputers and SRAMs. But the sale of Inmos ended any hope that a British-owned firm would be a leader in high-volume sales of integrated circuits.[90]

The Case of Plessey

Plessey, the fourth largest British electronics firm after GEC, Thorn-EMI, and STC, specialized in the production of telecommunications equipment and military electronics. Microelectronics and components constituted only 11 percent of its revenues in 1988. Plessey was a major supplier, along with GEC and STC, to the Post Office and later to British Telecom. Plessey focused the development of semiconductor products on application-specific integrated circuits for telecommunications and military electronics. Like all the other British firms, it was highly dependent on external sources of standardized circuitry.

In 1986, GEC offered 1.2 billion pounds for Plessey. This was a hostile takeover bid, and Plessey appealed to the Monopolies and Mergers Commission, and, with the support of the Ministry of Defense, convinced the commission to rule against the acquisition, a rare example

89. "Management Today Considers Thorn-EMI's Divestment of Income," *Management Today,* January 1989, p. 36.

90. Terry Dodsworth, "Thorn-EMI Sells Inmos to SGS-Thomson," *Financial Times,* March 14, 1989, p. 32; Hugo Dixon, "Thorn Selling Chipmaker to Thomson-SGS," *Financial Times,* December 12, 1988, p. 1.; and Terry Dodsworth, "SGS-Thomson Develops Taste for British Chips," *Financial Times,* December 13, 1988, p. 25.

of such rulings. Still, some incentive remained for merging the operations of the two firms in the area of central office switches. Both firms had been involved in developing a new switch, the System X digital switch, for British Telecom. In March 1988, the switch divisions were merged into a joint venture called GEC-Plessey Telecommunications.

In 1987, Plessey opened a new plant at Roborough for the fabrication of VLSI CMOS circuits. It included Europe's first facility for the fabrication of six-inch CMOS wafers. The cost of the new plant was 50 million pounds. In November 1988, GEC and Siemens teamed up to offer 1.7 billion pounds for Plessey. Again, Plessey appealed to the Monopolies and Mergers Commission and to the Commission of the European Community to block the merger as anticompetitive. This time, however, neither commission opposed the merger.[91]

The Case of Ferranti

Ferranti is a Scottish firm that was family-owned and managed until a financial crisis arose in 1975. In response, the National Enterprise Board purchased 75 percent of the firm's shares and injected new capital into its semiconductor business to keep it afloat. The main justification for this assistance was to preserve competition among the major suppliers to the Ministry of Defense and to ensure continued production of items that only Ferranti could manufacture such as advanced radar equipment and battlefield communication and control systems.[92] Ferranti was one of the first firms to be privatized by the Thatcher government. It has remained a major supplier of military electronic systems to the British government as well as an important exporter in world military electronics markets.

In the middle and late 1970s, Ferranti invented new kinds of ASICs that won it successes in semiconductor markets. Ferranti developed particular strengths in gate arrays, ASICs particularly in demand for use in large computers. When other firms entered the ASIC markets in the early 1980s, however, Ferranti's profits from semiconductors declined rapidly. In November 1987, Ferranti sold its semiconductor business to Plessey for 30 million pounds.

Since the mid-1980s, Ferranti has concentrated on developing products for four markets: military electronics systems, electronics for the oil industry, advanced software systems, and cellular telephones. Its profits have remained low but steady. In September 1987, Ferranti

91. The Monopolies and Mergers Commission approved the takeover in February and the European Community approved the following April.
92. Morgan and Sayer, *Microcircuits of Capital*, p. 126.

purchased a U.S. firm, International Signal and Control, for an undisclosed sum to gain better access to military electronics markets in the United States.[93]

The British semiconductor industry has been going through a painful process of shrinkage and consolidation through mergers. All the major domestically owned firms became overly dependent on sheltered military markets and therefore overly specialized in the production of low-volume products. The attempt to reenter markets for high-volume standardized circuitry through government funding of a start-up called Inmos ultimately failed because the Thatcher government believed that Inmos, like all other firms in the NEB portfolio, had to be sold to a private owner.

The British semiconductor market was increasingly dominated by foreign firms. Philips, through its Mullard subsidiary, has been in Britain since the industry began. Texas Instruments established a dominant presence in Britain in the early 1970s. Other American firms, such as Motorola, Intel, and Hewlett-Packard, have established major production facilities there, often with the intention of exporting some of their production to the rest of Europe. Some Japanese firms, such as NEC and Fujitsu, have limited production capabilities in Britain. In recent years, European firms such as SGS-Thomson and Siemens have entered the British market by acquiring British firms.

There is an important parallel between the auto and semiconductor industries in Britain. In both, the weakness of domestic firms, combined with an openness to inward foreign investment, preserved domestic revenues and employment, but control was lost to foreign firms. In both, Britain has increasingly come to look like a threat to the rest of Europe as a potential export platform for extra-European firms. It thus provides a built-in goad to devise European-level responses to competitive challenges from Japan and the United States.

CONCLUSIONS

The declining competitiveness of British firms in steel, automobiles, and semiconductors is a product of British state-societal arrangements. The weak British state regularly adopts ill-advised macroeconomic policies because it is too easily influenced by societal interests. Nation

---

93. "Ferranti and Plessey: The Better Kept Secret," *Economist*, September 26, 1987, p. 83; and Terry Dodsworth and Geoffrey Owen, "Ferranti: Seeking a Premium from a Defensive Strategy," *Financial Times*, November 4, 1988, p. 12.

alization in Britain is always desperation response to declining competitiveness and therefore does not give the state more power over the
economy. The British state, like the French, has overemphasized increasing the size of British firms at the expense of maintaining high
levels of domestic competition. Unlike France, however, the British
have rarely restricted foreign investment. The resulting competition
tends to be more favorable for the foreign investors than for British
firms in part because of the general inability of the British state or entrepreneurs to speed the adoption and diffusion of new technologies.

Even in its reduced position in the world economy, Britain makes
major contributions to science and technology. Since World War II,
however, it has been systematically unable to diffuse innovations into
the economy. Labor is a major factor because labor is powerful relative
to the state and business. British laborers resist innovations in the
workplace because they have been able to secure steady wage increases
without increased productivity. Unlike German labor, which is powerful because of its high skill level, British labor's power come from its
effective organization on the shop floor and in national politics. Thus
British labor has the power to block changes that is lacking in the other
four countries.

The drastic decline of British international competitiveness has
stimulated interest in and commitment to revitalizing competitiveness,
which goes a long way toward explaining the continued popularity of
Thatcherism despite historically high unemployment. Thatcherism
differs from earlier doctrines mainly in its emphasis on privatization.
Privatization has reduced the flow of public revenues into large enterprises, but it has not stemmed the decline in British competitiveness.
Rationalization efforts were accelerated, but that might have happened
without privatization.

Britain has not radically altered its state-societal arrangements since
World War II despite a major decline in international competitiveness.
The British have not fully recognized that continued reliance on military R&D and procurement as the main foundation for policies in
high technology is doomed to failure. They are hoping that liberal policies toward inward foreign investment will help them meet the challenges of international competitiveness. But with the growing presence
of foreign firms, mostly American and Japanese, Britain faces increased complaints from its partners in the European Community that
its territory is being used as an export platform into a "Europe without frontiers."

A weak and fragmented business sector and a strong but divided
trade union movement have delayed the diffusion of new technologies
in many industries. Business does not cooperate with the government

to speed the diffusion of new technologies as in Japan. Labor does not work with business to encourage the diffusion of technologies that would lead to increased and higher productivity as in Germany. The continuing battles among the state, business, and organized labor make it difficult for Britain to extricate itself from its predicaments.

FIVE

Germany

How did German manufacturing remain internationally competitive
in spite of the government's lack of any means for centralized industrial
policy making? To answer this key question requires examination of
the social mechanisms used to train factory workers and the institutions that promote the diffusion of knowledge from universities
(mostly funded by the state) to private businesses. This chapter lays the
foundation for a larger argument about what patterns of state-societal
arrangements are best for promoting international competitiveness.
The case of Germany provides evidence for an alternative to the Japanese pattern of strong state, strong business, and weak labor.

German macroeconomic performance was very strong until 1973.
Between 1954 and 1963, real growth in GDP averaged 6.5 percent, the
average increase in consumer prices was only 2.2 percent, and unemployment averaged 2.8 percent. Between 1964 and 1973, the growth
rate dropped slightly to 4.3 percent, inflation rose slightly to 3.6 percent, but unemployment averaged 0.6 percent (a rate matched only by
Japan among the major industrialized countries). Between 1974 and
1983, however, growth dropped to 1.9 percent, inflation rose to 5.0
percent, and unemployment averaged 3.6 percent. By the late 1980s,
unemployment was almost 9 percent.[1]

Despite the disappointing drop in aggregate growth and the rise in
unemployment in the 1980s, Germany continued to run a large trade
surplus and to remain competitive in strategic industries. Its current
account went from a deficit of around $15 billion in 1980 to a surplus
of over $40 billion in 1987. Production of raw steel remained stable,

---

1. All rates were calculated from data in the *Economic Report of the President* (Washington, D.C.: U.S. Government Printing Office, annual).

between 40 and 50 million tons, between 1960 and 1987. Employment in the industry was steadily reduced from about 400,000 in 1965 to about 180,000 in 1988. This reduction was lower and more gradual than that in all the other major industrial countries except Japan.[2] In the auto industry, production remained stable at an average a little above 4 million motor vehicles per year between 1970 and 1988. Total employment in the top three German firms (Volkswagen, BMW, and Daimler-Benz) increased from 357,000 in 1977 to 591,000 in 1986.[3] No firm statistics are available for production and employment in the German semiconductor industry. Nevertheless, the improved fortunes of Siemens and AEG by the end of the 1980s implies that there was modest growth over the decade.

STATE-SOCIETAL ARRANGEMENTS IN GERMANY

State-societal arrangements in post–World War II Germany were strongly shaped by the military defeat. During the Allied occupation, a new constitution—the Basic Law—was imposed on the German people, but many of the institutional changes it contained reflected the German desire to break with the Nazi past. The new German state was much less centralized and much more constrained in its powers than the Nazi state. The Nazis had suppressed regional governments and intermediary institutions of all kinds. The postwar German state was a genuinely federal one, and extensive powers were granted to the regional governments.[4]

The centralization of power in industry was reduced somewhat during the occupation. The prewar industrial cartels in coal, steel, and chemicals were broken up, and the occupation authorities encouraged strengthening the bargaining rights of noncommunist labor unions. Nevertheless, a recentralization occurred soon after the end of the occupation, under the leadership of the major banks. The "universal banking" system, which remained intact after World War II, was an important factor in this recentralization.

Labor was stronger in German politics after World War II than in any other major industrialized nation because German industry de-

2. American Iron and Steel Institute, *Annual Statistical Report* (Washington, D.C.: American Iron and Steel Institute various years); "West German Steel: In the Furnace," *Economist*, January 23, 1988, p. 62; and Michael Farr, "German Steel Makers Restructure," New York Times, June 8, 1988, p. C8.

3. *Ward's Automotive Yearbook* (Detroit: Ward's, various years); and annual reports of Volkswagen, BMW, and Daimler-Benz.

4. Here and elsewhere, my interpretation of postwar German history is based heavily on the work of Peter Katzenstein. See his *Power and Politics in West Germany: The Growth of the Semisovereign State* (Philadelphia: Temple University Press, 1987), chap. 1.

pended on its highly skilled work force to achieve export-led industrial growth. German unions' policy of wage restraint in exchange for greater shop-floor and national political power helped greatly in promoting postwar economic recovery.

Organization of the State

The most important government institutions are the chancellor's office; the Bundesbank; the ministries of Finance, Economics, and Research and Technology; the Council of Economic Experts (Sachverständigenrat); the Federal Cartel Office; the regional governments; and the universities. As in all large capitalist nations, government institutions work within a policy network that includes the political parties, the unions, employer associations, and other private actors.

The Chancellor

The chancellor of the Federal Republic is in a key position to propose new policies, especially because he is often also the head of the largest party in the ruling coalition. But the chancellor must win approval for all legislative changes in the parliament and has limited control over certain parts of the bureaucracy, as in many other industrial democracies. A particularly important limit on the chancellor's policy-making power in economic policy is the autonomy of the German central bank, the Bundesbank.

The Bundesbank

The Deutsche Bundesbank has sole control over monetary policy. It was created under the occupation in 1948, modeled after the Federal Reserve System in the United States, although it serves as a true central bank, unlike any of the branches of the Federal Reserve System. The Board of Directors (Zentralbankrat) is composed of the directors of the Bundesbank and the presidents of the central state banks (*Landeszentralbanken*). The Landeszentralbanken have no real independence, unlike the state banks (*Landesbanken*), but are merely administrative units of the Bundesbank. Members are appointed by the federal government for eight-year terms to assure the Bundesbank's independence from the chancellor and the ruling party.[5]

5. Peter A. Hall, "Patterns of Economic Policy: An Organizational Approach," in Steven Bornstein, David Held, and Joel Krieger, eds., *The State in Capitalist Europe* (London: Allen & Unwin, 1983), pp. 10–12; and Jeremiah M. Riemer, "Alterations in the Design of Model Germany," in André Markovits, ed., *The Political Economy of West Germany* (New York: Praeger, 1982), p. 60.

The Ministries

The Ministry of Economics and the Ministry of Finance share control over fiscal policy. The Ministry of Economics has been headed by relatively conservative political figures since World War II. Ludwig Erhard was the master of economic policy during the Adenauer administration. At that time, the Ministry of Economics had no rivals for control over economic or industrial policy in the federal government. In 1972, however, the creation of the Ministry of Research and Technology presented the Ministry of Economics with a rival of considerable importance. The Ministry of Research and Technology developed an elaborate research planning system and was given authority over administering a variety of technical aid programs for specific industries. During the 1970s, the majority of this aid went to the nuclear energy programs and to the state governments.[6]

The Council of Economic Experts

The Council of Economic Experts (Sachverständigenrat) was created in 1963 to produce an annual report on the economy. The federal government appoints its five members for five-year terms. The members are all academic economists, and usually all but one adhere to the neoclassical perspective within economics.[7]

The council has substantial autonomy from the government. For example, it has right of access to all relevant economic information produced by the federal government, which is required by law to issue a written discussion of the implications of the council's annual report for economic policy. The council disapproves of too much government involvement in domestic economic affairs and favors maintaining liberal free trade policies in external economic affairs. The council was an early proponent of national-level bargaining between management and labor and allocation of wage increases according to productivity criteria. It distrusts Keynesian demand management and blames inflation on excessive wage increases. Over the years, the council has been critical of both the Christian Democratic Union (CDU) and the Social Democratic Party (SPD). It is an institutional gadfly that promotes neoclassical views of economic policy.[8]

6. Jonathan Story, "The Federal Republic—A Conservative Revisionist," *West European Politics* 4 (1981): 64; Josef Esser and Wolfgang Fach with Kenneth Dyson, " 'Social Market' and Modernization Policy: West Germany," in Kenneth Dyson and Stephen Wilks, eds., *Industrial Crisis: A Comparative Study of State and Industry* (New York: St. Martin's Press, 1983), p. 122.

7. There is always one Social Democrat with less conservative economic views.

8. Karl-Georg Zinn, "Politik und Sachverständigenmeinung—Sachverständigenrat und Council of Economic Advisers in Vergleich," *Gewerkschaftliche Monatshefte* 29 (March

The Federal Cartel Office

Antitrust or competition policy is the province of the Federal Cartel Office (Bundeskartellamt), but, at least until recently, antitrust administration is largely a paper tiger. The Cartel Office can be overruled by the minister of economics. Nevertheless, it plays an important role in German industrial policy by placing one more barrier in the path of foreign firms that attempt to acquire German ones.[9]

The Regional Governments

The eleven regional governments (*Länder*) have the power to collect taxes, to distribute regional revenues (a certain percentage of which come from federal income taxes and over which regional assemblies have the power of the purse), and to use regional banks (*Landesbanken*) for development and aid purposes. Because regional governments have considerable power, economic policy in the Federal Republic is truly federal.

The Universities

All large universities in Germany are state institutions, and all professors are members of the civil service. Although the universities have a great deal of autonomy from the state, as in other major industrialized democracies, the state may use them as an instrument of economic and industrial policy through public financing of basic scientific research. A very important and often unremarked feature of the German system is the network of research institutes—particularly the Max Planck Institutes and Fraunhofer Institutes—that serve to deepen the basis of knowledge and to provide alternative channels for the diffusion of information and technology.

The Fraunhofer Institutes are of particular importance because they serve as a bridge between the universities and industry. There are thirty-five Fraunhofer Institutes, each associated with a major university. The directors of the institutes are generally faculty members in science, engineering, or the social sciences. Each institute has its research specialty and can form interdisciplinary teams to attack specific problems. Most of the employees of the institutes are not faculty members

1978): 181; Kenneth H. F. Dyson, "The Politics of Economic Management in West Germany," *West European Politics* 4 (May 1981): 36; Riemer, "Alterations," pp. 68–69; and Katzenstein, *Policy and Politics*, p. 63.

9. German firms generally acquire other German firms either to diversify their operations or to rescue a failing firm.

but possess advanced degrees and are employed under limited contracts, which gives the institutes much more flexibility in staffing than would be possible in a purely academic environment. Industrial firms can contract with any Fraunhofer Institute to do applied research. The Fraunhofer Institutes played a major role in helping German industry make the transition to semiconductor-based factory automation from the older mechanical engineering–based manufacturing.[10]

Organization of Business

West Germany's business community has three major peak associations: the Federation of Germany Industry (Bundesverband der Deutschen Industrie, or BDI), the Federation of German Employers' Associations (Bundesvereinigung der Deutschen Arbeitgeberverbände, or BDA), and the Diet of German Industry and Commerce (Deutscher Industrie- und Handelstag). The BDI is the central organization representing the overall economic policy objectives of German business. In 1973, the BDI was made up of thirty-nine industry-specific associations with a total of one hundred thousand member firms. The BDI represents between 80 and 90 percent of all firms, with around eight million employees. In the 1950s and 1960s, the leadership of the BDI was recruited from industry located in the Ruhr area. One of its most colorful leaders, Hanns Martin Schleyer, a former president of Daimler-Benz in Stuttgart and a somewhat heavy-handed opponent of labor, was assassinated by the Baader-Meinhof terrorist group in 1977.[11]

The BDA coordinates collective bargaining strategy of West German employers, administers a strike fund, gives legal advice, and deals with questions of social policy. Like the BDI, the BDA represents more than 80 percent of all German firms, but the two rarely have jurisdictional disputes because the BDA functions primarily in the arena of labor-management relations and leaves national policy matters largely to the BDI.

The DIHT represents mostly the smaller firms in the German economy. Membership in the regional branches of the DIHT is compulsory. Because the DIHT contains a diversity of regions and firms, it is much less likely than the BDI and BDA to arrive at a coherent policy position

10. Interview materials. Also see *Frauenhofer-Gesellschaft: Contract Research for Industry and Government* (Munich: Fraunhofer Gesellschaft, 1988).

11. See Gerard Braunthal, *The Federation of German Industry in Politics* (Ithaca, N.Y.: Cornell University Press, 1965); Volker R. Berghahn, *The Americanization of West German Industry, 1945–1973* (New York: Cambridge University Press, 1986), p. 327; and Wolfgang Streeck, "Between Pluralism and Corporatism: German Businesses Associations and the State," *Journal of Public Policy* 3 (1983): 265–84.

and is therefore generally less influential in German policy debates.[12]

The ties between house banks (*hausbanken*) and major industrial firms are an important element in the organization of German business. Under the universal banking system, banks can own shares in the corporations to which they loan money, and their representatives sit on the firms' boards of directors (*Vorstand*). Thus there is no analogue in Germany to the distant relationship between banks and firms in Britain and the United States.

Most share market dealings are concentrated in the investment departments of the Big Three banks: Deutsche Bank, Dresdner Bank, and Commerzbank. The power of the banks is reinforced by a law, dating from 1896, that prohibits a firm from dealing on the stock exchange or bond markets until one year after its registration. In other words, raising money on equity and bond markets is subject to a probationary period of one year, during which bank supervision and financing have to play the central role in the probation. According to Andrew Shonfield: "Here one catches a clear glimpse of the underlying vision of the law-makers who shaped the institutional structure of the German economy—the banks as prefects who will keep a watchful eye on a new company for a test period (one year), who will restrain the speculative excesses of undisciplined investors, and who have the authority, ultimately, through their control of shareholders' proxy votes, to tell the managers of German industry where they get off."[13]

Until 1984, foreign banks were not allowed to establish German subsidiaries, a prerequisite for doing business in Germany. German firms could borrow internationally for their foreign operations but had to finance domestic investments through German banks. After April 1984, the government eliminated a coupon tax that foreigners had to pay on the interest they got from investment in German bonds. In May 1985, foreign banks were allowed to establish subsidiaries, but these were limited to markets for innovative financial products such as swaps, floating-rate notes, and zero-coupon bonds. Liberalization of financial markets continued with some relaxation of the rules that made it difficult for small firms to obtain equity funding. In 1987, a new stock market tier, the *geregelte Markt*, was set up to encourage smaller firms to go public by lowering the costs of new stock offerings and relaxing the disclosure rules. But such liberalization has remained limited and incremental, and the banks continue to dominate financial markets.[14]

12. Katzenstein, *Policy and Politics*, pp. 25–26.
13. Andrew Shonfield, *Modern Capitalism: The Changing Balance of Public and Private Power* (New York: Oxford University Press, 1965), p. 240.
14. "Shritt für Schritt geöffnet," *Industriemagazin*, June 1988, p. 178; and "Sweeping Away Frankfurt's Old-Fashioned Habits," *Economist*, January 28, 1989, p. 73.

Not only does this system give German banks a great deal of influence over firms' decisions, but it makes it difficult to start new firms, especially in industries in which the banks already own equity because banks do not like to finance competitors to companies in which they own equity. Thus in Germany no venture capital market is independent of the other capital markets.

The banks play a central role in structuring relationships among businesses in specific industries. The federal government usually defers to the banks in responding to industry-specific challenges, stepping in, only if the banks are unable to respond. But government intervention occurs only after elaborate consultations with the banks, the firms, and regional governments, and the unions.

Organization of Labor

Seventeen unions organize about 7.5 million workers under the umbrella of the Federation of German Trade Unions (Deutscher Gewerkschaftsbund, or DGB). There are independent unions for white-collar employees and civil servants, but the DGB is the most powerful labor organization in German politics. Although the DGB has no formal connection with any major party, its natural inclination is to align itself with the SPD. An important Christian Democratic wing of the labor movement is represented in the upper reaches of the DGB and makes it possible for the DGB to work with CDU/CSU-dominated coalition governments.

The most influential of the seventeen unions that make up the DGB is the Industrie Gewerkschaft Metall, or IG Metall. With a membership of 2.5 million workers, it is the largest industrial union in any Western democratic society. It has set the agenda for the German labor movement in being the first to work for such goals as codetermination (*mitbestimmung*),[15] humanization of the workplace, and a thirty-five-hour workweek.[16]

German law has institutionalized the relatively strong position of organized labor in industry. Factory works councils operate under legal rules first established in 1920 and reaffirmed and amended in 1952 and 1972.[17] The number of employee representatives, the organiza-

15. Codetermination is joint (labor and management) decision making both at the workplace and in the corporate boardroom.

16. Katzenstein, *Policy and Politics*, pp. 26–28; and Otto Jacobi, "Economic Development and Trade Union Collective Bargaining Policy since the Middle of the 1970s," in Otto Jacobi, Bob Jessop, Hans Kastendiek, and Marino Regini, eds., *Economic Crisis, Trade Unions, and the State* (London: Croom Helm, 1986).

17. The historical background for the 1920 law is discussed in Berghahn, *Americanization*, pp. 13–16.

tion of elections, and the terms of office are specified by law. The works councils have far-reaching rights on decisions affecting personnel management: hiring, firing, layoffs, retirement, overtime, and vacations.

The works councils do not have the same rights as industrial unions. They may not act as collective bargaining agents for the workers, call strikes, or organize demonstrations. Their main function is to mediate conflicts that arise in specific factories. It might appear that unions and works councils would compete for influence with the workers, but in fact they collaborate closely, in part because about 80 percent of the councillors on works councils have been union members since the 1950s. The works council legislation gives the unions another legal channel for influencing what happens in the workplace.[18]

The German system of vocational education helps to preserve the influence of skilled labor. Students generally complete their compulsory schooling at age sixteen. For those who do not go on to universities, the next step is a combination of vocational school and on-the-job training. The latter is organized on a contractual basis between the school and a specific firm and is regulated under the Vocational Training Act of 1969. The firm provides most of the financing for the training and thus has a great deal of influence over its content. The student's skills are certified by chambers of industry and commerce (*kammerrecht*). After completing the training, the student generally enters an apprenticeship program, the length of which varies with occupation but ends with an examination and the preparation of a piece of practical work. The student who passes these tests is certified as a skilled worker (*facharbeiter*) and can decide whether to continue training in a master (*Meister*) course.[19]

State-societal arrangements in Germany reflect the high degree of centralization and influence of organized business and labor and the relative decentralization and fragmentation of power in the federal government. Banks play a key role in the organization of business because of Germany's universal banking rules. Labor has had a powerful influence because of Germany's long-standing specialization in mechanical engineering industries, which require a highly skilled work force. A well-trained and educated work force is the rock on which the unprecedented power of the German labor movement is built.

The German system compensates for the decentralization and fragmentation of the federal government in a variety of ways. First, and

18. Katzenstein, *Policy and Politics*, pp. 64–65.
19. Eric Owen Smith, *The West German Economy* (London: Croom Helm, 1983), pp. 171–72.

most important, much government power devolves on private and parapublic institutions. Much power in industrial policy making is in the hands of the banks, the BDI, and the DGB. Second, the regional governments can be expected to promote industry and help resolve industrial crises. Finally, public and parapublic institutions speed the introduction and diffusion of new technologies.

Policies for the Steel Industry

The steel industry has always been considered a strategic industry in Germany. The success of German specialization in metalworking and mechanical engineering is critically dependent on the availability of high-quality steel. Before World War II, the steel industry was responsible for Germany's superiority in certain military technologies. By the 1980s, however, the steel industry was viewed as not so central either to national security or to economic prosperity. It has remained highly competitive internationally because of the modernization of plants and products, but the global shrinkage of demand for steel led to low profitability and the need to close more plants than was comfortable, especially for regions like the Saar, Ruhr, and Rhine valleys, which were strongly dependent on the steel industry for employment.

The Failure of the Occupation's Decartelization Policy

In 1945, the occupation authorities confiscated two major German enterprises: IG Farben (a huge chemical combine) and the Krupp steel complex. The British military trusteeship controlled the iron and steel production of occupied Germany. The Allies planned to dismantle the Nazi-created Salzgitter iron and steel works, but they abandoned these plans when the workers protested. Labor unions were suppressed until 1947, when German workers were permitted to organize at the zonal level.

France, like Russia, wanted permanently to limit Germany's ability to resume world leadership in steel production and proposed that steel production in the Ruhr Valley, be internationalized. This proposal later helped gain political support for the creation of the European Coal and Steel Community. The initial concern of the United States, in contrast, was to break up the large combines in steel (and other industries) and to deconcentrate control over production through something resembling U.S. antitrust laws. The United States succeeded in codifying this system in the Potsdam Agreement, which called for breaking up trusts and cartels in postwar Germany. The Vereinigte

Stahlwerke (Unified Steelworks), created during the Weimar years and second in importance only to Krupp in the Nazi steel industry, was broken up into thirteen small firms. But the United States relaxed its position on the reconcentration of Germany industry in 1947–48 as the Cold War got under way. One of the basic ideas underlying the Marshall Plan was that the economic recovery of Western Europe depended on the economic development of Germany. Thus even the less ambitious policy of deconcentration lost its initial appeal to the occupation forces.[20]

The German steel industrialists believed that deconcentration of the steel industry would prevent it from resuming its prewar eminence. Thus their immediate response to the occupation efforts at decartelization was to form the *Walzstahlkontore* (steel consortia), which coordinated the production of the small firms created by the breakup of the larger combines so that they could continue to take advantage of scale economies.[21] The *Kontore* were partly the creation of the German banks. The occupation authorities realized that the deconcentration of control over steel production requires deconcentration of banking as well. The smaller banks formed after 1945 quickly began to merge to form larger financial institutions. Of particular importance for the steel industry was the emergence of the Deutsche Bank, whose directors sat on the supervisory boards of almost all major steel firms.[22]

After World War II, according to Josef Esser, "the steel bosses were willing to make concessions to the union to avoid even more threatening outcomes of the political realignment."[23] In an early form of codetermination called Montan codetermination, union representatives were added to the boards of directors of most of the major firms. The labor directors had to be selected by a union vote and were assigned responsibility for personnel and social policies of the firms. This form of codetermination in the steel industry has persisted despite numerous efforts to undermine it.

The German government, in collaboration with the Marshall Plan authorities, helped rebuild the steel industry in the years immediately following World War II. Marshall Plan aid was channeled into steel,

20. Ernst-Jürgen Horn, *Management of Industrial Change in the Federal Republic of Germany* (Brighton, Eng.: Sussex European Research Center, 1982), p. 13; Smith, *West German Economy*, pp. 13–17; Berghahn, *Americanization*, chap. 2; and William Manchester, *The Arms of Krupp, 1587–1968* (Boston: Little, Brown, 1968), esp. chaps. 26–33.

21. Domenico Moro, *Crisi e ristrutturazione dell'industria siderurgica italiana* (Varese: Giuffre, 1984), p. 88.

22. Shonfield, *Modern Capitalism*, p. 255; and Smith, *West German Economy*, p. 17.

23. Josef Esser and Wolfgang Fach, "Crisis Management 'Made in Germany': The Steel Industry," in Peter J. Katzenstein, ed., *Industry and Politics in West Germany* (Ithaca, N.Y.: Cornell University Press, 1990), pp. 237–38. See also Berghahn, *Americanization*, p. 311.

coal mining, shipbuilding, and electrical power generation. The German government adopted special tax credits and accelerated depreciation to encourage investments. The Investment Aid Law of 1952 required all German firms to contribute to a private fund of approximately 1 billion marks, to be administered by the Kreditanstalt für Wiederaufbau, for investment in basic industries.[24]

The Crises of 1962–1963 and 1967

In 1962–63, after a period of rapid growth, a crisis developed owing to an overcapacity of production of several million tons. The lead banks for the steel industry (especially Deutsche Bank) persuaded Mannesmann to abandon a planned increase in production of sheet steel in exchange for an eight-year contract with Thyssen to supply slabs for Thyssen's new sheet steel production.[25] The German banks were resuming their traditional role in structuring the nature of competition and specialization within the steel industry.

The Krupp steelworks was allowed to resume operations early in the Cold War. In 1967, the president of the Deutsche Bank, Herman Abs, took over the management of Krupp. The president of Thyssen, Hans-Günther Sohl, responded with the statement: "We don't want state intervention that submits our industry to external influences. . . . We hope that the time when prices and incomes in our sector were considered political factors belongs to the past."[26] The firms preferred intervention by banks rather than the state as a way of limiting the politicization of the industry. The banks had strong financial incentives to intervene, whereas the state had an ideological stake in avoiding overt intervention. Thus the major actors at this point agreed on a policy of bank-led restructuring.

Thus in 1967, the *Walzstahlkontore* were replaced with the *Rationalisierungsgruppen* (rationalization groups). The northern rationalization group, for example, consisted of Klöckner, Peine-Salzgitter, and Maximilianshutte. Klöckner had invested heavily in engineering and technology and owned 26 percent of Korf Engineering, which had pioneered a method of direct reduction by melting scrap iron and steel in electric furnaces.[27] Using the crude steel products supplied by Peine-Salzgitter and Maximilianshutte, Klöckner tried to carve out a

24. Esser and Fach, "Crisis Management," p. 239.
25. Shonfield, *Modern Capitalism*, p. 256.
26. Quote (in my translation) from Jean G. Padioleau, *Quand la France s'enferre* (Paris: Presses Universitaires de France, 1981), pp. 161–62.
27. This method of making steel is somewhat more expensive than that of basic-oxygen furnace or open-hearth steel manufacturing, but it allows much smaller plants to operate profitably in specialty steel markets.

niche in the speciality steel market. In 1977, Klöckner purchased a controlling share of Maximilianshutte. Although Klöckner had financial difficulties in the 1980s, the rationalization groups may have contributed to the reconcentration of control over steel production. In 1960, for example, the top two German firms controlled only 23 percent of production; by 1984, they controlled 52 percent.[28]

The Crisis of 1977: Krupp and the Saar Valley Firms

In the early 1970s, a Dutch holding company called Estel, jointly owned by Hoesch Werke AG (a German steel firm that was not doing very well) and Hoogovens BV (the largest Dutch steel concern), was established. Hoogovens was able to gain access to the German market in exchange for new investments Estel made in Germany. This was the first major attempt by the German industry to deal with problems of specific firms by internationalizing control.

The next major crisis occurred in 1977. The Deutsche Bank took a leading role in a second restructuring of Krupp. Three other banks and the federal minister of economics were involved in the bargaining. One result was the so-called Krupp discount—a lower interest rate paid by the firm to its major lenders, which was really a private subsidy.[29] The small steel firms of the Saar Valley were also particularly hard hit by reduced production. Between 1974 and 1977, employment fell by six thousand workers. In 1977, two firms—Roechling Burbach and Neunkircher Eisenwerke—threatened layoffs or bankruptcy. A round of negotiations ensued involving the firms, the state and federal governments, the unions (especially IG Metall), and eventually Arbed, a Luxembourg-based steel company. A complex restructuring plan was adopted in 1978. Arbed agreed to take control of the Saar Valley firms in exchange for 900 million marks in loan guarantees from the federal government. The Saarland state government contributed 120 million marks for the construction of a new foundry. The banks agreed to write off 60 million marks in outstanding loans. Arbed committed itself to contribute 120 million marks in new capital and to rationalize production in the region.[30]

IG Metall agreed to take all this even though it meant a drastic reduction in jobs (nine thousand over five years) because the union received guarantees of jobs for certain workers and social aid for those who would be displaced. Also, adjustment assistance was to come from the European Community under Article 56 of the Treaty of Rome, and

28. Moro, *Crisi e ristrutturazione*, pp. 88 and 95–96.
29. Esser, Fach, and Dyson, " 'Social Market' and Modernization Policy," p. 114.
30. Esser and Fach, "Crisis Management," p. 225.

older workers would be allowed to retire early without losing their pension benefits. Productive capacity declined by 20 percent as a result of the closing down of the least efficient units.

This restructuring plan caused some hardships, but it seems to have had some of the desired effects. Unemployment in the region decreased from 7.6 percent in 1977 to 6.6 percent in 1980.[31] Nevertheless, by November 1982, Arbed was in financial trouble and faced the possibility of going bankrupt. To avoid the loss of thirty thousand jobs in the Saar, a special bridging loan of 2.2 billion marks was arranged with some brokering on the part of the federal government. By 1982, the unemployment level in the region had soared to 12 percent.[32]

The Continuing Difficulties of the Ruhr Firms

The 1977–78 steel crisis also affected the Estel group and therefore the Ruhr Valley firm, Hoesch. The German government decided not to give loans to companies that were not 100 percent German-owned, so Estel received no assistance. The success of the Estel venture depended on movement toward implementing the Werner Plan, which had stabilized exchange rates between the German mark and the Dutch guilder, but no further movement was forthcoming. Thus, by 1982, the Estel venture was dead. Hoesch was incorporated into a new grouping of Ruhr Valley firms.

Bargaining over rationalization of the Ruhr was complex and by the mid-1980s had not resulted in a stable solution. The first step was taken by Krupp and Hoesch in 1981 in negotiations to form a firm called Ruhrstahl. This idea was supported by IG Metall and by state and federal economics ministers. Thyssen, however, opposed the merger and succeeded in blocking it.

In June 1982, the Ruhr steel industrialists approached requested 14 billion marks in investment assistance from the federal government. The request was so large because the steel firms had built up a collective debt of 10 million marks in the 1970s and early 1980s in attempting to meet increased competition from Japanese and European firms.[33] In January 1983, three mediators were appointed by the federal government to recommend a course of action for the Ruhr Valley. They suggested that the five Ruhr firms should merge into two groups: a "Rhine group" composed of Thyssen and Krupp and a "Ruhr group"

31. Gerhard Ollig, "Staat und Stahl in Deutschland," *Annalen der Gemeinwirtschaft* 49 (October–December 1980): 434; Esser, Fach, and Dyson, " 'Social Market' and Modernization Policy," pp. 112–13.
32. Esser, Fach, and Dyson, " 'Social Market' and Modernization Policy," p. 114.
33. Esser and Fach, "Crisis Management," p. 233.

composed of Hoesch, Klöckner, and Salzgitter. The federal and state governments would provide aid, but only 3 billion marks would be needed.

This solution was opposed by the North-Rhine Westphalian and Saarland state governments and the IG Metall because of the omission of Arbed and the likely inability of the two groups to become internationally competitive without massive restructuring. Krupp and Klöckner were the smallest of the major German steel firms in revenues and also the least profitable (see Figure 17). Klöckner was in trouble because of a badly timed investment in a new steel plant in Bremen. The Bremen plant opened in 1975, just in time for the slump in global demand for steel. By March 1983, Klöckner was nearly bankrupt. Pairing the strongest Ruhr Valley firm, Thyssen, with one of the weakest, Krupp, seemed highly inadvisable to the management and union representatives of Thyssen. Similarly, the management and unions of Hoesch and Salzgitter objected to a merger with Klöckner.

Thyssen's chairman, Dieter Spethmann, refused to merge with Krupp because Gerhard Stoltenberg, the finance minister, demanded that Thyssen pay cash to cover differences in valuation between the two firms. The lead banks were very unhappy with Spethmann's refusal because the collapse of the merger deal would make Thyssen ineligible for state subsidies. Thyssen lost $173.7 million between September 1983 and September 1984, mostly at its American subsidiary, the Budd Company, purchased in 1978, so Thyssen's bankers were particularly upset about the financial consequences of Spethmann's opposition to the merger with Krupp.

Klöckner Werke continued to have financial problems into the late 1980s. But the coup de grace was an unexpectedly large loss—more than 600 million marks—at the holding company Klöckner and Company in the oil futures market in October 1988. On October 29, 1988, the Deutsche Bank purchased the company for 400 million marks, of which 250 million would form a new equity base and 150 million would go into reserves. Joerg Henle, grandson of the founder, Peter Klöckner, remained chief executive, but Ulrich Cartellieri of Deutsche Bank took over as chairman of the supervisory board of the firm.

The Closure of Krupp's Rheinhausen Plant

In September 1987, an agreement was reached in negotiations involving the managements of the Ruhr firms and representatives of the IG Metall and of the federal and state governments to modernize production in the Ruhr and gradually eliminate thirty-five thousand jobs. Three firms—Thyssen, Krupp, and Mannesmann—secretly planned

Figure 17. Revenues and profits of major German steel firms

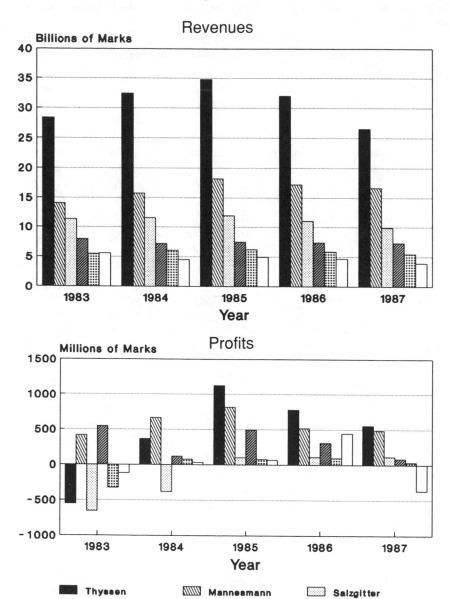

Sources: Reuters Dateline database; and *Moody's International Manual* (New York: various years).

for the closure of Krupp's Rheinhausen plant. The public announcement of this plan in February 1988 brought on demonstrations, traffic blockades, disruption of a meeting of the Krupp board of directors, and a brief occupation of the Krupp villa. Turkish workers at the plant invoked ties of Islamic fraternity by asking the government of Iran, which owned 25.1 percent of Krupp Stahl's parent firm, Friedrich Krupp GmbH, to stop the closure. Such labor militance had not been seen in the German steel industry since before World War II.

The Rheinhausen plant, which dated from before World War II, had originally employed more than thirty thousand workers. By 1988, the work force had dwindled to fifty-three hundred. It had been operating at about half its capacity of 4 million tons per year. Despite the demonstrations, the plant was closed in June 1988. The federal government refused to do anything to keep it open. The president of the IG Metall complained that he had been unable to meet with the appropriate minister in Bonn. Regional adjustment assistance of over a billion marks was provided, however, half from the federal government and the rest from the EC and the North-Rhine Westphalian government. Thus despite a growing tendency toward confrontation between labor and management in the steel industry, partly because of the intense desire of the Kohl government to stay out of the picture, the German steel industry continued to shrink slowly. The costs of adjustment for workers were eased by state, federal, and EC adjustment assistance.[34]

The German steel industry, like that of all other major industrial countries, had many problems in the late 1970s and 1980s. Attempts at internationalization in the Saar were only partially successful, as were attempts to close obsolete plants by forming regional groups in the Ruhr. The problems of the Ruhr were much more significant than those of the Saar because the largest and most modern steelmaking facilities were in the Ruhr and many more jobs were at stake there. The integrated steel companies of the Ruhr were prompt in adopting new steelmaking technologies such as basic-oxygen furnaces and continuous casters, but the smaller and older plants in the Saar were not well suited to the technologies that had been adopted in Japan.

State-societal arrangements helped Germany make the painful transition more rapidly than the United States and the other major European countries. Powerful labor unions, in this case the IG Metall, persuaded their members to accept rationalization schemes in exchange for concessions in other areas. In the case of the Saar Valley, the

34. Ibid., pp. 229–32.

IG Metall had to ask its members to accept the closing of many small plants and to work with the managements of foreign investors to increase productivity. Federal adjustment assistance played an important part in winning labor's acceptance of the necessity for closing obsolete factories in the Ruhr.

The German federal government was increasingly involved in negotiations for the restructuring of the industry because neither the banks nor the state governments were capable of handling it alone. Nevertheless, the German government avoided nationalizations and restrictive trade measures in its efforts to assist the industry, relying primarily on its ability to sanction mergers and to provide grants, loans, loan guarantees, and adjustment assistance. Thus the hand of the state was light relative to those of business and labor. Nevertheless, the necessary adjustments were made and in reasonably good time to preserve German international competitiveness.

POLICIES FOR THE AUTO INDUSTRY

The German auto industry is oligopolistic, dominated by a small number of firms: Volkswagen (VW), Fordwerke (the German subsidiary of Ford), BMW, Adam Opel (the German subsidiary of General Motors), Daimler-Benz, and Porsche. BMW, Daimler-Benz, and Porsche produce only high-priced autos, while Volkswagen, Ford and Opel produce lower-priced vehicles. Because Germans drive fast on the autoban and tend to calculate lifetime costs of owning an automobile, they are somewhat less inclined than consumers in other countries to buy the less expensive but less well-built and less powerful Japanese models. Nevertheless, Japanese imports accounted for about 15 percent of the domestic market by 1986.[35]

Until 1986, Volkswagen was the largest firm (in revenues) in the German automobile industry (see Figure 18). After 1986, however, Daimler-Benz's revenues grew faster than those of Volkswagen because of a series of acquisitions.[36] Daimler-Benz has been more profitable than Volkswagen in the 1980s. Its motor vehicle production is split roughly half and half between luxury cars and commercial vehicles

35. "West German Carmakers: Vibrations While Accelerating," *Economist*, March 21, 1987, p. 72.

36. Daimler acquired majority holdings in the following firms in 1985: AEG, Dornier, and Motoren und Turbinen Union (MTU). Dornier makes small aircraft; MTU makes jet engines. Daimler purchased a 30 percent share of Messerschmidt-Bölkow-Blohm (MBB) in 1988. MBB is the main German partner in the European Airbus consortium. See Christopher Lorenz, "Edzard Reuter Opens the Diversification Throttle," *Financial Times*, April 18, 1988, p. 10.

(trucks and buses), whereas Volkswagen produces only passenger vehicles. Volkswagen's main competitor in the European market is Fiat: both firms have held between 15 and 20 percent of that market since the 1970s. Volkswagen confronted intense competitive pressure from the Japanese and the Italians at the lower price ranges beginning in the 1970s, but Daimler-Benz has competed only with BMW and Porsche in the German market for luxury cars. Its main competitors in Europe are Saab and Volvo. The subsidiaries of U.S. firms—Fordwerke and Adam Opel—are smaller than Volkswagen and Daimler-Benz and have had more variable profits. Nevertheless, Ford's profits in Germany exceeded those of Volkswagen in 1987.

The German auto industry is an important source of export revenue. Roughly half of Germany's export revenue in the early 1980s came from motor vehicles. Net exports of motor vehicles produced a trade surplus of 58 billion marks in 1982. The importance of the motor vehicle industry in creating employment and export revenue, combined with the strong international competitiveness of German auto firms, reinforced the general tendency of the federal government to avoid industry-specific policies for the automobile industry. The state has been involved in the evolution of the auto industry during periods of crisis, however, as occurred with Volkswagen in the mid-1970s. A few government programs have been devised to promote the automobile industry.[37] But far more important is the role of the state as the rescuer of last resort during the infrequent financial crises that hit the industry.

The Origins of Volkswagen

The role of the German government in the auto industry was shaped in part by the formation of Volkswagen in May 1937 under the tutelage of the Nazi government.[38] After briefly considering inviting Ford and General Motors to participate in the production of a "people's car," the government "asked" the executive officers of several German firms, including Porsche and Daimler-Benz, to help the state form a new firm. These producers were reluctant to create a new competitor

37. An example is the CAR 2000 program administered by the Ministry of Research and Technology in which federal government funds were used to subsidize the development of exotic technologies relevant to the automative industry by funding projects proposed by the firms themselves.

38. The best single source on this subject is Simon Reich, *The Fruits of Fascism: Postwar Prosperity in Historical Perspective* (Ithaca, N.Y.: Cornell University Press, 1990), chap. 5. See also Reinhard Doleschal, "Zur geschichtlichen Entwicklung des Volkswagenskonzerns," in Reinhard Doleschal and Rainer Dombois, eds., *Wohin läuft VW? Die Automobilproduktion in der Wirtschaftskrise* (Reinbek bei Hamburg, Germany: Rowohlt, 1982).

Figure 18. Revenues and profits of major German auto firms

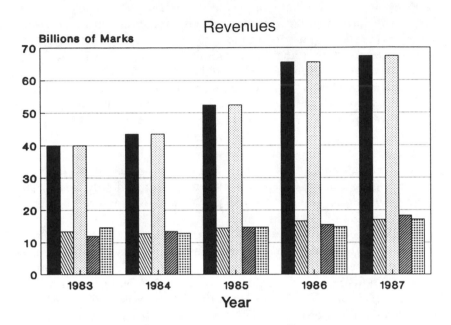

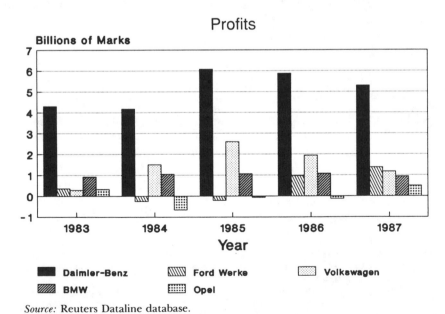

Source: Reuters Dataline database.

but went along when they were assured that American firms would be excluded and that they would receive other benefits from cooperating with the state.

The Nazi government wanted to demonstrate that Germany could produce mass-consumption items such as automobiles that could eventually compete on a world scale. Hitler's goal was to produce a car that cost less than 1,000 reichsmarks. The government was prepared to develop this capability through state subsidies, building a national highway system, confiscating the funds of independent trade unions and cooperative societies to form a new investment bank call the Bank der Deutschen Arbeit, and establishing a system of savings under which families would set aside small sums periodically so as to qualify for a vehicle at some later date.[39]

A large and very modern plant was build at Wolfsburg. By the end of 1939, 80 percent of the construction was completed at a cost of 215 million reichsmarks. Although no automobiles were produced at Wolfsburg before the outbreak of World War II, roughly 115,000 vehicles were produced during the war, of which more than half were for military use. A large percentage of the cost of the plant was the purchase of twenty-seven hundred specialized machine tools from the United States. Hitler was particularly grateful to Henry Ford for his help in arranging the sale of this equipment to Volkswagen. For this and for his public defense of anti-Semitism, Hitler awarded Ford a Grand Cross of the German Eagle, the highest award that could be bestowed on a foreigner, in July 1938.[40]

The work force at the Volkswagen plant was mostly German, but in 1938 Italian workers were imported through an agreement between Hitler and Mussolini. In 1941, 850 Soviet prisoners of war were added to the work force. In the next two years, slave labor from nearby concentration camps would augment the work force and be assigned the most dangerous jobs such as handling explosives for munitions production.

Volkswagen after World War II

After World War II, the British occupation authorities allowed Volkswagen to resume production. The Allies had extensively bombed the plant at Wolfsburg, but the company had saved most of the important

39. According to Simon Reich, the savings were put into a special bank account that was never used. After the war, a lawsuit was filed on behalf of the 336,000 people who had paid into the fund but never received an automobile. The suit was unsuccessful. See Reich, *Fruits of Fascism*, p. 158.
40. Robert Lacey, *Ford: The Men and the Machine* (New York: Ballantine Books, 1987), pp. 228–31, 405–6.

machine tools by hiding them in caves. The British occupation authorities allocated scarce food supplies to Volkswagen so the firm could attract and retain a highly skilled work force. During this time, getting enough to eat was a major problem and workers accepted very low wages in exchange for guaranteed food supplies.[41] Thus despite the general shortages of investment capital and food in postwar Germany, Volkswagen rapidly returned to production levels reached during the war.

In January 1948, the British authorities brought in Heinrich Nordhoff, a former executive at Adam Opel, to run the firm. Nordhoff had experience with high-volume production of low-priced vehicles and quickly recognized that such vehicles could be produced at Wolfsburg. Nordhoff decided to focus production on a single standardized vehicle, later known as the Beetle. By 1949, Volkswagen was producing more than 46,000 cars per year, 18,000 more than its closest rival in Germany, Adam Opel. Production increased to 762,000 vehicles per year in 1955. The price of the Beetle was reduced from 5,200 marks in 1948 to 3,790 marks in 1955. By 1965, 10 million Beetles had been produced.[42]

The Korean War stimulated demand for Volkswagen's products, which were being exported to more than eighty countries by the mid-1950s. Volkswagen quickly became an internationally oriented producer. A Canadian subsidiary was established in 1952; a Brazilian subsidiary, Volkswagen do Brasil, was established in 1953; Volkswagen of America was founded in 1955. Exports increased from around 200,000 vehicles per year in 1956 to 1 million in 1968. Overseas production increased from 150,000 vehicles per year in 1965 to 700,000 in 1974.[43]

In 1961, after a lengthy dispute about the ownership of the firm, 60 percent of Volkswagen's shares were offered to the public in a privatization scheme that was first proposed by Ludwig Erhard when he was minister of finance in 1957. The effort at privatization tested the Adenauer government's commitment to building a liberal economic system. The government passed the test, but just barely. Nordhoff and the minister of finance, Fritz Schäffer, supported by the government of Lower Saxony and the SPD, had lobbied hard and successfully to delay privatization until Volkswagen was on a firmer financial footing. But the government could not politically afford to maintain Volkswagen as

41. Reich, *Fruits of Fascism*, p. 182.

42. Doleschal, "Zur geschichtlichen Entwicklung," p. 45. See also the official history in the 1986 annual report of Volkswagen. The design for the Beetle apparently was done by Porsche in the 1930s.

43. Rolf Kasiske, "Krisen sind programmiert: Zur wirtschaftlichen Entwicklung der Automobilindustrie und von VW," in Doleschal and Dombois, *Wohin läuft VW?* p. 99.

a state enterprise indefinitely. After the public stock offering in 1961, the federal government and the regional government of Lower Saxony each retained 20 percent of the stock.[44]

After 1961, the federal government intervened in Volkswagen's affairs less than did the regional governments. The government of Lower Saxony in particular played an important role in the development of the firm. Franz-Josef Strauss, the CSU party leader and governor of Bavaria, was an especially vocal critic of the firm. In 1966, Volkswagen had a bad year because of the general recession brought on by the policies of the Bundesbank, and Strauss attacked Nordhoff for blocking efforts to find a successor model to the Beetle.

The 1974 Crisis at Volkswagen

Strauss was right. VW became increasingly vulnerable because of its overdependence on the Beetle. When Nordhoff died in 1968, Kurt Lotz became the new head of the company. Under Lotz, the firm tried to deal with the lack of new models by purchasing Audi from Daimler-Benz in 1965 and NSU (Neckarsulm) in 1969, but the new models acquired and produced before the 1970s were not successful. The resistance of minority stockholders of acquired firms to such mergers produced fairly intense political opposition to further acquisitions and eventually resulted in the dismissal of Lotz as head of VW in 1971. Rudolf Leiding, who replaced Lotz, tried to introduce new models, but by 1974 the firm was in serious financial trouble.

In 1974 VW sales fell by 11 percent. The firm was heavily dependent on exports, which in 1973 accounted for 70 percent of production. By 1975, this figure fell to 56 percent. A decline in demand in the United States provoked by the 1974 recession, the floating of the mark after 1972, and increased Japanese competition created grave difficulties for Volkswagen because the United States was its largest foreign market. Sales in other markets did not compensate for the loss of VW's share in the U.S. market. The firm began a series of expensive direct foreign investments to service foreign markets in the early 1970s. New plants were built in Belgium and Yugoslavia to service European markets. Labor costs in these new facilities were much lower than in Germany. New facilities in Mexico and Brazil were built to service Latin

---

44. For a discussion of the ownership dispute, see Reich, *Fruits of Fascism*, pp. 186–93. In 1985, Gerhard Stoltenberg, the minister of finance, placed Volkswagen on the list of state holdings to be privatized before the parliamentary elections in 1987. The initial plan was to reduce federal government holdings from 20 to 14 percent of equity by not participating in purchases of new stock issued by the firm. See John Tagliabue, "Bonn to Cut Stakes in 10 Companies," *New York Times*, March 27, 1985, p. 27; and "Why West Germany Is Selling Two Gems in the Crown Jewels," *Economist*, July 5, 1986, p. 57.

American markets but occasionally supplied VW-Europe with less expensive components. Somewhat smaller-scale plants, oriented primarily toward assembly operations, were operating in Nigeria and South Africa during this period. Of all these ventures, the ones in Mexico and Nigeria were the most profitable. Growth in overseas production remained relatively modest.

During the transition to multimodel production, Leiding had called for wage restraints from the autoworkers. This made him extremely unpopular with the IG Metall, which had five seats on the supervisory board (*Aufsichtsrat*) of VW as a result of the campaign for codetermination in the late 1960s. The displeasure of the workers was also expressed through the SPD coalition government. Leiding admitted that perhaps he had "underestimated the influence of the Federal and Lower Saxony SPD governments who are part-owners of VW." In 1974, Leiding was replaced by Toni Schmücker, who had been in charge of the reorganization of the Rheinstahl firm in the early 1970s and was trusted by the SPD and the unions.[45]

The representatives of the government of of Lower Saxony and of the IG Metall cochaired the supervisory board of VW in 1974. The firm secured an agreement with IG Metall to reduce the work force by forty thousand (roughly one-fourth of the total) in exchange for distributing layoffs across different plants and avoiding plant closures. Some of these workers were Turks, who had to leave Germany after being laid off. Under the Treaty of Rome, Italian workers could not be expelled from Germany so they were offered generous severance payments. The government of Lower Saxony and the federal government agreed to implement a special program to provide assistance for dismissed German workers. Older workers were encouraged to take early retirement. By 1976, VW was back in the black.[46]

Diversification and Internationalization at Volkswagen since 1974

Since 1974, VW has successfully introduced several new models, including the Rabbit (Or Golf, as it is called in Europe). VW made major investments in production facilities in the United States (which did not earn much money and were closed in 1987)[47] and began a joint venture with Nissan in 1981 to produce a new model in Japan called the Santana to be sold in Asia. VW expected to benefit greatly from increased access to Asian markets, Nissan's marketing expertise, and advanced automotive components produced in that region.

45. Smith, *West German Political Economy*, p. 209.
46. Esser, Fach, and Dyson, " 'Social Market' and Modernization Policy," pp. 114–18.
47. "The People's Car Struggles to Change Gear," *Economist*, October 24, 1981, p. 65.

In 1983, VW signed an accord with the Spanish national firm SEAT (Sociedad Español de Automóviles de Turismo) to produce several VW models in Spain, and in 1986, it acquired full control over SEAT. Production at SEAT increased from 279,000 motor vehicles in 1984 to 433,000 in 1988.[48] In 1985, the Shanghai-Volkswagen Automotive Company was formed to assemble Santanas in China. VW had a 50 percent share of gross sales in the Brazilian auto market in the late 1970s, which declined in the early 1980s to around 40 percent. In 1987, VW formed a 51-49 joint venture with Ford in Brazil and Argentina called Autolatina to merge the activities of the two firms in those countries. Thus VW had made major steps toward internationalization to supplement its strategy of diversifying its model lines.

Volkswagen's efforts to diversify into information technology were not so successful. In 1979, Volkswagen acquired Triumph-Adler, a German office equipment manufacturer that had been late in seeing the need to make a transition to microelectronics-based products. This venture ended in 1986 when Triumph-Adler was sold to Olivetti after VW lost over 2 billion marks. Nevertheless, VW made important innovations in microelectronics-based process technology. In 1983, VW opened a new assembly plant in Wolfsburg, Hall 54, which used advanced factory automation techniques to assemble the new Golf model.[49]

Carl Hahn, who became the head of Volkswagen in 1982, focused in the late 1980s on the problem of increasing competition from low-wage countries in Asia. "The Koreans," he said, "are now at the wage levels of Germany in 1950, and then the Germans worked as many hours as the Koreans do today. . . . They are as capable of producing and developing sophisticated high tech products as we are. . . . By the year 2000, Korea will be an automobile manufacturer of the size of Germany."[50] Accordingly, Hahn pursued a strategy of developing new models that were slightly more luxurious than VW's earlier models (such as the Passat, first produced in 1988), automating plants in Germany (the plant that produced the new Passat made extensive use of robots and factory automation equipment), and increasing production in Spain and China.

VW received only minimal government support for these strategies. Because organized labor in Germany is so strong, an explicit agreement with German unions was needed to permit the greater flexibility of the work force required for ambitious factory automation schemes.

48. Kevin Done, "Survival of the Fittest," *Financial Times*, February 22, 1989, p. 19.
49. Volkswagen, *Annual Report*, 1986, p. 55.
50. Quoted from Andrew Fisher, "Car Maker with an Eye on New Horizons," *Financial Times*, March 13, 1989, p. 38.

VW also needed the unions' approval for increasing the firm's investments outside of Germany. Both agreements were made without the intervention or direct involvement of the government.[51]

The Case of Daimler

The case of Daimler illustrates the importance of banks in the German system and the increasing government role in setting the rules for restructuring European industry in anticipation of the freer flows of trade and investment in the so-called Europe 1992. Daimler has been a highly profitable firm for more than two decades but recently has faced increased competition in its major motor vehicle markets: luxury cars and commercial vehicles. Since 1985, it has diversified into a range of high-technology areas, particularly electronics and aerospace.[52] Its main problem now is to integrate these new interests into its existing businesses.

The major stakeholders in Daimler-Benz are the Deutsche Bank and the government of Kuwait. Deutsche Banks owns 28 percent of the firm; the Kuwait Investment Office owns 14 percent. In 1987, the chairman of Daimler, Werner Breitschwerdt, was replaced by the former finance director Edzard Reuter. One reason for this change was that the Deutsche Bank believed that Reuter was more likely to pursue and aggressive high-technology strategy. He was the chief architect of the diversification plan, supported by Alfred Herrhausen, the head of Deutsche Bank, who was killed by a terrorist bomb in November 1989.

Daimler has rescued troubled firms twice in recent years. In October 1985, it purchased a majority of the shares of AEG for 1.6 billion marks; in 1988, it purchased 30 percent of Messerschmidt-Bölkow-Blohm (MBB) for 800 million marks. Although AEG returned to profitability in 1986, it had had serious financial difficulties since 1974 (see Figure 19). The rationale for purchasing AEG was mainly technological. According to Reuter, "You will not be able to produce a car in the future, at least in the luxury bracket of the market, without integrating your engine, your gearbox, your axles, with an electronic system."[53] The German government welcomed the deal because it gave a threatened electronics firm access to the deep pockets of a major automotive producer.

51. See Wolfgang Streeck, "Successful Adjustment to Turbulent Markets," in Peter Katzenstein, ed., *Industry and Politics in West Germany: Toward the Third Republic* (Ithaca, N.Y.: Cornell University Press, 1989).

52. In 1984, 95 percent of Daimler's revenues came from motor vehicles. By 1988, this had dropped to 69 percent because of the diversification efforts. See Steven Greenhouse, "Daimler on a New Road," *New York Times*, April 9, 1989, p. F1.

53. Quoted from Lorenz, "Edzard Reuter."

Figure 19. Profits and losses of AEG

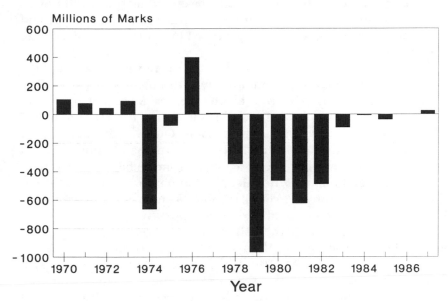

Sources: Doug Anderson, *AEG-Telefunken, A.G.* (Boston: Harvard Business School Press, 1981), case 1-381-187, p. 20; and "Der zweite Frühling in besseren Kreisen," *Industriemagazin,* June 1988, p. 39.

The purchase of AEG strained the traditionally close relationship between Daimler and Bosch, the automotive electronics and components firm. Daimler and Bosch are headquartered in Baden-Württemberg (Stuttgart), while BMW and Siemens are headquartered in Bavaria (Munich), which creates pressure for cooperation within the region and competition across the regions. The purchase of AEG upset this natural order. Bosch now fears that AEG will become a more serious competitor in supplying Daimler's automotive electronics needs. Daimler has tried to minimize the conflict by stressing the distinctive role of AEG in improving Daimler's factory automation capabilities but has not put pressure on AEG to focus its efforts in that direction.[54]

The acquisition of MBB was a rescue operation in which Daimler and the federal government shared the expense and the risk. Daimler paid 800 million marks for its 30 percent stake in MBB, but the federal government guaranteed Daimler against future losses connected with Airbus. The government agreed to provide up to 4.3 billion marks in subsidies in addition to the 10.7 billion already pledged to support the

54. Interview materials; and "Robert Bosch: Success by Stealth," *Economist,* July 9, 1988, p. 69.

Airbus program. A new holding company was set up to own West Germany's 37.9 percent share of the European Airbus consortium. This holding company was initially an 80-20 venture between Daimler and the federal government. Daimler promised to buy the government's 20 percent by 1999.[55]

Late in 1988, Daimler's acquisition of MBB ran into political difficulties when the Free Democratic Party (FDP) members of the CDU/FDP coalition government resisted the merger. Martin Bangemann, the minister of economics and a leading member of the FDP, was one of the principal architects of the deal. Count Otto von Lambsdorff returned to the leadership of the FDP late in 1988 and initially voiced strong distaste for it but later accepted its inevitability. In addition, both the Federal Cartel Office and the Commission of the European Community initially tried to block the deal. The Cartel Office was concerned that the merger would have anti-competitive effects on the German aerospace industry; the commission was concerned about the government subsidies that MBB would receive through Daimler in case of financial difficulties. But the EC approved the deal in March 1989 when it was satisfied that the subsidies would be limited and that new capital would be injected into MBB to increase its efficiency and international competitiveness. The Cartel Office vetoed the deal in April 1989, but Daimler then asked the new minister of economics, Helmut Haussmann, to override the veto, which he did.

The Daimler case illustrates some of the strengths and weaknesses of the German system. Working closely with Deutsche Bank, Daimler created a new focal point for German efforts to compete in a range of high technologies. It removed some of the fiscal burden from the federal government, which had been subsidizing both the aerospace and electronics industries. This strategy will be successful, however, only if Daimler can integrate the varied activities of its acquisitions into its existing activities without a major drop in overall profitability. In the German system industrial problems are often solved by merging less profitable firms into larger industrial units.

Policies for the Rest of the German Auto Industry

BMW had serious financial problems in the late 1950s but was restructured by the Bavarian state bank (which is controlled by the CSU) along with its major private lenders—another example of the general

55. Interview materials; "Daimler-Benz: Come Fly with Me," *Economist*, November *12*, *1988*, p. 77; and David Marsh, "West Germany Approves Daimler-Airbus Proposals," *Financial Times*, November 3, 1988, p. 20.

preference of the federal government to leave restructuring to the state governments and the banks.[56]

The German system of university-industry linkages and vocational education helped preserve the auto industry's competitiveness in the late 1970s and 1980s. The transition from mechanical machine tools to numerically controlled and computer numerically controlled machine tools in the small and medium enterprises that produce precision components for the auto industry was eased because German machine-tool firms could obtain technological assistance from the universities and could rely on high skill levels on the factory floor.[57]

State-societal arrangements have helped keep the German automobile industry competitive by easing the technological transitions. The pattern of weak government, strong business, and strong labor works because business responds quickly to changes in international competition and labor accepts changes in the workplace. Government provides a good macroeconomic environment and the necessary infrastructures for producing consumer durables for mass consumption.

The government seldom intervenes in the German auto industry. The main exceptions were in the bailout of BMW in the 1950s, the transition problems of Volkswagen in the mid-1970s, and the diversification efforts of Daimler-Benz in the middle and late 1980s. In the cases of BMW and VW, most of the restructuring was negotiated by the regional governments, the banks, the unions, and the firms themselves. Nor has the federal government been involved much in limiting inward foreign investment because of the inherent barriers created by the German financial system. Its most important role has been to create a skilled work force and a strong macroeconomic underpinning to upgrade the technological infrastructure.

German auto firms have relied on the high skill base of the work force to maintain as much high-value-added production in Germany as possible, shifting low-value-added processes to low-wage offshore production facilities. Almost all important production of components still occurs in Germany, mostly in small and medium-sized firms, because of the rapid diffusion of advanced machine tools. The training

56. Smith, *West German Economy*, p. 209. The federal government does not always let state banks do the rescuing. Because of the predominance of the CSU in Bavaria and of Franz-Josef Strauss in the CSU before his death, national party politics tend to be projected onto the policies of certain state banks. This is the only explanation for the recent 1 billion mark loan from the Bavarian state bank to the East German government.

57. Interview materials. See also Ira Magaziner and Mark Patinkin, *The Silent War: Inside the Global Business Battles Shaping America's Future* (New York: Random House, 1989), chap. 4.

programs designed and managed jointly by businesses, unions, and governments have helped to make this possible.

The German unions could have blocked the modernization and internationalization efforts of Volkswagen, Ford, and Opel, but they chose not to. They envisioned a future for themselves in the practices of the luxury car producers such as Daimler and BMW. Thus Volkswagen was able to combine intensive factory automation at home with heavy investments in offshore production.

Policies for the Semiconductor Industry

The German auto industry has been a pillar of strength and therefore relatively free of state intervention except in times of temporary crisis. The same cannot be said for the semiconductor industry. Germany is Europe's biggest market for semiconductors (32 percent in 1980, 29 percent in 1983).[58] Yet to date, only Siemens has managed to compete with other major suppliers in Europe and is fifth after Philips, Texas Instruments, SGS-Thomson, and Motorola. Other German firms such as AEG, SEL (Standard Elektrik Lorenz), and Bosch have semiconductor production units but do not compete in marks for high-volume circuits. The weakness of the semiconductor industry prompted the government first to support national champions (in this case, Siemens and AEG) and later to approve a series of cooperative arrangements between Siemens and other European firms.[59]

Semiconductor Firms in Germany

German semiconductor manufacturers include Siemens, AEG, Valvo (the German subsidiary of Philips), Bosch, Intermetall (a subsidiary of ITT), SEL (formerly a subsidiary of ITT, purchased by Alcatel of France in 1986), IBM-Deutschland, Texas Instruments, and Motorola. German-owned firms are in a weak position overall. They lagged behind U.S. and Japanese firms in integrating semiconductor technology into products and production processes and therefore had a smaller and less secure base for expansion than did firms in the United States and Japan (see Figure 20). Uwe Thomas, director of

58. "Siemens Is Set to Take on the World in Integrated Circuits," *Business Week*, August 6, 1984, p. 64.
59. Gerd Junne, "Multinationale Konzerne in 'High Technology'-Sektoren, Oder: Wie gut ist die Strategie vom guten Zweiten," in Peter H. Mettler, ed., *Wohin expandieren multinationale Konzerne?* (Frankfurt: Haag und Herchen, 1985), pp. 11–14.

Figure 20. Revenues and profits of German electronics firms

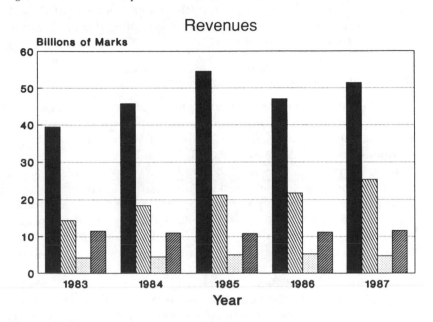

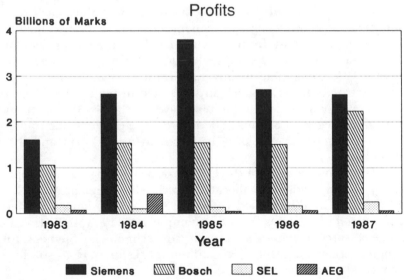

Source: Reuters Dataline database.

electronics research of the German Ministry of Technology and Research (BMFT), said in 1982 that "the main emphasis of this Ministry is to see what we can do in strengthening the application of microelectronics."[60]

Government Support for the Computer Industry

The German government began to worry about the data processing industry in the early 1960s. In 1964, over 60 percent of the mainframe computers in Germany had been made by IBM and only 11 percent by German producers (Siemens, AEG, SEL, and Zuse).[61] In August 1965, ministerial meetings were held to discuss ways to promote the national computer industry. Siemens and AEG prepared a joint memorandum in which they proposed a partnership for research and development in electronic calculators. The plan was supported by the Ministry of Scientific Research (a precursor of the BMFT) and the Ministry of Defense, and the Data Processing Program was approved by the cabinet in March 1967.

This program provided funding over fifteen years to finance development efforts by individual firms. Siemens and AEG received the lion's share, 995 million marks and 295 million marks, respectively. Nixdorf (founded in 1968), Kienzle, and Philips each received less than 50 million marks. Siemens decided to license mainframe computer technology from RCA rather than develop its own. When RCA abandoned the computer business, Siemens switched to marketing IBM-compatible mainframes from Fujitsu. None of the major electronics firms in Germany was able to match the innovations that were going on in the United States in the field of semiconductors and integrated circuits. The importance of microelectronic components was perceived slowly in Germany as in Japan and the rest of Europe.

A five-year extension of the Data Processing Program was approved in 1971, and funds were allocated for the development MOS devices. In the third funding period 1976–79, AEG was designated to develop high-speed LSI devices for use in computing. The BMFT also funded some research in generic semiconductor technologies. Siemens, for example, received a grant of 26 million marks in 1972 to subsidize its semiconductor research.

---

60. "Last Chance Tactics of European Chip Makers," *Business Week*, June 28, 1982, p. 117.

61. For the early days of the German computer industry, see Kenneth Flamm, *Creating the Computer: Government, Industry, and High Technology* (Washington, D.C.: Brookings Institution, 1988), pp. 159–62.

Government Support for Semiconductor Research

In 1974, BMFT announced grants of 376 million marks over five years to develop integrated circuits. Siemens was to develop MOS memory devices, and AEG was to work on computer-aided design tools. Gallium arsenide research was also funded, although at relatively low levels.

German firms were still not confident enough of their technological capabilities to rely solely on German technologies. Siemens began a long series of acquisitions of U.S. firms when it purchased Dickson in 1974. In 1975, Siemens licensed the 8080 microprocessor from Intel, AEG licensed microprocessors from Rockwell, and Nixdorf concluded a purchase agreement with Nitron, a subsidiary of McDonnell-Douglas. In 1977, Siemens acquired Litronix and 20 percent of Advanced Micro Devices. Bosch bought 25 percent of American Microsystems in 1977.

The BMFT's five-year program for 1979–84 reflected its recognition of the importance of semiconductors. The ministry's expenditures in information technology shifted dramatically during the 1970s from support of information processing such as computers to microelectronics.[62] Nevertheless, total expenditures for research in these two areas were relatively limited. As in other industrial countries, procurement policies were probably more important in promoting domestic firms than direct R&D subsidies.

The BMFT's five-year program for 1984–89 called for the expenditure of 1.2 billion marks to support research on integrated circuits, data processing, and industrial automation. The minister of technology and research, Heinz Riesenhuber, defended these efforts, saying: "If we want to be internationally competitive and create new jobs, we absolutely must use the big potential for innovation and growth in [electronics] technology."[63] Although Riesenhuber's statement reflects the federal government's concern about German competitiveness in high-technology electronics, its funding of semiconductor research remained relatively modest until 1984, when Siemens joined with Philips to initiate the Mega Project.

Procurement Policies to Promote Microelectronics

Part of the overall strategy for promoting German microelectronics was the use of the Bundespost—a state-owned monopoly that

62. *West Europe Report: Science and Technology; FRG [Federal Republic of Germany] Information Technology; Perspectives, Goals, Funded Programs,* JPRS-WST-86-013, Foreign Broadcast Information Service, Washington, D.C., March 28, 1986.

63. Quoted from "Bonn's Late Push in the High Tech Race," *Business Week,* April 9, 1984, p. 43.

controlled all main and telecommunications services—to purchase more advanced technological products. The Bundespost met with firms such as Siemens and AEG before establishing specifications for contracts to purchase telecommunications equipment. It paid premium prices for advanced semiconductors that helped the German firms realize dynamic economies of scale by increasing yields in semiconductor production. This use of the Bundespost was criticized in the mid-1980s both at home and abroad. Telecommunications users claimed that the Bundespost was not allowing them to create their own private telecommunications systems and was charging higher prices for services than did similar agencies in other countries. The postal workers union and the traditional telecommunications equipment suppliers (including Siemens) sided with the Bundespost in resisting attempts to liberalize telecommunications markets. The proponents of liberalization included rival telecommunications equipment suppliers (such as SEL), major users of telecommunications equipment, and a variety of professional, academic, and consumer groups. A compromise was worked out in 1988 permitting greater competition among major suppliers to the Bundespost and in markets for terminal equipment (telephones, modems, PBXs, and the like). The Bundespost's ability to subsidize technological development through its procurement policies diminished, and Siemens, which had benefited from preferential supplier arrangements, had to adjust to more competition in its core markets.[64]

Siemens and the Mega Project

In 1983, Siemens decided to make major new investments in the production of standard MOS memory devices especially DRAMs. Karlheinz Kaske who became head of Siemens in 1981, believed that dependence on Siemens's competitors for the supply of key components such as DRAMs was not in the firm's long-term interests. Apparently Siemens had had difficulty bringing new telecommunications products to the market when Japanese firms refused to sell their newest chips. According to Jürgen H. Knorr, head of Siemens's semiconductor unit, "We were being manipulated."[65]

The Mega Project would develop new integrated circuits in three phases: 1-megabit DRAMs at 1.2 micron line widths; 4-megabit DRAMs

---

64. Interview materials; Patrick Cogez, *Telecommunications in West Germany* (Berkeley: Berkeley Roundtable on the International Economy, 1985); and Jacob F. Blackburn, *The Telecommunications and Computer Industries in Western Europe* (Washington, D.C.: Department of Commerce, 1986).

65. Quoted from "Siemens: A Plodding Giant Starts to Pick Up Speed," *Business Week*, February 20, 1989, p. 136.

at 0.7 micron line widths; and devices with 0.3 micron line widths. The initial investment allocated for this project was 1.4 billion marks. The 1-megabit DRAM was to be developed at a Siemens facility in Regensburg. The firm hoped to bring the chip to market by 1986, but it encountered problems that made it decide on international collaboration.

In October 1984, Siemens and Philips agreed to work together on the Mega Project. In 1982 they had signed a long-range R&D agreement to develop submicron technology, computer-aided design, speech recognition, and new materials. The earliest agreement was to involve about fifty scientists from the two firms and only $3.7 million in funding. In 1984, the funding was increased to around $500 million with an additional $170 million to come from the Dutch and German governments. The two firms would work together to develop two submicron CMOS circuits by the end of 1988: a 1-megabit static RAM (SRAM) and a 4-megabit DRAM.

Problems in designing and manufacturing its 1-megabit DRAMs compelled Siemens to turn to Toshiba in July 1985 to supply the production equipment and circuit designs for these chips. Commercial production of the devices began in January 1987. The Toshiba production technology for 1-megabit DRAMs used five-inch silicon wafers. The Siemens engineers wanted to use six-inch wafers and purchased the wrong alignment equipment in the United States. The equipment had to be scrapped, and the 1-megabit production was badly off schedule, even with the purchase of technology from Toshiba.

Siemens sold 1.5 million units in 1987. The total demand in Europe for that year was 10 million units. Siemens's customers, including German computer firms such as Nixdorf, were very unhappy with its low output. But without the agreement with Toshiba, Siemens would have been even later in delivering its 1-megabit DRAMs. In 1988, Siemens sold around 3.5 million units at around $60 per unit. But both the Dutch and German governments were displeased at having helped subsidize the purchase of Japanese technology.[66]

Siemens was behind IBM and several Japanese firms in bringing 4-megabit DRAMs to market, but the lead of Siemens's competitors had decreased. By the end of the Mega Project, Siemens and Philips were widely recognized as being ahead of Japan and the United States in the development of x-ray lithography equipment and other technologies necessary for achieving submicron line widths. The final cost of the Mega Project was around 4 billion marks: 1.5 billion for research and 2.5 billion for fabrication facilities. The firms provided all of the funding for the latter. Of the total for research, 403 million marks

66. Interview materials.

came from the two governments: 243 million from the German government and 160 million from the Dutch government.[67]

The European Debate over JESSI

In 1986, Siemens, Philips, and Thomson began to discuss a follow-up to the Mega Project to be called the Joint European Submicron Silicon Initiative. The initial proposals called for an eight-year program budgeted at 3 to 4 billion marks to develop and design manufacturing technologies for the next generation of integrated circuits. As in the Mega Project, a large proportion of the total budget would come directly from the Dutch and German governments.

The French government and Thomson pressured SGS-Thomson to participate in JESSI,[68] but Siemens and Philips were not eager to include SGS-Thomson because Thomson had not invested in the Mega Project. The Siemens representative, Hermann Franz, said that "Philips and Siemens will develop the technology itself. But SGS-Thomson could be associated with work on design and equipment."[69] The French, however, insisted that SGS-Thomson should have equal status with Siemens and Philips.

In June 1988, the Dutch government announced that it would renew its subsidies for Philips's participation in the Mega Project and JESSI. In November, the European Community began to consider funding JESSI. When Karlheinz Kaske was asked on November 17 if he thought EC funding was essential, he said it was indicating that Plessey might participate in JESSI if the GEC-Siemens acquisition (see Chapter 4) was approved. In January 1989, Plessey officially joined the project. In April 1989, Heinz Dürr of the AEG subsidiary of Daimler announced that Daimler would like to join the project. The Mega Project had spawned a broad European effort to develop new semiconductor technologies within JESSI.

By the end of the 1980s, JESSI was widely recognized as a world leader in the development of the next generation of semiconductor manufacturing equipment. It was particularly strong in x-ray lithography. Both Japan and the United States were weak in this area. IBM petitioned JESSI for access to its research on x-ray lithography and con-

67. J. Nicholas Ziegler, "The Hare and Tortoise Revisited: Political Strategies for Technological Advance in the French and West German Semiconductor Industries," manuscript, Department of Government, Harvard University, December 12, 1987, p. 35.

68. The merger of Thomson's semiconductor operations with those of SGS in 1987 made SGS-Thomson, with sales of $859 million in 1987, the second largest European semiconductor firm, behind Philips ($1.6 billion) but ahead of Siemens ($657 million).

69. Quoted from Guy de Jonquieres, "European Chips Plan Clouded by Siemens, SGS-Thomson Dispute," Financial Times, April 5, 1988, p. 1.

tinued to support joint research on semiconductor manufacturing in the United States (see Chapter 6).

Siemens's dramatic and ultimately successful efforts to reserve its dependency on foreign suppliers of standard circuits helped end a period of "Europessimism" in Germany. The federal government provided subsidies and political support for the Mega Project and JESSI. Siemens's subsidies from the Bundespost for telecommunications equipment enabled the firm to make enormous investments required. The federal and regional governments helped indirectly by funding the Fraunhofer Institutes, which set the agenda for and did some of the basic research in both projects. German unions were flexible about working time at semiconductor and wafer fabrication facilities so they could be operated on a twenty-four-hour basis, as is the global norm. Finally, European institutions, particularly EUREKA, helped facilitate the formation of European R&D consortia.[70]

The Case of AEG

The biggest industrial crisis in electronics in Germany involved Siemens's nearest German competitor, AEG. The near collapse and rescue of AEG illustrates the tendency of the state to avoid involvement in rescues unless absolutely necessary and the relatively important role played by the private banks. It also illustrates the tendency of the German system to solve industrial problems by creating internationally oriented national champions.

AEG has deep roots in German industrial history. It was an early innovator in radio and electronics and the main rival of Siemens. By the 1970s, AEG had become a highly diversified holding company with equity participation in nuclear engineering, consumer electronics, and a variety of other businesses. In 1983, it was Europe's fourth largest electronics concern and the twelfth largest in the world.[71] It employed 120,000 workers, more than 100,000 of them in Germany. AEG has been crucial in establishing Germany as a major industrial nation. Thus its fall from grace in the late 1970s and early 1980s was a shock to most Germans. Trouble began in the mid-1970s, when AEG and Siemens, which were partners in the nuclear engineering concern Kraftwerk Union, took major losses in the restructuring of that firm. For AEG, the cost was between 1.0 and 1.5 billion marks.[72] But the

70. Interview materials.
71. Esser, Fach, and Dyson, " 'Social Market' and Modernization Policy," p. 118.
72. "Banking on Recovery: A Survey of International Banking," *Economist*, March 26, 1983, p. 49; and Doug Anderson, *AEG-Telefunken, A.G.* (Boston: Harvard Business School, 1981), case 1-381-187, p. 9.

main problem was that AEG, failing to see that its consumer electronics business could not compete with foreign firms, had delayed too long in diversifying out of consumer electronics and shoring up its other businesses. It also had serious weaknesses in microelectronics.

AEG paid no dividends after 1973. Losses in 1979 amounted to nearly 1 billion marks. On October 24, 1979, the chief executive officer, Walter Cipa, informed the supervisory board of the firm that there were big problems and that major layoffs of employees were likely. The next day, the IG Metall representatives of the organized workers at AEG issued a press release saying that large layoffs were anticipated and that the union opposed them. IG Metall representatives on the supervisory board were accused by representatives of major shareholders of leaking confidential internal information. The union representatives defended themselves by arguing that the management's first recourse was always to lay people off rather than find ways to maintain employment.

On November 8, 1979, four AEG representatives met with the minister of economics, Count Otto von Lambsdorff, and the minister of finance, Hans Matthöfer, to try to gain assistance from the federal government in resolving AEG's problems, but their efforts were to no avail. On December 4, 1979, a rescue plan put together by the major banks under the leadership of the Dresdner and Deutsche banks was announced. This plan included a major write-down of the nominal value of AEG shares, a restructuring of its debt, the layoff of twelve thousand employees, the closure of a gas turbine plant, and a "solidarity contribution" of German manufacturing firms (an agreement to purchase 200 to 450 million marks worth of unsecured debentures at less than the market rate of interest).[73]

The banks were anxious to avoid intervention by the federal government, as were some firms. A German businessman observed: "Small firms get into trouble all the time and go under. But a business of this size can't be allowed to fall. The State won't let it. We saw that the United States did not abandon Chrysler and Canada won't abandon Massey-Ferguson either. We were therefore of the opinion that in Germany, as well, the State would not allow a company like AEG to go bankrupt. We concluded that if we wanted to preserve our economic system, we had to make an attempt to save the company without leaving that task to government."[74] The problem of not encouraging other large firms to expect bailouts was dealt with by making the terms of the rescue less than generous. There was also concern that the AEG's failure would further reduce competition in the German market.

73. Anderson, *AEG-Telefunken*, pp. 1–2.
74. Ibid., p. 16.

In 1980, Hans Friderichs of the Dresdner Bank was elected chairman of the board of directors (*Vorstand*) and brought in a new manager for the firm, Heinz Dürr, who had previously run Robert Bosch GmbH, a producer of automobile components and electronic products. AEG, along with Bosch and Mannesmann, made some new investments in telecommunications, and the situation began to look a little brighter. In the summer of 1982, however, AEG rejected an offer from the British General Electric Corporation to purchase 40 percent of AEG's capital goods business, and the value of AEG stock fell precipitously.

By July 1982, AEG was once more on the edge of bankruptcy. A new rescue was devised with direct involvement of the federal government, which came up with 1.1 billion marks in loan guarantees and 85 percent of a 0.6 billion mark package of export credits. Because of the government guarantees, the banks agreed to grant the firm 1.1 billion in new loans. AEG then filed for "composition" (*Vergleich*), which is roughly equivalent to reorganization under Chapter 11 of the bankruptcy laws in the United States and can be done in Germany only if write-offs of debt are less than 65 percent of existing debt and 75 percent of all creditors agree to the package. A writer for the *Economist* observed: "West Germany's way of financing industry puts most of the burden of rescues on to the banks for two reasons. The universal banking system makes banks more deeply committed to industry than elsewhere. And the government's *laissez faire* approach to industrial finance leaves banks to pick up the tab when things go wrong."[75]

In the next episode of this sad story, AEG's consumer electronics subsidiary, AEG-Telefunken, was sold to the French firm Thomson-Brandt in March 1983 largely because the German Cartel Office blocked the sale to Thomson of a somewhat larger German consumer electronics firms, Grundig. The official story was that the purchase of Grundig would reduce competition in consumer electronics to an unacceptably low level, but a major reason why the federal government opposed the Thomson-Grundig deal was because Philips owned 24.5 percent of Grundig and Grundig was a major purchaser of semiconductors produced by Siemens.[76]

In the early 1980s AEG began to recover from the big losses of the late 1970s. In October 1985, Daimler-Benz announced that it was purchasing a majority share of AEG's stock for 1.6 billion marks. The purchase eliminated AEG's debt and gave it access to the ample cash reserves of Daimler-Benz. In turn, Daimler-Benz gained access to AEG's technology in semiconductors, telecommunications, military electronics, and satellite and space technology. With combined annual

75. "Banking on Recovery," p. 50.
76. Interview materials.

sales of 60 billion marks, the new firm would be Germany's largest industrial concern. In 1986, AEG reported a profit of around 1 million marks after three years of almost break-even performance.[77]

German government policy generally has been to let firms do whatever they can to become internationally competitive. The German government decided to became a major backer, through direct subsidies for the Mega Project and JESSI, of Siemens's efforts to produce high-volume integrated circuits. Like Volkswagen and Daimler-Benz, Siemens is a national champion firm. The financial difficulties of AEG, in contrast with the high profitability of Siemens, eventually led to the incorporation of AEG into the Daimler-Benz empire with the blessing of the Deutsche Bank. The role of the German government in that absorption was purely permissive. It was a move that made sense for Daimler-Benz independent of government aspirations for German electronics.

The German system has managed to preserve two internationally viable electronics firms in a highly competitive world market but at the cost of creating giant firms. Perhaps this was inevitable; the Japanese competition also created giants. But Japan has six giants, and Germany has only two and therefore competition within Germany is not as strong as it is within Japan. The German giants, furthermore, are much more dependent on the state than are the Japanese giants and much more in need of allies outside of their own country. Moreover, the German system's focus on giants has detracted from efforts to build the capacity for innovation in small and medium-sized concerns. Thus, though the ability of the German system to adapt to the changing competitive environment of recent years is impressive, it has areas of weakness that may come back to haunt it.

Conclusions

The pattern of state-societal arrangements in Germany of weak federal government, strong business, and strong labor has helped to increase or maintain international competitiveness in the steel and auto industries but has been less successful in the semiconductor industry. Still, Germany remains close to Japan in overall and industry-specific competitiveness since World War II, which shows that there is a real alternative to the Japanese pattern of strong state and strong business.

77. Jonathan Carr, "Daimler-Benz Buys Majority Stake in AEG," *Financial Times*, October 15, 1985, p. 1.

When both business and labor are strong, the response to changes in technologies is faster because business has the confidence to introduce new technologies in the workplace and labor has the confidence to accept them. Because organized labor participates in national and regional politics through its allies in the Social Democratic party, it takes a moderate stance on economic issues, which allows the government to pursue cautious but generally wise macroeconomic policies. Because organized labor has extensive power on the shop floor, it tends to be willing to accept new technologies in the workplace. German labor unions frequently cite productivity figures when bargaining for higher wages so technologies that increase productivity are generally more welcome there than in other large industrial countries.

The Germans have studiously avoided administrative guidance of the French or Japanese varieties. Indeed, because of the decentralized nature of the German system, that option is not open to them. They have compensated for the lack of a centralized bureaucratic structure with a combination of R&D subsidies, university-business linkages, mergers, bank-led rescues, and reliance on the high skill level of the work force. During the time of the SPD/FDP coalition, the federal government's capacity to intervene in specific regional and industrial crises was substantial, but the government remained firmly committed to allowing other social actors (especially the banks) to try their hand at resolving crises before it got involved.

On the whole, this system has worked well. Despite lower growth rates and higher unemployment in the 1980s, German trade surpluses are second only to those of Japan. The average German citizens, however, is far wealthier than the average Japanese citizen. German workers enjoy much greater influence in workplace and national politics than do Japanese workers. German industries have adjusted to changes in world markets much more successfully than those in other European countries. The ability of a few firms such as Siemens and Bosch to become internationally competitive in high-technology industries has created a new sense of optimism among the German population. Nevertheless, the German economy is too sluggish, too dependent on exports, and too oriented toward industries such as low-priced automobiles that may be threatened from external competition in the future.

German state-societal arrangements contribute to both the strengths and weaknesses of the system. They help to promote the rapid diffusion of new technologies, but they also help to preserve the "clubby" atmosphere of German business. They give Germany the advantage of a highly skilled work force, but they make that work force less flexible than might be desirable to meet international competition. The arrangements in the financial sphere help to slow the rate of inward foreign investment and to give firms the luxury of a long time horizon for decision making, but they also make it difficult for new, potentially more innovative German firms to get access to capital. Accordingly, there are likely to be battles over changes in these arrangements in the future.

The German case illustrates that it is not necessary to copy the Japanese model to be internationally competitive. Because of differences in the state-societal arrangements among the major industrialized nations, it may not be possible or desirable to copy the Japanese. Were it to do so, the German government would have to become much stronger, German labor would have to become much weaker, and German business would have to accept a much more interventionist state than presently exist. What precisely would be gained will be discussed in the concluding chapter.

SIX

The United States

People knowledgeable about economic policy making in the United States seldom admit that the country even has an industrial policy. Industrial policy, like planning, is not a popular subject with American elites. In academic discussions in the United States, industrial policy is often equated with direct subsidies, protectionism, and other market-distorting practices that a large number of people dislike. These practices are frequently referred to in a single abbreviated phrase: "picking winners and losers."

Since 1980, however, a variety of explicit industrial policies have been proposed, including export trading companies, ministries for trade and industry like MITI,[1] new versions of the Reconstruction Finance Corporation of the New Deal,[2] and radical revisions of antitrust laws.[3] These proposals have come from both of the major political parties and been supported by diverse interests. But a hard core of resistance to tinkering with time-cherished myths and institutions remains.

The main argument of this chapter is that the United States has a fragmented industrial policy that stresses the use of tax, defense,

1. Senator Adlai Stevenson III was the principal advocate of new ministries. He was later supported by Secretary of Commerce Malcolm Baldridge and other interested parties. See Lawrence Franko, "Japan's Multinational Challenge," *Harvard International Review*, January–February 1983, p. 18

2. Felix Rohatyn, "The Coming Emergency and What Can Be Done about It," *New York Review of Books*, December 4, 1980, p. 20.

3. Robert E. Taylor, "Reagan to Seek Cut in Damages for Trust Suits," *Wall Street Journal*, March 23, 1983, p. 3. See also 19 below. The proposals for antitrust reforms initiated by Attorney General Edwin Meese in 1985 were echoed in the 1991 proposals of Attorney General Richard Thornburgh.

procurement, and technology policies and relies mainly on the large size of the U.S. market and the enterprise of its firms to retain competitiveness in world markets. This policy has not been very successful in the apparel, steel, consumer electronics, automobiles, and, more recently, semiconductor and machine-tool industries.[4] A succession of difficulties in key industries has generated an active public debate since the late 1970s over new state-societal arrangements but has not produced major changes in the key institutions linking the state and society. The continuity of institutions despite proposed innovations requires an explanation. In this chapter, as in previous ones, the core of the explanation lies in preexisting state-societal arrangements.

THE INSTITUTIONAL FRAMEWORK

State-societal arrangements in the United States combine a highly fragmented government with strong business interests and relatively weak organized labor. Business strength vis-à-vis the state is firmly entrenched. Those who speak for business in the aggregate oppose almost all forms of government intervention beyond the setting of macroeconomic policy. Although firms and industries experiencing heightened international competition have been known to petition the government to intervene in their favor, usually by adopting tariffs or other import restrictions, these petitions have not been supported by fellow industrialists since the adoption of the Reciprocal Trade Agreement Act of 1934.[5]

Labor is weak in the United States, and its interests are only imperfectly represented in party politics and government agencies. This is not to say that the voice of labor is never heard. Organized labor played a central role in American politics in the 1960s as a cornerstone to the electoral coalitions for Presidents John Kennedy and Lyndon Johnson. Labor supported Keynesian demand management, desegregation, and the war on poverty. The leadership of organized labor—with the notable exception of the Teamsters Union—supported Hubert Humphrey over Richard Nixon and Jimmy Carter over Ronald Reagan, but

4. For an excellent documentation of the decline of these industries, see Michael L. Dertouzos, Richard K. Lester, and Robert M. Solow, *Made in America: Regaining the Productive Edge* (Cambridge, Mass.: MIT Press, 1989). Anticipating the developments described there is John Zysman and Laura Tyson, eds., *American Industry in International Competition: Government Policies and Corporate Strategies* (Ithaca, N.Y.: Cornell University Press, 1983).

5. See David A. Lake, *Power, Protection, and Free Trade: International Sources of U.S. Commercial Strategy, 1887–1939* (Ithaca, N.Y.: Cornell University Press, 1988), p. 7.

the rank and file did not. By the 1970s, labor spoke with many voices, all of them weak.

Though its overall influence fluctuates, organized labor shares many of the views of the business leadership about the role of the government. Labor does not want too much government intervention in the economy, especially in labor-management relations. Until the late 1970s, labor supported the open trade and investment policies favored by business. Even though business and labor increasingly disagree over trade and foreign investment, they continue to share the same vision of America as a global military power fueled by a vigorous and dynamic economy.

The American state evolved within a tradition of amateurism. There has never been recruitment of top-level bureaucrats solely from elite universities, as in Japan and France. There is no tradition of an elite civil service, as in Britain and Germany, with the possible exception of the notion held mostly by eastern white Anglo-Saxons of an obligation to "serve the public" by occupying high government posts. This idea suggests that serving the public requires sacrifices (for example, in income and prestige)—the reverse of the Japanese notion of *amakudari* (descent form heaven) and the French *pantoufflage* (putting on a slipper) to describe the move from public office to the private sector.

Although there is a general aversion to adopting explicit industrial or mesoeconomic policies, they are made through a variety of channels, probably the most important of which is the Department of Defense. The United States expends enormous resources in two other areas—agriculture and health—which strengthens the competitiveness of industries in both fields. These three fields increasingly bear the burden of reversing the decline of U.S. competitiveness in other areas. The inability of existing institutions to meet the challenges in nondefense, nonagricultural, and non-health-related industries provokes debates about institutional reform, but reform has been blocked by the ideological preferences of socially dominant coalitions and institutional inertia.

The Organization of the State

One of the distinguishing features of the organization of the American state is the fragmentation of power. The federal system gives extensive powers to the state and local governments (as in Germany), and the division of power among the executive, legislative, and judicial branches creates further fragmentation. The Congress carries more weight in economic policy making that does the legislature of any other large capitalist country. Within the executive branch, economic policy making is decentralized, further fragmenting the state's authority.[6]

The Executive Branch

The most important executive branch agencies with a role in making industrial policy, roughly in order of importance, are the president and his domestic policy advisers; the Office of Management and Budget (OMB); the Council of Economic Advisers (CEA); the Department of Defense (DOD); the Department of the Treasury; the Antitrust Division of the Department of Justice; the Office of the U.S. Trade Representative (USTR); the Department of Commerce; and various interagency task forces and coordinating committees. Because of the relatively open and decentralized nature of economic policy making, many other bureaucratic agencies can get involved in the formulation and implementation of industrial policies. The Department of Labor, for example, has administered programs for retraining workers and for providing adjustment assistance to workers in "trade-impacted" industries. The Department of Transportation gets involved in trade disputes involving the automobile industry. The Department of Energy has responsibilities for dealing with dependence on foreign sources of energy. The National Science Foundation helps to formulate national policies for research and development. The eight agencies enumerated above, however, are regularly involved in the making of industrial policies.[7]

The President and the Domestic Policy Advisers

The president plays a central role in economic policy making by the executive branch. All disputes that cannot be settled at a lower level

6. The thesis that power is fragmented in the American state owes much to Theodore Lowi, *The End of Liberalism: The Second Republic of the United States*, 2d ed. (New York: Norton, 1979), and Stephen S. Krasner, "United States Commercial and Monetary Policy: Unravelling the Paradox of External Strength and Internal Weakness," in Peter J. Katzenstein, ed., *Between Power and Plenty: Foreign Economic Policies of Advanced Industrial States* (Madison: University of Wisconsin Press, 1978).

7. I have left out the Federal Reserve Board because my focus is on industrial policy rather than macroeconomic policy. Discussions of U.S. economic policy making often omit the Department of Defense because that agency has little influence over macroeconomic policy. See, for example, George C. Edwards III and Stephen J. Wayne, *Presidential Leadership: Politics and Policy Making* (New York: St. Martin's Press, 1985), chap. 9; Roger B. Porter, *Presidential Decision Making: The Economic Policy Board* (Cambridge: Cambridge University Press, 1980); David C. Mowery, Mark S. Camlet, and John P. Crecine, "Presidential Management of Budgetary and Fiscal Policymaking," *Political Science Quarterly* 95 (Fall 1980): 395–426; Roger B. Porter, "Economic Advice to the President: From Eisenhower to Reagan," *Political Science Quarterly* 98 (Fall 1983): 403–26; and Herbert Stein, *Presidential Economics: The Making of Economic Policy from Roosevelt to Reagan and Beyond* (New York: Simon and Schuster, 1984).

eventually reach his office. The president cannot always end the bickering, but he can reduce internal squabbling by putting his prestige and power behind his chosen solution to a particular problem. The president's annual budget proposals, establishment of R&D priorities, and trade policy give him significant discretionary authority. Nevertheless, all policies are negotiated with Congress and other groups with particular interest in them.

Until the presidency of Franklin D. Roosevelt, the Office of the president was a simple affair, mostly consisting of a personal staff. Roosevelt made the office into a small bureaucracy, which now consists primarily of the Office of Policy Development, the Council of Economic Advisers, and the staff of the National Security Council.[8] The Office of Policy Development handles communications from domestic interest groups that want presidential intervention. It staffs the various cabinet councils, thus helping to mold the agenda for cabinet deliberations on economic policy. The head of the Office of Policy Development reports to the White House chief of staff, who controls access to the president and his top advisers.[9]

The Office of Management and Budget

The OMB deals with the minutiae of preparing the president's proposals for the national budget. The director of the OMB defends the president's budget before Congress. In addition, the OMB monitors the expenditures of the various agencies to make sure that they are staying within their budgets. The director of the OMB informs cabinet officers and other heads of agencies when they may be overcommitting themselves. The director needs to have a good relationship with the president so that he can speak authoritatively to the agency heads. The director is almost inevitably a key policy adviser to the president because of his familiarity with the multifarious activities of the government.[10]

8. The Domestic Council was established in the Executive Office of the President in 1970 under Richard Nixon's executive branch reorganization plan. The Domestic Council became the Domestic Policy Staff in 1977 under the Carter administration. In 1981, the Domestic Policy Staff was renamed the Office of Policy Development. See Larry Berman, *The New American Presidency* (Boston: Little, Brown, 1987), p. 121. For a good summary of the argument about the expansion of the powers of the presidency after FDR, see Fred I. Greenstein, "Continuity and Change in the Modern Presidency," in Anthony King, ed., *The New American Political System* (Washington, D.C.: American Enterprise Institute, 1979); John Helmer, "The Presidential Office: Velvet Fist in an Iron Glove," in Hugh Heclo and Lester M. Salamon, eds., *The Illusion of Presidential Government* (Boulder, Colo.: Westview Press, 1981), pp. 57–61.

9. See Berman, *New American Presidency*, pp. 113–21; and Edwards and Wayne, *Presidential Leadership*, pp. 246–51.

10. See Larry Berman, *The Office of Management and Budget and the Presidency, 1921–1979* (Princeton, N.J.: Princeton University Press, 1979).

The Council of Economic Advisers

The president selects a group of mostly academic economists to join the Council of Economic Advisers. The offices of the CEA are located in the Old Executive Office Building next to the White House. The chairman of the CEA is often a trusted friend of the president who had provided advice during electoral campaigns. The chairman of the CEA and the director of the OMB often join in opposing narrowly targeted economic policies.

The Department of Defense

The Department of Defense is the most important of all the cabinet agencies in the making of industry-specific policies. The sheer size of its personnel and budget make it a major force. More important, a tutelary relationship exists between the Department of Defense and the defense contractors, not unlike that between MITI and major Japanese firms or between the Ministry of Industry and major French firms. DOD works with both its major contractors and other firms to build industrial strength in areas that are deemed crucial for national security purposes by subsidizing R&D for the development of military or "dual-use"[11] technologies and by purchasing items for use by the various branches of the armed forces.

The DOD accounts for a significant fraction of the total R&D spending of the United States—some would argue too significant. Roughly 40 percent of total annual R&D spending is financed by the government, a larger share than in any other major industrial country. Military R&D makes up a substantial proportion of that 40 percent (the rest is primarily space, medical, energy, and agricultural research). In 1988, for example, DOD spent $33.1 billion for R&D. The same year, IBM's R&D expenditures were $4.4 billion. Thus DOD manages an R&D operation eight times the size of the largest corporate program.[12] Until recently, because of the byzantine nature of DOD procurement and contracting regulations, the department worked with a limited number of firms that specialized in supplying its needs. Recent efforts to liberalize the department's procurement and contracting arrangements have somewhat broadened the circle of defense suppliers.

DOD played a key role in the development of the U.S. aerospace and electronics industries. Its contracts for the development of jet fighters

11. Dual-use technologies can be used either in military weaponry or in civilian applications.

12. *Statistical Abstract of the United States, 1989* (Washington, D.C.: U.S. Government Printing Office, 1989), p. 326; and IBM annual report for 1989.

and bombers helped to create the technological and manufacturing base for America's civilian aerospace industry. Its procurements of integrated circuits for the Minuteman ballistic missiles in the 1960s helped semiconductor and integrated circuits firms realize economies of scale before selling their products to civilian customers. Its purchases of computers and software helped to make the U.S. computer industry internationally competitive.[13]

DOD has become increasing worried about what it calls the "defense industrial base" of the United States,[14] by which it means the ability of U.S.-owned firms to manufacture mechanical and electronic items needed for weapons. In particular, DOD is concerned about the weakness of the U.S. machine-tool industry and the competitive difficulties of the semiconductor industry. The U.S. is overly dependent on Europe (mainly Germany and Italy) and Japan for the production machinery required to make things out of metal. DOD does not like having to purchase important electronic components for weapons systems abroad, even from allied countries.[15] This concern over dependence on foreign countries for defense-related products puts DOD in the new and somewhat uncomfortable position of advocating more ambitious industrial policies.

In the section on policies toward semiconductors below, I will discuss DOD's programs for very high-speed integrated circuits (VHSIC) and for semiconductor manufacturing technology (Sematech). From 1979 to 1989, the VHSIC Program involved about twenty semiconductor firms and about $20 billion.[16] More recently, DOD co-funded with industry and R&D consortium called Sematech to improve semiconductor manufacturing techniques. DOD has also co-funded the National Center for Manufacturing Sciences to diagnose and remedy problems in the U.S. machine-tool and manufacturing equipment industries.

The Defense Advance Research Projects Agency (DARPA) became the administrative arm of the DOD in managing both the VHSIC and Sematech programs. VHSIC was administered by the VHSIC Program

13. See Michael Borrus, *Competing for Control: America's Stake in Microelectronics* (Cambridge, Mass.: Ballinger, 1988), chap. 4; and Kenneth Flamm, *Creating the Computer: Government, Industry, and High Technology* (Washington, D.C.: Brookings Institution, 1988).

14. David Dickson, *The New Politics of Science*, rev. ed. (Chicago: University of Chicago Press, 1988), pp. 130–31; and *Bolstering Defense Industrial Competitiveness: Preserving Our Heritage, the Industrial Base, Securing Our Future*, Report to the Secretary of Defense by the Under Secretary of Defense (Acquisition) (Washington, D.C.: Department of Defense, 1988).

15. Defense Science Board, "Report of the Defense Science Board Task Force on Defense Semiconductor Dependency," Office of the Undersecretary of Defense for Acquisition, Washington, D.C., 1987.

16. Glenn R. Fong, "The Potential for Industrial Policy: Lessons from the Very High Speed Integrated Circuit Program," *Journal of Policy Analysis and Management* 5 (Winter 1986): 264–91.

Office, which was located in the Office of the Undersecretary of Defense for Research and Engineering after its inception in 1979. It became a quasi-autonomous agency of DOD in the early 1980s. The head of the Program Office, E. D. (Sonny) Maynard, was the director of defense computer and electronics technology until he resigned in July 1988. All VHSIC program administration was transferred to DARPA in May 1988, which was already directing a follow-on program called the Microwave and Millimeter-Wave Monolithic Integrated Circuits Program.

The secretary of defense is an important figure in any U.S. administration. He is often a key foreign policy adviser to the president with at least as much weight as the secretary of state or the national security adviser. From the formation of the Department of the Defense in 1947 until the late 1970s, U.S. manufacturing was strong and the secretary had little involvement in domestic economic policy making except to preserve DOD's role as a promoter of defense-related industries. In recent years, the secretary of defense has become more involved in matters of economic policy and tended to side with the secretary of commerce on industrial concerns. As the threat of Soviet military competition recedes, there is a tendency for the secretary to worry less about military and strategic rivalries and more about economic ones.

The Department of the Treasury

Like ministries of finance in other major industrialized countries the Department of the Treasury is responsible for the formulation of domestic and international monetary policies. Its core function is to collect taxes (through the Internal Revenue Service) and to issue checks for government purchases and wages. It also has some responsibilities for monitoring and regulating the activities of banks and other financial intermediaries. Unlike the ministries of finance in Japan and France, the Treasury has little direct control over the allocation of credit. It influences monetary policy primarily by issuing government bonds and adjusting the discount rate.

The secretary of the treasury is often a friend of and close adviser to the president. He chairs important cabinet and interagency committees and represents the United States at annual meetings of the International Monetary Fund and other financially oriented international organizations. The secretary deals frequently with the private financial community and tends to mirror its concerns about inflation and the value of the dollar in international exchange. He also tends to oppose increased intervention of the government in the economy, often siding with the chairman of the CEA and the OMB director in preferring to avoid industry-specific measures.

The Antitrust Division of the Department of Justice

The United States has a long and deep tradition of promoting do-mestic competition through the enforcement of antitrust and fair-trading legislation. The Sherman Act of 1890, the Clayton Antitrust Act of 1914, the Federal Trade Commission (FTC) Act of 1914, and the Celler Antimerger Statute of 1950 provide the legal basis for this tradition.[17] The FTC was established to put muscle into the powers granted the government in the Sherman and Clayton acts to break up trusts and monopolies. The Anti-Trust Division of the Department of Justice and the FTC have sometimes clashed over the right to admin-ister these laws.

Several excellent studies of the history of competition policy exist.[18] For the purposes of this chapter the important points are that it is gov-erned primarily by the desire to prevent firms from controlling very large market shares (even locally) so they can extract monopoly rents or exercise market power; it includes collusive practices typical of oli-gopolies; and it is not concerned with foreign firms competing with U.S. firms in foreign markets or through imports rather than domestic production.

The result is that because of increasing international competition, U.S. entrepreneurs, aside from their normal and natural hatred for antitrust laws, have a particular grudge about the way these laws have been administered in the last decade. U.S. firms see themselves in com-petition with foreign firms that are not subject to the same strict com-petition policies, and may benefit from sheltered monopolistic or oligopolistic markets at home.

In the early 1980s, both Congress and the executive branch showed dissatisfaction with the existing antitrust regime. Egged on by the U.S. Chamber of Commerce, Congress was particularly exercised by the growing power of the FTC. In the Federal Trade Commission Im-provements Act of 1980, Congress attempted to give itself the right to veto trade rules adopted by the FTC, but in 1983, the Supreme Court

17. See M. L. Breenhut and Bruce Benson, *American Antitrust Laws in Theory and Prac-tice* (Brookfield, Vt.: Gower, 1989), p. 125.
18. See, for example, Douglas H. Ginsburg, "Antitrust, Uncertainty, and Technolog-ical Innovation," *Antitrust Bulletin* 24 (Winter 1979): 635–86; Thomas K. McCraw, *Proph-ets of Regulation* (Cambridge, Mass.: Belknap Press of Harvard University Press, 1984), chaps. 2–5; Thomas K. McCraw, "Mercantilism and the Market: Antecedents of Amer-ican Industrial Policy," in Claude E. Barfield and William A. Schambra, eds., *The Politics of Industrial Policy* (Washington, D.C.: American Enterprise Institute, 1986), pp. 41–52.

ruled that this law was unconstitutional because it provided for a "legislative veto." The Department of Justice dismissed a major antitrust suit against IBM in 1982. In 1985, the department proposed abolishing treble damages provisions for private antitrust suits. Because the vast majority of antitrust suits were filed by private firms, this would have resulted in a major reduction in suits.[19] In the National Cooperative Research Act in 1984 Congress tried to make it easier for U.S. firms to pool resources in R&D consortia.

Large mergers are subject to veto by antitrust authorities in the United States if they are challenged by a competing firm or some other party with legal standing. Mobil's merger with Marathon, for example, was blocked at least partly for this reason. In general, the government does not encourage mergers. Encouraging mergers would be seen as a violation of its mandate and would be politically costly for either party's candidates in the next election. Most antitrust issues involve whether to split up giant firms—and if so, how. The reorganization of AT&T after the mandated divestment of the regional operating companies in 1984 is a good example of this centripetal emphasis in U.S. attitudes toward giant firms. Nevertheless, in a world of increased international competition, former supporters of antitrust are far less certain that "big is bad." One such former supporter, Secretary of Commerce Malcolm Baldridge, was quoted as saying: "The Clayton Act 'reflects the prevailing view of the 1950s that "big is bad" while "small and many is good." . . . 'Try to get across that theory to Japan's Toyota Motor Corp. with $20 billion in sales, to West Germany's Hoechst AG with $14 billion in sales, to the United Kingdom's Unilever Group with $20 billion in sales, or to South Korea's Hyundai Group with $9 billion in sales.' "[20]

The Office of the U.S. Trade Representative (USTR)

The Office of the USTR is responsible for formulating and implementing U.S. strategies for trade negotiations. Because the staff consists of fewer than one hundred professional members, much of the preparatory work must be done by other government agencies. One of

19. Michael Pertschuk, *Revolt against Regulation* (Berkeley: University of California Press, 1982); Barry Weingast and Mark J. Moran, "Bureaucratic Discretion or Congressional Control? Regulatory Policymaking by the Federal Trade Commission," *Journal of Political Economy* 91 (1983): 765–800; Frank H. Easterbrook, "Detrebling Antitrust Damages," *Journal of Law and Economics* 28 (1985): 445–67; and A. Mitchell Polinsky, "Detrebling versus Decoupling Antitrust Damages: Lessons from the Theory of Enforcement," in Lawrence J. White, ed., *Private Antitrust Litigation: New Evidence, New Learning* (Cambridge, Mass.: MIT Press, 1988).

20. Quoted in Peter Behr, "Antitrust Act May Undergo Major Changes," *Washington Post*, January 1, 1986, p. H1.

the most important functions of the USTR is to meet with representatives of businesses to discuss strategy for trade negotiations. For this purpose, the Trade Act of 1974 authorized policy advisory committees and industry sector advisory committees, which meet frequently before and during multilateral trade negotiations and less frequently at other times to enable the USTR to gather information from business about problems of trade and competitiveness. The high standards for the recruitments of USTR personnel and their regular access to business representatives give the Office greater clout in Washington on trade matters than much larger agencies.[21]

The trade representative is an important adviser to the president on questions of international economic policy. Most of the president's economic policy advisers focus on economy-wide concerns, whereas firm- and industry-specific concerns are expressed through the trade representative. The trade representative has to recommend policies that benefit some industries at the expense of others to help the president make whatever trade-offs are necessary for a credible and coherent trade policy. The CEA and the State and Treasury departments can pursue vague policies of fostering liberal trade and investment without worrying too much about the impact on specific firms or industries; the office of the USTR cannot. Nor is the office as likely as the Departments of Transportation, Housing and Urban Development, or Energy to be "captured" by a limited set of business interests. If the Department of Commerce were stronger, the Office of the USTR would have less prestige and clout.

The Department of Commerce

If the U.S. government set civilian industrial policies, the Department of Commerce probably would be the responsible agency. In fact, it is an agency with residual functions—ones with no other logical location in the government. For example, the National Oceanic and Atmospheric Administration, the U.S. Customs Service, and National Bureau of Standards (recently renamed the National Institute for Science and Technology), and the International Trade Administration are under the Commerce Department. Since the passage of the Export Administration Act of 1979, the Department of Commerce has shared authority with DOD in administering export controls for dual-use products (those with both civilian and military applications).[22] One

21. See Gilbert R. Winham, *International Trade and the Tokyo Round Negotiation* (Princeton, N.J.: Princeton University Press, 1986), pp. 307–17.
22. The Department of State is responsible for controlling exports of weaponry under the Export Control Act of 1949 and the International Traffic in Arms Regulations. If the

consequence of this functional incoherence is low staff cohesiveness and morale. Commerce has traditionally been unable to recruit the excellent employees such as are found in the CEA, DOD, the Office of the USTR, Treasury, and other agencies.

Despite the incoherence of the agency, since 1981, when Malcolm Baldridge was appointed in the Reagan administration, the secretary of commerce has become an increasingly important advocate of industry-specific policies. The secretaries who succeeded Baldridge—William Verity and Robert Mosbacher—have been more influential than those who preceded him because they have had better access to the president than has been traditional. Before Baldridge, industry-specific policies advocated by the Commerce and Labor departments were usually opposed by a powerful coalition of advisers and cabinet officers, often including the domestic policy advisers, the chairman of the CEA, the head of OMB, the trade representative, and the secretaries of state and treasury. In recent years, however, the secretary of commerce has seen his position strengthened by increasing support for industry-specific measures from the domestic policy advisers, the secretary of defense, and the trade representative. This change is the result of growing concern over the international competitiveness of U.S. manufacturing.

The Legislative Branch

The struggle for control over economic policies is a constant in the relations between Congress and the president. This struggle is accentuated when the party that controls the presidency does not control both houses of Congress.[23] The needs, desires, and priorities of congressional constituencies differ from those of the president's constituency. The president has only partial control over the budget, for example, because the Congress modifies it before approving it.

Congress does not implement economic policies, but it has great influence over them because it is responsible for all legislation. It amends and authorizes the national budget. It has the power of oversight in the implementation of policies by executive branch agencies. Congress also

---

Department of State determines that a given product is a weapon, it is responsible for controlling exports of that product. The DOD creates and maintains a list of militarily critical technologies, which the Departments of State and Commerce use in their separate export-control efforts. See Michael Mastanduno, "Trade as a Strategic Weapon: American and Alliance Export Control Policy in the Early Postwar Period," in G. John Ikenberry, David A. Lake, and Michael Mastanduno, eds., *The State and American Foreign Economic Policy* (Ithaca, N.Y.: Cornell University Press, 1988).

23. See Berman, *New American Presidency*, pp. 8–10.

funds small bureaucracies that do not report to the president, including the Congressional Budget Office, the General Accounting Office, the Office of Technology Assessment, the National Science Foundation, the National Academy of Science, the National Academy of Engineering, and the Library of Congress.

Organization of Business

The two main peak associations in the United States are the U.S. Chamber of Commerce and the National Association of Manufacturers (NAM). The U.S. Chamber of Commerce had 180,000 member firms in 1990, up from 83,000 in 1974.[24] In 1981, its budget for research and lobbying was $69 million.[25] The National Association of Manufacturers had 13,500 member firms in 1988, representing around 80 percent of industrial output. In that same year, it had a total staff of 180—100 in its Washington office and 80 in its three regional offices.[26] The U.S. Chamber of Commerce represents both small and large enterprises, whereas NAM tends to represent only the interests of large enterprises. A small number of large firms belong to such groups as the Business Roundtable, the Conference Board, and the Committee for Economic Development. These groups speak authoritatively on economy-wide issues but rarely represent the interests of specific firms or industries and therefore receive a relatively small proportion of firms' total effort in business-government relations.

Because the American government is as fragmented, it is desirable for firms to try to influence policy making directly. As David Yoffie and Joseph Badaracco state: "A company with a politically active senior executive, a corporate public affairs staff, its own media identity, a Washington law firm, and a Washington office or lobbyist has an independent apparatus for political action. It has its own information, contacts, and bargaining chips. It can lobby in Congress, negotiate with executive agencies, and take court action. Such a company can still work, in the traditional ways, through its industry association or through umbrella groups like the Chamber of Commerce. But it can also act on its own."[27] Because of this fragmentation, the peak

24. Telephone query to the U.S. Chamber of Commerce on March 13, 1990; and Pertschuk, *Revolt against Regulation*, p. 57.

25. Ira Katznelson and Mark Kesselman, *The Politics of Power: A Critical Introduction to American Government*, 3d ed. (New York: Harcourt Brace Jovanovich, 1987), p. 131.

26. Pamela Babcock, "Watching Congress for NAM Is 'Opening Night' for Eisen," *Washington Post*, January 18, 1988, p. 11.

27. David Yoffie and Joseph Badaracco, "A Rational Model of Corporate Political Strategies," Working Paper, Division of Research, Harvard Business School, 1984, pp. 3–4. Also see David Vogel, *Fluctuating Fortunes: The Political Power of Business in America* (New York: Basic Books, 1989), p. 297.

associations are less important than in other major capitalist countries. This does not mean, however, that business interests are poorly represented. On the contrary, business views weigh heavily in the decisions made in all three branches of the government. Business influence has fluctuated over time, but very little, with the possible exception of a government flirtation with ambitious environmental policies in the early 1970s.[28]

Organization of Labor

Union membership increased from 3.5 million in 1935 to 18 million in 1985, but as a percentage of the labor force it peaked at around 33 percent in 1950 and then declined rapidly from 30 percent in 1975 to around 18 percent in 1985. The percentage of union members employed by the public sector increased dramatically between 1960 and 1986 because of successful organizing efforts.[29] The most important peak association for labor in the United States is the American Federation of Labor–Congress of Industrial Organizations (AFL-CIO), a federation of labor unions with a paid membership of 13 million in 1985. The largest industrial union within the AFL-CIO umbrella is the Teamsters with 2 million members, closely followed by the United Auto Workers (UAW) with 1.5 million members. The fastest-growing union is the Association of Federal, State, County, and Municipal Employees.[30]

The reasons for the weakness of organized labor in the United States are controversial. One interpretation is presented by Michael Goldfield:

> U.S. Labor is politically weak in comparison to labor movements in other economically developed capitalist countries because unionization in the United States exists mainly as a regional phenomenon. In the Northeast, the Midwest, and along the West Coast, labor unions have had until recently a density quite favorable in comparison to those in other coun-

28. Here I agree with the main thesis of David Vogel's *Fluctuating Fortunes* but disagree with his views about the significance of the variations in the political power of business over time. My disagreement arises from the comparative perspective adopted in this book. The variations that Vogel observes failed to convince me that business has ever been less powerful vis-à-vis government and labor in the United States in the postwar era than it is in Germany or Japan. For further discussion see Chapter 7.

29. Only 5 percent of state and local workers were unionized in 1960; around a third were unionized in 1986. See Kenneth R. Noble, "Public-Sector Unions Are Labor's Darlings," *New York Times*, March 8, 1987, p. E4.

30. The Teamsters is the largest single union in the United States, although there are around 2 million unionized workers in the textile and clothing industry. See David McKay, *Politics and Power in the USA: A Guide to the Basic Institutions of the American Federal Government* (Harmondsworth, Eng.: Penguin, 1987), p. 128; Michael Goldfield, *The Decline of Organized Labor in the United States* (Chicago: University of Chicago Press, 1987), pp. 8–22; and "Declining Force, Increasing Power," *Economist*, February 14, 1987, p. 23.

tries. . . . Nationally, however, their lack of political influence is a reflection of their negligible presence in much of the South, Southwest, and West. This regional isolation is readily traceable to events of the 1930s and 1940s. Second, the stifling of rank-and-file democracy in the late 1930s, the bureaucratization of major unions during World War II, the elimination of radical oppositions and unions from 1946 to 1955, and the political subordination of U.S. unions to the Democratic Party have all worked to undermine the ability of labor unions to extend themselves nationally. . . . Third, these limitations have been the result both of defeats suffered by the labor movement and of choices made by its leadership.[31]

State-societal arrangements in the United States are based on fragmented state, weak labor, and a highly influential but somewhat fragmented business sector. Business is influential despite the relative unimportance of peak associations. Because of the fragmented nature of the state, businesses pursue individual and small-group lobbying efforts outside the framework of peak associations. In addition, because of the large size and diversity of the U.S. economy it is hard for peak associations to represent a consensual view for business on most issues, with the possible exception of macroeconomic policies. The enormous political strength of internationally competitive firms enables them to resist efforts to strengthen the power of the state to make industry-specific policies. The weakness of labor biases state-societal arrangements against neocorporatist institutions that include labor such as exist in other major capitalist countries, especially Germany.

POLICIES FOR THE STEEL INDUSTRY

The steel industry in the United States was fully competitive with those of Britain and Germany from the end of the nineteenth century through World War II. The Japanese were a minor factor in the world steel industry until after the war. Investment decisions resulting from complacency and bad management in the 1950s, however, put the United States at a strong competitive disadvantage with respect to both Germany and Japan. The decline in competitiveness was not fully evident until the late 1960s, when imports of steel from Japan surged. Low profits in the 1970s—partly the result of the Nixon price controls and government antipollution requirements—delayed needed investments in new technologies. The U.S. industry was slow to switch from open-hearth to basic-oxygen furnaces and as late as the mid-1980s had

31. Goldfield, *Decline,* pp. 235–36.

still not converted the majority of their integrated steel operations to continuous casting.

The U.S. government contributed to the decline of the industry by failing to tie subsidies and trade barriers to investments in new technology. The U.S. steel industry finally restructured itself radically in the late 1980s, but the delay was very costly in lost revenues and jobs and the high prices paid by the customers of U.S. steel firms.

The Structure of the Steel Industry

The U.S. steel industry is dominated by three large firms: USX, LTV Steel, and Bethlehem Steel (see Figure 21), which have well over half of the total productive capacity of raw steel in the United States.[32] Nevertheless, the steel industry is highly competitive domestically, especially when compared with the domestic steel industries of other large industrialized nations. The competition among integrated producers has been supplemented with competition from foreign firms and from the rapidly growing minimill operators.

Profitability in the U.S. steel industry has been low since the late 1960s. As occurred in other major industrial countries, the stagnation of demand after 1973 resulted in overcapacity and poor financial returns. The recession that followed the tight monetary policies of the early 1980s produced unprecedented losses. Figure 21 shows the net income for selected firms between 1984 and 1988.

Steel Policies from 1917 to 1945

The U.S. government first intervened in the steel industry when the great trusts were being built at the end of the nineteenth century. Because of the close interrelationship between the railroad and steel industries, regulation of the railroads in the Interstate Commerce Act of 1887 and of the trusts in the Sherman Antitrust Act of 1890 was also aimed at the steel industry. This legislation made large conglomerations like United States Steel (now called USX) very wary of acquiring too much market share, but it did not prevent the establishment of an oligopolistic market structure in which the largest firms played a central role in setting prices.

During World War I, the steel and railroad industries were nationalized, but they were returned to private ownership after the war. The steel market in the United States was stable between 1917 and 1967.

32. See Donald F. Barnett and Robert W. Crandall, *Up from the Ashes: The Rise of the Steel Minimill in the United States* (Washington, D.C.: Brookings Institution, 1986), pp. 6–8.

Figure 21. Sales and net income of U.S. steel firms

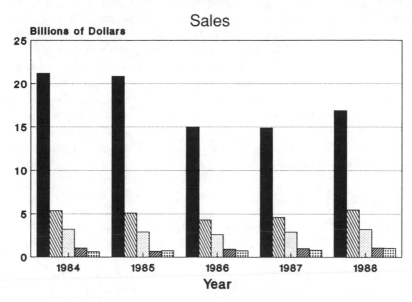

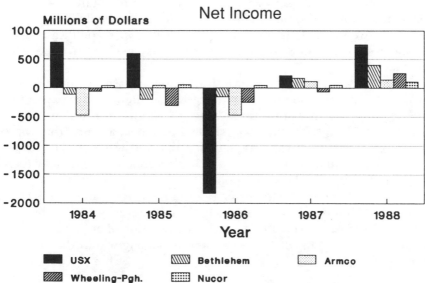

USX   Bethlehem   Armco
Wheeling-Pgh.   Nucor

Source: Disclosure database on CompuServe.

All but one of the thirteen largest companies operating in 1967 had been in business in 1917. Between the 1870s and the 1950s, the U.S. steel industry was the world leader in technology, plant size, and production. U.S. steel firms built their strength on the basis of large domestic markets and large plants with open-hearth furnaces.

Beyond enforcement of antitrust and regulation of the railroads, the main role of the government was to intervene occasionally in major strikes and other labor-management disputes. Until the New Deal, presidential administrations aligned themselves with the anti-union policies of the firms. But in the 1930s and 1940s the rise of organized labor in the steel industry was condoned and sometimes encouraged by government policy.

Truman's Seizure of the Plants of U.S. Steel

During the Korean War, the strong steel unions were the source of an unfortunate government intervention. In 1952, the prospect of a lengthy strike in the steel industry, which would idle workers and production capacity in many downstream industries and would probably accentuate inflationary pressures in the economy, induced Harry Truman to use army troops to seize the plants of United States Steel. The Supreme Court ruled this seizure to be unconstitutional, and a seven-week strike ensued. Truman's attempted seizure was so politically damaging to him that subsequent administrations tried not to repeat his mistakes.[33]

Based on a study that projected a rapid increase in domestic demand, the Truman administration urged that the industry expand its steelmaking capacity and threatened to build government-owned plants if it did not. The industry resisted this idea, arguing that there was already sufficient capacity and that demand was not likely to increase. The industry was correct, and its decision not to expand capacity turned out to be the wisest policy.

In the mid-1950s, the Kefauver Committee investigated allegations that the steel industry was subject to "administered prices." This was yet another unsuccessful attempt to find a violation of antitrust rules in an industry that had been very cautious in staying within the letter of the law.

Kennedy's Jawboning of the Industry

In the early 1960s, when steel price increases seemed likely at a moment when there was danger of a rise in inflation, John F. Kennedy

33. Grant McConnell, *The Steel Seizure of 1952* (Indianapolis: Bobbs-Merrill, 1960).

resorted to a practice used by previous and subsequent administrations called jawboning. He called in the presidents of the largest firms, including Roger Blough of U.S. Steel, and asked them not to increase prices. After one of these visits, Kennedy was reported to have said: "My father always told me that all businessmen were sons of bitches, but I never believed it until now."[34]

Kennedy's secretary of labor, Arthur Goldberg, was actively involved in the contract negotiations in 1962. Goldberg had been a principal adviser to the United Steelworkers in the 1950s. He argued that wage increases should be tied to growth in productivity and that firms should limit price increases if they could negotiate wage restraints with the unions. U.S. Steel's announcement of a major price increase after a moderate wage increase set off Kennedy's jawboning.[35] The upshot was that U.S. steel announced that it would not increase prices, and the rest of the industry followed suit.

The Industry Gets Voluntary Export Restraints

By the late 1960s, the growth of foreign imports was the main subject of government-industry exchanges. The industry leaders asserted that steel imports must be the result of unfair trade practices; they claimed to hold a strong technological advantage over their foreign competitors. In fact, the competitive balance had begun to shift toward Japanese and German producers because of their large investments in basic-oxygen technology. The industry petitioned for trade barriers. In 1968 the State Department negotiated a three-year voluntary export restraint agreement with Japan, which became effective in 1969 following a congressional threat of mandatory restrictions.[36] It was extended for three more years in 1972. Despite the agreements, however, imports from third countries increased and U.S. steel profits and investments remained low.

In the early 1970s, the steel industry, like many other heavy industries, became a target for environmentalists who wanted legal remedies against corporate polluters. The egregious dumping of toxic wastes into Lake Michigan by plants in the Chicago area, the asbestos pollution of the taconite ore producers in Michigan, and the obviously negative effects of the Pittsburgh mills on the air quality of that region

34. Quoted in Wallace Carol, "Steel: A 72-Hour Drama with an All Star Cast," *New York Times*, April 23, 1962, p. 25.

35. Donald F. Barnett and Louis Schorch, *Steel: Upheaval in a Basic Industry* (Cambridge, Mass.: Ballinger, 1983), p. 237.

36. Michael Borrus, "The Politics of Competitive Erosion in the U.S. Steel Industry," in John Zysman and Laura Tyson, eds., *American Industry in International Competition* (Ithaca, N.Y.: Cornell University Press, 1983), p. 84.

were frequently cited by critics who wished to change the laws. The resulting legislation required firms to adopt less polluting technologies—for example, using scrubbers in smokestacks to reduce air pollution, and disposing of toxic wastes in authorized dumps rather than in nearby bodies of water. The steel industry complained that these measures increased its production costs and would force it to raise prices.

In adopting price controls to combat inflation, the Nixon administration reduced the industry's profits during a period of booming demand and increased production costs. The steel boom died in 1973, however, and imports, which had reached a steady 15 percent of the domestic market, again became the focus of the industry's concern.

The Steel Industry and the Trade Act of 1974

During the maneuvering behind the 1974 Trade Act, the steel industry played a central role in lobbying for a separate industry-specific advisory council for steel and in incorporating stronger antidumping and countervailing duty remedies in the act. During the steel boom of 1972–74, the industry reduced its demands on the government for protection but made demands again in 1975 when demand slackened. In January 1975, U.S. Steel filed seven countervailing duty petitions with the Treasury Department against six EC producers and Austria. The Treasury dismissed the petitions so U.S. Steel took them to the customs court. In July 1975, American specialty steel producers and workers filed a petition with the International Trade Commission (ITC) for special relief against imports from stainless and alloy steel producers in the EC, Japan, Sweden, and Canada. The commission ruled in favor of the petition and recommended quotas, but President Gerald Ford decided instead to negotiate orderly marketing agreements with the countries involved.

In January 1976, steel was exempted from the Generalized System of Preferences (GSP) established under the 1974 Trade Act. This meant that Third World steel producers would not benefit from the lower tariffs made available to them through the GSP. In October 1976, the American Iron and Steel Institute, the trade association representing the industry, filed a petition under Section 301 of the 1974 Trade Act with USTR, alleging that a steel agreement between the EC and Japan would result in diversion of trade to the United States. Pressure mounted late in 1976 and early 1977 for more import restrictions.

The Trigger Price Mechanism

In 1977, another round of contract negotiations with the United Steelworkers (USW) took place. U.S. Steel's strategy was to trade higher wages and job security for greater control over workplace rules. The head of the USW, I. W. Abel, was inclined to agree, but he was challenged by a rank-and-file revolt under the leadership of more militant workers, including Ed Sadlowski. Thus the contract did not introduce as much flexibility into the workplace as the firms or the USW leadership wanted, but it did commit the firms to a large pay increase and new job security guarantees. This contract seriously diminished their ability to compete in the very rough markets of the late 1970s and early 1980s.

Immediately after the contract was negotiated, the firms began to lobby harder for import restrictions. From August 1977 until the end of September, fourteen major steel mills were closed and operations were cut back at many other plants. Twenty thousand jobs were lost in a few months. In mid-September, a group of public officials and local union leaders from sixty steel towns formed the Steel Communities Coalition to plead for assistance from Congress. The bipartisan Congressional Steel Caucus's membership swelled to 120 members by mid-October. Its purpose was to create a united front in Congress in defense of jobs and profits in the steel industry.

President Carter called a special White House Conference on Steel on October 13, 1977. Under Secretary of the Treasury Anthony Solomon was appointed to head a task force to devise a comprehensive program for the industry. Within the government it was widely recognized that whatever was done would have to include measures to increase profitability so the firms could adjust to increased competition. The government would also have to find ways to assist the unemployed workers and their communities. Carter administration members later asserted that an implicit bargain was involved: the government would restore the profitability of the industry in exchange for major restructuring. On December 5, 1977, Solomon announced a program establishing a trigger price mechanism for steel.[37]

The trigger price was based on a formula that combined Japanese domestic selling prices with estimated transportation costs to arrive at a floor price for imports. Japanese prices were used because they were the lowest in the world at the time. Japanese imports were the most troubling to U.S. firms, and it was felt that using Japanese prices biased the floor price in the direction of the more efficient producers in the United States.

The trigger price remained at the 1977 level for several years, thus sheltering U.S. firms from the price-cutting that was taking place elsewhere, notably in Europe. Additional protection for domestic firms

---

37. Much of the above depends on the excellent account of this period in Borrus, "The Politics of Competitive Erosion," pp. 83–96.

was provided by the rapid decline between 1977 and 1981 in the exchange rate of the dollar against the currencies of major steel exporters. When the exchange rate improved in 1981–82, imports from Europe increased rapidly. European imports became much more competitive not only because the dollar rose in value but because the trigger price level, dependent on Japanese selling prices, gave the Europeans more room for competing with U.S. firms.

The Voluntary Export Restraints of 1982

The U.S. steel industry filed a countervailing duty and injury petition against the major European steel producers in January 1982 (similar petitions had been filed in 1977 and 1980 against Japanese and European firms). The Reagan administration, invoking the informal agreements made at the time of the Solomon plan, canceled the trigger price mechanism temporarily to punish the industry for filing the petition, but the International Trade Commission issued a favorable ruling and the petition was forwarded to the Department of Commerce for its recommendations on countervailing duties.

The Commerce Department made a special study of the subsidization of steel production in Europe and announced its preliminary findings in the summer of 1982. Subsidies of from $2 to $200 per ton were assessed for the various firms. The Commission of the European Community claimed that all such subsidies were part of a larger agreement to restructure the European steel industries, and they should not be subject to countervailing duties. Negotiations between the United States and the EC culminated in November 1982 with a voluntary export restraint agreement limiting European imports.

Between the summer of 1982 and the summer of 1983, exports of steel to the United States from Australia, Brazil, Korea, Mexico, Taiwan, Argentina, and South Africa (countries not covered by the 1982 agreement) doubled. Foreign producers of stainless and specialty steels, which were not explicitly covered under the 1982 agreement, also increased their exports to the United States. In April 1983, the International Trade Commission recommended import quotas for stainless steel, and in July, the Reagan administration increased tariffs for four years to protect domestic specialty steel producers.

In 1984, the United Steelworkers and Bethlehem Steel sought escape-clause relief under Section 201 of the 1974 Trade Act. The main target in these petitions was not imports from Japan and Europe but from Canada and NICs such as Brazil and Korea. The United Steelworkers called for a limit of 15 percent on imports over domestic demand for steel; presidential candidate Walter Mondale favored a 17 percent limit. The International Trade Commission ruled that Bethlehem had been injured by increased imports and that imports of rolled steel should be limited. If the Reagan administration had accepted the ITC recommendations for quotas, the older arrangements with Europe and Japan would have had to be renegotiated. The administration ignored the quotas for rolled steel and recommended instead a target of 18.5 percent import penetration for all carbon steel imports.[38]

The VRAs of 1984

With the support of the Reagan administration, Congress passed the Steel Import Stabilization Act, Title VIII of the U.S. Trade and Tariff Act of 1984, which set a goal for import penetration in a range between 17 and 20.2 percent. This act set the scene for a new round of negotiations for a series of voluntary restraint agreements, which culminated in a five-year arrangement between the United States and the seven exporters that provided 30 percent of U.S. imports. But the agreement excluded one major exporter, Canada, and semifinished steel products. Thus further negotiations would be needed to broaden the coverage of both countries and products.[39]

In December 1984, U.S. Steel filed an unfair trade petition against ten uncovered countries, and by the end of January 1985 the ITC produced favorable rulings. The United States and the EC agreed on a limit of 7.6 percent for import penetration by EC steel but remained at odds over how to deal with certain products such as semifinished steel and pipes and tubes. The dispute over semifinished steel was not resolved until September 1986.

Because of the VRAs, the foreign share of the U.S. market dropped from 26.5 percent in 1984 to around 20 percent between 1985 and 1989 but the domestic industry continued to lose money until 1987. Between 1982 and 1986 the cumulative losses were $11.6 billion.[40] LTV Corporation, McLouth Steel Products Corporation, and Wheeling-Pittsburgh Steel Corporation filed for bankruptcy under Chapter 11. Kaiser Steel was closed. Weirton Steel was sold to its employees in 1984 through an employee stock ownership plan. Nevertheless, the VRAs gave the more profitable firms the confidence to make major new

38. Stephen Woolcook, Jeffrey Hart, and Hans van der Ven, *Interdependence in the Post-Multilateral Era* (Lanham, Md.: University Press of America, 1985), pp. 52–53.

39. Theresa Wetter, "Trade Policy Developments in the Steel Sector," *Journal of World Trade Law* 19 (1985): 485–96.

40. Robert Kuttner, "Why Scrap a Steel Policy That Works?" *Business Week*, May 22, 1989, p. 24.

investments in steel manufacturing technology, particularly in continuous casters, while reducing productive capacity.

Productive capacity was reduced from 154 million tons a year in 1982 to 112 million tons in 1987. A total of 444 mills were closed in the 1980s. USX alone reduced its capacity by nearly 50 percent to 19 million tons and reduced its work force from 149,172 employees in 1980 to 53,522 in 1987. Bethlehem reduced its work force from 84,200 to 34,400 in the same period. Around 200,000 workers in the industry lost their jobs between the end of the 1970s and 1989.

The reduction in productive capacity and in the work force enabled U.S. firms to achieve much higher productivity. New investments in plant modernization also helped. About $9 billion was spent on continuous casting in the U.S. steel industry in the 1980s. Bethlehem Steel, for example, invested about $1 billion on a continuous caster for its Sparrows Point plant. Inland Steel invested $400 million in new equipment for cold-rolled steel, with funds contributed by its new Japanese partner, Nippon Steel. U.S. steel firms concluded a variety of new arrangements with foreign firms in the form of joint ventures and equity sales. Many of these arrangements were with Japanese firms (see Table 6). By the late 1980s, the combination of new investments and joint ventures with Japanese firms had begun to pay off. U.S. steel manufacturing costs were $484 per ton in November 1988, lower than those of all the other major industrial countries. U.S. firms, on average, required only 6.3 man-hours to produce a ton of steel.[41]

The VRAs negotiated in 1984 were to expire on September 30, 1989. Steel industry executives argued strongly for extension because they had made impressive strides in productivity but needed five more years to recover from twenty years of unfair trade. LTV and Wheeling-Pittsburgh were still in Chapter 11 restructurings. The high subsidies for steel production in Europe were given as further reason for extending VRAs, or at least as a bargaining point for the reduction of subsidies. Steel consumers in the United States argued strongly for an end to VRAs on the grounds that the premium prices they had to pay for steel were making them less internationally competitive. The choice would be to extend the VRAs for five years, as the industry wanted, or for some shorter period. If the VRAs were not extended, the industry would no doubt file a new round of antidumping, countervailing duty, and injury petitions. In July 1989, the Bush administration agreed to extend the VRAs.

41. Barnett and Crandall, *Up from the Ashes*, p. 7; James Buchan, "A Hard Won but Fragile Prosperity," *Financial Times*, May 19, 1989, p. 16; Gregory L. Miles, "Forging the New Bethlehem," *Business Week*, June 5, 1989, p. 108; and "American Steel: Did You Say *De*-Industrializing?" *Economist*, December 17, 1988, p. 75.

Table 6. Major U.S.-Japanese joint ventures or equity sales in steel

Date	U.S. firm	Japanese firm	Description
1982	Wheeling-Pittsburgh	Nippon Steel Kawasaki	$150 million rail-making plant with continuous caster
1982	Rouge Steel	Nisshin Steel	$40 million offer to purchase refused
1984	National Intergroup	Nippon Kokan	$292 million purchase of 50% equity in National Steel
1984	Wheeling-Pittsburgh	Nisshin Steel	$17.5 million purchase of 10% equity in Wheeling-Pittsburgh
1985	LTV	Sumitomo Metals	$125 million plant to produce electrogalvanized steel
1986	Nucor	Yamato Kogyo	$220 million plant to produce heavy structural steel
1986	Wheeling-Pittsburgh	Nisshin Steel	$65 million plant to produce coated sheet steel
1987	Inland	Nippon Steel	$400 million plant to produce cold-roiled steel
1988	Armco	Kawasaki	$400 million joint venture Kawasaki to purchase 40% share of Armco

Source: Business press.

Policies for the steel indusry were strongly constrained by the industry's slowness in realizing that to remain internationally competitive it needed to adopt new steelmaking technologies. The gap betwen the United States and Japan in the adoption of basic-oxygen furnaces and continuous casting was a major reason for the decline of the U.S. steel industry. This occurred because of understandable but regrettable investment decisions on the part of the industry in the 1950s and 1960s, but it remained unbridged for much too long because government, management, and labor all failed to keep the issue of competitiveness in the forefront. Government was not able, as it was in Japan, to alert the industry to opportunities for technological change because it did not have the bureaucratic wherewithal to obtain an independent and accurate diagnosis of the industry's problems and then to act upon it in a forceful manner. Business was overly concerned with maintaining domestic price levels and a smooth working relationship with the United Steelworkers and was not paying sufficient attention to competitive threats from abroad. The United Steelworkers succeeded in raising wages above the average for the manufacturing sector, which made the jobs of steelworkers vulnerable to competition from countries where wage increases stayed more in line with advances in productivity.

U.S. trade policy responses were mostly protectionist toward steel from 1977 onward. The Carter administration's efforts to limit the damage to the multilateral trade regime succeeded for only a short time. The limited and temporary protection-for-restructuring bargain that was negotiated turned out to be a long-term commitment to shelter jobs and incomes in the industry firms by maintaining a quasi-permanent set of VRAs. The Carter administration had proposed a refundable investment tax credit in the summer of 1980 (which the Reagan administration opposed), and the Reagan administration had implemented an accelerated depreciation program in the Economic Recovery Tax Act of 1981 as fiscal policy aids to the steel and auto industries, but these macroeconomic measures were not sufficient to deal with the pressure for protection emanating from an industry that had fallen badly behind its major international competitors. The inability of the U.S. government to apply industry-specific measures such as subsidies for restructuring investments outside of trade policy gave it no other recourse than to engage in protectionist actions. Protection enabled U.S. firms to make new restructuring investments eventually, but it also encouraged Japanese firms to establish a significant manufacturing presence in the United States through joint ventures and acquisitions. By the end of the 1980s, the U.S. steel industry was leaner, meaner, and significantly more Japanese than it had ever intended to become. U.S. steelworkers paid a higher price than was necessary in lost jobs and income.

POLICIES FOR AUTOS

The U.S. auto industry was known for its strong entrepreneurialism and technical innovation from the 1920s through the 1950s. The industry was built on a strong base created by Ford's successful experiments with standardized components and assembly-line production of a single model, General Motors's successful innovations in the management of multimodel production, and Chrysler's innovations in the product itself. By the 1930s, few auto firms in the world could challenge the American "big three" in average production costs or quality of products. In 1950, the U.S. auto industry produced 76 percent of all the passenger cars in the world.[42] Only countries that adopted restrictive trade and investment measures could prevent the large U.S. firms from dominating their domestic markets. Later, countries that encouraged firms to export were able to challenge U.S. firms in world markets from a sheltered home base.

With the possible exception of the interstate highways legislation of the 1950s, the U.S. government has not been concerned with promot-

42. N. P. Kannan, Kathy K. Rebibo, and Donna L. Ellis, *Downsizing Detroit: The Future of the U.S. Automobile Industry* (New York: Praeger, 1982), p. 23.

Table 7. Shares of passenger cars sold in the U.S. market, 1980 and 1987 (in percentages)

Company	1980	1987
General Motors	45.8	36.3
Ford	16.4	20.1
Chrysler	8.8	10.7
Honda	4.2	7.2
Toyota	6.5	6.1
Nissan	5.8	5.6
Others	12.5	14.0
Total	100.0	100.0

Source: Reprinted from *Business Week*, April 25, 1988, by special permission, copyright © 1988 by McGraw-Hill, Inc.

ing the industry because the industry did not need to be promoted. Herbert Hoover, for example, wanted to make it possible for other industries to grow as fast as the auto industry had but left the auto industry itself alone.[43] In the early 1970s the government was more concerned with antitrust and environmental issues than with competitiveness. It first became evident that the auto industry was having competitive problems in the late 1970s, especially after the oil price increases of 1978. The financial collapse of the Chrysler Corporation in that year and the loan guarantee program that resulted provoked a reexamination of the premises behind government policies not just for the auto industry but for industry in general.

Structure of the Industry

The U.S. auto industry is highly concentrated, with production dominated by the big three firms: General Motors, Ford, and Chrysler. Table 7 shows the domestic market shares of the top six firms in 1980 and 1987. GM lost some of its dominant market position to the other large producers during this period, although it is still the largest producer, both globally and in the United States. Ford has gained steadily in market share and in profitability relative to GM. Its ratio of net income to sales was almost twice as high as GM's from 1984 to 1988.

General Motors is the largest manufacturing firm in the world. Its revenues in 1988 were over $123 billion. Ford is the second largest manufacturing firm in the world with revenues of over $92 billion in 1988. Chrysler shrank dramatically in the late 1970s and early 1980s but almost doubled its revenues between 1984 and 1988 (see Figure 22).

After its financial difficulties in the late 1970s and early 1980s, Chrysler emerged smaller but more competitive. It was the first of the

43. See Ellis Hawley, " 'Industrial Policy' in the 1920s and 1930s," in Barfield and Schambra, *Politics of Industrial Policy.*

Figure 22. Sales and net income of U.S. auto firms

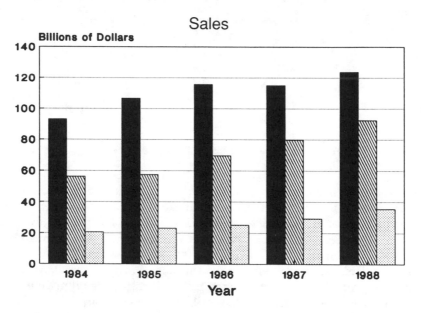

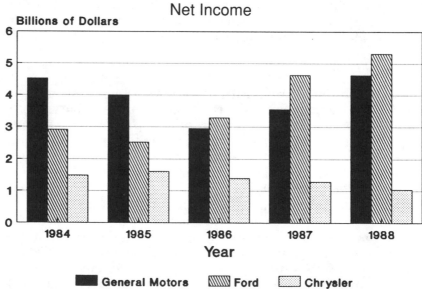

Source: Value Line Annual Reports on CompuServe.

big three to produce fuel-efficient, front-wheel-drive cars, the so-called K-cars, in the late 1970s. A large part of its profits since 1982 has come from sales of minivans and jeeps, not cars. Its current car models rely too much on the K-car designs of the late 1970s. Its sales and profits are not as impressive as GM's or Ford's, and it has not been able to spend as much on the development of new products and processes. Chrysler had to sell off its European subsidiaries during the financial restructuring of the late 1970s. Thus, unlike Ford and GM, it has no European operations to contribute to its global profits.[44]

Imports and Transplants

The share of imports in U.S. sales of motor vehicles grew from around 7 percent in 1966 to over 30 percent in 1987.[45] The growth in unit sales of imports has been steady despite the fluctuations in aggregate demand for motor vehicles. Imports from foreign-owned firms grew from 1.6 million in 1975 to 3.2 million in 1987. U.S. firms increased their imports of vehicles from Japan and other Asian countries for sale in the United States from 155,000 in 1975 to 348,000 in 1987.[46]

Since the conversion in 1982 of the Honda motorcycle plant in Marysville, Ohio, to the assembly of Honda automobiles, Japanese producers have become a major presence in the United States (see Table 8).[47] The new plants were built initially in response to congressional threats to establish local content requirements and the voluntary export restraint agreement of 1981. When the strong-dollar policies of the Reagan administration ended in 1985 and the yen/dollar exchange rate began to drop, Japanese firms could realize economies in assembling vehicles in the United States, especially given the success of Honda and Toyota in transferring Japanese production methods to U.S. plants.[48]

44. The profits of Ford-Europe in 1988 were $1.6 billion; those of GM-Europe were about $1.8 billion. See Kevin Done, "Sharp Recovery for GM in Europe," *Financial Times*, February 16, 1989, p. 22; Kevin Done, "Ford Races to European Record," *Financial Times*, February 18, 1989, p. 10.

45. Motor Vehicle Manufacturers Association, *World Motor Vehicle Data* (Detroit: MVMA, various years).

46. Motor Vehicle Manufacturers Association, *Motor Vehicle Facts and Figures '88* (Detroit: MVMA, 1988), p. 16.

47. Two recent journalistic works on this phenomenon are David Gelsanliter, *Jump Start: Japan Comes to the Heartland* (New York: Farrar Straus Giroux, 1990); and Joseph J. Fucini and Suzy Fucini, *Working for the Japanese: Mazda's American Auto Plant* (New York: Free Press, 1990).

48. In Japanese plants, 19.1 man-hours were required to produce the average vehicle in 1988, whereas in transplants the figure was 19.6 man-hours. In U.S.-owned plants in North America, 26.5 man-hours were required to produce the average vehicle. In European plants, 35.9 man-hours were required. The source for these data was J. D. Powers Associates, as cited by J. F. Krafcik, MIT International Motor Vehicles Project,

Table 8. Japanese assembly plants in the United States as of 1989

Company	Location	Date opened	Capacity	Models
Honda	Marysville, Ohio	1982	360,000	Accord
	E. Liberty, Ohio	1989	150,000	n.a.
Nissan	Smyrna, Tenn.	1983	265,000	Sentra and light trucks
Toyota-GM	Fremont, Calif.	1984	100,000	Corolla
Mazda	Flat Rock, Mich.	1987	240,000	MX-6
Mitsubishi	Normal, Ill.	1988	120,000	Eclipse
Toyota	Georgetown, Ky.	1988	200,000	Camry
Subaru-Isuzu	Lafayette, Ind.	1989	240,000	n.a.

Source: Reprinted from *Business Week,* April 25, 1988, by special permission, copyright © 1988 by McGraw-Hill, Inc.

The U.S. press called the new plants transplants. Their production capacity rose to about 1.8 million units per year by 1989 (including the plants in Canada brings North American capacity up to 2 million), but actual production was only around 750,000 units in early 1989.[49] During the boom sales years of 1985 and 1986, the growing capacity of the transplants was hardly noticed, but when demand slowed in 1987, the U.S. market began to experience some problems of overcapacity.

If Japanese firms keep exports to the United States at over 2 million units and use their U.S. plants at high capacity, they may have as much as 30 percent of the U.S. market by the early 1990s. If demand stabilizes at 10 to 11 million units per year, as is likely, more U.S.-owned plants will have to close to keep profit rates at acceptable levels.[50] Not only do the transplants raise the specter of further U.S. plant closings, but they also threaten to reduce the market share of U.S.-owned components firms. Japanese auto producers in the United States tend to acquire major components either from the parent firm in Japan or from Japanese components producers, which are also building plants in the United States. The Japanese auto firms claim that they cannot get the same quality and on-time delivery from U.S.-owned components firms. In 1980, only 18 Japanese firms made parts in the United States; by 1989, there were 232.[51] Japanese-produced vehicles in the United States generally have less than 60 percent domestic content,

---

presentation at a conference on Europe 1992, University of California, Berkeley, January 9, 1989. A graphical representation of the data can be found in Dertouzos, Lester, and Solow, *Made in America,* p. 185.

49. Anatole Kaletsky, "Detroit in a Struggle with the Sceptics," *Financial Times,* February 22, 1989, p. 21.

50. See also James P. Womack, Daniel T. Jones, and Daniel Roos, *The Machine That Changed the World* (New York: Rawson Associates, 1990), pp. 202–3.

51. "American Carmakers: Reinventing the Wheel," *Economist,* April 8, 1989, p. 78.

whereas for U.S.-owned firms the figure is greater than 90 percent. Some Japanese firms, like Honda and Mazda, are trying to increase the domestic content of their products, but Toyota and Nissan are less likely to do so without threats from the U.S. government.

The U.S. auto industry has been internationalized from within. It is still possible to tell the difference between U.S.-owned auto firms and others, but the differences are getting hazier. U.S. firms are more and more dependent on their overseas operations and alliances with foreign firms, which in turn are more and more dependent on their U.S. operations. This intermingling resulted from a combination of open trade and investment policies and the inability of the U.S. industry to respond to the market's demand for small, fuel-efficient automobiles in a timely fashion.

Legacies of the Industry's Origins

The attitudes of the auto industrialists were shaped by events in the early days of the industry. Henry Ford never forgave the banks for refusing to finance his earlier ventures. All the major firms (as in other countries) found it necessary or advantageous to have their own financial systems to offer loans to consumers at favorable rates. Mistrust of banks led most auto firms to finance the main part of their investments from internal sources (reinvested profits). As the labor militancy of the 1930s receded and autoworkers' wages rose above the average manufacturing wage, a populist tone crept into the rhetoric of auto management which sometimes created conflict with their brethren in more traditional industries (such as steel) and the financial community. On the whole, the successful U.S. auto industry did not want or need help from the government. A fierce spirit of independence and a strong ideological commitment to free enterprise characterized the industry.

This history made it all the more difficult for the industry to accept the environmental concerns of government in the early 1970s and the assistance of the government when Chrysler began to fail in the late 1970s. But by that time, a complacency had set in about the superiority of American products and processes that was belied first by the success of European firms in the 1960s and then by the greater success of Japanese producers in the U.S. market in the 1970s. Again, trade policy was the U.S. government's main instrument for dealing with increased international competition.

European and Japanese Competitors in North American Markets

Historically, the North American market had been insulated from those of other regions, because of the preference of North American consumers for larger cars than those demanded elsewhere (mainly a function of greater average wealth and lower fuel prices), the ability of North American producers to make large cars more cheaply than any other producers, and the barriers to entry into the large car market because of North American dominance.[52]

VW and the Japanese firms used product and process innovations to position themselves in the small car market. The U.S. firms responded by introducing new products and increasing efforts to internationalize production. The early compact and subcompact models such as the Ford Falcon and the Chevy Vega were responses to the VW Beetle. Speeding up the assembly process caused problems with quality control, and the first attempts to meet foreign competition were mostly unsuccessful. GM turned to greater outsourcing of components and to offshore assembly to meet the increased competition, achieving greater success eventually with the Chevrolet Chevette. Ford's European operation was somewhat more aggressive in developing new products than was the North American branch; it spearheaded the production of the Ford Fiesta model, which was later imported to meet demand in the U.S. market.

The Initial Response: Downsizing

U.S. firms in the late 1970s and early 1980s tried to downsize existing models—that is, to produce more or less the same cars but with lower body weight and size to increase their fuel efficiency without major redesigning or reengineering. The U.S. firms had recognized their vulnerability in the small car segment of the North American market and hoped that downsizing would meet the demand for smaller cars. Downsizing was only partly successful. The average U.S. consumer continued to believe that foreign models of comparable price were higher in quality. Downsizing could not eliminate the price differentials between U.S. and foreign (mostly Japanese) models in the lower price ranges because it did not address the innovations in car manufacturing that were adopted by the Japanese firms. Finally, downsized cars were not as fuel efficient as the Japanese or European models, although they were considerably better than standard U.S. models. Without downsizing, the results would have been even worse, but with downsizing they were not impressive.[53]

52. These arguments are made in Alan A. Altshuler, Martin Anderson, Daniel Jones, Daniel Roos, and James Womack, *The Future of the Automobile* (Cambridge, Mass.: MIT Press, 1984).

53. Gilbert R. Winham, *The Automobile Trade Crisis of 1980* (Halifax, Nova Scotia: Center for Foreign Policy Studies, Dalhousie University, 1981).

The Development of New Models

By the end of the 1970s, the U.S. firms began developing new models, but only Chrysler produced a line of small, fuel-efficient cars, the K-cars.[54] General Motors began work on X-cars, which would combine fuel efficiency with excellent engineering to recapture the customers lost to imports, putting its main efforts into developing a new line of midsize cars. In the interim, GM imported a small car, the Chevette, produced by its subsidiary in Brazil. Ford imported the Fiesta from Ford-Europe and in the early 1980s introduced a new compact model, the Escort, which was developed for sale in both Europe and North America.

Ford would design midsize models somewhat later but more successfully than GM. The Ford Taurus and Mercury Sable, for example, were introduced in December 1985 with great success. The GM-10 line of midsize models was late and had to be cut back to ten from an original plan for twelve different models. Begun in 1984, the GM-10 program cost around $8 billion. The first three models (the Buick Regal, Oldsmobile Cutlass Supreme, and Pontiac Grand Prix) were introduced in 1987. They did not sell as well as the new Ford models, and not until May 1989 did GM market a product that directly competed with Taurus and Sable—the Chevrolet Lumina.

Ford's Attempts to Build a World Car

A "world car" is a model produced in a variety of locations and sold on a variety of markets, thus taking advantage both of economies of scale resulting from standardization of models and components and of lower factor costs (especially lower wages) in different locations. Under this conception, the ideal world car would be a VW Beetle-like automobile engineered in Detroit, Japan, or Germany, with components coming from wherever they could be made with acceptable quality at the lowest cost and assembled in a low-wage region.

54. Under the supervision of the Department of the Treasury through the Chrysler Loan Guarantee Board between 1978 and 1981, Chrysler was strongly encouraged to develop K-cars and to shift production toward the smaller car segments and away from large cars, despite the contrary opinion of earlier Chrysler managements. The appointment of Lee Iacocca as president and general manager of Chrysler, a series of very restrictive wage restraint agreements with the United Auto Workers, a drastic cutback in the work force and closure of inefficient plants, the loan guarantees of the federal government, the sale of Chrysler's defense businesses and foreign subsidiaries, and the voluntary export restraint negotiated with Japan in 1981 helped Chrysler to turn a profit after three years of losses. See Robert B. Reich and John D. Donahue, *New Deals: The Chrysler Revival and the American System* (New York: Times Books, 1985); David Abodaher, *Iacocca* (New York: Zebra Books, 1982).

There is much to be said for this concept considering that it costs as much as \$1 billion to develop a single new car model from scratch; engine, transaxle, and transmission plants typically require output of 2 million units per year to realize minimum scale economies; and huge budgets are required for advertising and marketing to build enthusiasm for new products. If the same model could be developed for many markets, firms that operate across markets could save on development, production, and marketing costs. In a sense, this is what VW did in the 1960s and what Toyota and Nissan did in the 1970s. But VW, Toyota, and Nissan pursued a world-car strategy at the low end of the market. Once a firm has moved upmarket, it may no longer be so easy to sell standardized products. Middle- and upper-income car buyers often call for some form of customization to distinguish their product from others. Regional differences in consumers' tastes are more pronounced in the higher end of the market. What sells in Germany may not sell in Ohio.

This was the reality Ford ran into in its first attempts to pursue a world-car strategy in the early 1980s. The Escort was supposed to be designed cooperatively by engineers in Europe and the United States so that both versions would be very similar. The managers of Ford-Europe were so convinced that the design proposed by the U.S. team would not sell in Europe that they produced a European version that shared only two minor components with the American one.

A realistic alternative to a world-car strategy is to standardize at the level of high value-added components—chassis, engine, drive shaft or transaxle, and transmissions—so that many different models can be built on the same platform of basic components. Economies of scale are much more important in production of major components than in final assembly, where production runs of as low as two hundred thousand units per year realize minimum scale economies. Thus an internationally competitive car manufacturer will take advantage of large production runs in components while maintaining some customization of assembled automobiles to meet the distinct tastes and preferences of consumers in different regional markets.

Another way to realize economies is to develop more than one model at a time. This was the principle behind the development of the Chrysler K-cars, the Ford Taurus and Mercury Sable line, and the GM-10 line. The main problem with this strategy is marketing: how to convince consumers to buy the different models that spring from the same base. Chrysler proved a master at selling K-cars by putting slightly different body shapes on the same components and frame and by appealing to specific tastes and life-styles in its advertising. The Taurus and Sable were so different from what was already on the market that they did not require so much marketing effort. The Ford management got a distinctive look and a higher-quality product by giving the designers a freer hand to create the car they had always wanted to build. They instructed the designers to take manufacturability into account so that they could reduce average manufacturing costs to improve profit margins.[55] The GM-10 cars, in contrast, looked too much like one another and too much like the older GM products. GM was slower than Chrysler and Ford to make the transition to new ways of designing models and marketing products but faster in investing in new factory automation systems.[56]

Linkages between Auto Firms and Their Suppliers

Over the decades, U.S. auto firms purchased a large number of independent components producers so as to capture the value added of components manufacturing for themselves. GM, for example, produced around 70 percent of the manufacturing value per vehicle in-house. The same figure for Ford was around 50 percent, for Chrysler around 30 percent.[57] U.S. firms have not always been successful in managing their components businesses and in the past few years have sold the least profitable ones. The Japanese firms, in contrast, surrounded themselves with large numbers of subcontracting components suppliers, which were given demanding specifications for price, delivery times, and quality. The Japanese automakers were thus able to get lower prices, higher quality, and faster product innovation from their components producers than U.S. firms did. In addition, because workers in auto-company-owned component production plants tended to be United Auto Workers members, their average wages were much higher than those of comparable Japanese workers.

International competition pushed U.S. firms to reorganize or sell their domestic components subsidiaries, to reduce the number of suppliers, to purchase more components from foreign and nonunionized domestic companies, and to work more closely with an inner circle of components firms to implement just-in-time production methods. For example, in 1979, Ford purchased components from thirty-seven hundred different factories. In 1989, that number was reduced to twenty-one hundred.[58] GM installed a new computer network in 1988

55. Alton F. Doody and Ron Bingaman, *Reinventing the Wheels: Ford's Spectacular Comeback* (Cambridge, Mass.: Ballinger, 1988), chap. 3.
56. For a detailed examination of GM strategies, see Maryann Keller, *Rude Awakenings: The Rise, Fall, and Struggle for Recovery of General Motors* (New York: Morrow, 1989).
57. Nick Garnett, "The Long Hard Road to Automation," *Financial Times*, October 21, 1988, p. 18.
58. "American Carmakers."

to link its production plants with two thousand of its suppliers and began to purchase entire subassemblies instead of individual parts from suppliers.[59]

Acquisitions and Efforts at Diversification

GM and Ford had major subsidiaries in Europe and important equity holdings in Japan. The most important GM subsidiaries were Vauxhall in Britain and Adam Opel in Germany; Ford's were Ford-UK and Fordwerke in Germany. Chrysler bought into European firms later than GM and Ford and burdened itself with weak firms: Simca of France in 1963 and Rootes of Britain in 1967. Chrysler had to sell off its European subsidiares to Peugeot in 1978 as part of its financial restructuring.

A brief liberalization of restrictions on inward foreign investment in Japan allowed the big three U.S. firms to buy stakes in the three weakest Japanese firms. Chrysler bought 15 percent of the shares of Mitsubishi Motors in 1970. GM purchased 34 percent of the shares of Isuzu in 1971 and 5.3 percent of Suzuki in 1981. GM bought another 5 percent of Isuzu's shares in 1981 to bring its total holdings up to 39 percent. Ford purchased 24 percent of the shares of Toyo Kogyo (now called Mazda Motors) in 1979.[60]

In the late 1970s, the U.S. auto firms began to invest in high technology to assure access to the latest advances in factory and office automation. All three firms had divisions that serviced government and military accounts. Only Ford had an aerospace division until GM purchased Hughes and Chrysler bought Gulfstream in 1985. GM purchased Electronic Data Systems (EDS) in 1984 to help develop its new factory automation systems and telecommunications networks, but because of EDS's size and profitability, this acquisition also provided GM with an important financial boost.

Sustained Weakness in Small Cars

Despite downsizing, the development of new models, and major new acquisitions, the U.S. firms still could not compete with the Japanese in the production of small cars by the late 1980s. They were slow to accept the defection of a large part of the U.S. domestic market from the

59. François Bar, "Configuring Telecommunications Infrastructure for the Computer Age: The Economics of Network Control" (Ph.D. diss., University of California, Berkeley, 1990), chap. 3.

60. Michael A. Cusumano, *The Japanese Automobile Industry* (Cambridge, Mass.: Harvard University Press, 1985), pp. 24–25.

larger models, asserting that consumers would come back to bigger cars when gasoline prices stabilized. But even when they realized that the shift was long-lasting, they could not narrow the gaps in average production costs and vehicle quality between themselves and the Japanese.

It was widely conceded in the early 1980s that the Japanese firms could produce small cars for $1,500 to $2,000 per unit less than the U.S. firms. Even after the rise in the value of the yen, Japanese firms still produced small cars for a few hundred dollars less than their U.S. and European competitors. To compensate for the decreased advantage in manufacturing costs and for the quantitative restrictions on imports from Japan, Japanese firms moved upmarket with more expensive and higher-quality products. During most of the 1980s, Japanese cars were judged to be of greater overall quality than comparable U.S. cars.[61]

The Role of Government Policies in the 1970s and 1980s

U.S. firms' inability to match Japanese production costs and product quality in small cars caused their domestic market share to shrink, and they lost around $2 billion between 1980 and 1982. Between 1979 and 1982, employment in the motor vehicle and equipment industry declined by three hundred thousand.[62] Laid-off workers often were unable to find jobs at comparable wage levels. The high level of Japanese auto imports wounded American national pride and weakened elite and mass public support for free trade. It was not surprising that the fiercely independent industrialists of Detroit turned to the government for help.

The Energy Policy and Conservation Act of 1975 preceded and possibly added to the problems of the auto industry in the late 1970s. This law established a program called corporate average fuel economy (CAFE) that gradually raised the average fuel efficiency of vehicles

61. Some evidence for the perceived increase in quality of Japanese products can be found in the *Index to International Public Opinion, 1980–1981* (Westport, Conn.: Greenwood Press, 1982), p. 47. J. D. Powers Associates surveys consumers' satisfaction with their car purchases. These surveys consistently show U.S. cars rated lower than Japanese cars, although the gap began to decrease by the late 1980s. *Consumer Reports* compiles statistics on reported frequency of repairs from nonrandom samples of readers. These statistics show that Japanese cars had much lower rates of repair beginning in the early 1970s and continuing into the mid-1980s. See Robert Crandall et al., *Regulating the Auto* (Washington, D.C.: Brookings Institution, 1986), p. 151.

62. Motor Vehicle Manufacturers Association, *Motor Vehicle Facts and Figures '88* (Detroit: MVMA, 1988), pp. 63 and 70. Some of the decline in jobs and profits must be attributed to the recession that followed the very high interest rates imposed on the U.S. economy by the Federal Reserve Board in 1980.

built by U.S. firms to 27.5 miles per gallon by 1986. Failure to meet the standards set out under the law would result in substantial fines. The Carter administration relaxed the CAFE requirements for Chrysler in 1977 when it began to experience financial problems. CAFE created an adversarial relationship between the industry and the government. The industry complained constantly about the program and asked for relief. It tended to attribute a greater portion of its problems to government overregulation in the coming years and did not pay sufficient attention to other factors.[63]

Amendments to the Clean Air Act of 1970 in 1976–77 upset the auto industry managements who did not think they could meet the 1978 deadline for reducing nitrogen oxide emissions. The industry asked for relaxation of the deadline, and with the support of the UAW and the National Automobile Dealers Association, got it set back to 1980. Resistance to these maneuvers on the part of the Senate and the Carter administration exacerbated the adversarial atmosphere of the late 1970s.[64]

Chrysler suffered a net loss in 1975 of $260 million during an auto industry recession, but the company had been headed for financial disaster since the beginning of the 1970s. Lynn Townsend, president of Chrysler from 1961 to 1966 and chairman of the board from 1966 to 1975, had revived the company in the 1960s by increasing the quality of products and engaging in a major expansion, which included establishment of production facilities in Europe and Latin America and created a very large debt. The firm was particularly vulnerable, as a result, to slowdowns in demand and was plagued even in good years with surplus capacity. When John J. Riccardo became president of Chrysler in 1970, he recognized the problem of overcapacity and began to cut budgets, personnel, and dividends. These cuts enabled the firm to survive but could not prevent the financial crisis of the late 1970s.

Chrysler's earnings recovered sharply in 1976 but dropped precipitously in 1977 and 1978. By 1979, the firm was headed toward bankruptcy. The eventual bailout of Chrysler by the federal government, in the form of the Chrysler Loan Guarantee Act of 1979, became an important element in U.S. debates over industrial policy. Because Chrysler returned to profitability in 1982 and the costs of the bailout for the federal government were minimal, advocates of industrial policy held up the Chrysler bailout as a model of intelligent policy making. But critics of industrial policy, including Ronald Reagan and influen-

63. See Davis Dyer, Malcolm S. Salter, and Alan M. Webber, *Changing Alliances* (Boston: Harvard Business School Press, 1987), p. 220.
64. Vogel, *Fluctuating Fortunes*, pp. 182–86.

tial members of his administration, argued that the cost of the bailout far exceeded its benefits and that, in any case, industrial policy was always a bad idea.[65]

A rapid jump in imports in the 1979 model year, combined with a recession induced by government policies to reduce the inflationary effects of the petroleum price increases of 1979, resulted in the temporary layoffs of more than two hundred thousand auto industry employees. The managements of the most severely affected firms, Chrysler and Ford, petitioned the federal government for tax reductions and import restrictions, as well as regulatory relief. The United Auto Workers also asked for import restrictions and suggested that the government should try to influence the Japanese government to encourage Japanese firms to invest in automobile production in the United States.

The Carter administration responded to the demands of the auto industry by sending its complaints about unfair competition to the International Trade Commission for a ruling on whether the Japanese firms were "dumping" or were causing injury to the U.S. industry under the terms of the 1974 and 1979 trade acts. The ITC issued a negative ruling in the summer of 1980. The Carter administration integrated discussion of the auto industry into its overall review of industrial policies in the United States. The refundable investment tax credit, an idea the Reagan administration rejected, was proposed partly to deal with the problems of the auto industry.[66]

Even before the inauguration, the Reagan administration was involved in decisions concerning the auto industry. In December 1980, Douglas Fraser, president of the UAW, visited Reagan to discuss trade restrictions with focus on Japanese imports. By that time, approximately three hundred thousand autoworkers had been laid off. Reagan promised to do something about the problem and asked his nominees for cabinet offices for recommendations. David Stockman, the new director of the Office of Management and Budget, and Murray Weidenbaum, the new chairman of the Council of Economic Advisers, opposed trade restrictions but favored relaxing environmental and safety regulations. Malcolm Baldrige, the new secretary of commerce, and Drew Lewis, the new secretary of transportation, favored trade restrictions. Reagan asked his trade representative, William Brock, and the secretary of commerce to negotiate a new voluntary export

---

65. For the definitive treatment of this incident, see Reich and Donahue, *New Deals.* See also Abodaher, *Iacocca;* Michael Moritz and Barrett Seaman, *Going for Broke: The Chrysler Story* (New York: Doubleday, 1981); and David Halberstam, *The Reckoning* (New York: Avon Books, 1986), chap. 34.

66. Interview materials.

restraint with Japan.[67] The VER negotiated in 1981 limited exports to the United States to 1.68 million vehicles per year. It expired annually but was renewed annually. In April 1984, the import limit was raised to 1.86 million vehicles to allow Japan to benefit somewhat from the U.S. economic recovery.

President Reagan allowed the VER agreement with Japan to lapse on March 31, 1985. This move was interpreted as a victory for GM over Ford and Chrysler because GM had been lobbying for relaxation of trade restrictions so it could import more cars from Isuzu and Suzuki. But just as important for the Reagan administration was that the auto firms' profits had reached record levels and there was no longer an electoral reason to support the VER.[68] The move was timed to put pressure on Japan to make further concessions on trade in agriculture and high-technology products. The trade deficit with Japan had worsened considerably (to around $34 billion in 1984), and there was strong pressure from Congress to threaten an import surcharge if Japan failed to make concessions on trade liberalization.

The end of the VER was likely to result in a significant increase in exports from Japan and consequently in Japanese penetration of the U.S. car market. The *Economist* estimated that Japanese car imports would increase from 1.85 million units to at least 2.2 million units. U.S. consumers were likely to be immediate beneficiaries of the end of the VER, but unless production could be maintained at current levels despite increased imports (which would be possible only if overall economic growth remained high), autoworkers would eventually have to be laid off again, perhaps repeating the cycle that began in 1978.[69]

Despite the formal ending of the VER, the Japanese announced in 1985 that they would continue to limit exports of automobiles. The Japanese government set an upper limit of 2.3 million units for export from April 1, 1985, to March 31, 1986. On February 12, 1986, MITI announced that it would extend the voluntary limits until March 1987. The 2.3 million limit held through March 1989.

The effects of the VER were widely debated within the United States. Like all fixed quantitative import restrictions, it created incentives for the exporting country both to increase the unit price (because demand exceeded supply) and gradually to upgrade the quality and therefore the unit price of each item exported so that revenues and profits would increase even though volume would not. The results were an increase

---

67. See David A. Stockman, *The Triumph of Politics* (New York: Harper & Row, 1986), pp. 154–58; and William A. Niskanen, *Reaganomics: An Insider's Account of the Policies and the People* (New York: Oxford University Press, 1988), p. 139.

68. Niskanen, *Reaganomics*, p. 140.

69. "A Victory for Car Buyers," *Economist*, March 9, 1985, p. 69.

of at least $1,000 per car on the average price of Japanese cars to con-
sumers, long waits for the delivery of vehicles, and steady or increasing
profits for Japanese firms, which were reinvested for the next round of
international competition. The profits of U.S. firms between 1981 and
1984 jumped by $8.9 billion, mainly because of the effects of the VER.
The profits of the Japanese firms increased by about $2 billion because
they could charge higher prices for their exports. The main losers were
the consumers who had to pay the higher prices.[70]

Some opponents of the VER thought the United States should have
used a tariff instead of a quantitative restriction so that all the revenue from the higher prices would go to the United States instead of
some going to Japan. This was not a likely alternative, however, because the U.S. government had avoided tariffs since the 1960s, U.S.
firms were becoming interested in selling Japanese imports under
their own labels, and there was fear of Japanese retaliation. At the end
of 1983, GM lobbied for a higher quota for Japan so it could import
more cars from Isuzu.[71] The VER pacified protectionist interests at
home without severely injuring the foreign exporters.

Prodded by the UAW, Congress initiated a series of debates over local content requirements for vehicles sold on the U.S. market. The
UAW demanded that 90 percent of the average value of vehicles sold
by a given manufacturer should consist of U.S.-made parts. In a few
years, not even the large U.S. firms would be able to meet this criterion
because of their increased use of foreign suppliers. Less extreme content requirements could have been adopted that would have hurt the
Japanese firms because the domestic content of their automobiles was
roughly 30 to 90 percent less than that of cars produced by U.S. firms.
Japanese fears of the consequences of content requirements had a noticeable effect on their production location decisions (see Table 8). The
mere hint that VERs would be replaced with content requirements induced the Japanese firms to invest in transplants.

The case of the auto industry illustrates one of the main points of this
chapter—that the lack of a full array of industrial policy instruments
forces the U.S. government to use restrictive trade and investment

70. See, for example, David Tarr and Morris Morkre, *Aggregate Costs to the United States
of Tariffs and Quotas on Exports* (Washington, D.C.: Federal Trade Commission, 1984);
Fred Mannering and Clifford Winston, "Economic Effects of Voluntary Export Restrictions," in Clifford Winston et al., *Blind Intersection? Policy and the Automobile Industry*
(Washington, D.C.: Brookings Institution, 1987); and José A. Gomez-Ibañez, Robert A.
Leone, and Stephen A. McConnell, "Restraining Auto Imports: Does Anyone Win?"
Journal of Policy Analysis and Management 2 (1983): 196–219.
71. Amal Nag, "GM Seeks Higher Japanese-Import Quotas So That It Can Sell Af-
filiates' Cars in the U.S." *Wall Street Journal*, September 12, 1983, p. 17.

policies to deal with the problems of specific industries. In the case of autos, as in steel, efforts were made to use tax policies to assist the industry. But because of the immediacy of the problem of import penetration and the inability of the firms to adjust rapidly to competition in small car markets, trade restrictions became the only effective way to deal with the severe short-term consequences of the crisis.

The industry deserves much of the blame for its failure to adjust to increased competition. Bad management at all three firms caused them to be slow in responding. They were also slow to understand that the new conditions of the market called not only for new models and new production technology but also for a new industrial culture in which designers would work with manufacturing engineers, suppliers would work closely with manufacturers, and labor would cooperate with management to introduce new work techniques. Each of the big three firms got part of the formula right, but none of them got it all right, at least not until the middle or late 1980s.

The reluctance to consider change in industrial culture is at least partly the result of preexisting state-societal arrangements in the United States, particularly the marginalization of organized labor and the unusual strength of business relative to government. Unlike German unions, American unions could not bargain for an equal say in the implementation of new factory systems. Unlike German industrialists, U.S. industrialists could not install advanced automation equipment, confident that workers would accept it and quickly learn to use it. Unlike the Japanese government, the U.S. government could not demand a quid pro quo in restructuring efforts in exchange for trade restrictions and relaxation of environmental regulations.

POLICIES FOR SEMICONDUCTORS

The U.S. semiconductor industry seemed invincible as late as 1984. Although it had lost some global market share to Japan in the late 1970s, it was still predominant in most major segments. But after a deep drop in demand for semiconductors that began in late 1984, the industry came under withering competition from Japan, and was in disarray by the end of the 1985 downturn. Many firms left formerly profitable markets for random access memories, several firms folded, thousands of workers were laid off, and production capacity was reduced. In Japan, in contrast, massive new investments in R&D and new production facilities were made during the same period.

The fragmented U.S. semiconductor industry suffered from having to compete with large and highly integrated Japanese firms that benefited from lax enforcement of antidumping laws and the ambivalence of the Reagan administration about meeting the challenge of Japanese competition. After the semiconductor trade dispute of 1986, however, even the anti-interventionists in the Reagan administration agreed to support special measures to buttress the competitiveness of the U.S. industry. This new mood resulted in public support for an R&D consortium for semiconductor manufacturing technology (Sematech) and a general reexamination of the premises behind U.S. economic policies. Nevertheless, few lasting institutional changes emerged. Rather than facing up to the need for institutional changes, the U.S. government increased its dependence on defense spending for the promotion of high-technology industries just at the time when long overdue shrinking of the budget deficit would eventually force reductions in military spending.

Structure of the Industry

The U.S. semiconductor industry is organized somewhat differently from that in other major industrial countries. There is a sharp distinction between "captive" producers such as IBM and AT&T that make semiconductors solely for internal consumption and "merchant" producers such as Motorola and Texas Instruments that produce them mainly for sale to other firms. Figure 23 shows the sales of the largest merchant firms. In 1988, the largest merchant firm, Motorola, had total sales of over $8 billion whereas IBM earned around $60 billion.

In Japan, in contrast, all the major semiconductor producers are integrated electronics firms and depend on semiconductor sales for less than 30 percent of their total revenues (see Table 5 in Chapter 2). These firms have "deeper pockets" (access to more capital) and have access to more patient capital than do the U.S. merchant firms. They invested in semiconductor production in the late 1970s and early 1980s with the full support of a government to which strengthening its position in high-technology electronics was a national economic priority.[72]

In the early 1980s, semiconductors accounted for over 80 percent of total sales for National Semiconductor, AMD, and Mostek and more than 65 percent for Fairchild and Intel. Texas Instruments and

72. See Borrus, *Competing for Control,* chaps. 5–7; and Flamm, *Creating the Computer,* chap. 6. Patient capital is that which does not require a high rate of return immediately but can afford to wait. A major factor in the patience of capital is the prevailing interest rates for loans. If the prevailing interest rate (and, by extension, the cost of capital) is high, capital will be impatient because it can be assured a high return in the short term from a variety of investments, including relatively low-risk ones such as bank accounts and government securities. Whatever else besides interest rates raises the cost of capital increases its impatience accordingly.

Figure 23. Sales and net income of U.S. semiconductor firms

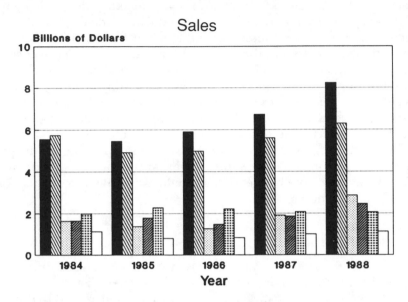

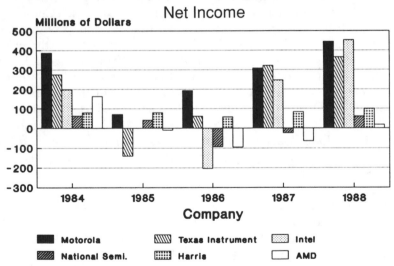

Source: Disclosure database on CD-ROM.

Motorola, the two largest firms in the merchant group, have been the most diversified, keeping semiconductors in the range of 30 to 40 percent of total sales. Texas Instruments branched out into consumer products such as calculators and personal computers, and Motorola

remains a major producer of communications equipment and consumer products. Texas Instruments tried to break into the mini- and
microcomputer markets as well, although the microcomputer effort
was a disaster. There is some evidence that other merchant firms—Intel, for example—have been trying to integrate downstream into computers, starting with add-on circuit boards for IBM-PCs and PC clones
and with advanced workstations for the computer industry.[73]

The Role of Offshore Production

Besides downstream vertical integration, most of the important merchant firms began to use foreign subsidiaries, mainly in Southeast Asia
but also in Latin America, to reduce costs in portions of the production
process. In the late 1970s, Intel, for example, after separating chips on
silicon wafers, sent them to its overseas affiliates for insertion in and
bonding to the plastic or ceramic packages that protect them from heat
and dust. The partially assembled integrated circuits would then be
shipped back to the United States for final assembly and testing. After
1982, most merchant firms did final testing at overseas facilities. Overseas affiliates were used not just to reduce labor costs but also to make
it possible to maintain steady production levels and work forces in the
United States despite fluctuations in world demand.

This strategy of production was adopted by AMD, National Semiconductor, Texas Instruments, Motorola, and others. The Japanese
firms, however, opted to automate assembly of products and, for the
most part, did not use overseas subsidiaries for manufacturing. It has
been argued that this choice of domestic automation over foreign investment was useful to the Japanese firms in the next round of competition because they were able to gain valuable knowledge about how
to improve the overall production process and, in particular, to increase the reliability of their products. Nevertheless, the U.S. firms
that remained competitive with the Japanese were not handicapped by
their overseas operations. When they began to automate the production process it was in domestic facilities but with the full intention of
applying the new processes overseas as soon as possible.[74]

73. See also "Intel May Soon Compete with Its Customers," *Business Week*, March 22,
1982, p. 63.
74. Interview materials; Sabina Dietrich, "Semiconductors," in François Bar, Michael
Borrus, Sabina Dietrich, Jeffrey A. Hart, and Jay Stowsky, *Case Studies on Manufacturing
and Overseas Production in Semiconductors and Related Industries*, Contract No. H3-5495.0
for the Office of Technology Assessment, June 15, 1988; Kenneth Flamm, "Internationalization in the Semiconductor Industry," in Joseph Grunwald and Kenneth Flamm, *The
Global Factory* (Washington, D.C.: Brookings Institution, 1985); and Dieter Ernst, "Automation, Employment and the Third World—The Case of the Electronics Industry,"
ISS Working Paper No. 29 (The Hague: Institute of Social Studies, 1985).

Historical Background

The U.S. government was involved in the semiconductor industry from its inception because of the importance of electronics for military technology. Semiconductors were invented in Bell Laboratories as part of an effort to develop new defensive radar technologies. The owner of Bell Labs, AT&T, was a regulated private monopoly, and the regulatory arrangement between AT&T and the federal government required Bell Labs to license all of its technological innovations to other firms. The earliest applications for semiconductors were military, and the assured military market for certain devices allowed firms to realize economies of scale so as to produce devices at prices that eventually would be attractive to industrial markets. As a major purchaser of business computers and other downstream civilian products, the government was an important promoter of the industry.

The government's role in the industry became less important in the late 1960s and early 1970s as the commercial markets for semiconductors—particularly in computers and telecommunications equipment—expanded more rapidly than the military and government markets. Scale economies led to rapid reductions in the cost per function of semiconductor devices, and average production costs declined steadily with cumulative production. Sales to the military and NASA in the 1960s helped U.S. semiconductor firms reduce costs so that by the late 1960s, they could find civilian customers in the computer and telecommunications industries who would pay a premium for early production of advanced devices.[75]

In the 1970s, the semiconductor industry seemed blessed. Its average annual rate of growth was over 20 percent. Profits were high, and employment in semiconductor-producing regions such as the Silicon Valley of northern California was booming. In the late 1970s, it was suggested that America's industrial problems might be solved if people moved from the Rustbelt (the Northeast and Midwest) to the Sunbelt (the West and Southwest) to take advantage of the rapid expansion of high-technology industries. One group of such proponents, the so-called Atari Democrats, first became a political factor in the 1980 elections.

The VHSIC Program

One early government attempt to promote the U.S. semiconductor industry (see Chapter 2) was the Very High-Speed Integrated Circuit Project begun in 1979. Funded by the Department of Defense and run

75. Again, the two main sources are Borrus, *Competing for Control*, and Flamm, *Creating the Computer*.

out of the Office of the Undersecretary of Defense for Research and Engineering, VHSIC was an officially sanctioned corporate research consortium in which most firms worked jointly on their contracts. VHSIC was supported by Secretary of Defense Harold Brown as a response to Soviet advances in microelectronics. In addition, VHSIC was to make is easier for military contractors and the armed services to bring the applications of microelectronics in defense systems closer to the technological frontier. Most military electronic systems were not using the latest semiconductor technology. As time went on, however, policy makers saw in VHSIC a way of supporting commercially relevant R&D in the semiconductor industry. The program quickly focused on reducing the line width of circuits to increase their speed of operation.

A problem in using VHSIC to advance the industry at this time was that military specifications for electronic circuits differed substantially from the normal industrial specifications. Military circuitry had to be fast, durable, and able to survive under combat conditions, Circuits used in computers, the largest industrial market, also needed to be fast (although manufacturers would not be willing to pay too large a premium for speed for most business applications) but did not have to be particularly durable. They certainly did not have to be able to survive nuclear attack. The key question for VHSIC, then, was whether the government would agree to civilian specifications.

The industry was able to get the military specifications set in such a way that the devices produced would be attractive to industrial customers. For example, the initial VHSIC focus on gallium arsenide as a substitute for silicon in chips was dropped after the firms argued that their customers would not be willing to pay a premium for these chips. Many of the final specifications dealt with generic technologies that would be useful for both civilian and military production such as circuit design, computer-aided design, lithography, testing, and packaging. Nevertheless, because much VHSIC work was classified, VHSIC personnel were isolated from other personnel in each VHSIC contracting firm. The VHSIC program thus made little contribution to civilian technology in semiconductors.[76]

The Semiconductor Slump of 1985

In 1985, employment at U.S.-based semiconductor companies decreased by fifty-five thousand workers and the industry as a whole

76. See Fong, "The Potential for Industrial Policy"; and Michael Y. Yoshino and Glenn R. Fong, "The Very High Speed Integrated Circuit Program: Lessons for Industrial Policy," in Bruce R. Scott and George C. Lodge, eds., *U.S. Competitiveness in the World Economy* (Boston: Harvard Business School Press, 1985).

suffered a loss of $1 billion.[77] Even profitable firms suffered a sharp reduction in profits (see Figure 23). Important U.S. firms such as Intel, Texas Instruments, Motorola, and AMD were losing money and dropping production lines in certain products. Mostek was nearly liquidated before its purchase by Thomson (of France) in 1985. Even the computer and telecommunications equipment manufacturers in the United States were beginning to worry. Their desire to buy cheap components had to be weighed against their interest in being assured access to the most advanced devices (particularly worrisome in light of the growing strength of Japanese computer and telecommunications firms).

In June 1985, a small firm called Micron Technology, headquartered in Boise, Idaho, filed an antidumping petition before the International Trade Commission against Fujitsu, Hitachi, Matsushita, Mitsubishi, NEC, Oki, and Toshiba, asking that countervailing duties of up to 94 percent be imposed on these firms retroactively for dumping (selling below the cost of production) 64K DRAMs. Although several members of the Semiconductor Industry Association (SIA) supported the Micron petition, the SIA as a whole remained neutral.[78]

A few days later, however, the SIA filed a Section 301 (unfair trade) petition against Japan, claiming that its members had been denied access to the Japanese market and repeating its earlier charges that the Japanese government had targeted the semiconductor industry and U.S. firms were suffering the consequences. Apparently, a draft version of the Section 301 petition called for import restrictions against Japan until U.S. firms were granted access to Japanese markets. IBM and other larger firms opposed this more. Intel, AMD, Hewlett-Packard, and some of the other merchant firms had favored either import restraints or countervailing duties. The final version did not include this demand.[79]

On September 30, 1985, Intel, AMD, and National Semiconductor filed an antidumping petition against eight Japanese firms for dumping erasable programmable read-only memories (EPROMs). The petitioners claimed that Japanese production costs were at least $6 per device but the sold them in the United States for only $4 to $5. They argued that dumping margins of from 77 to 227 percent should be assigned.

77. Dataquest data cited in Intel Corporation, *Annual Shareholders Meeting Report*, April 16, 1986, Figure 11.

78. Interview materials; and Andrew Pollack, "Japan Seen Target of Chip Plea," *New York Times*, September 28, 1985, p. 21.

79. See David B. Yoffie, "How an Industry Builds Political Advantage: Silicon Valley Goes to Capitol Hill," *Harvard Business Review* 66 (May–June 1988): 82–89.

The International Trade Commission ruled that the U.S. industry had been injured by the trade practices of the Japanese firms in all three cases. The ruling on 64K DRAMs was made in August and that on EPROMS in November. The ruling on 256K (and above) DRAMs was not made until March 1986 after an unprecedented antidumping investigation in January 1986 by the secretary of commerce, who apparently felt the need to accelerate the process behind the DRAM petition and to change the complaint to provide greater bargaining leverage with the Japanese government.[80]

On March 14, 1986, Commerce and the ITC ruled that Japanese firms had indeed dumped 256K DRAMs and 1-megabit DRAMs and that the dumping margins for at least two firms, Mitsubishi and NEC, exceeded 100 percent. Commerce had ruled similarly on 64K DRAMs in January so the second ruling was not a surprise. Nevertheless, the addition of a government-initiated investigation to private antidumping and Section 301 complaints signaled the intent of the Reagan administration to make trade in semiconductors a major thrust in its diplomacy with Japan.[81]

The Japanese government responded to the changed mood in Washington by sending MITI officials to meet with industry representatives on January 20, 1986. At this meeting, MITI offered to establish floor prices for devices sold by Japanese firms in the United States. The U.S. firms rejected this offer, claiming that the Japanese could still dump in third-country markets, which would be an incentive for U.S. equipment firms to locate their production outside the United States. In addition, the U.S. firms claimed that floor prices would violate antitrust laws. What they wanted, they said, was for Japan to stop dumping on a worldwide basis.

After the ITC and Commerce rulings on the antidumping and unfair trade petitions, the Japanese firms raised their selling prices in the United States in a belated and unsuccessful effort to mollify the U.S. semiconductor producers. Hitachi announced a special program to increase imports into Japan of electronic components and other items from the United States and to increase contributions to the U.S.-based Hitachi Foundation. But most U.S. observers considered these offers to be mere window dressing.

In late May 1986, the ITC recommended that countervailing duties be imposed on Japanese semiconductor firms; the dumping margins varied from firm to firm for 64K and 256K DRAMs. On May 27, the ITC ruled that Micron Technology had suffered economic injury as a

---

80. Evidence for this can be found in Clyde W. Prestowitz, Jr., *Trading Places: How We Allowed Japan to Take the Lead* (New York: Basic Books, 1988), p. 57.

81. Ibid., pp. 57–61.

result of sales of Japanese 64K DRAMs on the U.S. market. The six largest Japanese producers were named in the ruling.[82]

The U.S.-Japanese Semiconductor Trade Agreement of 1986

On July 30, 1986, the U.S. trade representative and MITI reached agreement on the semiconductor trade issue. The agreement barely beat a legislatively mandated deadline for new penalties and sanctions. MITI agreed to help administer a floor-price system based on fair market value (FMV) and, in a confidential side letter, agreed to adopt measures to raise U.S. firms' share of the Japanese market from 10 to 20 percent.[83] The U.S. government and firms agreed to drop the anti-dumping and Section 301 petitions against Japan. The specifics of the agreement were left to later negotiations.

The U.S. semiconductor industry received the news of this agreement with some skepticism. Concern was expressed about how fair market value would be established, the treatment of third parties to which semiconductors might be sold at lower than FMV, and the inclusion of other devices besides 64K and 256K DRAMs and EPROMs in the agreement. Conflict continued between the merchant semiconductor firms and the industrial consumers of semiconductors (mostly computer and electronics firms) about the terms of the agreement. The consumers wanted to maintain their right to purchase devices at low prices and worried that Japanese integrated firms would have an advantage over them if they could not. They were particularly anxious to exclude 1-megabit DRAMs from the FMV price system.

One immediate effect of the agreement was to raise DRAM prices dramatically (see Figure 24). By late September 256K DRAM prices had increased from $2.25 to about $5.00 per device.[84] Makers of printed circuit boards for computers and electronic equipment threatened to move their board assembly operations overseas, where prices of components could not be so closely monitored. Part of the problem may have been that the prices established by the Department of Commerce for the FMV system were inaccurate. The American Electronics Association and the Semiconductor Industry Association worked together to provide data to Commerce to revise the system so as to bring prices down to more realistic levels. By the end of the first quarter of 1987, the prices of 256K DRAMs dropped again to about $4 per unit.

---

82. These producers were Toshiba, Matsushita, NEC, Hitachi, Fujitsu, and Mitsubishi. Oki was not named.

83. Prestowitz, *Changing Places*, pp. 65–66.

84. Tom Moran, "Chip Pact Said to Imperil Board Assembly in U.S.," *Infoworld*, September 22, 1986, p. 1.

Figure 24. Unit prices for 256K DRAMs

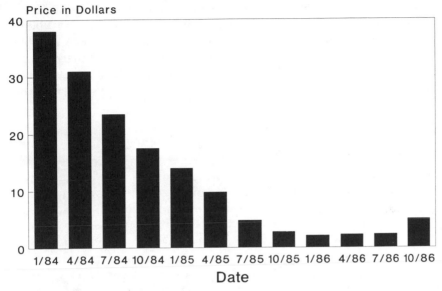

Price in Dollars

Source: Dataquest pricing data as cited in *Infoworld*, February 3, 1986, p. 1. The October 1986 figure was an estimate.

The Breakdown of the Semiconductor Agreement

Japanese firms began to complain in the fall of 1986 that the FMV system gave a relative advantage to Korean and European firms. They contended that complying with the paperwork for administering the FMV system was raising their production costs and suggested that stabilizing prices would remove incentives to innovate.[85] U.S. firms began to complain about Japanese dumping in third markets and about noncompliance with the FMV system in the U.S. market. In November, the U.S. government warned the Japanese government that dumping in third countries would result in the termination of the July agreement.[86]

In mid-March 1987, MITI asked Japanese firms to cut production by 10 percent an effort to reduce price-cutting in third-country markets. It also tightened up its export licensing system to make it harder to send small batches of semiconductors through third parties. The 10

85. Susan Chira, "Japanese Uneasy on Chip Pact," *New York Times*, August 2, 1986, p. 17.
86. Clyde Farnsworth, "Japan to Cut U.S. Textile Exports," *New York Times*, November 15, 1986, p. 17.

percent cutback in Japanese production created shortages in DRAMs because no U.S. firms had been willing to reenter the DRAM market after the slump in 1985. The profitability of Japanese firms improved dramatically. Between 1985 and 1987, they had lost about $4 billion (compared with about $2 billion for U.S. firms). Not only did the MITI-mandated cutbacks allow the Japanese firms to make large profits, they also deepened the differences between semiconductor and systems producers in the United States. The latter began to blame the trade agreement for the high prices of DRAMs.[87]

Imposition of Trade Sanctions

Access to the Japanese market had not improved and dumping in third countries continued.[88] The Japanese government claimed that there was no agreement on market access and denied the existence of the confidential side letter. On March 23, 1987, the Senate Finance Committee passed a nonbinding resolution by voice vote calling on the president to retaliate against Japan for failing to live up to the semiconductor trade agreement. On March 27, 1987, President Reagan announced that $300 million in trade sanctions would be imposed on Japanese firms for violating the July 1986 agreement and for restricting access to the Japanese market. The sanctions affected some Japanese consumer electronic products, power tools, and desktop and laptop personal computers, but not semiconductors. U.S. computer and electronics firms wanted to avoid increased costs for Japanese components and hoped also to avoid Japanese retaliation against U.S. products. The SIA agreed to the sanctions to placate the various computer and electronics industry associations, feeling that the message would get across in any case.[89]

The president's move increased the tension in an already strained relationship with Japan. The Japanese government threatened to retaliate if the trade sanctions were implemented (the president had given the Japanese government a few weeks to respond).[90] In the end, no agreement could be worked out and sanctions were imposed on April 17.

87. Interview materials.
88. Semiconductor Industry Association, *Four Years of Experience under the U.S.-Semiconductor Agreement: "A Deal Is a Deal,"* Fourth Annual Report to the President (San José, Calif.: SIA, 1990), pp. 59–62.
89. Interview materials. See also Lee Smith, "Let's Not Bash the Japanese," *Fortune,* April 27, 1987, p. 175; Rachel Parker, "Industry Associations Applaud Sanctions against Japanese," *Infoworld,* April 6, 1987, p. 28.
90. Susan Chira, "U.S. Given Warning by Japan," *New York Times,* April 16, 1987, p. 23.

The Rise of Sematech

The U.S.-Japanese dispute over semiconductor trade in 1985–87 was an initial battle in what was to become a much wider trade war. A Defense Science Board Task Force on Semiconductor Dependency was convened in mid-February 1986 to assess the "impact on U.S. national security if any leading edge of technologies are no longer in this country." The executive secretary of the task force, E. D. (Sonny) Maynard, was also director of the Department of Defense's (VHSIC) Program. The chairman was Norman Augustine, head of Rockwell. The task force also included representatives from a variety of electronics and defense-oriented firms, a former under secretary of defense, a former under secretary of commerce, and the director of the National Science Foundation.[91] Several of the reports done for the task force were so depressing and controversial that they were classified.[92]

The Department of Defense decided, on the basis of these reports, to support a new effort to bolster U.S. technology: Sematech, short for Semiconductor Manufacturing Technology. Sematech was originally proposed by Charles Sporck, president and CEO of National Semiconductor. Sematech would be jointly funded by SIA members and the Department of Defense and would draw on the resources of the Semiconductor Research Corporation, a consortium set up by the SIA in North Carolina. The Defense Science Board recommended that the Department of Defense provide $200 million per year over the 1987–92 period, but the actual level of funding for 1988 ended by being only $100 million.[93]

Sematech has thirteen core members: IBM, AT&T, Harris, Micron Technology, Rockwell, Texas Instruments, Motorola, AMD, Intel, LSI Logic, Hewlett-Packard, Digital Equipment Corporation, and National Semiconductor. Sematech's charter allows only 100 percent U.S.-owned firms to be members. All the large merchant semiconductor firms plus four large computer manufacturers—IBM, AT&T, Digital Equipment Corporation, and Hewlett-Packard—are represented in Sematech's core. The purpose of Sematech is to put U.S. firms back on the technological frontier in semiconductor manufacturing. Its goal is to produce circuits with smaller and smaller line widths in three stages:

91. Jack Robertson, "DOD Task Force Eyes Impact of IC Technology Offshore," *Electronic News*, February 24, 1986, p. 1.

92. One study that was unclassified was Richard Van Atta, Erland Heginbotham, Forrest Frank, Albert Perrella, and Andrew Hull, *Technical Assessment of U.S. Electronics Dependency* (Alexandria, Va.: Institute for Defense Analyses, 1985).

93. Jeffrey Bairstow, "Can the U.S. Semiconductor Industry be Saved?" *High Technology*, May 1987, p. 34; David E. Sanger, "Chip Makers in Accord on Plan for Consortium," *New York Times*, March 5, 1987, p. 29; and "Conferees OK $100M for Sematech," *Electronic News*, December 21, 1987, p. 1.

0.7 microns, 0.5 microns, and 0.35 microns. Sematech works only with U.S.-owned semiconductor manufacturing equipment producers in pursuit of this goal.[94]

Sematech is an R&D consortium. Therefore, it has to be registered with and monitored by the Department of Justice under the National Cooperative Research Act of 1984 so that it does not violate antitrust laws. Roughly half of the operating funds for Sematech come from the Department of Defense and are administered by the Defense Advanced Research Projects Agency. To avoid some of the problems connected with the diffusion of technologies that were associated with the VHSIC Program, DARPA has administered the Sematech effort with a light hand. Although there have been some disputes between the companies and DARPA over the goals and objectives of the program, increased competition from Japan created greater solidarity between government and industry than existed for the VHSIC Program.[95]

IBM and AT&T were instrumental in initiating Sematech. An IBM executive, Sanford Kane, was the chairman of the executive committee of Sematech. Another IBM employee, Paul Castrucci, was chief operating officer of the venture until his resignation in April 1989. IBM licensed its 4-megabit DRAMs for production at the Sematech facility in Austin, Texas. Similarly, AT&T licensed a 64K SRAM to Sematech and donated its own proprietary 0.7-micron CMOS production process for use in the early stages of the project.[96]

The chief executive officer of Sematech from 1987 until his death in June 1990 was Robert Noyce, formerly of Intel and one of the founding fathers of Silicon Valley. Noyce was a firm advocate of the use of R&D consortia to deal with competitive challenges from abroad. Opponents of industrial policy challenged the necessity for R&D consortia and criticized Sematech for its high costs and its potentially anticompetitive effects. Sematech was also criticized for being slow in recognizing the need to reverse the rapid decline of the U.S. semiconductor production equipment industry.[97] Supporters of industrial

94. Presentation by Sanford Kane at a meeting on the U.S. Semiconductor Industry at Stanford University, October 21, 1988.

95. Interview materials.

96. Brian Santo and Waren Rappleya, "Sematech Front End: 4-MB DRAM, 64K SRAM Recipes Will Be Donated to Consortium," *Electronic News*, February 1, 1988, p. 1.

97. See Jay Stowsky, "Weak Links, Strong Bonds: U.S.-Japanese Competition in Semiconductor Production Equipment," in Chalmers Johnson, Laura D'Andrea Tyson, and John Zysman, eds., *Politics and Productivity: The Real Story of Why Japan Works* (Cambridge, Mass.: Ballinger, 1989); *Using R&D Consortia for Commercial Innovation: Sematech, X-Ray Lithography, and High-Resolution Systems* (Washington, D.C.: Congressional Budget Office, 1990); and Claude Barfield, statement before the Sub-committee on Science, Research, and Technology, *The Government Role in Joint Production Ventures* (Washington, D.C.: U.S. Government Printing Office, 1989), p. 63.

policy defended R&D consortia as a necessary response to the increasing competitiveness of both Japan and Western Europe in advanced electronics.[98] Some advocates of R&D consortia argued that cooperation should be extended to joint production, which would require further modification of antitrust laws.[99]

It was not clear that Sematech would achieve all of its goals, but the project had nearly universal support from the major computer and semiconductor firms in the United States. This support sprang from their concern about growing U.S. dependence on foreign sources of advanced integrated circuits. The semiconductor industry continued to have problems with the electronics systems manufacturers over the negative consequences of the 1986 Trade Agreement. After a series of difficult negotiations, the computer and semiconductor firms agreed to recommend the termination of the FMV system. The SIA turned its attention to problems other than preventing dumping and building modern manufacturing facilities: achieving greater market access in Japan, getting U.S. firms to reenter the market for DRAMs, and formulating a constructive response to the challenge from Japan and Europe in downstream industries such as consumer and automotive electronics.[100]

Increased international competition in semiconductors has forced the United States government and other major institutions to make changes that allow U.S.-owned firms to compensate for the greater fragmentation of the electronics industry relative to its major competitors in Japan and Europe. These changes have been strongly constrained by the preexisting bias against industry-specific policies. The main government policy initiatives for the semiconductor industry have been in trade policy and defense spending (VHSIC and Sematech). Portraying challenges to industrial competitiveness and threats to national security so as to build support for action appears to be a constant in state-societal arrangements in the United States.

The case of the semiconductor industry suggests that the U.S. government can act despite its fragmentation when competitiveness concerns a broad coalition of interests. The coalition that supported VHSIC and Sematech, for example, included representatives of industry, the defense establishment, and the bureaucracy responsible for trade

98. See Dertouzos, Lester, and Solow, *Made in America,* p. 140.
99. See Thomas Jorde and David Teece, "Competition and Cooperation: Striking the Right Balance," *California Management Review* 32 (Spring 1989): 25–37.
100. Interview materials. As attempt to deal with reentry into DRAM markets by forming a DRAM consortium called U.S. Memories failed for lack of funding in January 1990. See SIA, *Four Years of Experience.*

negotiations. The question of whether the U.S. system can respond to challenges that are not directly linked to national security concerns is still open.

CONCLUSIONS

The United States was only partially successful by the late 1980s in responding to challenges of international competitiveness. The response was slowest and weakest in steel, which endured a drastic shrinkage of revenues and employment. The auto industry needed less downsizing, and employment returned to its pre-1978 level albeit with some reductions in real wages and benefits. As in the steel industry, however, the adoption of voluntary export restraints and other trade barriers to protect jobs and revenues resulted in a major influx of foreign firms. In semiconductors, the response to declining competitiveness was rapid and strong because economic competitiveness was closely related to national security, but it is not yet clear whether the policies adopted would reverse the decline.

The United States was not in nearly as bad shape as Britain by the late 1980s. Although the policies of the Reagan and Thatcher administrations bear a superficial resemblance, the results were different. The United States enjoyed higher growth, lower unemployment, and much higher per capita income. U.S. industries had declined markedly in the face of international competition, starting from a position of global leadership after World War II. British industries emerged from World War II in a much weaker position, and the postwar decline brought them to an even lower state.

Yet the United States did not respond as well as Japan or Germany to the competitive challenges of the 1970s and early 1980s. Its government was more uncertain about how to respond, its firms were slower to adopt needed changes in technology and workplace arrangements, and the nation did not build the skills of its work force to deal with future challenges. In short, the United States had much to learn from its major competitors.

But the key question, to be considered in the final chapter of this book, is, What should be learned? I will argue that the citizens of the United States need to decide whether they want a future American more like Japan or more like Germany. The debate over institutional change in the United States has focused too much on the desirability of emulating Japan. This focus has led one prominent author, James Fallows, to argue that the United States should not copy Japan but can succeed best by being itself.[101] Clearly, whatever the United States does, it has to remain true to its history and to its citizens' sense of collective identity. But there is an alternative to blindly emulating Japan—or any other country.

101. James Fallows, *More Like Us: Making America Great Again* (Boston: Houghton Mifflin, 1989).

SEVEN

Conclusions

The main argument of this book is that state-societal arrangements are the key to explaining recent changes in international competitiveness. State-societal arrangements matter because they can accelerate or impede the development and diffusion of technological innovations that are crucial for competitiveness (see Figure 1 in Chapter 1), especially during technological transitions.[1]

International competitiveness in steel, autos, and semiconductors has been heavily dependent on the diffusion of new technologies. In the case of steel, the new technologies were basic-oxygen furnaces and continuous casting. For autos, they were just-in-time (or *kanban*) production systems and automated assembly systems. The critical new semiconductor technologies were the production techniques needed to move from one generation of semiconductors to another (e.g., from transistors to integrated circuits, from integrated circuits to LSI, and from LSI to VLSI).

The first countries to develop and diffuse these technologies widely were most likely to increase their share of world production, to maintain or increase employment, and to experience fewer financial crises. By these criteria, the best performers overall were Japan and Germany. Germany, like the other major European countries, was an underperformer in semiconductors, whereas Japan was remarkably successful in that industry from the late 1970s on. The competitiveness of Britain

1. I have not said much about the issue of technological transition, but my position is similar to those in James Kurth, "The Political Consequences of the Product Cycle: Industrial History and Political Outcomes," *International Organization* 33 (Winter 1979): 1–34; and Stephen S. Cohen and John Zysman, *Manufacturing Matters: The Myth of the Post-Industrial Economy* (New York: Basic Books, 1987).

and the United States declined in all three industries, although the United States started from a much better position. France's performance was somewhere in between. Until the 1970s, France grew almost as rapidly in industrial and technological competence as Japan. That growth virtually stopped in the late 1970s and resumed at a slower pace after 1986.

VARIATION IN STATE-SOCIETAL ARRANGEMENTS

Figure 25 summarizes the information in Chapters 2 to 6 concerning the organization of state, business, and labor in the five industrial countries. The five countries are placed on the faces or vertices of a triangle that represents the influence of the government, business, and labor in state-societal arrangements. A country on the labor vertex has strong labor, weak government, and weak business. A country on the business vertex has strong business, weak labor, and weak government. A country between the labor and business vertices has strong labor and business and weak government. Each country has a distinctive pattern. That is, Japan has a pattern of high influence for the state and business but low influence for labor; Germany has a pattern of high influence of business and labor but low influence for the state (although the federal government is in a weaker position than the regional governments in dealing with specific industries).

Some of the judgments implicit in Figure 25 need to be qualified because of important changes that have occurred since World War II.

Figure 25. State-societal arrangements in the five countries

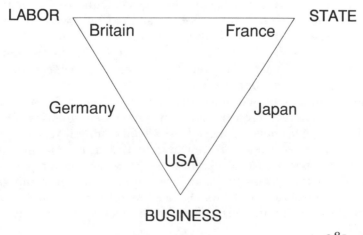

LABOR — Britain — France — STATE

Germany — Japan

USA

BUSINESS

For example, the influence of labor in Britain was greatly reduced during the Thatcher administration, from 1979 to 1990, and the state became more assertive in carrying out its program of privatization. Similarly, labor in Germany had somewhat less influence under the Kohl administration than in previous SPD governments. Labor may have gained some influence in Japan with the unification of the Sohyo and Domei. Labor was temporarily influential in France immediately after the strike in 1968 and had greater say in French politics during the Mitterrand presidency than under previous presidents.

In Britain, both the degree of centralization and the influence of the state increased markedly after the institutional changes introduced by the Conservatives in 1972, but both remained low compared with France and Japan. The trend in the United States toward greater use of government resources to support civilian industries in the late 1980s is not reflected in Figure 25, nor is the move away from the use of state enterprises in Britain and France under the Thatcher and Chirac governments.

The influence of business increased in Japan during the period in question, but it has been high relative to the other industrialized countries for the entire period because of the *keiretsu* form of organization. Business influence has fluctuated substantially over time in both the United States and Germany, but relative to other countries it was high throughout the period. In Britain, services and financial interests have always had substantial influence, and manufacturing has had its ups and downs. Thus the influence of business as a whole has been weakened by its diversity and lack of a single voice. In Britain and the United States business has few incentives to create centralized peak associations because of the fragmented nature of the state. It is not necessary to centralize to influence public policies, and doing so may even be counterproductive. In Germany, business is centralized primarily as a counterweight to centralized labor but also partially as a consequence of the large role played by the big three universal banks in financing industrial activities and the legal environment that creates national forums for tripartite bargaining among government, business, and labor for wages and other labor market issues.

France, like Britain, scores low on business influence because of the high dependency of French firms on government policies. Because most French firms never achieved the global competitiveness enjoyed by Japanese firms, they were not able to rival the influence of the state. France has industrial families, but they have never played the same role as the *keiretsu* in Japan in creating domestic competition. The high centralization of French business reflects the high concentration of ownership in most industries and owners' need to deal with the government in a relatively unified way: it stems from their relative weakness and is not (as in Japan and Germany) a source of strength.

In short, the relative influence of government, business, and labor in the five countries creates a distinctive pattern. Britain had the least successful pattern: low government and business influence combined with highly influential labor. Japan and Germany, with very different state-societal arrangements, both increased their international competitiveness. France, with its state-dominant pattern, performed well until the late 1970s, which suggests that this pattern is not well suited for the technological transition connected with innovations in microelectronics. The business-dominant pattern of the United States also did poorly when compared with all the other large industrial countries except Britain.

State-Societal Arrangements and the Creation and Diffusion of Technologies

The relative power of the state, business, and labor in setting industrial policy is closely linked with the creation and diffusion of new technologies. Labor must be receptive to the introduction of new technologies at the workplace, business must be prepared to adopt new technologies in a timely manner, and the state must be able to work with both business and labor to ensure the rapid creation and diffusion of new technologies.

Whether labor will be receptive to the introduction of new technologies in the workplace depends on how confident it is that it will receive higher wages when productivity increases. This confidence depends on labor's political power in the system, which in turn seems to depend on the level of skills possessed by the average laborer. Even if it lacks political power, labor may still accept new technologies if guaranteed job security and opportunities for training, but the upgrading of production technologies will be limited by a low average level of skills in the work force.

The ability of business to adopt new technologies rapidly depends on its access to information about technological change, which can be positively affected by the direct actions of an influential state (as in Japan) or by the transmission of this information by institutions, especially educational ones, that link state and society (as in Germany).

In Japan, the close working relationship between government agencies and the larger firms, which is a result of the weakness of organized labor and of the long dominance of the Liberal Democratic party, allows private and public resources to be combined to pursue technological and economic priorities established jointly by government and business. The main payoff to labor has been job security and steadily increasing wages. A societal commitment to upgrading the skills of workers has been part of the arrangement, but this commitment is not as deep in Japan as it is in Germany. The big loser under the Japanese system is the average consumer (who is also the average worker), who tends to pay higher prices than those in other industrialized countries for equivalent consumer goods and receives lower interest on personal savings and investments. This set of arrangements, which could be upset in the future if labor and consumer interests organize effectively, has been the basis of the dominance of the Liberal Democratic Party in Japanese politics since the 1950s.

The Japanese system is well organized for joint state and business efforts to bring Japan to the technological frontier in strategic industries and keep it there. There is very little room for labor to resist the introduction of new product and process technologies. So far, these innovations have benefited labor as a whole because they have had a positive effect on employment and wages. Business can block government measures that it perceives are against its interests, especially measures that appear to favor a limited number of *keiretsu* over others, but has enough weight in government-business forums to assure that government initiatives in creation of technology enhance individual and collective competitiveness.

In Germany, government plays a much less important role than in Japan and labor is much more important. The strength of the German system is built on the high skill level of German workers, the result of educational efforts that can be traced back to the Wilhelmine era. After World War II, the traditional power of skilled labor in the workplace was reinforced by the growing power of organized labor in the political system and its embodiment in legal institutions that guaranteed labor a voice in important policy-making forums.

The high influence of labor in the German system, combined with its higher than average level of skills, has resulted in strong support for technological improvements in established industries to guaranteed continued growth in wages. German laborers have been somewhat less enthusiastic about encouraging the growth of new industries such as microelectronics because they are concerned that new process technologies will replace labor with machines. Nevertheless, increasing competition within the European Community and from the newly industrializing countries has made it clear to both business and labor that the rapid introduction of technological innovations is the key to continued German competitiveness.

Although the German government plays a minor role relative to others, it is responsible for the educational system that transmits skills to the work force, and it funds many of the activities of universities and the Fraunhofer Institutes, which help to assure the transmission of university-created knowledge to businesses. Finally, the German government, like that of Japan, has created a stable macroeconomic climate for business investments. Thus the German system has worked nearly as well as the Japanese because it encourages the creation and diffusion of technologies.

In sharp contrast, the British system has not encouraged the diffusion of technologies, despite the continued importance of Britain in developing new technologies. The uncertainty created by fluctuating political and macroeconomic climates has clearly worked to delay diffusion of new technologies. The relative weakness of both government and business in the face of a relatively unified and militant labor movement provides a further disincentive. Britain's competitive decline is partly, but not wholly, a function of poor management. But even wise management was confronted with important constraints not present in other industrial countries.

In the United States, the political weakness of labor, closely connected with the low average skill level of the work force, has impeded the diffusion of new production technologies. The fragmentation of the American state makes it difficult for the state to act as a partner with business in the creation of new technologies, especially those that have no military application. Business may impose its wishes on both the government and organized labor in the United States, but it is strongly constrained in the competitive strategies it can adopt.

In France, the main impediments to the creation and diffusion of new technologies have been the lack of domestic competition in important markets and the marginalization of labor. The lack of domestic competition will become less important as French firms deal with the problem of surviving in the increasingly open European market, but they will still have to grow out of their current dependence on the tutelary relationship with the powerful French state. The state has learned the lesson of being overly dependent on one or two national champions per industry. But the political fragmentation of organized labor is likely to continue, and there seems to be no major move toward upgrading the skills of the work force. Nevertheless, state-societal arrangements have not been as much of a handicap to making the technological transition in France as they have been in Britain and the United States.

Why Alternative Explanations Do Not Work as Well

Chapter 1 discussed five categories of alternative explanations: macroeconomic, culturalist, statist, corporatist, and coalitional. Each of these is inferior to the state-societal approach for reasons already sketched out. Here, some further criticisms will be added to the list.

Macroeconomic variables are important for international competitiveness. Factor prices, aggregate demand, levels of savings and investment, and exchange rates have a major impact on trade performance, employment and wage levels, profitability, and other indicators of competitiveness. For example, recent research published by the Institute for International Economics suggests that shifts in trade balances in the late 1980s closely reflected changes in exchange rates. Both the direction and the magnitude of changes were as predicted in leading theories of adjustment. Exchange rates were posited to be strongly affected by underlying macroeconomic conditions.[2]

The connection between macroeconomic policy instruments and macroeconomic outcomes, however, is less certain. Policy instruments vary across countries because the economic institutions that are associated with state-societal arrangements vary. Some countries give government agencies the power to allocate capital, others do not; some have firm control over interest rates, others have only limited control. There are significant differences on the fiscal side as well. Because of this variance in macroeconomic policy instruments and their effects, it would be very difficult for the major industrial countries to coordinate their macroeconomic policies even if they wanted to.[3]

Since macroeconomic policy instruments are so closely constrained by state-societal arrangements and are linked in such an uncertain way to outcomes because of institutional mediation, it makes sense to explain changes in competitiveness not in terms of macroeconomic policy but of state-societal arrangements. Thus I argue that state-societal arrangements account for most of the variance explained by macroeconomic variables as well as some of the variance not explained by them.

I have argued that culturalist explanations, unlike macroeconomic explanations, cannot be considered true rivals to state-societal explanations. Cultural explanations cannot account for changes in competitiveness in such relatively short time periods as those involved in this study. Culture is rarely defined in a precise enough way to permit an adequate test, but when it is, what is called culture is usually epiphenomenal rather than fundamental. This is the case in recent work linking culture and competitiveness because the attitudes or ideologies

2. Fred Bergsten, ed., *International Adjustment in Finance: Lessons of 1985 through 1990* (Washington, D.C.: Institute of International Economics, 1991).

3. William H. Branson, The Limits of Monetary Coordination as Exchange Rate Policy," *Brookings Papers on Economic Activity* 1 (1986): 175–94; and Jeffrey Frankel and Catharine Rockett, "International Macroeconomic Policy Coordination: When Policymakers Do Not Agree on the True Model," *American Economic Review* 78 (June 1988): 318–40.

that are posited to reflect differences in culture probably reflect differences in state-societal arrangements or other variables not so deeply rooted in history as the term "culture" implies.

It has to be admitted, however, that culture as embodied in "habits of mind" may have played a role in the persistence of certain state-societal arrangements. Why do Americans distrust the state so much? Why did the British accept the blocking role of organized labor? Why do the Americans and the British accept high spending for military R&D? Why do Japanese workers accept their subordinate status in society? Why don't Japanese consumers band together to protect their interests as they do elsewhere? Why is it so hard to reform the French educational system? There are no easy answers to these questions, and I would not like to say that it is simply a matter of pursuing personal and group interests.

The statist, corporatist, and coalitional approaches are all less general than the state-societal approach because they focus on a proper subset of the pattern of relationship among the three "actors" that are the concern of the state-societal approach: the state, business, and organized labor. The statist approach focuses on the state exclusively and therefore misses the important role of business and labor in competitiveness. The corporatist approach posits a connection between state, business, and labor that does not exist in most large industrial countries. The coalitional approach does not consider the possible role of a relatively autonomous state in explaining country-level outcomes. These three approaches, therefore, do not fit the data. We are left, then, with the conclusion that the state-societal approach is the most general approach and the one that best fits the data at hand. This does not mean that the alternative approaches are not useful for other purposes but that they are less useful in this context.

IMPLICATIONS FOR THEORIES OF DOMESTIC INSTITUTIONAL CHANGE

One of the main failings of earlier work on state-societal arrangements is its emphasis on stasis or inertia and hence its inability to account for change. This book attempts to remedy that failing by looking for evidence of such change and finding convincing explanations for it. Although there was not a great deal of institutional change during the period addressed in this book, there was enough to suggest some new lines of inquiry.

Some institutional change was imposed on Japan and Germany by the occupations that followed World War II. Not all the changes desired by the occupation authorities were effected in the two countries, and both had their own ideas about how to reorder themselves in light of the disasters that had befallen them. Defeat in war made possible changes in state-societal arrangements. What changes actually occurred depended on additional factors.

In Germany, for example, the nationalist and militarist elites were not allowed to participate in building the postwar order. The authoritarian and corporatist methods of the Nazi state were discredited. The postwar order, therefore, combined a desire for a competitive market with a highly weakened and federalized state to guarantee that the excesses of the recent past would not be repeated. The political power of labor was institutionalized in a new legal regime to prevent the legitimation crises that preceded the rise of the Nazis. Although the new arrangements were inconsistent with granting mesoeconomic policy-making instruments to the state, the German system compensated by emphasizing the training of skilled workers and the transfer of university-created technologies to businesses in areas that were crucial for maintaining or increasing competitiveness.

In Japan, the conservative elite were not so thoroughly discredited as they were in Germany. Some bureaucracies, in particular MITI's predecessor agency, the Ministry of Commerce and Industry, wanted to apply some of the lessons learned during the military occupation of Manchuria in guiding the development of heavy industry after the war. They were not prevented from doing this by major changes in the institutions governing the exercise of state power. Some of the reforms introduced by the occupation authorities took root—the introduction of greater competition in Japanese politics and markets, the legalization of trade unions, the breakup of Nippon Steel, the enfranchisement of women, and others—but postwar state-societal arrangements were not as radically different from those of the prewar period as they were in Germany.

Less significant changes in state-societal arrangements occurred in Britain, France, and the United States after World War II. In Britain, the main turning points were 1972 and 1979, corresponding to the adoption of the Industry Act of 1972 and the election of Margaret Thatcher. The Industry Act of 1972 attempted to institutionalize a greater centralization of mesoeconomic policy making and confirmed a growing societal consensus over the desirability of reducing conflict between labor and business. These institutional reforms did not succeed, however. The election of Thatcher meant a shift away from the use of state enterprises to privatization as a response to the weakness of private British firms in international competition. Because of the continued erosion of British manufacturing and the altered but still substantial role of British organized labor, this process had reached its limits by the end of the 1980s.

288

In France, the 1980s were troubled times. The system that had worked so well to build French competitiveness in steel and automobiles was failing to maintain that competitiveness and impeded the development of high-technology electronics. The Socialists experimented with neo-Keynesian macroeconomic policies, a major increase in R&D expenditures, and nationalization. The macroeconomic policies were badly timed; the nationalizations were mostly reversed by Jacques Chirac (but not until after they had injected some badly needed capital into some strategic industries). By the late 1980s, France had recovered somewhat and was facing the changes that would be imposed by Europe 1992 with renewed confidence.

In the United States, starting in the late 1970s, serious proposals were put forward for institutional changes that would allow the government to make and implement mesoeconomic policies outside of the traditional realms of defense, agriculture, and health. These proposals were seriously debated through the late 1980s and rejected by three different administrations. But the increasingly obvious growth of Japanese economic strength and the declining threat of a Soviet Union preoccupied with *glasnost* and *perestroika* meant that the debate over institutional change was far from over.

In short, movement occurred in state-societal arrangements within the bounds established by the underlying distribution of power among major societal groupings. That movement was likely to continue in the two least favored countries—Britain and the United States—with further debate on giving the state instruments to pursue mesoeconomic policies to respond more effectively to the challenges from Japan and Germany.

The competitive success of Japan and Germany also affected state-societal arrangements. In Japan, business had achieved greater autonomy and the agencies of the state began to compete for mesoeconomic influence to deal with the increasingly complex domestic economy. By the end of the 1980s, MITI was no longer the prime mover of mesoeconomic policy, especially in high-technology electronics, and businesses did not depend on its guidance as much as in the 1950s and 1960s. The Japanese system began to undergo pressure from below to grant greater influence to workers and consumers so that the societal gains from greater international competitiveness could be distributed more equitably.

In Germany, continued problems of competing with low-wage countries in older industries combined with the forces behind Europe 1992 were bringing certain established institutions into question. The dominance of the three largest universal banks was under attack, as was the resistance of German labor to Japanese- and American-style production practices in high-technology industries. The lack of meso-economic policy instruments at the federal level resulted in mesoeco-nomic policy experiments at the provincial level.

What emerges from this study, therefore, is a greater sense of the dy-namism and room for maneuver in state-societal arrangements within the broad constraints imposed by the domestic balance of power. Never-theless, the variance in state-societal arrangements across nations was not diminishing, nor were they becoming less closely connected to in-ternational competitiveness.

WHERE DO WE GO FROM HERE?

The two countries that experienced increased competitiveness in the last two decades—Japan and Germany—are not on the vertices of the state-business-labor triangle in Figure 25 but on the sides linking the state and business and business and labor respectively. The country that experienced the greatest decline in competitiveness—Britain—is on the labor corner, which suggests that this is a position to avoid in the future if possible. There is no example of a country on the side linking state and labor, although this might be an option in countries under-going a "populist" phase (e.g., Brazil under João Goulart or Poland af-ter the election of the Solidarity government). Neither populism nor full-fledged tripartite concertation (see the discussion on neocorporat-ism in Chapter 1) appears to have been an option for large industrial-ized capitalist countries during the postwar period.

It seems reasonable to argue that it is easier to move from a corner of the state-business-labor triangle to an adjacent side or from a side to an adjacent corner than to a nonadjacent position. A move to a non-adjacent position means removing one societal grouping from a posi-tion of influence and replacing it with at least one other grouping. Such a change would probably involve a lengthy and perhaps violent struggle. If one assumes that Japanese- and German-style state-societal arrangements are likely to continue to be connected with increasing competitiveness in the world economy (this assumption will be reex-amined below), then each of the other three countries faces a different set of choices about which of the two models to emulate in reforming its domestic institutions.

If the assumptions in the previous paragraph are correct, then the main option for France is to emulate Japan and for Britain to emulate Germany. To do this, France will have to build a much more compet-itive domestic market around competing industrial families. Given the position of France in the European Community, it is likely that the

"Frenchness" of those industrial families will be even more broadly defined than it is at present. In addition, the French state will have to give up some of its prerogatives in the allocation of credit and focus more of its efforts on promoting the creation and diffusion of new technologies outside of the charmed circle of champion firms. Finally, the French state will have to work with business to create a more stable macroeconomic climate.

In Britain, there will have to be major efforts to increase the skills of the work force. A major overhaul of the educational system will be required, with heavy involvement of both business and labor. New investments in manufacturing will be required, and the most likely sources of new capital will be Japan and Germany. The government will have to focus its efforts on assuring that state-funded universities are creating technologies oriented toward manufacturing and can transfer those technologies to business, a task already begun under the Thatcher government. A new political coalition would have to form around the joint interests of business and labor, which would mean a centrist party and an avoidance of either the Thatcherism or laborism of the recent past. There are indications that Britain is currently headed in this direction.

The United States is fortunate in having a choice between the Japanese and German models. If it chooses the Japanese model, there will have to be a major upgrading of government agencies and centralization of industrial policy making in a single agency. At the very minimum, there will have to be a civilian equivalent to the role of the Department of Defense in supporting the development of defense-related products and technologies. If the United States chooses the German model, there will have to be a major upgrading of the role of unions in government policy making and in labor-management relations. A significantly increased commitment to the training and retraining of workers will also be needed. The transition to the German style of state-societal arrangements will take longer because of the need to narrow the gap in skill levels between the United States and Germany, whereas a transition to a Japanese style would encounter strong resistance from those Americans (the vast majority) who are suspicious of strong central government.

SUMMING UP

How can we explain changes in international competitiveness among the major industrial nations in the last twenty years or so? The answer lies in the political and social institutions that establish the fundamental relationships among government, business, and labor in each society. These state-societal arrangements vary substantially from country to country. Variations in state-societal arrangements affect competitiveness mainly through their effect on the creation and diffusion of new technologies.

One of the great ironies of this book is that systems with only one major dominant social actor in the realm of industrial policy (Britain, France, and the United States) tended to do worse in postwar international competition than systems with two (Germany and Japan). A coalition of either the state and business (Japan) or business and labor (Germany) seems to be more conducive to the diffusion of new technologies than one-actor dominance.

One might think that a business-dominant system like that of the United States would be ideal for maintaining competitiveness, but that is not so. In a technological age, when the weakness of labor is the result of a low societal commitment to raising the level of skills in the work force, there will be extensive resistance to the introduction of new technologies in factories and offices. Similarly, one might think that systems with a dominant state such as France would do well in international competition. But a strong state acting alone without strong allies in the private sector will be limited in its ability to anticipate shifts in markets and to respond correctly to them.

Thus we are left with a choice between two models currently embodied in the German and Japanese systems. I have argued that the United States and Britain should opt for a German-style system and France might pursue a Japanese-style approach. I have indicated that both the German and Japanese approaches contain certain problematic features. In any case, I expect variations in state-societal arrangements to persist and to continue to be a source of debate within and between countries. One could argue convincingly, based on historical evidence, that changes in state-societal arrangements are at the center of all domestic debates and that it takes more than relative economic decline to change the outcome of such debates. The increasing bitterness of economic disputes among the major industrialized countries, however, creates an important incentive for them to consider all possible mechanisms for reducing international economic tensions—even domestic change.

Glossary

Aufsichtsrat	Supervisory board (Germany).
Brownfield plants	Industrial plants that have been modernized or renovated (compare "Greenfield plants").
Captive firms	Firms that produce semiconductors for use in their own electronics products and sell a very low percentage of them outside the firm (compare "Merchant firms").
Domei	The trade union federation that covers the bulk of private industry in Japan.
Endaka	The decline of the value of the Japanese yen versus the dollar after 1985.
Greenfield plants	Industrial plants built on sites that had no previous industrial facilities (compare "Brownfield plants").
Kanban	Literally, "card." The term refers to the just-in-time method of production in Japan.
Kanji	The Japanese writing system derived from Chinese characters.
Keidanren	A federation of more than 110 leading Japanese industrial associations.
Keiretsu	An industrial group of large Japanese firms associated with one of the major Japanese banks.
Keizai Doyukai	The Japanese Committee for Economic Development.
Merchant firms	Firms that use a relatively low percentage of their semiconductor production for electronics end products (compare "Captive firms").

Kikkeiren   The Japanese Federation of Employers Associations.

Peak association   An association that aspires to represent all organizations of a specific type, e.g., business trade associations, in a given society. Examples of business peak associations include the U.S. Chamber of Commerce, the Keidanren (Japan), and the Bundesverband der Deutschen Industrie (Germany).

Shitauke   A major Japanese firm and its circle of smaller suppliers and subcontractors.

Sohyo   The federation of public-sector unions in Japan

Vorstand   Board of directors (Germany).

Zaibatsu   Japanese industrial combines dominated by old industrial families or government contractors.

Zaikai   Literally, "financial circle," but actually a club made up of the CEOs of major Japanese companies usually with close ties to the leaders of the Liberal Democratic party.

Zenji   The All-Japan Automobile Industry Labor Union.

Abbreviations

ACARD	Advisory Council for Applied Research and Development (U.K.)
AEG	Algemeine Elektricitäts Gesellschaft (Germany)
AEI	Associated Electrical Industries (U.K.)
AFL–CIO	American Federation of Labor–Congress of Industrial Organizations
AMC	American Motors Corporation
ANVAR	Agence Nationale de Valorisation de la Recherche (France)
ASIC	application-specific integrated circuit
AT&T	American Telegraph and Telephone
BDA	Bundesvereinigung der Deutschen Arbeitgeberverbände
BDI	Bundesverband der Deutschen Industrie
BL	British Leyland Motor Company
BMC	British Motor Company
BMFT	Bundesministerium für Forschung und Technologie (Germany)
BMH	British Motor Holdings
BMW	Bayerische Motoren Werke (Germany)
BOF	basic-oxygen furnace (technology for making steel)
BOJ	Bank of Japan
BSC	British Steel Corporation
BTG	British Technology Group
CAFE	corporate average fuel economy
CBI	Confederation of British Industries
CDU	Christlich Demokratisches Union (Germany)
CEA	Commissariat à l'Énergie Atomique (French)

CEO	chief executive officer
CFDT	Confédération Française Démocratique du Travail
CGE	Compagnie Générale d'Electricité (France)
CGP	Commissariat Général du Plan (France)
CGT	Confédération Générale du Travail (France)
CIASI	Comité Interministériel pour l'Amenagement des Structures Industrielles (France)
CIDISE	Comité Interministériel pour le Développement des Investissements et le Soutien de l'Emploi (France)
CII-HB	Compagnie Internationale de l'Informatique–Honeywell-Bull (France)
CIMATEL	Circuits Integrés Matra-Intel (France)
CIRI	Comité Interministériel pour les Restructurations Industrielles (France)
CMOS	complementary metal oxide on silicon
CNCA	Caisse National du Crédit Agricole (France)
CNPF	Conseil National du Patronat Français (France)
CODIS	Comité d'Orientation pour le Développement des Industries Stratégiques (France)
CPRS	Central Policy Review Staff (U.K.)
CSF	Compagnie Générale de Télégraphie sans Fil (France)
CSSF	Chambre Syndicale de la Sidérurgie Française
CSU	Christlich Soziale Union (Germany)
DARPA	Defense Advance Research Projects Agency (U.S.A.)
DGB	Deutscher Gewerkschaftsbund (Germany)
DGT	Direction Générale des Télécommunications (France)
DIHT	Deutscher Industrie- und Handelstag (Germany)
DIPS	Denden Information Processing System (Japan)
DOD	Department of Defense (U.S.A.)
DRAM	dynamic random access memory
EC	European Community
ECSC	European Coal and Steel Community
EDS	Electronic Data Systems (U.S.A.)
EEC	European Economic Community
EFCIS	Societé pour l'Étude et la Fabrication des Circuits Integrés Speciaux (France)
EPROM	erasable programmable read-only memory
ESPRIT	European Strategic Program for Research and Development in Information Technologies (EC)
ETL	Electro-Technical Laboratory (Japan)
EUREKA	European Research Coordination Agency
FDP	Free Democratic party (Germany)
FDES	Economic and Social Development Fund (France)

FMI	Fond de Modernisation Industriel
FMV	Fair Market Value
FSAI	Fonds Spécial d'Adaptation Industrielle (France)
FTC	Federal Trade Commission (U.S.A.)
GATT	General Agreement on Tariffs and Trade
GE	General Electric (U.S.A.)
GEC	General Electric Corporation (U.K.)
GM	General Motors (U.S.A.)
GmbH	Gesellschaft mit beschränkter Haftung [a private limited company] (Germany)
GNP	gross national product
GSP	Generalized System of Preferences
IBM	International Business Machines (U.S.A.)
ICL	International Computers Ltd. (U.K.)
IG Metall	Industrie Gewerkschaft Metall (Germany)
IP	Investissements et Participations (France)
IRC	Industrial Reorganization Corporation (U.K.)
ITC	International Trade Commission (U.S.A.)
JCCI	Japanese Chamber of Commerce and Industry (Japan)
JECC	Japan Electronics Computer Corporation (Japan)
JESSI	Joint European Submicron Silicon Initiative
LSI	large-scale integrated [circuits]
MAP	Microprocessor Applications Project (U.K.)
MBB	Messerschmidt-Bölkow-Blohm (Germany)
MCI	Ministry of Commerce and Industry (Japan)
MEDL	Marconi Electronic Devices Ltd. (U.K.)
MF	Monnaie et Finance (France)
MHS	Matra-Harris Semiconducteurs (France)
MISP	Microlectronics Industries Support Program (U.K.)
MITI	Ministry for International Trade and Industry (Japan)
MMC	Monopolies and Mergers Commission (U.K.)
MOS	metal oxide on silicon
NAM	National Association of Manufacturers (U.S.A.)
NEB	National Enterprise Board (U.K.)
NEC	Nippon Electric Company (Japan)
NEDC	National Economic Development Council (U.K.)
NEDO	National Economic Development Office (U.K.)
NIC	newly industrializing country
NMOS	N-channel metal oxide on silicon
NRDC	National Research and Development Corporation (U.K.)
NSU	Neckarsulm (Germany)
NTT	Nippon Telegraph and Telephone (Japan)
OMB	Office of Management and Budget (U.S.A.)

OPEC	Organization of Petroleum Exporting Countries
PCM	plug compatible machine
PIPS	Pattern Information Processing System (Japan)
PSA	Peugeot Société Anonyme (France)
RAM	random access memory
RCA	Radio Corporation of America (U.S.A.)
R&D	research and development
SEL	Standard Elektrik Lorenz (Germany)
Sematech	Semiconductor Manufacturing Technology (U.S.A.)
SIA	Semiconductor Industry Association (U.S.A.)
SNCF	Société Nationale des Chemins de Fer (France)
SPD	Sozialdemokratische Partei Deutschland (Germany)
STC	Standard Telephone and Cables (U.K.)
SWP	sector working party (U.K.)
TI	Texas Instruments (U.S.A.)
TRW	Thompson Ramo Woolridge (U.S.A.)
TUC	Trades Union Congress (U.K.)
UAW	United Auto Workers (U.S.A.)
USTR	[Office of the] United States Trade Representative
USW	United Steelworkers (U.S.A.)
VCR	videocassette recorder
VER	voluntary export restraint
VHSIC	very high-speed integrated circuits
VLSI	very-large-scale integrated [circuits]
VRA	voluntary restraint agreement
VW	Volkswagen (Germany)

Index

Cornell Studies in Political Economy

EDITED BY PETER J. KATZENSTEIN

Democracy at Work: Changing World Markets and the Future of Labor Unions, by Lowell Turner

National Styles of Regulation: Environmental Policy in Great Britain and the United States, by David Vogel

International Cooperation: Building Regimes for Natural Resources and the Environment, by Oran R. Young

Governments, Markets, and Growth: Financial Systems and the Politics of Industrial Change, by John Zysman

American Industry in International Competition: Government Policies and Corporate Strategies, edited by John Zysman and Laura Tyson

Library of Congress Cataloging-in-Publication Data

Hart, Jeffrey A.
  Rival capitalists : international competitiveness in the United States, Japan, and Western Europe / Jeffrey A. Hart.
    p. cm. — (Cornell studies in political economy)
  Includes bibliographical references and index.
  ISBN 0-8014-2649-9 (alk. paper). — ISBN 0-8014-9949-6 (pbk.)
    1. Japan—Industries. 2. European Economic Community countries—Industries. 3. United States—Industries. 4. Industry and state—Japan. 5. Industry and state—European Economic Community countries. 6. Industry and state—United States. 7. Competition, International. I. Title. II. Series.
HC462.9.H2274 1992
338.09—dc20
                                                                          92-52757